The Quarrel of
Macaulay and Croker

The Quarrel of Macaulay and Croker

Politics and History in the Age of Reform

WILLIAM THOMAS

OXFORD

UNIVERSITY PRESS

OXFORD
UNIVERSITY PRESS

Great Clarendon Street, Oxford OX2 6DP
Oxford University Press is a department of the University of Oxford.
It furthers the University's objective of excellence in research, scholarship,
and education by publishing worldwide in
Oxford New York

Athens Auckland Bangkok Bogotá Buenos Aires Calcutta
Cape Town Chennai Dar es Salaam Delhi Florence Hong Kong Istanbul
Karachi Kuala Lumpur Madrid Melbourne Mexico City Mumbai
Nairobi Paris São Paulo Shanghai Singapore Taipei Tokyo Toronto Warsaw
and associated companies in Berlin Ibadan

Oxford is a registered trade mark of Oxford University Press
in the UK and certain other countries

Published in the United States
by Oxford University Press Inc., New York

© William Thomas 2000

The moral rights of the author have been asserted
Database right Oxford University Press (maker)

First published 2000

British Library Cataloguing in Publication Data
Data available

Library of Congress Cataloging in Publication Data
Thomas, William, 1936–
The quarrel of Macaulay and Croker : politics and history in the age of reform /
William Thomas.
p. cm.
Includes bibliographical references (p.) and index.
1. Macaulay, Thomas Babington Macaulay, Baron, 1800–1859—Political and social
views. 2. Macaulay, Thomas Babington Macaulay, Baron, 1800–1859. History of
England. 3. Croker, John Wilson, 1780–1857—Political and social views. 4. Literary
quarrels—Great Britain—History—19th century. 5. Historiography—Great
Britain—History—19th century. 6. Great Britain—Politics and government—1830–1837.
7. Great Britain—Historiography. I. Title.
DA3.M3 T47 2000
941.081'092—dc21   00–037499
ISBN 0–19–820864–2

3 5 7 9 10 8 6 4 2

Typeset by Graphicraft Limited, Hong Kong
Printed in Great Britain
on acid-free paper by
Biddles Ltd., Guildford and King's Lynn

Acknowledgements

I have to thank several institutions and friends for helping me to write this book. My first debt is to Christ Church, which has met all my expenses as they occurred, except one. That was the cost of a month's visit to the Huntington Library, San Marino, California to read Zachary Macaulay's papers, which was made possible by a grant from the British Academy and a Mayer Fellowship awarded by the Library's Trustees. I have also had much help from librarians and archivists wherever I have sought material, but I am specially indebted to Arlene Shy and John Dann of the William Clements Library, Ann Arbor, Michigan, to William Erwin and Linda McCurdy of the William Perkins Library in Duke University, and Thomas and Sherrill Pinney in Pomona, California, who all sweetened toil with warm hospitality and kindness. In Britain, I have enjoyed the princely hospitality of the Master and Fellows of Trinity College, Cambridge, Macaulay's college, and special help from the late Robert Robson, the Librarian David McKitterick, and my old friend Boyd Hilton. The Earl of Lonsdale gave me permission to see the letters and journals of the second Earl in the Cumbria Record Office, Carlisle. John and Virginia Murray gave me access to all their papers relating to Croker, Lockhart, and the *Quarterly Review*, which I read in the historic drawing-room in Albemarle Street beneath the portraits of some of the characters in these pages. Theodore Landon gave generously of his large store of genealogical knowledge of Crokers, Pennells, Giffards, and Landons and helped me clarify Croker's family connections. Grace Dempsey showed me the whole Croker pamphlet collection in its old quarters in the British Museum. Anthony Browne scoured the records of Christie's to make sure that Peel's letters to Croker really had not survived. Adrian le Harivel opened the stores of the National Gallery in Dublin to show me the Lawrence portrait of J. W. Croker which is here gratefully reproduced with the Gallery's permission.

I have had help and advice from many scholars. The late John Clive first gave me an idea of the treasures of material buried in the Victorian reviews, and his work on Macaulay was an early inspiration. Christopher Breiseth was very generous in letting me read his Cornell Ph.D. on Croker and the additions he has made to it since. In my work on materials in Britain I have benefited from conversations with Marilyn Butler, James Cameron, Michael Drolet, Peter Ghosh, Iain Hamilton, Norman Hampson, Colin Matthew, Roger Morriss, Lucy Newlyn, and Pat Rogers. In my daily round in college I have tried the patience of many colleagues with questions relating to their respective fields, and am specially grateful to Peter Parsons for saving me from errors relating to classical scholarship, to Ronald Truman for his cosmopolitan reading in European literature, and to Henry Harris for general encouragement. Three friends, John Walsh, Thomas Pinney, and Bruce Kinzer read the manuscript right through, correcting errors and convincing me it could make a book. It took shape under the patient vigilance and skilful fingers of Jackie Webber and Jennifer Smith, who never reproached me even for last-minute changes. I am deeply indebted to the editors of the OUP, Ruth Parr and Anne Gelling, and to their expert copy-editor for guiding this manuscript through the processes of publication.

Finally, my wife Deborah has not only helped with travel plans, but transcribed whole series of microfilms and xeroxes and ensured that, wherever I had to work, my surroundings would be beautiful, restful, and conducive to composition. I dedicate this book to her with love and gratitude.

Contents

List of Plates

Abbreviations

Add. MSS.	Additional manuscripts, British Library
Brightfield	Myron F. Brightfield, *John Wilson Croker* (Berkeley, Calif., and London, 1940).
CHE	*Critical and Historical Essays* of Thomas Babington Macaulay, 3 vols. (London, 1846).
Clive	John Clive, *Thomas Babington Macaulay: The Shaping of the Historian* (London, 1973).
CPC	J. W. Croker Papers, William L. Clements Library, Ann Arbor, Michigan.
CPD	J. W. Croker Papers, Duke University, Special Collections.
ER	*Edinburgh Review*
Greville	*The Greville Memoirs, 1814–1860*, ed. L. Strachey & R. Fulford, 8 vols. (London, 1938).
HE	Lord Macaulay, *The History of England from the Accession of James II*, 3 vols. (London, Everyman edn. 1906).
Jennings	Louis J. Jennings, *Correspondence and Diaries of the Rt. Hon. John Wilson Croker*, 3 vols. (London, 1884).
LM	*The Letters of Thomas Babington Macaulay*, ed. Thomas Pinney, 6 vols. (Cambridge, 1974–81).
MC	*Morning Chronicle*
MW	*Miscellaneous Writings of Lord Macaulay* (London, 1860).
NLS	National Library of Scotland
PD	*Parliamentary Debates*
QR	*Quarterly Review*
S.D.U.K.	Society for the Diffusion of Useful Knowledge
TCM	Macaulay MSS, Trinity College, Cambridge.
Trevelyan	G. O. Trevelyan, *Life and Letters of Lord Macaulay*, 2 vols. (Oxford 1961, 1978).
ZM	Zachary Macaulay Papers, Henry E. Huntington Library, San Marino, Ca.

Introduction

This book tells the story of a quarrel, which began in the House of Commons during the debates on the great Reform Bill, and was carried over into the reviews and the newspapers in the 1830s and 1840s. If it had been confined to parliament and to politicians it would be rather dry and trivial. But the antagonists were a young man whose work has since made his name a household word, and a veteran politician who is remembered, if at all, as a severe reviewer and editor of historical memoirs. The quarrel began in a political crisis, and its original motivation was political. But the clash in the Commons left an abiding mutual dislike and a rivalry which long outlasted the political argument. Time added a third ingredient. Both men were skilled writers of invective, but while Macaulay sought a wider fame as a narrative historian, Croker remained fascinated by the political arena and in so far as he could separate politics from history proper, he concentrated on leaving accurate records of the past. It is this which gives the quarrel a historiographical interest. Anyone who writes conscientiously about the past experiences a tension between actuality and relevance, between the duty of finding out what people in the past really did and thought, and the duty of persuading the contemporary reader that what he has found is interesting. Today most historians lay the stress on the first. It is considered rather the mark of the amateur and journalist to tell a good story well. The professional historian prides himself on accurate research and analysis. In Victorian England most historians concentrated on the second duty, of making the past vivid for a lay readership. Croker, the editor and unsparing critic of any writer who thought the past made a good story, seems to belong in spirit to the analytical and professional side; Macaulay to the narrative and amateur. As Sir Charles Firth, writing as the Victorian fashion for grand narrative was faltering, put it, 'Other historians enlarge on the difficulty of finding out the truth. Macaulay enlarges on the difficulty of stating it.' Throughout this study I have been aware of this tension and have tried to keep a balance. From a respect for his readers, Macaulay takes great liberties with the sources. From a respect for the sources, Croker lays a great burden on his readers. Macaulay is a historian every reader can enjoy, but Croker is a historian the professional must respect.

Of course, reputations are never wholly undeserved, and I have been asked when writing this book why I have not concentrated on the greater man and given his antagonist an appropriately minor place. My first reason is that it would have been unjust. Biographers are usually conscious or unconscious partisans of their subjects, and one spur to my earliest researches was the way the evidence of even the printed record was misinterpreted by the biographers on both sides. This is the theme of my first chapter. But so strong was the tendency among the first biographers to assimilate each man to the values of late Victorian politics, that I have followed this chapter with four more in which I have tried to re-examine their different backgrounds and the outlooks so formed. In many ways it was a conflict of different generations; Croker's outlook was shaped by the struggle with revolutionary and Napoleonic France, Macaulay's by the challenges of prosperity and peace. Macaulay was not, as I shall show, a typical Whig, but he belonged to a generation which was impatient with the pieties which had justified the long war and which the Government would invoke again to guide the nation at peace. His disagreement with Croker was in that sense inevitable, since to Croker every Whig was suspect, for his party's opposition to the war and its ill-concealed sympathies with revolutionary principles. But in Croker's case his deep distrust of Whiggism was compromised by his friendship with Peel, the most important connection of his political life. For a long time I debated whether this should go in a separate study. In the end I decided that, as it was so closely bound up with Disraeli's attack on Peel and consequently with the libellous portrait of Croker in *Coningsby*, it should be included in this book. It forms Chapter 4, but strict historiographers may treat it as Lady Bracknell treated the chapter on the fall of the rupee, and omit it as too sensational.

The second reason follows from the first. Macaulay got a drubbing during the reform debates, not only from Croker but also from Peel. He took his revenge in a manner more suited to his talents, the anonymous review. But the two great reviews, the *Edinburgh* and the *Quarterly*, were strongly political. No contributor to them could write entirely for himself, though Macaulay contrived to achieve greater independence than most reviewers. Not only did the reviews prolong the quarrel: they also ensured it had more participants. Reviewing brought in John Murray and J. G. Lockhart, the *Quarterly*'s publisher and editor, as well as the other visitors to 50 Albermarle Street; and on the Whig side Macvey Napier and Longman with their partisans on the *Edinburgh*. The dispute was the talk of the clubs and the country houses and the country vicarages where the quarterlies were most avidly read. So any full account of the later ramifications of the quarrel entails a study of the higher journalism in early Victorian England and each man's position in it. At this stage in their careers, both men were reluctant politicians. Croker never sat in the reformed parliament and always insisted that he preferred a retirement among his books and his French revolutionary researches. Macaulay went to India to make his fortune so as to enjoy the independence of a man of letters. But both men were drawn back into politics; Croker to writing political articles for his old party, Macaulay taking a seat in parliament and a ministerial post. Though both aspired, oddly enough, to write history free of the loyalties of contemporary politics, they failed, and not unexpectedly the failure was more marked in Croker the veteran politician than in Macaulay the fair-weather one. How much Macaulay's work was affected by his Whig allegiance was always the central question for students of the *History of England*, but equally important for my story is Croker's motive for attacking it. So I examine their different conceptions of history in Chapters 6 and 7.

My third reason for choosing to describe a quarrel is more conjectural. We would all, if challenged, agree with J. S. Mill's dictum, that he who knows only his own case knows little of that. But when we approach the controversies of the past we seem to feel no obligation to apply it. We do not shrink from amassing evidence, indeed we amass more than the scholars of any previous generation. But once we have amassed it, the controversial issues we address are primarily those raised by other scholars, rather than those which agitated the men and women we study. Our students are encouraged to arrange their knowledge according to these scholarly debates and to ask whether Dr A is right in his criticism of the assertion made by Professor B, rather than to put themselves in the position of this or that figure in the period studied. We engage in debate about the past, but it is often driven by our arguments in our own society, and it seldom leads us to the dialogues of the past. Yet if Mill is right, such dialogues should be a more fruitful way of acquiring genuine historical understanding than the study of this or that scholarly thesis; which, after all deductions are made for the energy and integrity of academic work, are often only the fashionable formulations of a few experts, especially when they acquire the status of what is called 'a scholarly consensus', that is, the entrenched authority of experts only one yawn away from what Mill called 'the deep sleep of a decided opinion'. One learns more of a man's outlook and motivation by studying him as he argued with antagonists than by following a scholarly consensus however learned. How many scholars trotting out the tired old truism that Macaulay was a Whig have noticed that he was a passionate nationalist and imperialist? How many who categorize Croker as a hardline Tory are prepared to take account of the fact that he, a Protestant, actually favoured the emancipation of the Catholics and the payment of the Irish Catholic priesthood?

In this study I have tried to explain why Croker and Macaulay disagreed, and what has struck me about the evidence as I have gathered it is the way hasty commentators have misread each man's real motives and substituted others which they could not possibly have professed. Of course, each generation rewrites the past to harmonize with its ideals and aversions, but that commonplace may help conceal and even justify the fact that the 'scholarly consensus' often elaborately and solemnly misses the real issues as men saw them in their own day. To recapture those issues in their original form is not an easy task, and it can be disheartening. For it shows that the social and political changes which we are supposed to welcome as a bracing challenge and a goad to fresh thinking, can actually sharpen antagonisms and put them beyond reconciliation. This is the tragedy of Macaulay's quarrel with Croker: the bitterness of their political differences actually concealed from each the large number of opinions and experiences they had in common.

If this were all, it would be a rather barren conclusion to a long narrative. But there is a more positive consequence. Because historians have so seldom doubted Macaulay's Whiggism they have generally assumed, or implied, that the vividness and popularity of the *History of England* have a political explanation, which was that the Victorian reader was already disposed to accept the political message Macaulay conveyed with such colour and force. My reading of Macaulay's letters and articles differs from this view. I suggest that he formed the idea of the *History of England* before he entered politics, and his political career was an interruption of the original plan. Experience of office altered his perception of human motive, and his political duties made him realize that writing the story of a whole society was not as straightforward a matter as he had first supposed. He disliked Carlyle's manner, but by a different route he had discovered the truth of Carlyle's dictum that narrative was 'linear' but action was 'solid'. But politics was not the primary purpose of the *History*, only an impediment to its completion. The original aim of the work, to convey to ordinary readers the importance past events had *for them*, remained essentially unchanged. The question then arises, what *is* the secret of the *History*'s success if it was, politically speaking, neutral? Together Chapters 7 and 8 try to answer that question.

My argument depends heavily on a distinction between the political and the historiographical uses of the words Whig and Tory. The Whig party was a confederacy of aristocratic politicians knit together by kinship as much as by ideology. Lord Melbourne once said that the key to the Whigs was that they were all cousins. Macaulay joined the party when it had actually passed its period of greatest influence, and he died the year after its remnants merged into the Liberal party of late Victorian England. But in the *History of England* he tried to be above party: its hero is William III, a stranger to English political strife, and one of its villains, John Churchill, first Duke of Marlborough, was a Whig. There is a doctrine of progress in the *History*, along with a rather materialistic, utilitarian claim that their free institutions made Englishmen more vigorous and richer than their European contemporaries, and this is sometimes taken to be the essence of 'the whig interpretation of history'. But this is to use the term in a very attenuated sense, confusing it with classical liberal economics and utilitarianism. In this book I call the political party and its members Whig with a capital, and the historiographical tradition whig in lower case. Similarly, there is a political and a historiographical meaning to the word Tory, the second of which I prefer to call conservative. Burke was a Whig but his *Reflections* conveyed a conservative view of politics and society which proved more congenial to a Tory like Lord Sidmouth than to a Whig like Lord Holland.

The Quarrel and the Biographers

Parties in wit attend on those of state
And public faction doubles private hate
POPE

I

The Great Reform Act of 1832 is usually celebrated as a very English triumph. Our ancestors, so the story goes, long accustomed to working a traditional set of institutions, came at last to realize that these were unsuited to the times they lived in, and they set about with a heroic pragmatism to alter them to meet the needs of the day. A minor extension of the franchise, the lopping off of rotten boroughs long overdue for disqualification, a scattering of new seats through the industrial areas, and it was all over. Even the major obstacle, the House of Lords, was persuaded in the end to alter the basis of its power, and revolution was avoided. The whole story is heavily infused with the spirit of compromise and it seems to have no place for theory, for ideology, or even for serious constitutional discussion. Schoolchildren ever since have been led to understand the episode as a matter merely of giving the vote to ten-pound householders, copyholders, and tenants-at-will. The difficulty has always been to understand what all the fuss was about.

We need to remember that, for most Englishmen of the unreformed political system, political authority was inseparable from an historic constitution, in which power had been shared out, in a manner quite unlike the arrangements of any other European state, between the monarch, the aristocracy, and the Commons. Understanding this distribution was a matter of reading English history since the Civil War. Of course there was a variety of versions of the most recent past, each finding favour with a particular group in society. There was a high Tory version stemming from Clarendon's *History of the Rebellion*. There was a Whig version in which John Hampden, Algernon Sidney, and Lord William Russell were heroes and martyrs. There was a more popular version of the struggle for civil and religious liberty which prevailed in Protestant dissenting circles and which ran from Foxe through Bunyan to Godwin. There was a lowland Scottish version which, as befitted a people living between barbarism and imperial prosperity, presented the story as a progress through stages of civilization. There was even an English pastoral version which stressed the lost innocence of rural life and the corruption of commerce. All these had their adherents. But they all agreed that knowing what happened in the past was the key to political understanding. Having no knowledge of history was to be politically illiterate. Denying the appropriateness of historic precedent and starting out from first principles was to be something worse; it was to declare oneself foreign, and subversive of established order. If one wanted to question the actual distribution of power the correct procedure among the politically literate was to argue from historic precedent. Everyone was aware that the Bills in their successive versions served or harmed particular interests in the state, but if the debates had been concerned with those issues only, they would have been a comparatively low-key series of bargains. What gave the bargaining its passion and the debates their high rhetorical flavour was the sense, on both sides of the House, that a venerable historic constitution was being irrevocably changed. By one side the change was presented as consolidation and improvement; to the other it seemed to threaten disorder and destruction. Both visions summoned up historical example and precedent, not only to the French Revolution of 1789 (repeated as its themes had been by the events in Paris in July 1830) but to the English Revolution of 1688 and the Civil War which had preceded it.

This study begins with one of the more striking clashes of historical interpretation during the reform debates. On 20 September 1831 Macaulay delivered his speech on the Third Reading of the Bill, before it went up to the House of Lords. He had only been in the House eighteen months but already men would hurry into the Chamber to hear him. They would have seen a short, stout figure, a 'shapeless little dumpling of a fellow', in a badly-tied neckcloth, delivering a brilliant harangue in a voice which occasionally approached a scream. The delivery was rapid, the prose cadence monotonous and repetitive, but the whole composition was so replete with vivid imagery, so loaded with historical illustration, that old men told their juniors that hearing him was some compensation for missing the eloquence of Pitt and Fox. It was a rather flattering parallel. Fox and Pitt were debaters who charmed with plain language. Macaulay was a preacher who aimed to overwhelm, who memorized his speech days ahead, and when delivering it left no time for interruption, let alone contradiction. This speech, his third on the Reform issue, was constructed around the historical parallel of the first French Revolution. It closed with a warning to the peers to heed the precedent of the French Revolution, which had destroyed the French nobility because they had not recognized till too late the need to make concessions. Why, he asked, had the French aristocrats been 'scattered over the face of the earth, their parks wasted, their palaces dismantled, their heritage given to strangers'? Because, he said, 'they refused all concession till the time had arrived when no concession would avail'.[1]

Macaulay was answered by J. W. Croker, till recently Secretary to the Admiralty, now the most searching critic of the Reform Bill on the Opposition benches, and an authority on the French Revolution. A frail man of middle height, slightly balding, he was now engaged in the last parliamentary battle of his career. He was not a natural orator (in fact he had overcome a childhood stammer) but he had served as an official under five Prime Ministers and was accustomed to prepare his brief and was skilled at meeting opposition objections. No one knew better than he how thinly the debating talent was spread on the government benches. Already he had savaged the new Lord Advocate, Francis Jeffrey. He had prepared an exposure of the inconsistencies in the Whigs' plan of reform. But Macaulay's version of the French Revolution stirred him to an impromptu rebuttal. The French nobility, he said, did indeed provide the House of Lords with a precedent and an example, but not because they had resisted reform. On the contrary, they had initiated it.

---

[1] *PD*, 3rd ser. vii (20 Sept. 1831), 308–9.

'Good God! Sir, where has the learned gentleman lived,—what works must he have read,—with what authorities must he have communed, when he attributes the downfall of the French nobility to an injudicious and obstinate resistance to popular opinion? The direct reverse is the notorious fact—so notorious, that it is one of the commonplaces of modern history.'

On the eve of the great Revolution the French nobility had welcomed the junction of their own order with the third estate in a way which anticipated the Whig peers' present enthusiasm for reform. Many French nobles had joined the third estate impulsively and at once; the rest had followed after a few days; and then those Macaulay had called 'obstinate bigots to privilege and power, abandoned their most effective privilege and most undoubted power, and were seen to march in melancholy procession to the funeral of the constitution'.[2] The Lords should indeed take note of the conduct of their French counterparts, but that pointed to a policy of resisting, not complying with popular demands.

For Macaulay this was only the heaviest in a series of glancing attacks. He had actually been to Paris with a view to writing a history of Restoration France. This he now abandoned. But his parliamentary position was also cruelly exposed. It was a major theme of Croker's criticism of the Whig government that its reform of the representative system aimed to destroy the borough seats owned by Tory proprietors and to save those owned by Whig ones. The charge was made more plausible by the fact that the government used figures from the 1821 Census in preference to the most recent ones of 1831. Macaulay sat for Calne, a borough in the gift of Lord Lansdowne. Croker sat for Aldeburgh which he owed to the Marquis of Hertford. Aldeburgh was to lose its member along with the other rotten boroughs in Schedule A of the Reform Bill. Calne was to keep one of its members through the addition of a few voters from the neighbouring hundred. Macaulay was undoubtedly embarrassed by the fact that he owed his seat, in effect, to a Whig magnate, and Croker's habit of referring to the seat by its full name, 'Calne and the liberty

[2] PD, 3rd ser. vii (20 Sept. 1831), 314–16. Quoted in part in L. J. Jennings, *Correspondence and Diaries of John Wilson Croker* (1st edn. 1884, hereafter 'Jennings'), ii. 130–3. Quote here § in Clive, 174 top, §2, but from Hansard.

of Bowood' (Lansdowne's country house) was calculated to increase his discomfort.[3] He had not been in the confidence of those who had devised the Reform Bill. His speeches dealt less in legislative details than in broad historical comparisons and his French historical learning now looked rather damaged. As a polemicist his forte was the anonymous review, where he had already prepared his riposte to Croker. 'See whether I do not dust that lying varlet's jacket for him in the next number of the Blue and Yellow. I detest him more than cold boiled veal'.[4] The 'Blue and Yellow' was the *Edinburgh Review* which soon after the 20 September exchange carried Macaulay's review of Croker's edition of Boswell's *Life of Johnson*.

It is a good example of Macaulay's talent for ridicule by tendentious quotation. Much of it was devoted to an amusing portrait of Johnson and his oddities; but the first half is a catalogue of Croker's supposed editorial blunders in matters of fact, in dates, in genealogy, in the classical languages and in literary and moral taste. Macaulay's technique was to present a list of factual errors (most of which were quite trivial and, for a work in five volumes, not very numerous) as if they were elementary and obvious:

Many of his blunders are such as we should be surprised to hear any well educated gentleman commit, even in conversation. The notes absolutely swarm with mis-statements into which the editor never would have fallen, if he had taken the slightest pains to investigate the truth of his assertions . . .[5]

Or again:

We have made no curious researches. The Work itself, and a very common knowledge of literary and political history, have enabled us to detect the mistakes we have pointed out, and many other mistakes of the same kind . . .[6]

He later boasted he had 'smashed' the book[7]. In fact it sold out in a few months. Croker published a sharp rebuttal of the criticisms in *Blackwood's Magazine*,[8] but his letters show he was

[3] *PD*, 3rd ser. iii. 98 (4 Mar. 1831); and v. 56–62 (19 July 1831).
[4] *LM*, ii. 84.   [5] *CHE*, i. 353–4.   [6] Ibid., 363.   [7] *LM*, ii. 106.
[8] Vol. 30, no. 187 (Nov. 1831), 829–38, where it is part of one of the 'Noctes Ambrosianae' and the defender is 'Christopher North'. A pamphlet version

smarting from Macaulay's criticisms thirteen years later when he was preparing a second edition.[9]

There were three still more acrimonious exchanges between the two men in the House of Commons, but thereafter, the quarrel was conducted at long distance. They never met socially, or if they did, there is no record of it.[10] Croker retired from the House of Commons after the Reform Act, and Macaulay went away to India to make his fortune. But each added to his dossier of the other's faults.

In 1848 Croker had a chance for revenge with the appearance of the first two volumes of Macaulay's *History of England*. He reviewed them in an eighty-page article in the *Quarterly* in 1849. It is, by any standards, a very severe review. Croker begins by saying that he had hoped that, as Whigs and Tories must alike approve of the beneficial effects of the Revolution of 1688, he would be able 'without any sacrifice of our political feelings' to enjoy Macaulay's narrative:

That hope has been deceived: Mr Macaulay's historical narrative is poisoned with a rancour more violent than even the passions of the time; and the literary qualities of the work, though in some respects very remarkable, are far from redeeming its substantial defects. There is hardly a page ... that does not contain something objectionable either in substance or in colour: and the whole of the brilliant and at first captivating narrative is perceived on examination to be impregnated to a really marvellous degree with bad taste, bad feeling, and, we are under the painful necessity of adding—bad faith.[11]

There followed an unremitting exposure of Macaulay's text, his political prejudices, his plagiarism of secondary authorities, his liberties with his sources, and his style. Macaulay thought that

appeared about the same time with charges and rebuttals in double columns entitled '*Answers to the Edinburgh Reviewer of Croker's Boswell* ...'. This was separately published as *Answers to Mr Macaulay's Criticism in the Edinburgh Review on Mr Croker's Edition of Boswell's Life of Johnson selected from Blackwood's Magazine* (London, 1847).

[9] NLS Lockhart, MS. 927, no. 46, fos. 63–4, 21 Jan. 1845, fo. 84, no. 56, 4 Nov. 1845.

[10] In his journal for 29 Jan. 1850 TBM records a meeting to elect a new member of the Athenaeum. Croker was in the Chair. 'I never was in a room with him before, saving the House of Commons. I took no notice of his existence.' (Journal II, 219).

[11] *QR*, lxxxiv, no. 168 (Mar. 1849), 550.

in its length and tediousness the review had done him a service. One wag said that Croker had attempted murder and achieved suicide. But Tory friends of Croker felt it was conclusive and crushing. What it did not do was damage the sales of the *History of England*, which has been continuously in print from that day to this.

II

Of the two men, Macaulay has had the better press. This is only in part because the historian who backs the forces of change keeps the attention of his readers. Of course, Macaulay's conviction that the history of England was 'emphatically the history of progress'[12] earned him a place in the esteem of late Victorian and early twentieth century liberals which lasted until the 'whig interpretation of history' came under attack between the two World Wars. Croker backed the losing side and his works slipped out of the reading lists of all but specialists on the French Revolution. So it is not surprising that during the heyday of political liberalism his stock was low. What is surprising is that it should not have seen a revival as the 'whig interpretation' lost its appeal. For one effect of the waning of whig history is that a good many of Croker's attitudes have come back into fashion. His defence of the unreformed representative system and his dislike of the Whigs now have many sympathizers: even sixth-formers assert that the Whigs who brought in the first Reform Bill were (as Croker said) acting from the merest opportunism. There is a better understanding too of the protectionist cause which Croker thought Peel had betrayed. Yet, despite these changes, the habit has persisted into quite recent times of thinking that the reactionary cannot be as morally right as the progressive, and of seeing the conflict between the two men as one of moral incompatibility. For this habit, blame lies largely with the first biographers.

Late Victorian biography was saturated with family piety, and it was the domestic virtues celebrated in the great 'three-decker' biographies rather than their boring bulk which provoked the iconoclasm of a later generation. But both the original piety

[12] *CHE*, ii. 226.

and the later iconoclasm had the effect of enhancing Macaulay's reputation and obscuring Croker's.

In middle-class families the writers of letters and the custodians of family history were generally the women, who were not as well informed about the professional activities of their menfolk as they were about the doings of uncles and aunts, nephews and nieces and other domestic matters. Middle-class families moreover moved from house to house, and lacked the continuity and centrality which enabled landed families to keep records from generation to generation. The Macaulay family moved, as their fortunes declined, from an opulent mansion in Cadogan Place to rented houses in Bloomsbury. We owe the survival of Zachary Macaulay's letters to the hoarding instinct of his last surviving daughter Frances. Her younger sister Hannah Trevelyan collected her brother's papers and handed them on to her son, George Otto Trevelyan. Frances outlived Hannah, and her collection of Zachary's papers went eventually to George Otto's sister Margaret, Lady Knutsford. So it would be fair to say that the main materials for the lives of Zachary Macaulay and his historian son were collected by two affectionate women, daughters of the one and sisters of the other. Family protectiveness was the dominant reason for preservation, and the materials were ample enough to make both biographers feel they need not look very much further afield.

Lord Macaulay's biographer George Otto Trevelyan was born in 1838, the year his uncle returned from India. He had a conventional education in the classics, and he became a fluent writer, but he was no scholar. He became a Gladstonian liberal, and he began the biography of his uncle in 1874, when Disraeli's second ministry gave him a break from office. As we shall see, he wanted to play down those elements in his uncle's career which were at odds with the Victorian ideal of manliness; and to explain away the evangelicalism of the Clapham sect in which Macaulay had been bred, by presenting its members as the originators of the style of agitation which the liberals had adopted under Gladstone.[13] But these concerns were not obtrusive. Trevelyan balanced them with copious quotations from

---

[13] Trevelyan 1. 64. For Trevelyan as biographer, see Christopher Tolley, *Domestic Biography: The Legacy of Evangelicalism in Four Nineteenth-Century Families* (Oxford, 1997), ch. 5.

Macaulay's letters, the vividness and charm of which make the *Life and Letters* a minor classic.

On his death the papers passed to his son, George Macaulay Trevelyan, whose historical writing represents the quintessence of 'the whig interpretation', and whose volumes on the reign of Queen Anne are a sort of continuation of Macaulay's *History of England*. He was a finer scholar than his father, and a very cursory comparison of the biography with the originals of the letters would have told him how negligent in dating and transcription George Otto had been, yet he frequently told enquirers after the originals that his father had omitted nothing of importance. This defensiveness was largely due to his dislike of Bloomsbury, and in particular of the fashion inaugurated by Lytton Strachey's *Eminent Victorians* of finding cracks in the most heroic reputations, and of reducing the art of biography to an affair of condensed and malicious caricature. Strachey wrote only a short essay on Macaulay,[14] but it is easy to imagine what he would have made of, for instance, Macaulay's letters to his sisters Hannah and Margaret. At any rate they were denied him. 'I'm not going to have those Bloomsbury people laughing at my great uncle' said Trevelyan.[15] His protectiveness certainly prolonged the reputation of his father's biography. Eminent historians from H. A. L. Fisher to Dom David Knowles showed no suspicion that they were dealing with a work of family piety. The centenary of Macaulay's death brought a crop of laudatory essays which were no more than *rechauffés* of G. O. Trevelyan's *Life*.[16] Only in the 1970s, a hundred years after G. M. Trevelyan's birth, has Professor Pinney's complete edition of Macaulay's letters made it possible to study in detail what the *Life and Letters* concealed.

Croker's literary reputation had by contrast no protectors. His only son had died in 1820, a fact which did much to quench his political ambition. Hardly less than Macaulay, he depended on

---

[14] *Literary Essays* (1948), 195–201.

[15] S. C. Roberts, *Adventures with Authors* (Cambridge, 1966) 121, quoted by D. Cannadine, *G. M. Trevelyan: A Life in History* (1992), 45.

[16] e.g. Mark A. Thompson, *Macaulay* (1959); A. Browning, 'Macaulay', *Historical Journal*, ii. (1959), 149–60, David Knowles, *Lord Macaulay 1800–1859* (Cambridge, 1960). E. S. De Beer's 'Macaulay and Croker', *Review of English Studies*, n.s., x. 40. (1959), 388–97 is an attack on Croker wholly based on Trevelyan.

a secure family life, but his family included no literary talent. He had in 1815 adopted as his daughter his wife's youngest sister Rosamund. She married George, the son of Sir John Barrow, Croker's colleague at the Admiralty. Sir John Barrow wrote many books, of which the best known is *The Mutiny of the 'Bounty'*. Perhaps he might have edited his friend's remains. In fact, Croker outlived him, as he did most of his literary friends. Whereas Macaulay died at the height of his reputation, Croker's misfortune was that he lived on into a world which had no firsthand knowledge of his career, in which even young Tories looked on him as a curious but irrelevant fossil.[17]

Looking at the quarrel with Croker, G. O. Trevelyan relied wholly on his uncle's hostile testimony, and as that rested largely on hearsay, the nephew eked it out with fiction. The fiction however did draw on an episode in which Croker had given hostages to fortune. In 1842 Croker was left £26,000 in the will of his friend and patron the Marquess of Hertford. Croker's friendship with Hertford went back to the Regency when the latter was still Lord Yarmouth, an active, witty man of fashion whose passion for painting and sculpture had already laid the foundation of what we know as the Wallace Collection. The two men became close in the 1820s when Yarmouth succeeded to his father's vast estates, and needed a man of business to advise him. Croker became that man of business, paying regular visits to Hertford's estate at Sudbourne in Suffolk, advising him about his property, particularly his parliamentary boroughs, running his errands, and when Hertford went abroad, keeping him informed in long gossipy letters. As Hertford's interest in politics waned, he trusted more and more to a man whose political experience and connections raised him above mere paid agents. The fall of the Tories and the loss of his boroughs gave him the excuse to believe that his country had no use for him; but there were also social constraints to avoid at home.[18] His family life was so disturbed (his mother had been the Regent's mistress and he himself was estranged from his wife and lived openly with a Lady Strachan) that he could never hope for a life of domestic

---

[17] e.g. Lord Stanley's account, 17 Mar. 1857, in J. R. Vincent (ed.), *Disraeli, Derby and the Conservative Party: The Political Journals of Lord Stanley* (1978), 57.

[18] Cf. Lonsdale MSS., J. W. Croker to Viscount Lowther, 12 Sept. [1832].

calm.[19] But after 1830 his restlessness increased with illness, and he roamed with his household from spa to spa seeking cures, for gout, for a hydrocele, and perhaps worse ailments still. Lady Strachan left him for an Italian; her daughters, on whom he had settled huge sums as if they were his own, married and departed. The third and youngest, Charlotte, who became Countess Zichy de Ferraris, was more affectionate, and seems to have had some hopes of reforming Hertford's private life and helping him recover his health. He made his last journey home from France in October 1841, and Charlotte Zichy and her husband came to stay at Dorchester House in the hope of overseeing and improving his lifestyle.[20] He was now sixty-four, but his health was shattered. His diction was at times unintelligible, and he had difficulty breathing. He needed rest and expert medical attention. But he had insisted on bringing to England the various *demimondaines* with whom he had toured the Continent, and these were settled nearby. So in his last months there developed a struggle for his loyalties between two sorts of associate.[21] The kept women wanted to extract what money and gifts they could while he lived. The 'respectable' associates headed by the Zichys and political cronies like Spencer de Horsey and Captain Meynell, hoped the Marquess would repudiate these hussies (though they would have been satisfied if they had kept discreetly out of sight) and make an honest end. One could say that in this, the penultimate battle, the *demimondaines* won. Hertford himself asked the Zichys to leave him, and when they had, he called out his women in the last debauch which killed him.[22]

Croker, whatever his motives, was one of the few friends to remain loyal through Hertford's decline. He later said that Hertford's 'was not a *moral* but a *medical* case—a disorder of the brain'.[23] Certainly his behaviour in his last years was extraordinarily erratic. Lonely and ill, with only his money to

---

[19] Bernard Falk, *Old Q's Daughter: The History of a Strange Family* (rev. edn. 1957) is in effect a history of the Seymour-Conways. For Hertford's connoisseurship see J. Ingamells, *The Third Marquess of Hertford as a Collector* (1982).

[20] CPD, Spencer de Horsey to J. W. Croker, 18, 19 Oct. 1841.

[21] Ibid., Charlotte Zichy de Ferraris to J. W. Croker, 11 Nov. 1841, making very clear her suspicions.

[22] Ibid., S. de Horsey to J. W. Croker, 16 Feb. 1842, and n.d. 'Thursday'; Falk, *Old Q's Daughter*, 158–9 using Greville vol. v, 18–21 (19 Mar. 1842).

[23] Brougham MSS, Croker to Brougham, 27 Sept. 1842.

reward favours and repay slights, he had developed a morbid habit, when stopping at a place for any length of time, of adding a codicil to his will. At his death on 1 March 1842, there were thirty-five of these, some contradicting others. There was also a great deal of money in cash and securities which Hertford had entrusted to his valet, Nicolas Suisse, who drew cheques, paid tradesmen, and saw that his master always had cash for his increasingly wayward needs. Given Hertford's restless life, Suisse was quite accustomed to dealing in French securities and with French and Italian banks. But it seems that he had also been transferring money to a private account against his return to France.[24] Though certain of a large legacy in his master's will, Suisse was suspected by the executors of defrauding the estate, and they charged him with embezzlement. In the trial, Suisse's counsel, Thesiger, questioned whether a man who had served so long and faithfully in expectation of a large reward could have had any motive to defraud, and instead called witnesses to prove that Hertford's dissolute habits amply explained the confusion in the accounts. In particular, Hertford had used Suisse to procure him the women on whom he liked to lavish large sums. One of these, Angelique Borel, who planned to set up house with Suisse, testified to having lived with Hertford for several years and been paid £7,000 or £8,000 a year. She also said she had often dined at Dorchester House with Croker.[25] In his testimony, Croker had said she had appeared to him to be more like a nurse than anything else.[26] The case provided a glimpse (no more) into the private life of a corrupted old grandee, but no details of Croker's relationship with Hertford other than that he was, with four others, discharging the duties of an executor. Suisse was acquitted. The executors however continued the prosecution in the French courts, and in 1844 they succeeded. Suisse was required to pay back £80,000 to Hertford's heir.[27] So the last round was won by the respectable party.

[24] Croker believed Suisse had plundered 'at least £150,000' from Hertford's bureau, and that he was to share this with a hotelier called Cailliez or Calliez. Brougham MSS, Croker to Brougham, 13 Sept. 1847; *The Times* 27 Aug. 1842, 7, where the hotelier is given as Caillé.

[25] *The Times*, 25 Aug. 1842; *MC* 25 Aug. 1842.

[26] *MC*, 7 July 1842, 7.

[27] CPD, Lady Strachan & Salza to J. W. Croker, 18 Aug. 1844; and a document, *Quelques Mots pour M. le Marquis de Hertford . . . Contre le Sieur Suisse*; forwarded

Disraeli took a close interest in the Hertford will[28] and its beneficiaries, and in 1844 he published *Coningsby*, in which the character of Rigby and his patron Lord Monmouth were plainly and deliberately based on Croker and Hertford. Rigby is introduced thus:

Mr Rigby was member for one of Lord Monmouth's boroughs. He was the manager of Lord Monmouth's parliamentary influence, and the auditor of his vast estates. He was more; he was Lord Monmouth's companion when in England, his correspondent when abroad; hardly his counsellor, for Lord Monmouth never required advice; but Mr Rigby could instruct him in matters of detail, which Mr Rigby made amusing. Rigby was not a professional man; indeed, his origin, education, early pursuits, and studies, were equally obscure; but he had contrived in good time to squeeze himself into parliament, by means which no one could ever comprehend, and then set up to be a perfect man of business. The world took him at his word, for he was bold, acute, and voluble; with no thought, but a good deal of desultory information; and though destitute of all imagination and noble sentiment, was blessed with a vigorous, mendacious fancy, fruitful in small expedients, and never happier than when devising shifts for great men's scrapes.[29]

Rigby is also a reviewer:

Mr Rigby had a classical retreat . . . which he esteemed a Tusculum. There, surrounded by his busts and books, he wrote his lampoons and articles; massacred a she liberal (it was thought that no one could lash a woman like Rigby), cut up a rising genius whose politics were different from his own, or scarified some unhappy wretch who had brought his claims before parliament, proving, by garbled extracts from official correspondence that no one could refer to, that the malcontent instead of being a victim, was, on the contrary, a defaulter . . .[30]

Croker was indifferent to fictional portraits of himself, but his family were not. In 1876 Trevelyan's biography of Macaulay

by Messrs. Perin & Gombert, advocates, to Capron & Co., Hertford's solicitors, and dated 29 July 1844, which is the indictment of Suisse before the Cour Royale; *Gazette des Tribunaux*, 19e année, no. 5393, dimanche 4 août 1844, 977. I owe this reference to the kindness of M. Robert Beck. See also CPD Capron, Brabant & Capron to J. W. Croker, 5 Aug. 1844, enclosing copy of a letter from Thomas Lawson (Capron's agent in Paris). Suisse was condemned by the Cour Royale to a further repayment of 77,000 fr. Lawson to Capron & Co., 14 May 1847.

[28] In *Disraeli Letters*, ed. G. Wiebe (Toronto, 1982), iv. 24, 32–4, 36–7.
[29] *Coningsby* (Bradenham edn., 1927), 11.   [30] Ibid., 12.

appeared, and it offered, as an explanation of Macaulay's early hatred of Croker, a letter written, eleven years after their first encounter, to Macvey Napier, the editor of the *Edinburgh Review*. Napier had been reading the manuscript of Macaulay's essay on Fanny Burney, and he objected to a reference in it to Croker, which he thought libellous. Macaulay's defence of his remarks (which however he consented to withdraw) shows how his imagination had already worked the banal details of the Suisse case into a Hogarthian horror. Croker, he claimed, was 'the most intimate confidant of Lord Hertford, at a time when Lord Hertford's House was as scandalous a nuisance as ever the Key in Chandos Street or the White House in Soho Square were. It was sworn by the girls of Lord Hertford's harem before Lord Abinger that Croker used to dine with them. By compliances of this sort he has obtained a legacy from an old debauchee whose name is held in as much abhorrence by the country as ever was that of Colonel Charteris'.[31] Trevelyan's comment on this letter (of 1843) was to say that it was endorsed by Disraeli's portrait of Rigby, which proved that the antagonism between the two men arose (in 1831) from 'incompatibility of moral sentiments and not of political opinions'. The implication was that Croker was a willing accessory to Hertford's vicious habits. In fact, the surviving correspondence shows that Hertford sought his advice on matters connected with his property, and that Croker deplored as much as any other member of the circle the aberrations of Hertford's last illness. He was actually a good deal more strait-laced than Hertford's friend Lord Lowther or the deplorably venal Strachans. Croker's widow was, understandably, upset by the passage in Trevelyan's book, and her neighbour, Sir Algernon West, persuaded him to omit the offending passage in later editions.[32] What was omitted, however, was the quotation from Macaulay's letter, not the approving reference

---

[31] *LM*, iv. 89, which renders TBM's spelling as 'Chartres'. The Key Coffee House and Hotel in Chandos Street was a notorious 'resort of rakes'. B. Lillywhite, *London Coffee Houses* (1962), 708. The White House, once the residence of Mary Cromwell, Lady Fauconberg, became in 1776 'the property of Thomas Hooper, and . . . won unsavoury notoriety'. C. S. Terry, *John Christian Bach* (1962), 89. Colonel Charteris appears in the first engraving of Hogarth's *A Harlot's Progress*. I am indebted to Pat Rogers for this information.

[32] Sir Algernon West, *Recollections 1832 to 1886* (2 vols., 1899), ii. 74–5. Mrs Croker died in 1880, at the age of 91.

to *Coningsby*. West also prevailed on Gladstone to defend Croker in his fine review of Trevelyan's biography in the *Quarterly* for 1876.[33] Gladstone tried, in what must surely be the fairest assessment of Macaulay ever written by a victim; but while he made shrewd comments on the reasons for Macaulay's popularity over that of his critics, he could hardly, so late in his career, attempt a defence of Croker's outlook, and of Disraeli's opinion he said not a word.

The Trustees of Croker's estate eventually found a sympathetic biographer in Louis J. Jennings, an experienced journalist who was to become a Tory MP. He worked for two years on the papers and published the *Correspondence and Diaries* in three volumes in 1884. Unlike Macaulay, whose official career was brief, and whose surviving letters were the intimate ones preserved by an adoring family circle, Croker's correspondence was largely official and political. He did not neglect his family. In fact his generosity to numerous relatives whom he had placed in various public posts contributed largely to make them a sort of bureaucratic clan which ramified through most of the departments of government and the law. But there seems to have been no domestic 'culture' with its family lore, its peculiar customs and its private language such as large families develop, and which gave Zachary Macaulay's children an emotional solidarity so close that it tended to inhibit his eldest son's public career. Croker valued his family life, and undoubtedly it took first place in his loyalties, but he also had a social life outside the family circle. We read of him amusing distinguished company in clubs and country houses, but usually he is alone. Mrs Croker did not go into society, and evidently could not shine in it as her husband did.

Jennings therefore faced a more difficult task than G. O. Trevelyan, a vast and varied correspondence on public affairs, undiminished by well-meaning solicitude, but with relatively few private materials. His brief was evidently to defend Croker from his detractors, but he realized that the papers contained a mass of material about major political figures of the time, which promised a biography of much wider appeal than a mere vindication of the man. Besides, conservatism had changed a good

---

[33] *QR*, cxlii no. 283 (July 1876), 1–48, repr. in *Gleanings of Past Years, 1844–78* (1879), ii. 265–340.

deal since Croker's day. Disraeli was dead. His successors were looking to 'villa toryism' for votes. They were not interested in protecting agriculture. They would be for the Empire and against Home Rule for Ireland. Jennings could share Croker's lifelong dislike of Whigs and liberalism generally, but as a 'Tory Democrat', shortly to enlist as a follower of Lord Randolph Churchill, he could hardly set out the full extent of Croker's distrust of democracy. He was also too anti-Irish (rabidly so, according to one authority)[34] to examine sympathetically Croker's Irish roots. As a busy journalist, he was not prepared to plough through hundreds of Croker's *Quarterly* articles, written in a *démodé* style on topics (like the French Revolution) which had lost all their resonance. So he concentrated on Croker's contacts in high politics and society, quoting copiously from the correspondence with the minimum of contextual explanation, and essentially his 'defence' is that a man who enjoyed the esteem and even intimacy of George IV, of Canning and Castlereagh, Wellington and Peel, Derby and Lonsdale, could hardly need defending from the criticisms of mere hack writers. Jennings did attribute Disraeli's portrait of Rigby to malice and spite, but he did not discuss its details and was content to show that Croker had not read the novel and bore no malice towards its author.[35] The Croker that emerges from the *Correspondence and Diaries* is a late Victorian edition of the Regency gossip, clubman and frequenter of country houses, not the reviewer, the political analyst, or the historian.

Not surprisingly, some of its readers thought Disraeli's version had not been confuted. 'I have been reading Croker', wrote A. V. Dicey in 1884 to his friend James Bryce, 'he was a bad bold man when all is said and done and I don't think that Disraeli did him gross injustice in the picture of Rigby'.[36] John Morley's review of Jennings was almost a defence of the portrait in *Coningsby*, finding that Rigby was 'not far from being Croker

[34] R. F. Foster, *Lord Randolph Churchill: A Political Life* (Oxford, 1981), 358.
[35] Jennings, iii. 255–6; 261–5. J.W.C. to an unnamed correspondent, 11 Feb. [1853]. The correspondent is Lady Hardwicke, and the letter answers hers to J.W.C. of 8 Feb. 1853; MS. in CPD.
[36] Bryce MSS., Bodleian Library, 13 Dec. 1884, fo. 62. The injustice, however, as Dicey's contemporary Goldwin Smith pointed out, lay in its cowardice and the fact that 'the person assailed cannot defend himself without seeming to countenance the libel' (*Reminiscences*, [New York, 1910], 138).

to the life'.[37] All that Jennings had done was to show that Croker had ignored Disraeli's libel, and even that claim Morley found implausible.

Jennings was, as far as I know, the last to use the MSS before they were dispersed. Even as he compiled the *Diaries and Correspondence* their dispersal was decreed. Rosamund Croker's will is the most significant of the scattered signs that she did not understand her husband's life-work. As we shall see, Croker was dogged by the fear that the events he had witnessed and the men he had known would be forgotten, or where remembered, misunderstood and traduced; and much of his writing was directed to setting the record right. Even after he had retired from politics he kept contact with the men he had known, constituting himself their vindicator against the ignorance and malice of posterity. His letters are full of his own memoranda as well as requests to the leading actors in certain transactions to state what they did or saw, and he would often use their testimony in his reviews. It is no coincidence that he felt impelled to edit Boswell's *Johnson*: Boswell's recording impulse anticipated his own. But Mrs Croker, having no children of her own, and evidently faced with competing claims on her affection, decided to divide the papers between a Barrow and a Pennell nephew, the former having first choice.[38] As often happens with the progeny of self-made men, the Barrow children lived by patronage, and they were the first to sell. In the 1920s the bulk of the papers were bought by an American millionaire, William L. Clements, and it would not be too much to say that, despite the fact that Clements was a much more generous custodian than G. M. Trevelyan, they passed out of the range of most British students of the nineteenth century.[39] Even after their acquisition by the University of Michigan, they remained scarcely touched by scholars from this side of the Atlantic. Many who liberally quote Jennings and are aware of the furtive excisions of other

[37] *Macmillan's Magazine*, vol. 51, no. 302, 110 (Dec. 1884). Most liberal reviewers thought the same, while Tory ones denied it. An exception was T. E. Kebbel in *Fortnightly Review* vol. 42, no. 105 o.s.; vol. 36, no. 252 n.s. (Nov. 1884) 688–702; but Kebbel edited Disraeli's *Speeches*, and so may have had an interest in upholding Disraeli's veracity.

[38] Mrs Rosamund Croker's will: Principal Registry, 30 Nov. 1880, fo. 848.

[39] Clements bought them in 1924. See Margaret Maxwell, *Shaping a Library: William L. Clements as Collector* (Amsterdam, 1973), 338.

Victorian editors have lacked the curiosity or the means to consult the originals. The other portion of the MSS, however, consisting of the letters of the less famous and a good deal of personal material, were not in Clements' purchase. They have been trickling on to the market in small instalments, some as late as the 1970s, and most of them have been bought by the Perkins Library of Duke University.

Jennings was probably the last person to read right through and select for publication the letters of Croker's most intimate political associate, Peel. Had Peel been more fortunate in his biographers, Croker's reputation might have been very different. But it was not easy to write the life of a man whose reputation, at the very end of his career, had changed from that of saviour of Conservatism to Liberal martyr. Besides, Peel was a reticent man whose idea of a Memoir was a collection of letters written during the three political crises of his career, the passing of Catholic Emancipation, the first ministry of 1834–5, and the Repeal of the Corn Laws; and he chose as editors of this work and Trustees of his papers, two men who did not know him well, and whose scope he further inhibited by a series of conditions.[40] Lord Mahon had abandoned a political career to devote himself to historical writing.[41] Edward Cardwell had a political career ahead of him as a Liberal. Neither relished the task they had been given, and they cloaked their reluctance with an air of reverent awe. They agreed the Memoir would make two volumes, one on 1829 and the other on 1834–5 and 1845–6. But Mahon was afraid that publishing the first would offend the Duke of Wellington,[42] and Cardwell wanted to delay both until the controversy over corn law repeal had died down. Something like a determination *not* to understand Peel's critics appears in Cardwell's argument for delaying both volumes together. If they published the first, on Catholic Emancipation and kept back the second, he told Mahon, 'Croker and Disraeli w^d be at once

---

[40] Lord Stanhope and E. Cardwell, *Memoirs of the Rt. Hon. Sir Robert Peel, Bart.*, 2 vols. (1856, 1857). The codicil giving them their commission is vi–xii of vol. i. For Lockhart's comments on the will see CPC Lockhart to Croker, 18 July 1850. Lockhart letters vol. iv. fos. 137–8.

[41] Aubrey Newman, *The Stanhopes of Chevening* (1969) is the nearest thing to a biography.

[42] Cardwell MSS, PRO 30/48/53, fos. 61–6, 11 Oct. 1851. Copy in Stanhope MSS, 54/4.

unchained. Our act would provoke, and w^d seem to justify a renewal of that malignity which the awful event of his death has silenced.'[43]

In this spirit they not only preserved Peel's reputation from hostile scrutiny for as long as possible; they also sought to placate the feelings of Peel's allies. The Memoir was shown in manuscript to the Duke of Wellington's son, the Duke of Newcastle, and the Prince Consort, who all asked for excisions which the editors were only too eager to grant. In this way a collection of letters which even with its original commentary could never have made lively reading, was further drained of its human content, and its publication delayed until almost all those who could have filled in its omissions were dead.[44]

After publication in 1857, Mahon thought his duty was done, but Cardwell was more alert to the Trustees' other obligation, the mass of Peel's papers from which they were to produce a selection. At first the sorting of these papers was entrusted to Cardwell's nephew, a young don at Oxford, C. S. Parker.[45] But neither Mahon nor Cardwell had any inclination to supervise, much less write, a biography. For some years the task was given to the historian Goldwin Smith, in spite of the stipulation he made that he should write a biography proper, and not the conventional 'Life and Letters'. Smith however was offered a chair at Cornell in 1868, and gave up his commission.[46] Parker was his obvious successor, and he produced the first

---

[43] Stanhope MSS, 54/15. Cardwell to Mahon, 7 Oct. 1851. Ibid., 54/4, Lord Douro to Stanhope, 28 Aug. 1856 and 1 Sept. 1856; Duke of Newcastle to Stanhope, 27 June, 23 July, 16 Aug. 1856; Mahon to Prince Consort, 2 Apr. 1852, and 22 Nov. 1856.

[44] Of all criticisms of the *Memoirs* the most penetrating was Macaulay's. He thought they confirmed Peel's 'obstinate determination not to understand what the charge was which I, and others who agreed with me, brought against him. He always affected to think that we blamed him for his conduct in 1829 . . . what we blamed was his conduct in 1825, and still more in 1827.' Trevelyan, ii. 378.

[45] Stanhope MSS, 54/15, Cardwell to Stanhope, 14 Jan. 1856.

[46] Goldwin Smith recommended that the task of sorting Peel's papers be given to T. J. Blackford of 85 High St., Oxford, the Under-Secretary to the Oxford Commission. Stanhope told Cardwell on 27 Oct. [1868] that he was sorry that they had ever allowed Goldwin Smith 'any access to our [sic] papers', & that he would 'have done great injustice to the memory of our departed chief [Peel] if he had treated of it at length'. (Cardwell MSS, PRO 30/48/52, fos. 129–30.) Smith's 'Peel' in *Macmillan's Magazine* xix (Dec. 1868) 97–106 suggests he had done very little with his commission.

volume in 1890. By that time, Jennings had produced his Croker volumes, which printed many letters from Peel. Those letters are only a selection from 620 letters written by Peel to Croker between 1812 and 1846, a correspondence now lost, but regular enough to suggest close friendship. But Parker seems not to have consulted any of this material, making his excuse that what Jennings had printed was full enough to save him the trouble.

It was in Clements' house in Bay City, Michigan, that Myron F. Brightfield read the bulk of the papers Jennings had used, to produce what is still the best study of Croker. Jennings had been interested in politics. Brightfield, a student of the Victorian novel, concentrated on Croker's literary career. He analysed with great accuracy and care the origins and issues of Croker's literary battles, in the course of a shrewd and extremely full account of the politics of the *Quarterly Review*. He was the first scholar to show that Disraeli's animus against Croker had its roots in a discreditable escapade in 1825, when Disraeli had sought to persuade John Murray to put up the money for a newspaper which he proposed J. G. Lockhart should edit. Croker was a friend of Murray, and though he had not as much responsibility for trying to save the publisher from a huge financial loss, as had his friend and colleague Barrow, Disraeli always cherished a prejudice against the Murray circle and what was thought its organ, the *Quarterly*.[47] This did not prevent him from trying to flatter Croker in *Vivian Grey* (1826). By the time he wrote *Coningsby*, however, his main target was Peel's leadership. Peel's Tamworth manifesto was 'an attempt to construct a party without principles' and its effect is 'political infidelity'. In office he had betrayed conservatism by making it a rule 'to consent to no change, until it is clamorously called for, and then instantly to yield'. It is not clear what Croker has to do with all this. *Coningsby* is an awkward blend of political tract and *roman-à-clef*, and in the latter genre characters need to be outwardly identifiable rather than inwardly plausible. Croker was no longer in parliament and led a retired life. Disraeli did not know him well, but he would have had access to what was publicly known of the man, his parliamentary career, his visits to aristocratic

---

[47] Brightfield, 184–95, where Croker's advice that Murray should not launch the newspaper is somewhat played down. Croker to Lockhart of 19 Nov. 1825, NLS, Lockhart MSS, 927, no. 11, fos. 13–15.

houses, literary gossip about his friendships with journalists like Theodore Hook[48] (Lucian Gay in *Coningsby*), and above all his reputation as a severe reviewer. All this could be woven together to make a plausible portrait of a narrow and obsequious intriguer. And up to a point the character of Rigby does resemble Croker. Croker did 'devise shifts for great men's scrapes'. He did have a retreat at Molesey, where he wrote his reviews in a book-lined room. He did savage 'she-liberals' like Lady Morgan, Maria Edgeworth, and Harriet Martineau. He wrote squibs and pasquinades. One might go further and say that, as Disraeli had firsthand experience of literary toadyism, he may well have put something of his own relations with Lyndhurst into his description of Rigby and Lord Monmouth. But Rigby is a hanger-on: Croker was not. Rigby has 'no thought, but a good deal of desultory information'. Croker had an elaborate political philosophy which bore some resemblance to Disraeli's own, but drew less upon fancy than upon a lifetime's experience of politics deepened by considerable historical scholarship. After 1846, they found themselves together in the Protectionist camp, a result which a closer observer than Disraeli might have foreseen and guarded against. But though the two men shared many political opinions, one would not guess it from *Coningsby*, where Rigby is a mere pliant toady to Lord Monmouth's will, and where the case against Peel, so like Croker's eventual position, is not made through the characters, but in long historical disquisitions (written, as one radical critic said, like leaders in the *Morning Chronicle*)[49] while the narrative is suspended.

In fact Croker's role in shaping the opinion of the rank and file of the Tory party was much more important than a restless opportunist like Disraeli could have appreciated. It was indeed Croker's position in Tory journalism that gave the quarrel with Macaulay its political significance. Both men came out as champions for their respective camps. Their review articles were anonymous, but among the politicians, in the salons and the clubs, each writer's identity was well known. Outside the fashionable world however, the reviews were read as party organs, their political articles having the status of ministerial and opposition

---

[48] For Hook, see M. F. Brightfield, *Theodore Hook and his Novels* (Harvard, 1928).
[49] Mrs Grote to R. M. Milnes, 17 Sept. 1844, Houghton MSS, Trinity College, Cambridge.

manifestos; and the crowd of weekly and daily newspapers would fill their leader columns, especially in the parliamentary recess, with extracts from the most striking articles in each quarter, so that a controversy would draw comments in the provincial press. For this reason it was vital for a review to have some agent among the leading politicians, who could give it advance hints of policy changes, and even exposition of current policy, and lend its articles the air of being privy to government secrets.

There was a long tradition of rivalry between the two quarterlies. The *Edinburgh* had been founded in 1802 by four clever but impecunious young men, and it quickly established itself as the ablest as well as the most learned journal of its kind. Its first editor, Francis Jeffrey, set its tone of intelligence tempered with sprightly wit, and he started the custom of 'cutting up' one victim in each number, which Macaulay was to carry on so loyally. At first the *Edinburgh Review* was politically neutral, but in the last years of the war its politics had borne the stamp of the great Whig salon, Holland House, and it was moderate Whig in its politics. Its early reputation for being cleverly written was largely due to the fact that its leading writers had been free of the trammels of office and the obligation to defend a parliamentary party, and its editor could take talent where he found it. Jeffrey was something of a literary purist, but he recruited the radical William Hazlitt and encouraged the early work of Thomas Carlyle. These men show that writing for Jeffrey was a form of literary recognition for its own sake, not a political commitment. The *Edinburgh* was read by reform-minded politicians and progressive lawyers, and its main provincial readership was among the middle class and the less bigoted areas of Dissent. It was by general consent the most prestigious literary periodical in Britain.[50]

The *Quarterly* was from the outset a more expressly political journal, called into existence in 1809, in protest at the *Edinburgh*'s too outspoken criticism of the government's conduct of the war. Its politics reflected official reaction to a year of disasters, starting with Moore's last stand at Corunna, continued with the fiasco of the Walcheren expedition and ending

---

[50] The best account of the early years of the *Edinburgh* is still John Clive, *Scotch Reviewers* (1957). But see also S. Collini, J. Burrow, and D. Winch, *That Noble Science of Politics* (Cambridge, 1983) ch. 2.

with the scandal of Mrs Clark and the Duke of York. Its first editor, William Gifford, took his political cue from Canning, and made the journal into a critical scourge of francophile Whigs and radicals and a staunch defender of the supremacy of monarchy and church. Its literary criticism was strongly tinged with this toryism.[51] Gifford became ill in 1822 and was succeeded for a few months by J. T. Coleridge and then by J. G. Lockhart, who relied on Croker for political guidance. Lockhart was, like Croker, unfortunate in his first biographer and as he plays a significant part in my story, he deserves a digression.[52] His family were lowland gentry from Lanarkshire and, like Jeffrey, he was educated at Glasgow, where his father was minister to the College Kirk. From Glasgow he went to Oxford on a Snell exhibition to Balliol. Oxford drew him to Anglicanism, but Balliol kept him from dissipation and, more surprisingly, from religious scepticism.[53] He returned to Scotland an accomplished classical scholar (an exception to Sydney Smith's joke that 'Greek never crossed the Tweed in any force') and well read in Spanish and Italian literature. On a visit to Germany he mastered German well enough to translate Schlegel, and his familiarity with the German romantic writers gave him a perspective on Scottish culture and especially Scottish Whiggism which was first expressed in *Peter's Letters to his Kinsfolk*.[54] He greatly admired Sir Walter Scott, whose daughter he married and whose executor and biographer he became. But the connection, while it raised his status in the literary world, may well have stifled his real talent. Scott disapproved of his journalism and his novels but approved of his editing the *Quarterly*, as an occupation suited to a gentleman, above newspaper writing with its 'temptation to drop into the *gown and slippers* garb of life'.[55]

[51] For Gifford, see Hill and Helen Shine, *The Quarterly Review under Gifford: Identification of Contributors 1809–1824* (Chapel Hill, 1949) and Brightfield, *Croker*, ch. vi.

[52] Andrew Lang, *Life of J. G. Lockhart* 2 vols. (1897) admitted that he had made no use of Lockhart's letters to Croker or to Murray (I.ix, II.3–4).

[53] CPC, Lockhart to Croker (vol. iii., fo. 42) 7 June 1845. 'In Balliol in my day certainly there was very regular religious instruction. We had lecture[s] in Greek Testament, Articles &c on Sunday & the tutor always made the lecture both critical and doctrinal.'

[54] By 'Peter Morris', 1819. The 'second edition' of this year was actually the first.

[55] Lang., i. 373.

In many ways he was a fine editor. He was an acute critic, and unlike most critics had a direct experience of the creative process. His cosmopolitan feeling for the wider trends in European literature made him alert to new and untried talent, while his precise classical learning enabled him to be ruthless with parochial or mediocre contributors. He had not Gifford's hard aggression, or his suspicion of dissent. In religion he inclined to broad churchmanship, to Coleridgeans rather than Tractarians, and he was more aware of movements in German biblical scholarship than most English writers. His main handicap as an editor was his political naïvety. He was ill at ease in society (where a slight deafness put him at a disadvantage) and unaccustomed to English party loyalties. The *Quarterly* was read in country houses and rectories all over the country, in the heartland of what would become protectionist toryism, and though its circulation was small, its influence was great, since it could claim to direct the minds of the rulers of the shires and parishes. He wanted the *Quarterly* to be the arbiter of taste to the higher classes; he did not relish one consequence of this, that it had to be partisan. As he told John Murray:

We are a Nation of parties. The Q.R. by its hold on the Conservatives, commands the eager attention of their opponents. *Society* is to an immeasurable extent under the indirect influence of *party*. The leaders of parties are also the leaders of Society. Your talkers of the first flight are subservient to the hints of their political oracles. A word of L^d. Landsdowne is reechoed by all the Sydneys & even Hallams—and if I wished to get every Tory wit to praise a particular paper I shd ask nothing but that the Duke or Peel shd give it a smile or a whisper.[56]

That expressed the problem of the editor of either quarterly. They would have liked to be read for the quality of their contributions alone, but the political affiliation prevented it. Because a review was thought to speak for one party or the other, its writers were tempted to carry their polemics into areas which we would consider politically neutral. Between the French Revolution and the first Reform Act English letters were more polarized by political antagonism than ever before or since. When some notable writer on one side wrote a book, a pamphlet or even a poem, it was a matter of pride on the other to

[56] Murray MSS, 30 Aug. 1838.

write it down. It was in this spirit that Macaulay wrote his piti-less dissections of Southey's *Colloquies*, Sadler on population, or Gladstone on Church and State, and Croker excoriated his more numerous victims, from Godwin, Leigh Hunt, and Keats to Whig aristocrats like Lord Holland and Lord John Russell. There is a sense therefore, in which the quarrel, begun during the reform debates by two formidably equipped partisans, could hardly be abandoned by either while each remained a reviewer. The reviews prolonged the quarrel and exacerbated it.

It is this fact which has led many writers (especially in Macaulay's case) to suppose that the quarrel was nothing more than one between a Whig and a Tory, as if each man's political loyalties were simple and constant, affecting his outlook and development in an unproblematical way, like a defect of vision.[57] In fact, of course, most political labels conceal as much as they describe, and a closer investigation of our pair shows that neither was a mere party writer. For one thing, neither would have admitted that he served his party for the transient purposes of gaining or maintaining political office. Both saw party as an instrument of a higher political, or rather moral purpose; indeed what lifts their disagreement above the concerns of the hack journalists and time-serving politicians who worked for party as a livelihood, is that each brought to his writing acute critical intelligence, deep learning, and an independent mind, which lend his political views not only originality, but also a certain nobility and altruism.

[57] 'In public life the two men personified the clash between Whig and Tory, between the *Edinburgh* and the *Quarterly* reviews'. Christopher Lloyd, *Mr Barrow of the Admiralty* (1970), 87.

2

Croker's Political Opinions

You know I never learnt to trust
The wisdom of the Scotch Review
I worship not Napoleon's bust;
I could not blush for Waterloo:

I'm proud of England's glory still,
Of laurels won on land and sea
Call me a Bigot if you will
But pray don't make a Whig of me.

W. M. PRAED

I

Party politics involved different sorts of loyalty for each man, and if we are to see in their dispute more than a crude confrontation of Whig and Tory, we need to try to be more precise about the difference. Croker had a longer political career than Macaulay. He had formed his political opinions in their essentials before Macaulay was born, and had still thirteen years of active political commentary ahead of him when Macaulay retired, from his first and last cabinet office, to write the *History of England*. So Croker's career covers a longer stretch of political history than his rival's and serves to display more conveniently the successive phases in the development of party politics.

It is possible, if a little artificial, to distinguish four such phases. The first, dating from 1790 to 1807, has been called the 'false dawn' of the party system,[1] and it was marked by the personal rivalry of Pitt and Fox which gained a wider audience because it was played out against the great political and social conflict provoked by the French Revolution. It was a false dawn, because party rivalry meant little to the mass of the people

---

[1] M. Roberts, *The Whig Party 1807–1812* (1939), 330.

outside the political classes, and when the war against French hegemony drew the propertied together in a common fear of radical change, the differences between Whig and Tory came to seem less important to the majority than the things they had in common.

In the second phase, from 1807 to 1830, the prevailing mood may be called 'non-party loyalism', because the ministries which historians have loosely called Tory turn out on closer scrutiny to be really coalitions, their ministers being appointed formally by the Crown, to which their allegiance, in official parlance at least, took precedence over their loyalty to one another. The king's government regularly overrode popular demands. No ministry lost a general election before 1841, and defeats in the Commons did not necessarily lead to a government's fall. A small electorate scattered through an ancient representative system which defied recent shifts of wealth and population shielded MPs from the harsher draughts of public opinion, and if governments wanted to know what the country wanted, they did not study by-election returns or Commons' divisions, but consulted experts of their own choice. Much ministerial correspondence of the period seems to be devoted to keeping different interests satisfied and avoiding new departures, but a reforming minister like Peel could effect major changes by negotiating directly with the interested parties and avoiding parliamentary debate altogether. There were parties, but no official party of opposition, and when a radical MP coined the phrase 'His Majesty's Opposition', it was taken as an ironic reference to ministerial weakness. 'Whig' and 'Tory' really ceased to describe parliamentary combinations. The first term contracted into a label for a coterie of borough-owning aristocrats who met exclusion from power with disdain for the compromises of government; the other expanded to mean any active politician satisfied with the traditional institutions of Church and State.

The third phase was ushered in by the Grey ministry in 1830, with a proposal for parliamentary reform which was, by contemporary standards, so radical that it divided opinion, inside and outside parliament, into reformers and conservatives. For sixteen years, until the split in the Tory party in 1846, there was a two-party system, corresponding roughly to an ideological division in the country at large. But though historians of a liberal persuasion have often taken this to have been a period which

1. *John Wilson Croker*, by Sir Thomas Lawrence.

saw the birth of the modern two-party system, the division into parties was shallow and short-lived. Both the Whig governments of Grey and Melbourne and the Tory government of Peel offended, and in the latter case repudiated the doctrinaires among their followers. Melbourne relied on Tory votes to hamper further reform; Peel used liberal votes to advance economic policies displeasing to most Tories. Indeed in the evolution of party politics, Peel was a much more disruptive force than his Whig predecessors. His policies in five years split the party which had returned him to power in 1841, and from 1846 conservatives had to choose between two parties, Protectionists and Peelites, and Britain entered a fourth period, of weak governments with no clear party complexion, which lasted until 1858, one year after Croker's death and one before Macaulay's.

If we consider the careers of our two antagonists in the light of these four phases, it looks as if their political differences were rooted in the fact that they belonged to different generations. Croker formed his political allegiances in the second phase of non-party loyalism, and Macaulay formed his in the third. That was what made their contemporaries think of one as a Tory and the other as a Whig. In fact however each man's political allegiance was highly idiosyncratic, untypical and unserviceable to later generations. Neither lived long enough to see the popular franchise which was the essential condition of the modern party system. They had faced each other briefly across the floor of the House of Commons during a period of acute party antagonism. Then they had gone their different ways. Croker had retired, to write against the Whigs and their policies, with their inevitable sequel, unrestricted democracy. Macaulay had stayed in politics for another decade, but reluctantly and always hankering after the independence of a man of letters. Each man's political conviction was fed by different assumptions and experiences which produced different degrees of intensity in their partisanship. Croker, even in retirement, was a close observer of political developments, who remained emotionally committed to the defence of the aristocratic order, and watched with mounting despair as one by one its defences gave way or were abandoned. Macaulay's early polemics suggest a still more remorseless partisanship, but their subjects are actually more personal than political, and quite early in his career he ceased to write about politics altogether. More and more he wrote with 'a remote past and a remote future' before his mind, ignoring that middle area of compromise and expediency which make up the world of the party politician. To try to turn either of these men into a founder or even forerunner of a modern political party was likely to be an artificial and anachronistic exercise. It was indeed less implausible in Macaulay's case because he was apparently more disposed to welcome change as progress than Croker. But, as we shall see, even this attitude has been exaggerated. When the first volumes of the *History of England* appeared, their political message no more echoed the Whiggism of Fox than it anticipated the liberalism of Asquith. As for Croker, though his views were more directly partisan, they were expressed in support of a party and a society which had disappeared.

II

Croker traced his political opinions to the impact of the French Revolution. 'I was in my ninth year when the Bastille was taken', he recalled at the end of his life, 'it naturally made a great impression on me, and the bloody scenes that so rapidly followed rendered that impression unfavourable'.[2] This is certainly true as far as it goes, but it does not explain why the French Revolution occupied a far more central place in his political outlook than it did in that of other equally reflective contemporaries, Coleridge, for example, or Southey. For this we have to look at his Irish background. Long before he knew of party divisions at Westminster, he was shaped by membership of a peculiar political system.

He was born in Galway in 1780, and his whole education took place in Ireland, first at schools in Cork and finally at Trinity College, Dublin. We know very little about these years of Croker's childhood. He left Ireland when he was quite young, and he soon became what his friends there would have regarded as a great man. He did not look back on his early years with nostalgia, and though he was very kind to his own relatives, he was also careful to distance himself from the more raffish of his countrymen who sought his patronage. 'We Irish', he once said, 'are sad, improvident fellows'.[3] So even when it tells us of his

---

[2] Croker, *Essays on the Early Period of the French Revolution* (1858), v.

[3] NLS, Lockhart MSS, 928, fos. 20–3 (no. 15) to Lockhart, 23 Jan. 1835. See also for instance his comments on William Maginn to Canning, 22, 23 July 1827 (Canning MSS, WYAS, Leeds) and on Prior's *Life of Goldsmith* (J.W.C. to James Prior, 20 Dec. 1836 [copy] C.P.D.) 'I certainly think that of all literary labourers the Irish appear to be the most contitutionally improvident, and to add to the inevitable difficulties of their situation by peculiar bad taste.'

Irish roots, his correspondence reveals little of his feelings. We can only be sure of some general factors.

Croker's upbringing affected his underlying assumptions in at least two ways. One was social. He was brought up in a predominantly agrarian society, where power was vested in landowners and property meant landed property. He once distinguished (in a letter to Robert Peel, of all people) between property and wealth. Great landowners had property and it was this that made them 'essentially conservative'; whereas 'mere manufacturing wealth was fleeting and uncertain and had a tendency the reverse of aristocratical'.[4] He does not seem to have felt at home in the industrial cities, and he did not sympathize with their new wealth, their chapel religion or their earnest ethic of self-help. In fact, because the Irish gentry were poor, and terribly prone to seek favours from government in the form of sinecures and pensions (even opposition 'patriots' forgetting their anti-government rhetoric when offered a place) Croker's early formative experience was of a society which intensified and prolonged the patronage system of the eighteenth century. His father had been an exciseman and rose to be Surveyor-General of the port of Dublin, a post which reverted to one of his sons. Croker himself had a sinecure in the customs which he thought he should have been allowed to retain to defray the expense of being elected.[5] In Ireland such jobbery was a way of life. Croker was like many of his class in regarding as completely natural an aristocrat's duty to dispense patronage and a dependant's right to seek it. The best aspect of this attitude was the loyalty it inculcated in superiors and dependants. The worst aspect was its incapacity to recognize the worth of talent and opinion from outside the charmed circle of patronage.

The other important factor in Croker's background was religious. He was an Irish Protestant.[6] In Ireland that meant belonging to the church of the ruling minority and having privileged access to political and legal appointments. It was not an intolerant minority. In outlook the Protestant clergy resembled

---

[4] Add. MSS. 40320, fos. 233–6, 3 Mar. 1833.
[5] R. G. Thorne, (ed.), *History of Parliament: the House of Commons, 1790–1820*, 534–5; cf. Add. MSS. 40184, Croker to Peel, 9 Aug. 1817, where he sets out the claims of the sitting member to the post.
[6] He was the grandson of a Protestant clergyman called Rathbone.

their English brethren in their mild rationalism and aversion to enthusiasm—a fact which the later alliance of democracy with catholicism in modern Ireland has tended to conceal. Many of the penal laws of the seventeenth century had been repealed or relaxed.[7] Catholics could own land, and in Croker's boyhood they were given the right to vote. As the Catholic middle class grew, many Protestants came to feel that doctrinal differences were outmoded and that those that remained would disappear, as Catholics moved more in 'polite' society. The removal of the disabilities suffered by Catholics was urged by many Protestant leaders, lay and clerical, who felt that it would not only put right a long-standing injustice, but also help Catholics shed those superstitions which Protestants had shed at the Reformation.

This optimism was shattered by the events of 1796 to 1800, the years Croker was an undergraduate at Trinity. The Volunteer movement had already led to an agitation for political reform which the old jobbing machinery of the Ascendancy could barely control. In Croker's childhood, the 'patriots' of a moderate separatism—giving more power to the Irish parliament, but not breaking the ties with Westminster or widening the franchise—were left behind by the extremist activities of the United Irishmen and Wolfe Tone, who demanded complete independence for Ireland and sought to get it with the help of Revolutionary France. The Rebellion of 1798 seemed to show even the most liberal Irishmen of the Ascendancy what violence and fanaticism lurked beneath the surface of polite society, awaiting ignition by any firebrand, Catholic or Protestant. 'The Dissenter fought', Croker wrote later, 'the papist massacred, the Loyalist cut down both'.[8] The threat of French intervention presented the governments of Dublin and London with a stark choice: union of the two parliaments, or a rebellious Ireland which invoked the protection of the French republic.

The Act of Union of 1801 is supposed to have detached the Protestants of the Ascendancy from the separatist cause, making criticism of the union a Catholic monopoly. In fact the process was neither as swift nor as complete as is often claimed.

---

[7] R. F. Foster, *Modern Ireland, 1600–1972* (1988), 203–11.
[8] *A Sketch of the State of Ireland, Past and Present* (1808), repr. in Jennings, 2nd edn. (1885), i. 443. Croker told Lord Londonderry in 1847 that he 'actually served against the rebels in 1798' but gave no details (CPD, 18 Aug. 1847).

'Catholic emancipation', or the admission of Catholics to full political rights, was the survivor of the old inter-denominational
tolerance, and it was advocated by those who felt that the Union
would be complete and secure only when the Catholics in Ireland
had been granted the rights which were their reward for supporting the Union. Croker consistently supported it, indeed he went
further. In a pamphlet in 1808 he said that the doctrinal differences between educated Anglican and Catholic were slight. 'In
all that regards happiness and power you find them [the Pro-
testants] to be Catholics, reading the liturgy; as Catholics are
Protestants, singing the mass'. Admission to office would, he
thought, affect relatively few Catholics: 'at most six lords, one
hundred and fifty commoners and twenty ecclesiastics' and these
would only be freed 'from four or five disabilities, which reach
not, interest not, the mass of the community'. The real problem
lay with the uneducated Catholic majority, among whom

the Irish language, a barbarous jargon, is generally, and in some
districts exclusively spoken: and with it are retained customs and
superstitions as barbarous. Popish legend and pagan tradition are confounded, and revered: for certain holy wells, and sacred places, they
have extraordinary respect; thither crowd, the sick for cure, and the
sinful for expiation; and their priests, deluded or deluding, enjoin
those pilgrimages as penance, or applaud them, when voluntary, as piety.
The religion of such a people is not to be confounded with one of the
same name professed by the enlightened nations of Europe.

For this reason Croker advocated the payment of the Catholic
priesthood by the state, and a property tax, which would replace
the contentious tithe, since 'the enlightening of two millions of
Catholics is more important than indulging two hundred'.[9]

The Act of Union hastened Croker's political rise, but it
had the effect of alienating him from his native country without
making him a comfortably assimilated member of the English
establishment. To Englishmen of the Napoleonic era, union with
Ireland projected into the heart of English politics a horde of needy
Irish adventurers, the most loyal of whom had place-seeking habits
which consorted badly with the prevailing ideal of 'independence'.
Croker was simply one of the most able of these, and the fact

[9] Ibid., 451–2. It is characteristic of Croker's self-conscious classicism that this
pamphlet was written in the style of Tacitus.

that his political and social aspirations were often questioned needs to be set against the fact that the Union merged two political systems at different stages of development. As a barrister, he had to eat the regulation number of dinners at one of the Inns of Court in London, and though he began his legal practice in Ireland, he experienced the same pull of the metropolis which Burke and Grattan had known before him. In his case however, the Union made an Irish legal practice much less attractive. Before it, he might have lived out an obscure career in Dublin. After it, he was, within two years of becoming an MP, given the important post of Secretary to the Admiralty. His return to parliament for Downpatrick was a piece of luck, and it was followed by another, when he was asked by Sir Arthur Wellesley to deputize for him as Irish Secretary while Wellesley was in the Peninsula. He did that very well, and the Admiralty job followed. In 1812 he lost his seat at Downpatrick, significantly to a 'Protestant', but he was valuable enough to the administration to be found a safe seat at Athlone. A later attempt to become member for his own university in 1817–18 also failed, and he fell back on a Hertford borough, first Yarmouth, Isle of Wight and then Bodmin, in Cornwall. He succeeded in a second attempt on Trinity in 1827, but his support for Catholic emancipation lost him the seat within three years. This time Aldeburgh was the safety net.

From a survey of Croker's political career it looks as if he was too liberal for Irish electoral conditions after 1801, yet too Irish ever to think of standing for an open English borough, much less a county. His rise in status apparently brought him no enduring satisfaction. For one thing, his politics lost a regional, not to say a national dimension. He had shared the condescending Ascendancy view, common to separatist and unionist, of the Irish masses. 'He thought them vulgar, lacking in spirit and prone to graft and deceit. He had little sympathy with the romantic cultural nationalism which was beginning to develop in his own day'. Those words were written of Wolfe Tone[10] but they could equally well apply to Croker. His Ireland was the Ireland of the Protestant minority; but his loyalty to it was political rather than religious, and his early experience of its shaky foundations gave him a fellow-feeling with ruling minorities everywhere.

---

[10] Marianne Elliott, *Wolfe Tone: Prophet of Irish Independence* (Yale, 1989), 418.

Protestant Ireland may have been too intolerant for him, but he remained an Irish Protestant, and this basic loyalty explains his want of sympathy for two tributary streams in English Conservative thought. He could not sentimentalize the masses, and so had no sympathy for Tory radicalism; and as Catholicism was the superstition of the Irish peasant, he ran no danger of being, in Newman's words, 'smitten with the love of the Theocratic church', like the Tractarians.[11] He was not moved by Coleridge's argument for a clerisy, nor by Southey's elaborate historical apology for Anglicanism. His defence of the Anglican establishment was political and constitutional: it was 'by law established', it offered a *via media* and its popular appeal was an irrelevance.[12] Many of his critics noticed that Croker's Toryism was hard, unsentimental and legalistic; actually it closely resembled that of more famous Protestant Irishmen such as Wellington and Castlereagh, but no one, as far as I know, identified it as what it was, the outlook of an uprooted member of the Protestant ascendancy.

The events leading to the Union gave him a suspicion of revolution and Jacobinism more intense than that of most English Tories. They also left him with an ineradicable dislike of the English Whigs, since they had colluded with the leaders of the United Irishmen. While the war with France lasted, what I have called non-party loyalism (sometimes inaccurately called 'anti-jacobinism') was to some extent an official philosophy, much closer to the sentiments of ordinary Englishmen than the liberal pacifism which marked (and politically disabled) the Foxite Whigs. Croker would have met it in a simple and uncompromising form among naval officers like Sir Edward Pellew and Sir George Cockburn, and, with suitable literary and historical embellishments, it was the keynote of the politics of the Murray circle. Their organ, the *Quarterly*, was founded to defend what Croker once called 'principles of morality, loyalty, respect for constitutional authorities'.[13] But it was not merely the creed of a party. Croker resembled many of the other uprooted men of his generation such as Gentz, Metternich, Stein, Chateaubriand, and Guizot, in adopting a conservatism which sought to defend not just one country, but a whole society, which the French

---

[11] Newman's *Apologia*, (Oxford, World's Classics edn. 1964), 26.
[12] Murray MSS, Croker to John Murray III, 6 Aug. 1843.
[13] CPC, Croker to Lockhart, 18 Nov. 1819.

Revolution and its sympathizers threatened to sweep away. He wrote in defence, not of a political party but of a whole social order, and hatred of the revolutionary movement ran through his literary work and his politics. His learning strengthened his power as a political writer and advocate, but in both literature and politics he wanted to direct his countrymen away from local concerns to the larger views of the European moral and political order.

It was this more than anything else that attracted Croker to the writings of Burke. Burke, we used to be told, inspired the writers of the English romantic movement against the rationalism of the eighteenth century.[14] Croker's debt to Burke was probably much more profound than that of the Lake Poets. For one thing, Burke was a friend of his family, and his kinsman by marriage. But more importantly, his writings offered a complete political education, and the younger man, treading the same path forty years on, read him as an Irishman, a precursor as well as a prophet. Something of Burke's admiration for the English landed aristocracy informs Croker's relations with Hertford and Lowther, particularly in his anxiety that they should take the place in government to which their birth and wealth entitled them. There is a clear parallel between Burke's attack on the Duke of Bedford in *A Letter to a Noble Lord*, and Croker's own opinion of the Russells as 'the very blackest blood of unchangeable Whiggery'.[15] But these affinities were local and comparatively trivial. Much more important to Croker's outlook was Burke's sense that in the French Revolution what was at stake was the stability of an international order. He once called Burke 'the patriarch of rational reform', and it seems likely that it was from Burke that he derived not only his approval of Catholic relief, but also his view that moderate reform was the best way to frustrate violent revolution, that 'a state without the means of some change is without the means of its conservation'.[16] Burke may have taught the English Jacobins to be nationalists: he taught Croker to be an internationalist.

[14]   A. Cobban, *Edmund Burke and the Revolt against the Eighteenth Century* (1960); J. Godechot, *La Contre-revolution: doctrine et action, 1789–1801* (1962), 65, 74.
[15]   Add. MSS. 40321 fos. 305–6, Croker to Peel, 21 Dec. 1838.
[16]   Burke, *Reflections on the Revolution in France*, in *Works* (Oxford, World's Classics edn. (1907)), iv. 23.

III

At the start of his career Croker probably had to be discreet about his political opinions. When he entered parliament, the old party labels were losing their relevance, and the great issues of political principle, far from being rallying points for particular groups, divided ministries as much as their opponents. The issue of Catholic relief, which had profound implications for the relations of church and state, had so bedevilled the construction of cabinets since 1801 that ministerial stability was only achieved in 1812 by a 'gentleman's agreement' to make it an open question. Equally, the opposition could never agree for long on any policy, least of all the reform of the representative system. Most MPs paid lip service to the ideal of independence, and if they gave this up for office, they did so with an eye on those political figures with whom they would be expected to act. When offered the Secretaryship of the Admiralty, Croker did not ask himself if his opinions were Tory or Whig, but how his accepting an office from Perceval would affect his obligations to Wellington (then commanding the army in Spain) and Canning (who had just fought a duel with Castlereagh).[17] A political outsider—a *novus homo* as he called himself—had to be clear about the terms on which he acknowledged a patron and what that patron's prospects were. A cabinet, from one aspect, was a group of such patrons united in the service of the Crown. But the Crown, in the last active years of George III and the Regency which followed, steadily lost the power of appointing cabinets. Ministers had to be chosen from those active politicians who combined experience of official business with the eloquence to steer it through parliament. More and more they were professionals, knowing one another and appreciating one another's talents, and the experience of war gave them a solidarity and mutual respect which were stronger than the ties of party. They were, when set against the wider society, an oligarchy; but it was an oligarchy refreshed by co-optation and enlightened by the limited but intense exposure which its acts received in parliament.

In his years at the Admiralty, Croker was at its centre. He knew most of the officials in Whitehall, and nearly all the ministers in

---

[17] Croker Coll., University of Florida, Gainesville, Croker to T. Casey, 27 Sept. 1809.

four successive governments. If the Foreign Office wanted to send an ambassador abroad, the request for a ship came to him. If the Secretary at War wanted to transport troops or provisions to the continent, he applied to the Admiralty. Croker knew most of the senior naval officers, through whose good offices he exercised a good deal of patronage, and his correspondence, particularly from Ireland, is full of requests for promotion, and expressions of gratitude for help received. As Secretary, he was the Admiralty's spokesman in the Commons, and in order to explain policy and meet opposition criticism on the administration of the Navy, he had to have all the facts at his command. He was seldom at a loss. Early in 1816, when the Whigs, led by Tierney, launched a sudden attack on the Navy estimates, Croker had to speak at short notice for his colleague as Treasurer of the Navy, and made a reply so conclusive and crushing that it was long remembered as a parliamentary *tour de force*.[18]

Even as a mere official his influence would have been great. But he was also a man of learning and culture, whose company and conversation made him a social asset, the sort of guest hostesses asked to make a dinner memorable, or who could be relied on to enliven a party at a country house weekend. Nothing is more impermanent than witty talk, and if Croker had been in demand for this alone, like his friend Hook, we would be in the dark about the nature of his contribution to society. But the tributes that survive show he was much more. He was amusing company, and he wrote long, informative letters which the recipients kept in large quantities. These show he was valued not merely as a gossip, but also for his candour, shrewdness, and discretion. One does not find in his observations deep thoughts about the import of his experiences or philosophic musings about the trends in society, which might not have been to his readers' taste. One does find accurate narrative by a man concerned to record what he had seen and heard, with an unrefracted judgement which even at this distance commands respect. It certainly did then. When George IV wanted to correct what he considered an unfair slur on himself in Moore's *Life of Sheridan*, he summoned Croker and gave him a long account of his relations with Sheridan, inviting him to take notes.[19] Croker knew

---

[18] Jennings, ii. 80–4.   [19] Jennings, ii. 288–312.

how to get things done. When Lord Lowther at the Office of Woods and Forests in 1829 was struggling with the financial ir-regularities of Nash, the architect of Regent Street, he told Croker that it would be 'a comfort and a blessing to me, if you could come up and direct my conduct at this time'; and he added, 'There is no one, on whose opinion I so much rely as yours'.[20] Tributes like this explain why Croker had so many correspondents in high positions. He wrote with the same easy respectful fluency to people of every rank not, as his enemies imagined, to curry favour, but because they valued his opinion and he had grown accus-tomed to giving it.

Long experience of office, and the habit of making, or par-ticipating in decisions, does tend to generate a feeling of con-tempt for the hostile critic who approaches politics from the outside, even if he does so with the help of some compelling abstract theory; and Croker did not need Burke's attack on the *philosophes* to be distrustful of Whig and radical theory. But he was not a reactionary. Rather, he assumed and generalized the experience of the 1820s, when Whig hopes of office faded, and such liberal measures as were passed came from the adminis-tration. Provided change was proposed by those best qualified to judge, addressed real grievances, and was moderate in scope, Croker did approve it. When Brougham once made fun of his Toryism, he replied with a list to prove that he had always been a reformer:

'I was an early emancipator, when Emancipation would have done good instead of mischief. I was, in 1820 & again in 1829 far in advance of Huskisson Palmerston [&] Melbourne in my opinions of the expediency of *some* Parliamentary reform. In 1820 I urged on Lord Liverpool in writing & by calculations the giving members to Manchester, Birmingham, Leeds &, I think, Sheffield. I advocated a general registration act. I proposed the introduction of the decimal prin-ciple in our coinage and measures. I have been officially a promoter of steam navigation and gas light, & in a more private way of railroads & all other *material* improvements. I have endeavoured to open & extend museums & libraries & to promote the arts. I have been more busy with the erection of public monuments than any individual I recollect, & I think, on the whole, I belong to the class of *rational reformers*. My aversion is to touch the *roots*—to meddle with the foundations,

[20] CPC, Lowther to Croker, 6 June 1829.

but I have no objection to prune the tree to improve the fruit—nor to enlarge & repair the house as our family wants encrease . . .'[21]

What he disapproved of was popular pressure, or Whig or radical leaders acting under its influence. This is of course very much the attitude of the permanent official, whose accumulated experience of his office leads him to distrust the 'amateur' politician. But Croker was so familiar with the members of the Liverpool ministry, that he trusted no others, even on matters of reform. So, for instance, he thought that in the middle 1820s parliamentary reform was not a popular demand at all, but one drummed up by demagogues and agitators. He thought that the most practical grievances of reformers could be met, and the extremer programme frustrated, by the disfranchisement piecemeal of the most objectionable and corrupt boroughs and the transfer of the seats to a few large towns, but that giving in to popular demands for a wider measure of reform would be disastrous.[22] He could not believe that the Whig leadership, which retained its parliamentary influence largely through its ownership of proprietary and nomination boroughs, could ever be sincere in its advocacy of a major reform in the representative system. Few historians who now make this assertion realize who made it first.

Croker's explanation of the origin of the reform crisis of 1830 is in tune with this low estimate of the Whigs. He thought their revival as a political party with prospects of office was brought about only because the Tories had split over the premiership of Canning.[23] He foresaw quite clearly that those who resigned with Wellington in 1827 would force Canning to make overtures to the Whigs and that would do more to revive Whig prospects of office than anything else.[24] When in 1830 Wellington's Ministry proved too weak to ride out the further effects of Catholic emancipation, the Whigs were able to form an administration, but again one too weak to last without some

---

[21] Brougham MSS, 22 Aug. 1842 and 21 Feb. 1851; CPC Box 22, memo of 27 Aug. 1838. For his views on piecemeal disenfranchisement of rotten boroughs, see Add. MSS. 40320, fos. 7–11, C. to Peel, 14 Mar. 1828 and Jennings, ii. 54–5.

[22] Brougham MSS, Croker to Brougham, 22 Aug. 1842, and 21 Feb. 1851; Croker MSS Clements, Box 22, memo d. 'West Molesey 27 October 1838'.

[23] Aspinall, A. (ed.), *The Formation of Canning's Ministry* (Camden Society, 1937), 127.

[24] Lonsdale MSS, J. W. Croker to Viscount Lowther, 11 May 1827.

popular appeal. Parliamentary reform, which Croker held had been a dormant issue from 1824 to 1829, was the form the appeal took. He thought the Whigs proposed it not for its own sake (for they had never agreed on it) but as a way of gaining popularity. Croker's central contention, in explaining how these men had come to form a government after twenty years in the wilderness, was that the old coalition of the forces of order, formed by Pitt and continued by Liverpool, had broken up. He denied (and here he is echoed by Namierite historians) that reform resulted from a great liberalizing movement in the public mind. It was, he declared, 'the state of parties which waked the spirit of Reform, and not Reform which created the state of parties'.[25]

Convinced that popular radicalism was a close ally of revolution, and Whigs at best treacherous friends of traditional institutions, Croker was horrified at the spectacle of a Whig ministry weakly giving way (as he thought) to the political unions and the mob. If his forebodings seem absurd to us, this is partly because we assume the permanence of a peaceful supersession in government, one party following another according to well-worn procedures. For Croker and his friends the change was unprecedented and therefore much more easy to invest with the air of catastrophe. A Whig government meant the removal from office of nearly all the prominent politicians he had known, and the popular vilification of the two he knew best, Wellington and Peel. In the Admiralty he had had a premonitory glimpse of the new reign, when the future William IV had succeeded the tirelessly efficient Lord Melville, been made Lord High Admiral (Melville had been First Lord) and then proceeded to quarrel, first with Sir George Cockburn, and then with Croker himself. When William ascended the throne, Croker was one of a small group of officials who had experienced him in his exercise of authority and they were, not surprisingly, apprehensive. A king who behaved like a liberal bull in a china shop seemed all the more dangerous because the new ministers seemed unlikely to be able to restrain him, being hardly more experienced than their master. 'I cannot express to you', Croker told Hertford, then abroad, 'the indignation which I feel at seeing the destinies of this great empire become the play things of such *chaps* as yellow

<hr>

[25] QR, xlv, no. 90 (July 1831), 'Friendly Advice to the Lords', 525.

Lambton and Johnny Russell, people whom a *club* would not trust to manage their concerns. We are indeed fallen on the days of little men.'[26] They were little men, of course, because the great men, magnates like Hertford and Lowther, men of political weight like Wellington and Peel, seemed not so much replaced as proscribed. His mind full of French revolutionary parallels, Croker feared a repetition in the England of 1831 of the events in France in 1789. The Whigs were leaders of an English *révolte nobiliaire*, and they would be ruthlessly trodden down together with the order to which they belonged, by the mob they had conjured into political life. Croker wrote as if the guillotine were prepared and the tumbrils audible. He drew up in parallel columns a chronology of the events leading up to the execution of Louis XVI and the events to date in what he expected to be the short reign of William IV. The second column was incomplete, but the article's title 'Stages of the Revolution' left little doubt what he thought would be the British monarch's fate.[27] Lockhart had to protest that even *Quarterly* readers needed something more cheering than a diet of doom-laden prophecy.[28]

There is no doubt that Croker sincerely believed that England was on the verge of revolution. The very thoroughness of his researches into the French Revolution, combined with his conviction that 'like causes produce like effects' gave him a more vivid sense than most of his English contemporaries of the parallels, and he was tormented by visions of a slide into tumult, disorder, and confiscation. But what gave his criticism of the Reform Bill and its advocates an almost reckless vehemence was the fact that he had already, before the fall of Wellington's government, decided to retire from politics. His years at the Admiralty had earned him a pension, he had no ambition for cabinet office, and he was in poor health. He stayed in parliament merely to fight the Reform Bill, and his criticism had a sharper edge because he knew he need have no fear of compromising a future career. He justified his retirement by revolutionary precedent. As successive stages of the French Revolution had involved in its errors and crimes more and more people, of varying shades of conviction, leaving scarcely any but the earliest exiles

---

[26] CPC, Letterbooks, 5 Apr. 1831.
[27] *QR*, xlvii, no. 94 (July 1832), 559–589.
[28] CPC, Lockhart letters, vol. I. fo. 61, J.G.L. to C., 20 June 1832.

free of guilt, the only safe and honest thing to do at the onset of the English revolution would be to refuse to participate from the beginning until the whole revolutionary cycle—abstract enthusiasm, naïve concession, administrative confusion, popular tumult, anarchy, and military dictatorship—had run its course.[29] He would only preserve his virtue as a spectator in a private situation: and that meant refusing to sit in 'the assembly which they mean to call the House of Commons'.[30]

What he had not reckoned on was that his speeches against the reform of parliament would raise his political reputation to new heights. From being a mere spokesman for a department, he became the defender of a whole system, and being the foremost critic of the Whig ministries, he was naturally considered a likely member of a future Tory ministry. Friends wrote reproaching him for deserting the cause of order when it most needed him.[31] He had offers of safe seats in the reformed parliament which he refused.[32] He was deep in the counsels of Wellington and Peel, who both treated him as an equal who would play an important part in a future ministry.

For a time, he held to his resolution. Writing to Peel in November 1832, he enthused about his friend's plans for rebuilding Drayton Manor, and then described his own retreat at West Molesey:

I have at last retired into my pretty den here and am as happy, as one can be with the prospect of seeing little of the friends of my early & better days & with the appaling [sic] visions of a bloody anarchy striding towards us. I wish you could see my library here. I think it a model for a book-drawing-room; 'tis but just finished, and all in the very cheapest way; but every one who has seen or sat in it are delighted with it; 'tis rather odd, and would frighten poor Smirke by its angles and irregularities; but it is warm and comfortable, and holds 3,000 volumes, without diminishing the size of the room, and without having, I think, any of the sombre formality of a library. I have besides a little den which holds 1,000 volumes more, and in which I *work*. In short, with the two

[29] Lonsdale MSS, Croker to Lowther, 13 Aug. 1830.
[30] Add. MSS. 40320, fos. 217–19 to Peel, 11 Oct. 1832.
[31] e.g. CPC, T. Elrington (Bishop of Ferns) to J.W.C., 16 Aug. 1832.
[32] One was from Nottingham, another from Wells, which he admitted was 'one of the few places in which the two bills (Reform and Boundary) seem to have left the interest of the gentry and clergy almost in statu quo'. (Add. MSS. 40320, fos. 210–13 to Peel, 8 Aug. 1832).

(very serious ones I admit) drawbacks which I have mentioned, I am as happy in my mind, as satisfied with my very moderate fortunes, & as contented with my humble location & still humbler vocations, as it is possible to be—but how long is the pleasing dream to last?[33]

It did not last long. He kept his resolution in form, but he breached it in spirit. He may have thought he could stay in his 'den' and work at his revolutionary and Johnsonian studies, but he was temperamentally quite unable to keep out of politics. He may have wanted to stay uncontaminated by the impending anarchy, but he was sensitive to the charge of deserting his friends, and he decided to help them with his pen. So what he had originally conceived as occasional prophetic warnings from a recluse became a formal agreement with Murray and Lockhart for a regular political article in the Quarterly. This meant that any political crisis would pull him out of his study and back into the world of politics. At the news of a resignation or a vital division, he would pour out a stream of inquisitive letters to the friends of his 'early and better days' and hasten up to town, do his rounds of the drawing-rooms, sound out opinion in the Carlton and the Athenaeum, and then rush off a political article for Lockhart, packed with advice for the men whose responsibilities he had earlier announced he could not share.

One might think an effort to combine politics and literature would have been fatal to success in either, and in one sense it was. But we should be careful not to invoke modern assumptions about specialization and scholarly objectivity in a milieu where the readership for either was negligible. With Croker especially, it was not a question of politics *versus* literature, because he thought both callings carried a social responsibility and were to be judged by the same criterion, whether or not they contributed to social stability. So he was not perplexed by the dilemma which, as we shall see, made Macaulay so concerned with the example of Mackintosh, whether political commitment was compatible with lasting literary fame. It seems likely that he turned from politics to literature because he thought he would be more useful as a writer than as an official, but his aims were much the same in both. In any case, as I shall try to show when con-

[33] Jennings, ii. 194-5; Brightfield, 113; Add. MSS. 40320, fos. 225-8.

sidering his historical writing, his conception of the historian's role was closer to that of the scholarly editor and archivist than to that of the writer of memorable narrative or prose epic, and he did not dream, as Macaulay did, of leaving some immortal work for posterity. Rather, he felt he could be useful over a wide range of activities, doing them as the occasions arose, as best he could. 'I have no *amour propre d'auteur*', he once told Peel.[34] He was certainly not seduced from writing by a love of society: in fact he carried into retirement a habit of unremitting literary activity, and once admitted that he retained from his official life a constant sense of guilt at not working.[35]

Still, the decision to return to the political battle as a writer had two serious consequences. One was that everything he wrote would be judged as a contribution to politics rather than to literature. In a period in which a growing reading public would turn away from party politics, demanding more amusement from its writers, and even in its serious moods seek solutions to wider social problems than the traditional political rhetoric was fitted to deal with, Croker's exclusively political treatment of public issues and his conception of the critic as a sort of literary police, would come to seem more and more antiquated. Moreover, his contacts in the clubs and country houses where he formed his political views would tend to keep him out of the mainstream of metropolitan literary life. Men who depended on their writing for a living (and he did not) were not likely to welcome as one of their own fraternity a man who wrote as a spokesman for the old aristocracy, or be grateful for such patronage as his political contacts might enable him to put in their way. For his knowledge of the literary world after 1832 Croker depended on Lockhart, just as Lockhart depended on him for guidance in political matters. 'My life has been spent between high politics and the most retired domesticity', he told Lockhart, adding: 'I never was in literary society and have fewer literary acquaintance [*sic*] or associations than any one would believe'.[36] But in retirement he never formed any close friendships with the prominent men of letters who were to shape the public's taste; a younger generation of writers came into being which could not understand

[34] Add. MSS. 40321, fos. 64–5, endorsed by Peel '25 Jan. 1835'.
[35] CPC, J.W.C. to John Murray (Copy) 7 June 1838.
[36] NLS, Lockhart MS. 928, fos. 20–3 [no. 15] 23 Jan. [1835].

his assumptions, and the result was an increasing tendency to self-parody in what he wrote.

On the other hand, his refusal to sit in the reformed parliament, despite his abiding interest in politics, reduced his value as a commentator. Being removed from the rough and tumble of party conflict lost him some of the cool, practical judgement of men and policies which made his letters on politics before 1830 so interesting. It also necessarily reduced his tolerance for opponents. He had to reconcile his concern for the political process with his new role as spectator, by saying that the constitution was heading for disaster, and that the revolution he had predicted was making rapid strides. Every turn of events had to be interpreted to confirm the wisdom of his motive for retirement. He lived more and more in the historic past, his prose becoming clotted with French and Latin tags, his standards of measurement literary rather than practical. The effect was irritating to the working politicians of his own generation and incomprehensible to the political newcomer. In the 1820s he had often made self-deprecating puns on his own name, the word 'croaker' being current slang for a complainer or pessimist.[37] But after 1832 he could hardly joke about it, and the politicians who were struggling to create a new equilibrium naturally resented their efforts being condemned as doomed to failure. Peel's endorsement on one of Croker's letters indicates that this irritation was felt even by an old friend: it reads, 'Mr Croker, *croaking*'.[38] On his side, Croker had to adopt an attitude of deference in order to get at the information he wanted, and the effect was to destroy any impression of objectivity: he became willy-nilly a political apologist. His liberal victims took him to be no more than the advocate of a party, and the question we shall have to ask is, whether they were right.

In the event the demise of the Whig ministry of Grey and Melbourne lifted Croker's gloom. He had expected it to be the prelude to a more radical one, just as the National Assembly had followed the Estates General.[39] Peel's recall in November 1834 was therefore a cheering sign that public opinion was returning to a state of health. But it did not last. Peel's 'Hundred Days'

---

[37] Wellington MSS, WP i/852/11, J.W.C. to Duke of Wellington, 20 Mar. 1826; cf. Elizabeth Longford, *Wellington: The Years of the Sword* (1969) 218.

[38] Add. MSS. 40321, fo. 99, 22 Feb. 1835.

[39] *QR*, vol. liv, no. 107, 284.

showed the radical virus had taken root in the electoral system: evidence of a Tory revival gave no comfort. Croker thought that the damage done by the Reform Act was irreparable, in that it had created a House of Commons which was 'not one of a *triad* of powers—not *tertius*, nor even *primus inter pares*—but the sole essential authority; and that the prerogatives of the other two estates must dwindle at first to a mere nominal existence, and eventually, cease to exist at all'.[40] Moreover, most members of the reformed house were delegates rather than representatives, pledged in effect, if not by formal undertakings, to do the bidding of their constituents, and so unfitted for the task of un-hurried and unbiased deliberation for the public good. It was government's task to legislate, but Melbourne's government, which succeeded Peel's first ministry, would, Croker thought, cravenly capitulate to the demands of its radical supporters. Peel's true role, therefore, was in opposition. There he could render radical measures harmless. But in government, he would have to trim his sails to the prevailing wind. So, paradoxically, the best hope of the opponents of radicalism was a strong Tory party in opposition.[41]

Being unreconciled to the reformed electoral system, Croker did not think he was called on to contribute to devising policies calculated to appeal to the electorate. He had himself used, if he had not coined, the word 'conservative' to describe men of *any* party who saw the need to preserve established institutions against the forces of radicalism and revolution. But conservat-ism was not Toryism. Croker as a historian was too sharply aware of the changes which the word 'Tory' had undergone since the reign of Queen Anne to fall into the pleasing illusion of a con-tinuity of party doctrine or tradition. In the very article in which he reviewed Peel's Tamworth Manifesto, he quoted approvingly a passage from Lord Mahon showing that, just as Tories under Anne supported policies the very opposite of those supported by Tories under George III and George IV, so modern Whigs had completely reversed what their forebears had stood for in the days of Marlborough and Walpole.[42] In a review of a life of

[40] Ibid., vol. liii, no. 106 (Apr. 1835), 551.
[41] Add. MSS. 40321, fos. 179–181, Croker to Peel, 14 Jan. 1836, replying to that in Jennings, ii. 303–6.
[42] QR, vol. liii, no. 105 (Feb. 1835), 281–2.

Bolingbroke later the same year he wrote that in the century since, Whigs and Tories had virtually exchanged tenets, so that 'a Whig of that day very much resembled a Tory of ours, and *vice versa*'.[43]

What then was the real, essential difference between Whig and Tory? Croker's answer is that there is a permanent battle of principle between those who are dissatisfied with the existing system and those who are not.

The party which . . . *would not have things so*—who are for *change*, and of course the advancement of the democratic principle which leads to change, are *Whigs*; those, on the contrary, who think that time is the best and safest reformer, who are averse to sudden and popular change, and who in all dubious cases think it safest to keep *things as they are*, are Tories.[44]

That he conceived this as a conflict based on differences of temperament, becomes clear in a letter he wrote to Brougham, in which he claimed that there were 'two great antagonistic principles at the root of all government—*stability* and *experiment*'. The human mind, he contended, divided as naturally into these as it did into 'indolence and activity, obstinacy and indecision' or any other 'contradictory moods of mind'. The basic disposition showed through all political circumstances, making it possible to say that a man was in the *wrong* party. He illustrated this from their own two cases. 'I don't believe that any circumstances', he told Brougham, 'could have made *you* a Tory or *me* a *Whig*. We might very easily have been thrown into those parties. You might have attached yourself to Pitt, and I might have been a humble follower of Fox, but amongst our more homogeneous associates, we should have been considered as crotchety, troublesome fellows, always hankering after the opposite doctrine'.[45] This view has important implications for party organization and for the eventual breach between Croker and Peel in 1846. For if a political party necessarily comprised men whose real inclinations ran in contrary directions, it could hardly be a reliable instrument of order and stability.

Croker's assumption that politics involved a conflict between a party of stability and a party of change has a reassuringly

[43] *QR*, vol. liv, no. 108 (Sept. 1835), 370.
[44] Ibid., vol. lix, no. 118 (Oct. 1837), 556.
[45] Brougham MSS, 14 Mar. 1839; Jennings, ii. 352–4.

modern ring. But this is misleading. Unlike later exponents of a two-party system, he did not think this conflict healthy, because he thought that the elements which represented stability in his own time—a landed gentry, led by a territorial aristocracy and constrained and civilized by an established church—were inherently more fitted to rule than their rivals for power. So he could never take comfort in the idea of parliamentary conflict as a form of gentlemanly rivalry between one group of interests and another, over which should supervise a set of institutions on the general excellence of which they were both agreed. On the contrary, his own experiences and his French revolutionary studies led him to regard those institutions, monarchy, landed aristocracy, and church, as being permanently on the defensive against their critics, republicans, democrats, and atheists. No fair-seeming aspirations to co-operation, no stress on moderation could conceal the fact that these two groups were fundamentally hostile. Beneath the parliamentary courtesies and constitutional proprieties was a deeper conflict, between order and disorder, stability and anarchy.

In using the word 'conservative' to rally the party of order, Croker did not mean a grouping whose members held approximately the same principles which they would, if called on, sacrifice for party advantage, but rather an all-or-nothing solidarity characterized by a system under siege. Agreements with the opposition were only temporary truces; no agreement in principle could be other than contaminating. There could be no compromise in the battle against subversive ideas: a truce was a chance for the enemy to spread his views peaceably, but the views themselves were no less dangerous.

IV

The main puzzle of Croker's career is that such a thoroughly political mind never attained cabinet rank and lived to see less able men achieve greater outward success. Disraeli's charges, obsequiousness and 'a restless instinct for adroit baseness',[46] do not take us very far. For the fact is that Croker was not very adroit in his own advancement. He refused a place in the cabinet and

[46] *Coningsby*, 83.

endured much reproach for doing so. He twice refused a Privy Councillorship before accepting it as a recognition of his services. He openly disapproved of the way men asked for honours and knighthoods at the start of a new ministry, earning Peel's approval for preferring 'an unadorned name'.[47] Disraeli's 'portrait' was out of date in another respect. The parliamentary influence of Lord Hertford and Lord Lowther (Eskdale in *Coningsby*) had been destroyed by the Reform Act, yet Croker continued the loyal friend of both. Borough patrons on that scale had been a feature of the unreformed constitution. Disraeli misrepresented what was surely a much more modern phenomenon.

Many references to Croker in memoirs and diaries suggest that he could be overbearing and opinionated.[48] But after all, he had been twenty years at the Admiralty, doing work involving vast responsibility and a seat in parliament where that responsibility was often under close public scrutiny. The Navy was an exception to the prevailing aristocratic values: it was a career open to talents, and its senior officers were closer to their often humble origins than their counterparts in political life. Croker had grown accustomed to speaking and being spoken to trenchantly and plainly, and this official habit is likely to have given him that confidence in his own grasp of fact and powers of forecast, which often grated on the sensibilities of his literary friends like Lockhart and Southey. But it had not always been so. Quite early in his career he admitted to an old college friend that he suffered from a diffidence about his merits and a pride in wanting them to be recognized.[49] He was also aware that in aristocratic society the parvenu was judged by severer standards than the man born to wealth and position. His path could not be all conformity and tame compromise. He had his integrity to preserve, and as he could not invoke title or estate, he had to do this by a more rigid observation of forms and conventions. In office, he must be more efficient and disinterested than the norm. Outside it, he must give no advantages to hostile critics. So the combination of diffidence and pride had an interesting effect. He liked

---

[47] Add. MSS. 40494, fos. 136–7 [7 Nov. 1841].
[48] *Mrs Arbuthnot's Journal*, ii. 431–2; *Journal of Sir Walter Scott* (ed. Anderson; Oxford, 1972), 469, *Journal of Thomas Moore* (ed. W. S. Dowden) ii. 351–2.
[49] Croker MSS, Gainsville, Croker to Thomas Casey, 12 Aug. 1811.

to be in complete command of the business in hand, but he liked to cloak his mastery with the formal authority of a superior. In other words, he remained the indispensable but discreet permanent secretary, and his relationships with the Admiralty Commissioner, Sir George Cockburn, and the First Lord, Melville, set the pattern of his relationships with his other patrons.[50]

With Hertford, as I have noted, Croker was an indispensable and trusted adviser rather than a paid employee. He seems to have hoped that his influence might bring his patron back into the political role for which his enormous wealth and influence qualified him, and he was very disappointed at his decision in September 1832 to go abroad and stay there.[51] But even at the end of Hertford's life, Croker's advice was sought as that of a sort of outside umpire, whose word carried more weight than that of any of Hertford's intimates. Fragmentary as it is, the evidence suggests Croker was trusted for his judgement.[52] It is noticeable too that he was deferred to by all the executors appointed under Hertford's will, not only the banker Hopkinson but also the solicitors Capron & Co., and that he bore the brunt of the work in clearing up the estate. The year 1842 is almost a blank in Croker's other correspondence.

Viscount Lowther, the future second Earl of Lonsdale, was another aristocrat who leaned on Croker's judgement.[53] The son of parents who lived apart, he had been brought up by family retainers, and all his life he preferred the company of farmers, stable boys, and jockeys to that of politicians and political hostesses. His journals record an energetic life divided pretty equally between his enthusiasm for horses, farming and estate management, and the company of actresses and opera singers.[54] He preferred his farm near Newmarket to the grandeur of Lowther Castle and when obliged to visit the latter, he preferred

---

[50] Roger Morriss, *Cockburn and the British Navy in Transition* (Exeter, 1997), esp. ch. 5.

[51] Lonsdale MSS, Cumbria R.O. Croker to Viscount Lowther, 12 Sept. 1832.

[52] CPD has correspondence from Hertford's entourage to J.W.C. A letter from Spencer de Horsey to Croker is typical: of Hertford's anger against the Government he writes; 'but when you come up to town a word from you will be all powerful in setting his mind right again.' (Dec. 1841).

[53] Hugh Owen, *The Lowther Family* (Chichester, 1990), 390–3 contains a short sketch. My information is from the long series of letters from Lowther to Croker in CPC. Croker's replies in Lowther MSS, Cumbria R.O. do not go beyond 1837.

[54] Lowther MSS, Lowther Estate Office.

to look over the family property in Whitehaven and its neighbourhood to entertaining his neighbours. Not a great reader, the only writer he spoke of in superlatives was Arthur Young. Though his position and the nine parliamentary seats (Lowther's Ninepins) made him a natural member of Tory administrations, politics bored him. A comment in his journal for January 1836 is typical. 'I dined at Lord Lyndhurst's—there is nothing more boring than an English dinner party'.[55] For all his wealth, he knew he was not equipped for major political decisions. He resigned from the ministry over Catholic Emancipation; more, one suspects, to escape from politics than from any real regard for the Protestant constitution.

Gradually Croker seems to have realized that Lowther's ambition was not to be kindled by politics. But they remained good friends. When in Paris, Lowther would give up his opera singer of the moment to pursue some revolutionary literature Croker wanted, or else to measure the size of one of the rooms which had witnessed some part of the drama of the Committee of Public Safety.[56] At home, he would send Croker impulsive gifts like a pony for the Crokers' adopted daughter, or an offer of a villa on Ullswater. To the end, he resisted his friend's advice to get married and to settle down.[57] By the 1830s however, Croker was absorbed in advancing the career of his third political ally, Sir Robert Peel. That relationship, fraught with fatal consequences for everything he had hoped for, must be the subject of a later chapter.

[55] Journal No. 23, Jan. to Aug. 1836.
[56] CPC, Box 20, folder 25, Lowther to Croker 22, 26, 28 Nov. and 2 Dec. 1835.
[57] Ibid., Box 22, folder 3, 18 July 1837.

3
Macaulay's Politics: From Clapham to Bowood

Fathers have flinty hearts
MACAULAY TO ELLIS,
2 September 1849

Macaulay's Whiggism was no more typical than Croker's Toryism, but strangely, for so clear a writer, it has been much more misrepresented. Trevelyan claimed that his uncle 'left college a staunch and vehement Whig, eager to maintain against all comers . . . that none but Whig opinions had a leg to stand upon'.[1] To make this seem more plausible, he stressed the deep Toryism of the Clapham background and played down the emotional side of Macaulay's inner life as it was revealed in his letters to his family. In this way the differences between Zachary Macaulay and his son could seem more political than temperamental,[2] and the effects of being 'bred a Pharisee' less decisive in shaping his mature outlook. Many writers have followed this lead, assuming that Macaulay's clear, untroubled intellect produced a steadfast, unwavering political allegiance.[3] In fact, Macaulay was rather a late convert to the Whig cause, and it was as much the collapse of the Toryism so much lamented by Croker as a positive commitment to Whig values which shaped his course. He formed a low opinion of the Whig leaders during the crisis leading to the Reform Act, and when it was over he saw the post of Legal Member of the Governor's Council in India not only as a road to financial independence but also as a way of escaping his political obligations. It was only on his return from India that he was persuaded to stand as parliamentary candidate for Edinburgh and, once in parliament, to take a post in

[1] Trevelyan, i. 113.   [2] Ibid., i. 63–4.
[3] e.g. H. A. L. Fisher, *The Whig Historians* (1928), 20.

a Whig ministry tottering for want of talent. When it fell, he went back with relief to his historical work. Even the *History of England* is less whiggish than is commonly held: even there, Trevelyan's pointers have helped conceal from readers the other elements in Macaulay's outlook. So the political career is worth a fresh examination.

Macaulay's upbringing was in its emphasis neither Whig nor Tory. The leading figures of the Clapham Sect who formed his first ideals and impressions of public life were mostly members of the established Church, but they were not dogged defenders of its political privileges. They had to co-operate with members of other Christian denominations in the anti-slavery cause and in the missionary work they supported. In his work in Sierra Leone, Zachary Macaulay had had to deal with Methodists and Baptists as well as pagans, and soon learned that in bringing Christianity to Africa, doctrinal differences were secondary. The earliest success of the Saints, the abolition of the slave trade, was less a matter of arousing public opinion than of lobbying ministers and members of parliament. The larger cause which followed, the abolition of slavery itself, depended rather more on an appeal to public opinion on the central ethical issue, but also involved the persuasion of other governments and hence an appeal to a still wider range of religious opinion and practice. By the time Macaulay was in his teens his father's associates could hardly be called a sect, since they included such men as the Quaker William Allen and the Unitarian William Smith. Zachary Macaulay had, as we shall see, some rigidities of outlook, but he could hardly have acquired the reputation of a good organizer if he had been an intolerant sectarian.[4] As the peace brought the leaders of the anti-slavery cause the opportunities of wider diplomacy and travel in Europe, we find him in close touch with a variety of influential foreigners such as Alexander von Humboldt, Louis Dumont, a highly placed French official, Albert de Staël, his brother-in-law the Duc de Broglie, and even Burke's 'reverend patriarch of sedition,' the Abbé Grégoire.[5]

---

[4] In trying to persuade Stephen to stand for parliament, for instance, Zachary Macaulay said he had 'got the heads of the religious bodies—Church, Quakers, Methodists and also some strong Abolitionists both ministerial and opposition, to reserve themselves for him.' Z.M. to Hannah More, 30 Jan. 1816; Knutsford, 328–30.

[5] Z.M. to Hannah More, 26 Sept. 1820; Knutsford, op. cit., 359.

2. *Thomas Babington Macaulay*, by I. N. Rhodes.

Traditionally, the Saints in parliament had been politically neutral, trying to regulate their conduct by the precepts of the Gospel, and supporting measures not men. 'I voted today,' said Henry Thornton, 'so that if my Master had come again at that moment I might have been able to give an account of my stewardship'.[6] Perhaps not all held to this standard, but it represented their ideal. Party politicians must have found it irritating, and official men like Croker would have preferred them to have supported government through thick and thin. On public order indeed they generally did. The Pauline injunction that the powers that be are ordained of God had lain behind their approval of war with atheistic France and this survived into the peace in the form of a horror of radicalism and disorder which always had for them an atheistic aura. On other issues such as Catholic emancipation they took their own line. Voting according to their conscience was in fact the hallmark of the evangelical politician, and this should be set against claims of political consistency made in retrospect by a generation which no longer felt the same religious fervour. Hannah Trevelyan recalled that her family had until about 1820 been Tory, but that when her father 'found that only the very liberal section of Parliament would support his Anti-Slavery views, he gradually more and more became a decided Whig.'[7] Outwardly this was true. In the 1820s he worked with prominent Whigs, in the Anti-Slavery Society founded in 1823, in the movement for popular education, and in the foundation of the University of London. But in doing so, he did not lay aside his religious convictions. Two of these causes could hardly have made much headway without the support of religious groups, but in his first and central concern, of abolitionism, Zachary seems to have been as pleased to note the support of prominent Tories such as Lord Bexley and Lord Harrowby (whose brother Henry Ryder, the evangelical Bishop of Gloucester, was always 'our bishop' in Zachary's correspondence with Hannah More), as of leading Whigs like Lord Lansdowne and Henry Brougham. In any political crisis, it was the abolitionist cause, 'our cause', that mattered. When Canning died in 1827, most liberals regretted the setback to liberal principles in foreign and economic policy and the cause of Catholic emancipation, but Zachary Macaulay was more concerned that the departed statesman had made a Christian end; and while Whigs and their allies despaired when they saw the weakness of the cabinet which followed, he told Hannah More that his 'great solicitude' was 'to know how

[6] Quoted by I. C. Bradley, 'The Politics of Godliness: Evangelicals in Parliament, 1784–1832', Oxford D.Phil. thesis 1974, 43.
[7] TCM, Hannah Trevelyan's MS journal, fos. 28–9.

the new Cabinet will be affected towards our slavery question. Huskisson is the Colonial Secretary and I confess I have my fears that he is, to say the least, very cold [or] lukewarm in our cause, if not secretly hostile'.[8] Far from being converted to Whig principles, he judged governments by the same criterion as before, and evidently the rule of conscience was observed by his son, who, on abolitionist issues at least, was prepared to resign from the government in which he held an office.

Zachary's religious dogmatism is sometimes assumed to have made his son Thomas a Whig, but there is really very little evidence for this before the latter's Cambridge début in 1818, and after that other influences came into play. It is not even very easy to discern, in the materials that survive, anything like a rebellion against paternal authority. Not that the elder Macaulay was an easy man to love. He discouraged expressions of feeling as self-indulgent. His manner was usually rather grim. He worked unremittingly hard and expected others to do the same. His efficiency drew upon him more than his fair share of work, but the effect of this upon his family does not seem to have concerned him. 'It is no compensation to me', his wife once complained, 'to be told by every Body, that you do the work of four men'.[9] Like many evangelicals he thought life only a short period of probation for eternity, that our earthly sufferings and disappointments were so many obstacles laid out by the divine wisdom to test and improve us, and that happiness was at most a casual benefit and not the central aim. Probably his abolitionist associates heard less of this doctrine than his intimates like Wilberforce, James Stephen, and Hannah More, to whom he wrote his revealing letters. Certain recurrent themes in these would strike the modern reader as rather morbid. They show, for instance, a preoccupation, almost a relish, for deathbed scenes, in which the focus is less upon the sufferer's physical than upon his spiritual state. 'I hope she makes progress', he writes of a mortally ill old lady in Hannah More's circle, 'and, as many months may yet elapse before her sharp trial terminates, I hope the work may yet be perfected.'[10] 'Progress' here means stages of repentance,

---

[8] Z.M. to Hannah More, 24 Aug. 1827 (partly in Knutsford, 443–4); 10 Oct. 1827.
[9] ZM, 26 July 1823. [10] Z.M. to Hannah More, 18 May 1816.

not of physical recovery. Another theme is that worldly reverses
are really occasions for inward scrutiny leading to joyous
sacrifice: the victim had to reflect on what he had done to
deserve the trial, and the result would bring him nearer God.
This belief undoubtedly helped Zachary Macaulay to sustain the
loss of his fortune with great courage and without recrimina-
tion against those relatives to whom he had entrusted his business affairs and whose negligence and incompetence ruined him.[11]
But one is bound to ask if it was not his other-worldly outlook
which had originally led him to lay such responsibilities on
people quite unfit to bear them, and whether his wife and children shared his resignation when the deteriorating business
forced them to move to a humbler neighbourhood and adjust
to more restricted prospects.

One might have expected his uncompromising severity to
have provoked a sharp reaction in his children, but it did not,
even in the eldest. There seem to have been no religious disputes
to divide them. Although the boys were sent to school and the
girls taught at home, there seems to have been no jealousy. The
Macaulay household was a very happy one, and even the financial collapse which scattered the children did not estrange them.
One has only to read their letters with their expressions of warm
affection and especially of grief at parting to see that the family
meant more to them than anything else. One reason for this was
that Zachary Macaulay was too absorbed in his causes, which
often took him away from home for long periods, to pay much
attention to household matters, and was inclined to intervene only
occasionally in his children's lives. But the main reason was that
his wife Selina was more interested in the education and development of her children than in the great causes which absorbed
her husband. His letters show fairly clearly that he was prepared
to sacrifice his children's affection to uphold a principle. He knew
that constant admonition alienated his eldest son, but he kept
it up, and when Tom was at Cambridge even consulted other
undergraduates about his shortcomings.[12] Selina by contrast
put her children's affections first and their opinions second. She

---

[11] The story is told in Knutsford, ch. XII.
[12] Z.M. to Selina Macaulay, 28 Sept. 1821. The informant mentioned here was
Baptist Noel.

encouraged them to be frank so that, as she once put it, they would have no secrets from her and she would know the worst.[13] Their letters show that she shielded Thomas more than once from his father's wrath.[14] Zachary in short represented the great overriding principle of duty, but she personified family affection. The children respected and obeyed him, but they loved and confided in her.

Thomas's education was quite unlike that of his brothers and sisters. As the eldest and most precocious he was marked out as the inheritor of Zachary's mantle. He had a gentleman's education, and the stress on classical languages and rhetorical debating, together with a liberal disdain for trade may have been part of his father's plan that he would succeed Wilberforce and Buxton and lead the abolitionist cause. Like many precocious intellects however, he remained endearingly impractical and dependent. When he was twenty-one, his mother could still make the coach journey from Bristol to London in order to prepare his clothes in time for Cambridge. At twenty-four, he still depended on his father for money. Above all, he was emotionally dependent on his family. Home had been for him what games, parties and especially theatre, were to other boys, and he never ceased to miss it. His family gave him the admiring audience he craved, and sheltered him from a world which, for some years, he found so much more baffling than the books he devoured. As he grew older, his response to its encroaching demands was a mixture of public feats of academic brilliance and more private mockery and satire of its pomposity and cant. His father saw portents of conceit in the one and of frivolity in the other. When the boy was fourteen, Zachary was 'labouring . . . to abate his self-confidence and his proneness unduly to estimate talent in others as compared with moral excellence'. He also worried about his son's 'tendency to laugh at whatever is capable of being made ridiculous in others—and therefore to caricature little faults and defects that he may laugh and make others laugh more heartily'.[15] In this of course he anticipated the two salient features of the famous reviewing style, its confident dogmatism

---

[13] Ibid., Selina Macaulay to Zachary Macaulay, 19 June 1822.
[14] An earlier occasion was in 1811; Z.M. to T.B.M. 6 June 1811 (an unfinished rebuke, explained by Selina to Zachary of the same date).
[15] Z.M. to Hannah More, 24 Jan. 1814.

and its sardonic humour; but the point to note is that he wanted to curb these qualities, not channel them into creative expression. Seven years later, Zachary was still admitting that Tom caused his parents more anxiety than their other children because he was 'in greater danger of aberration'. He went on: 'But his habits of respect and deference and the delight his affectionate heart feels in giving us pleasure form strong ties. If to all this were added deep seated principle, the fear and the love of God, we should be more than content'. The chief obstacle to such piety was what he called the young man's 'ill-timed passion for desultory reading',[16] or in other words, the imaginative literature of antiquity and of modern Europe which his son soaked up like a sponge.

It does not seem to have occurred to Zachary that his son's genius lay in literature, not politics, or law, or religious observance. His own ideal of young manhood was embodied in such evangelicals of the second generation as his son's Trinity contemporary Baptist Noel, or George Stephen, the most eager abolitionist among James Stephen's sons, and it is no surprise to find Thomas disliked such people intensely.[17] They had, as it were, reached their envied place in his father's esteem by a pious imposture, whereas he, the eldest son, with more originality and more learning, had to hide his real opinions behind a mask of deference and conformity, while casting about for a career which, whatever direction it took, could not be assured of his father's approval. One effect of Zachary's lack of sympathy was that Thomas looked to his mother and sisters for the praise he craved, and their responses were not overcritical. It would not be too much to say that his fondness for the centre stage and his habit of bearing down upon his audience were nurtured in the domestic circle. Until quite a late age he read aloud his articles in draft to his mothers and sisters, a fact which surely accounts for their extraordinary clarity and rhetorical force. One imagines him writing to compete with the embroidery and sewing and a hundred household chores, and deliberately inserting his paradoxes to raise a laugh.

---

[16] Z.M. to Hannah More, 30 Nov. 1821.
[17] Ibid., to Hannah More, 27 Dec. 1821 (partially repr. in Knutsford, 376–7) and 1 May 1827. For Noel, see Zachary Macaulay to Selina Macaulay, 28 Sept. 1821, ibid.

Soon after he had settled down in Cambridge, Thomas wrote his father a formal declaration in which he said that he would rather have his applause than university honours, and pledged himself to acquire 'those accomplishments and that information which may qualify me to inherit your public objects, and to succeed to your benevolent enterprises'.[18] Outwardly he kept the pledge, but inwardly he lost the conviction which prompted it and which would have given its fulfilment the single-minded force which informed Zachary's philanthropy. It is easier to identify the effects of this change of outlook than to trace their causes, for outwardly there was no overt act of rebellion. But two influences are fairly clear, one not much noticed by any of Macaulay's admirers, the other noticed even by Trevelyan, but left unexplored.

It is well known that Macaulay disliked mathematics and withdrew from his examination for honours rather than be placed low in the class list. But he excelled at Latin and Greek, and devoured the classical authors with the appetite of a gourmet and the discrimination of a connoisseur. It was inevitable that a Trinity man should have looked with awe to one of the greatest figures of classical scholarship, Richard Bentley.[19] Macaulay's tutor was J. H. Monk, Bentley's first biographer, who probably infected Macaulay with his admiration. But for an evangelical, the sort of prodigies of textual exegesis which made Bentley so remarkable generated a dangerous habit of mind not necessarily favourable to the simple apprehension of scripture required for the Christian life. Textual analysis could be used, and had been used since the Renaissance, to purge the texts of all the careless and ignorant transcriptions of the monkish annotators who had preserved them for posterity. But the same technique could be applied to the foundation documents of the Christian religion, and then the question arose, would the philological scrutiny of the sacred texts strengthen or weaken faith? Did not Gibbon stand as an awful warning of what happened to those who preferred the pagan to the Christian classics? There were scholars in Cambridge who did not fear the effects of textual study of the

---

[18] *LM*, i. 344–6; reported by Zachary Macaulay to Hannah More, 26 Oct. 1818 (ZM).
[19] His measured tribute to Bentley is in his essay on Sir William Temple, *CHE*, iii. 97–106, but see also J. N. A. Munby, *Macaulay's Library* (1966), 22–3.

Bible. One of them was Herbert Marsh, Lady Margaret Professor of Divinity in Cambridge until his appointment to a bishopric in 1816, who was among the first English divines to take seriously the work of German scholars, notably Michaelis, and whose own comparative work on the texts of the Gospels worried High Churchmen and offended evangelicals. Marsh's most outspoken critics among the latter were Charles Simeon and Isaac Milner, the two men whose influence at Cambridge had been Zachary Macaulay's chief reason for sending his son there.[20] It was Milner who, as Dean of Queen's College, had entertained the young Macaulay in 1813. Both Zachary and Hannah More admired Milner's work, and took his part in the controversy with Marsh. When Marsh became a bishop she declared, 'we are fallen on evil tongues and evil days', adding, 'these things reconcile me to leaving the world'.[21] Marsh's first see was Llandaff, where there was no cathedral and no bishop's residence, and his duties probably did not require long absences from Cambridge,[22] but when promoted to Peterborough he issued the famous eighty-seven questions, 'cobwebs to catch Calvinists', which he required his clergy to answer before he would ordain them or confirm them in their livings. They were attacked in the *Christian Observer*.[23] Outwardly, Macaulay was discreetly equivocal on the controversy: an early article of his described the eighty-seven questions as 'unanswerable', and said Marsh's theory of the origin of the Gospels showed the impossibility of reaching doctrinal agreement.[24] But as in the cases of George Stephen and Noel, he gave vent to his feelings in private. It is well known for instance that he took a large library to India which he read and re-read, but there were two books in it which he could not read. One was Pliny's *Natural History*. The other was the *History of the Church of Christ*, begun by Joseph Milner and completed by his brother Isaac. At the end of Volume 1, Macaulay wrote:

[20] For Simeon, see H. E. Hopkins, *Charles Simeon of Cambridge* (1977).

[21] ZM, Hannah More to Zachary Macaulay, 18 July 1816; 23 July 1816, Zachary's reply.

[22] Information from Dr Peter Searby and Professor Keith Robbins.

[23] Vol. xx. no. 3 (Mar. 1821), 160–90; no. 4 (Apr. 1821), 235–58; no. 5 (May 1821), 295–316.

[24] *ER*, xlii, no. 86 (Feb. 1826), 320–1; repr. in Clive & Pinney, *Selected Writings*, 10–11; note: 'with the truth or falsehood of the hypothesis we have nothing to do'.

My quarrel with you is that you are ridiculously credulous; that you wrest everything to your own purpose in defiance of all the rules of sound construction; that you are profoundly ignorant of your subject; that your information is secondhand, and that your style is nauseous . . .

In the second volume he stopped at page 217, writing in the margin:

Here I give in. I have done my best—But the monotonous absurdity, dishonesty and malevolence of this man are beyond me. November 13 [1836][25]

Macaulay never explicitly repudiated his father's beliefs, but he made up for the sacrifice of honesty by roundly condemning many of the men and things Zachary most admired.

The other influence which Macaulay encountered at Cambridge was utilitarianism, but its effect on him has usually been treated rather impressionistically.[26] As so often with Macaulay the difficulties begin when we move outside the orbit of the family. The man who influenced him most was Charles Austin, who is said to have enjoyed expressing the doctrines of utilitarianism in their most paradoxical form. Unfortunately Austin left nothing behind except the reputation of making a fortune at the bar.[27] On the other hand we have Macaulay's own attacks on James Mill's *Essay on Government*, the work which the younger utilitarians regarded as 'a masterpiece of political wisdom', attacks which many take as a wholesale repudiation of the utilitarian system and proof that Austin's impact on Macaulay was short-lived and superficial. An exception is sometimes made for Macaulay's views on India. He had attacked James Mill for the absurdly schematic deductivism of the *Essay on Government*, but he went out of his way in parliament to praise the *History of British India*. In his speech of 10 July 1833 on the renewal of the East India Company's Charter, he called Mill's book 'on the whole the greatest historical work which has appeared in our language since that of Gibbon'.[28] Once in India he adopted

---

[25] Quoted by J. N. L. Munby, *Macaulay's Library* (1966), 9. This did not prevent him from writing a charming account of his meetings with the Dean for Milner's daughter when she came to write his biography. *LM*, vi. 75–8.

[26] cf. J. Clive, 61–95.

[27] J. S. Mill, *Autobiography*, ed. J. Stillinger (Boston, 1969), 48–9.

[28] *Speeches*, 135.

views on the government of the country very similar to Mill's; he consulted Mill while working on the Indian Penal Code, and the most famous of the papers he wrote as Law Member of the Governor's Council was the *Minute on Education*, which has been aptly called 'James Mill's philosophy expressed in Macaulayese'.[29] One writer explains this apparent inconsistency by saying that when considering England's institutions Macaulay expressed himself with the warmth and reverence of a Burkean Whig, but in India where 'reverence had no political value', he could afford to be a utilitarian.[30]

Was Macaulay then a Whig in England but a utilitarian in India? Even in the realm of ideas, there is something to be said for a strict attention to chronology. Macaulay's early essays suggest that he felt the strong pull of utilitarianism long before he considered himself a Whig. Indeed, if we consider the pervasiveness of evangelical morality and practice in the Macaulay family circle, and the comparative naïvety with which the abolitionists pursued their aims regardless of the ties of party, it seems much more likely that the first and most acute conflict which Macaulay experienced was not that between Toryism and Whiggism, but between the evangelical outlook of his family and their friends and the hardly less unworldly philosophy of Bentham and Mill which he met at college. It was a conflict, moreover, less about what his political allegiance was to be (for as we shall see, that was determined by factors outside his control) than about finding his own characteristic voice.

His earliest writings show that the utilitarian doctrine made a much deeper impact than has been generally realized. The basic proposition of utilitarianism is that men call that good which gives pleasure and that bad which gives pain. A good act is an act the consequences of which involve more pleasure than pain, not only to the agent but to those his act affects. The virtuous man is therefore, in Bentham's phrase, the exact calculator; he acts upon a rational assessment of the consequences of his act in pleasure and pain. The more exact his calculation, the more

[29] Duncan Forbes, 'James Mill and India', in *Cambridge Journal* Oct. 1951, 23. But cf. Eric Stokes, *The English Utilitarians and India* (1959).

[30] D. Winch in J. W. Burrow, D. Winch, and S. Collini, *That Noble Science of Politics: a Study in Nineteenth Century History* (Cambridge, 1983), 124.

readily he will be able to discriminate between the short-term gratification he will get and the long-term gratification he will give others. He may covet his neighbour's goods, but a proper foresight will convince him that he has more to gain from a general respect for other people's property. He will then be consulting, not his own happiness but 'the greatest happiness of the greatest number'.

To the evangelical, already familiar with the idea that rational action involved abstinence now for the sake of rewards hereafter, what was new and refreshing was not the morality of calculation (which underpinned the whole scheme of domestic discipline) but the idea that one could have this together with a measure of harmless hedonism. You could pursue pleasure if you liked and if you were prepared to live with society's disapproval, but you need not be plagued with a bad conscience as well, because what men called their consciences amounted to no more than their experiences of pleasure and pain reduced by the laws of associationism into settled habits expressed as general rules. The utilitarian was not less high-minded than the evangelical: he was just less credulous about where he got the rules from.

Of course the calculation of consequences, easy enough in our own domestic circle where we know the likely effect of an act upon friends and familiars, becomes more difficult when applied to changes in society at large. How do we know, for instance, that redistributive taxation does more harm than good to the poor it is intended to benefit? The utilitarians thought that the laws of political economy supplemented the felicific calculus, by showing us what was objectively best for 'the greatest number' without eroding our own freedom of choice. One reason indeed why classical political economy enjoyed such success in Protestant Britain was that it seemed to offer an old and faltering religious morality a new scientific authority. Why, for example, should people be chaste? Because the law of population demonstrated that humans multiplied much faster than the food supply to feed them. So chastity, or continence, was a virtue because it was essential to survival. It showed, as the scriptures did not, why rising pauperism should be met not by more charity but by less. Very soon after the political economists, the moralists seized upon the new science for their own purposes, and the lessons of political economy were being taught in dialogue form by Mrs Marcet,[31] and in fictional form by Harriet Martineau, whose *Illustrations of Political Economy*[32] made her the Hannah More of the new liberal creed.

The third strand which made up utilitarianism was associationist psychology, and this gave it its radical edge. It held that the human mind was a passive receptacle of sensations, from which alone we derived our knowledge. We had no innate ideas. Our abstract ideas were formed in the last analysis by the association of pleasure and pain with particular experiences. We were in fact shaped by our environment, and if teachers could control the environment of their pupils from an early enough age, associating pleasurable experiences with good behaviour and painful ones with bad, then literally anything could be taught, cheaply and effectively, to any one. This was the conviction (very summarily expressed) behind the education James Mill gave his son, and in part it accounts for that astonishing confidence in the power of education to justify and consolidate political reform which began to appear in England in the 1820s. It was expressed in cant phrases like 'the progress of intelligence' and 'the March of Mind', and its practical effects are to be seen in the Mechanics Institute Movement, the Society for the Diffusion of Useful Knowledge, and the new University of London.

Macaulay's early essays show that he had absorbed the whole utilitarian system. In *Machiavelli* (1827) he says that the immorality of the Italian Renaissance was due to the fact that ethics was 'not a science but a taste';[33] in other words that men took up moral positions for aesthetic reasons, not scientifically, knowing their physical effects. Machiavelli was judged by the utilitarian standard, his failing to see 'the great principle, that societies and laws exist only for the purpose of increasing the sum of private happiness'.[34] In the review of Mitford's *History of Greece* (1824) is an application of the utilitarian principle to proving that it is only in a democracy that the interest of the governors and the governed is likely to coincide, an argument taken from James Mill's famous *Essay*.[35] In the *Milton* essay (1825) Macaulay adopted the utilitarians' tone of brisk contempt

---

[31] J. Marcet, *Conversations on Political Economy* (1817).
[32] Ibid., 3rd edn. 11 vols. (1832).   [33] *CHE*, i. 14.
[34] Ibid., 31.   [35] *MW*, i. 160–1.

for traditional maxims in morals and politics. Political economy, he declares, has made such progress, that children can solve problems that baffled the ablest of their forebears. 'Every girl who has read Mrs Marcet's little dialogues on Political Economy could teach Montague or Walpole many lessons in finance'.[36] The phrase 'every schoolboy knows', which recurs in many variants in Macaulay's writing is often taken as a sign that he naïvely expected every young person to match his own precocity. 'Every schoolboy knows who imprisoned Montezuma, and who strangled Atahualpa'.[37] A more likely origin is the simple empiricism which derives from the associationist theory. The mere exposure of the mind to facts precipitates understanding; the increase of intelligence (or as we would say, information) meant that more people were better informed than ever before, so social progress was irreversible, and modern children were bound to know much more than adults a hundred years ago.

The same essay shows how far Macaulay was prepared to go along with the utilitarians' denigration of poetry. Judged by the criteria of science, poetry was misrepresentation, and a fondness for it a symptom of intellectual backwardness. This was the argument James Mill had used in the *History of British India* against Sir William Jones and the orientalists, to prove that the Hindus were in fact very low on the ladder of civilization; and it was extended by Mill's followers to discredit the admirers of the English romantic poets with their high conception of the poet as religious teacher. Macaulay's *Milton* is built around the problem how, if poetry is the characteristic utterance of a primitive culture, Milton could have been a great poet *and* a republican. Nations advance, he says, as they learn to generalize from their observations and, instead of feeling strongly, reason abstractly. In their literature they 'advance from particular images to general terms'. So 'the vocabulary of an enlightened society is philosophical, that of a half-civilized people is poetical'. As knowledge advances, so does the generalizing habit: men look less at individuals and more at classes. 'They therefore make better theories and worse poems.'[38]

---

[36] *CHE*, i. 6.   [37] Ibid., iii. 109.
[38] Ibid., i. 6. Macaulay's essay on Dryden shows the same concern how, in Dryden's case, purity of poetic practice could be reconciled with royalist politics.

But Macaulay's family loyalties set a limit upon his appetite for rejection and demolition, and as an evangelical education could not but be resistant to the utilitarian ethos, there were severe tensions. These are evident to any attentive reading of the early essays. The essay on Milton, for example, has a criticism of Gibbon's five causes of the spread of Christianity. Macaulay has clearly been reading Hume on the natural history of religion, but he deftly uses Hume's argument against Gibbon. A philosophical conception of God, Macaulay admits, 'attracted few worshippers' in the early years of the Church. People cannot worship abstractions; they need to embody their objects of devotion in concrete, palpable forms. But then he adds, that is exactly why the gospel of Jesus spread so quickly.

It was before Deity embodied in a human form, walking among men, partaking of their infirmities, leaning on their bosoms, weeping over their graves, slumbering in the manger, bleeding on the cross, that the prejudices of the Synagogue, and the doubts of the Academy, and the pride of the Portico, and the fasces of the lictor, and the swords of thirty legions, were humbled in the dust.[39]

The habit of metonymy is Gibbon's, but this is an evangelical Christian reply to Gibbon's Chapter XV.

Macaulay never publicly repudiated his religious background, even when mocking the effects of religious wishful thinking or bigotry. The review of Southey's *Colloquies* starts with a powerful utilitarian attack on the idea that religious belief is the basis of society, but it also has a moving passage on the way the alliance with the temporal power had always harmed the Church.[40] There is a similar passage in the first attack on Sadler.[41] There cannot be much doubt that his religious upbringing marked Macaulay very deeply. His prose may derive its brisk, dismissive clarity from a utilitarian scepticism, but its moral depth and force come from the Authorized Version of the Bible. Perhaps the tension between the two may account for those violent antitheses which became the distinguishing mark of Macaulay's prose.[42] Too fastidious to imitate the evangelical preacher's habit of drawing lessons direct from scripture, yet too earnest to adopt

[39] *CHE*, i. 22–3.   [40] Ibid., i. 254–5.   [41] *MW*, i. 15–16.
[42] cf. however George Levine's view in *The Boundaries of Fiction: Carlyle, Macaulay, Newman* (Princeton, 1968), 83 ff.

the light, non-committal irony of Gibbon or Hume, Macaulay expresses the tension within himself by setting opposites in startling juxtaposition. An early example is actually in verse, and comes in a letter to his father. It is about Voltaire.

> Teacher of truth, and lies, and good, and crime,
> Martyr, and knave, and moralist, and rake,
> Most weak, most wise, most abject, most sublime,
> The guardian Angel, the seducing Snake . . .

and so on.[43] The contrasts occur very frequently in his prose, and their function is the same: to have a little of each world, without committing himself to either. When he tells his father of his visit to Sydney Smith for example, the antithesis is a mere mask to hide his affection for the man.

His misfortune is to have chosen a profession at once above and below him. Zeal would have made him a prodigy. Formality and bigotry would have made him bishop. But he could neither rise to the duties of his order, nor stoop to its degradations.[44]

Zachary would certainly have disapproved of Sydney Smith. His son as certainly would have preferred him as a wit than as a prodigy of zeal. But he gives his father a description which gestures at the ideal of an evangelical preacher, as well as the evangelical suspicion of bishops, and conceals the real source of enjoyment, Sydney Smith's sense of humour.

After leaving Cambridge and starting to earn his living as a barrister then, Macaulay was hardly a 'staunch and vehement Whig', but rather an uneasy mixture of evangelical and utilitarian. Neither creed involved him in any clear commitment to party, for two reasons. One is that for him politics had always taken second place to literature. It may be that this preference was the result of his evangelical upbringing with its stress on the transient nature of merely human institutions. But in any case his extraordinary precocity meant that even in his boyhood his learning and his vocabulary ran ahead of his experience, and the decisive influences upon him derived not from his surroundings but from his inner life, his reading and the huge storehouse of imagery and example which that reading gathered. When he told his father, after the 'Peterloo Massacre', that he took his

---

[43] *LM*, i. 209.   [44] Ibid., i. 216.

inspiration not from Hunt and Waithman but from Cicero, Tacitus, and Milton, he may have sounded pompous but he was reporting a fact.[45] His political ideas came from books and not from life, and even in his early writings he maintained that political achievements were less lasting than literary ones. Bonaparte, he told his father in 1821, had done no more than 'force the often reluctant service of a few thousand hands for ten or twelve years', whereas Homer had 'through six and twenty centuries . . . influenced the feelings, interested the sympathies, governed and fixed the standard of taste of vast and enlightened empires'.[46] The idea is first broached as a defence of his own privacy against his father's killjoy suspicions that his son was wasting time better spent on his appointed studies: but later it is developed into the doctrine that such attacks on art and literature are fatal to the attackers, and the latter are identified with religious asceticism. In the *Milton*, for instance, he says that the political victories of the Puritans were nullified by the art which they spurned and which survived them:

Though they were the conquerors, their enemies were the painters. As a body, the Roundheads had done their utmost to decry and ruin literature; and literature was even with them, as in the long run, it always is with its enemies.[47]

As we shall presently see, it was not long before he found the same unpleasant puritanism in the work of the French Jacobins, and after them in the English utilitarians. By then, his emancipation would be nearly complete, but its achievement would take the form, not of a choice of political creed, but as a vindication of literature and freedom of expression against political interference.

The second reason for doubting an early political commitment is that, while Macaulay probably assumed that his education was to be in some way a preparation for public life, it was by no means clear in 1824 that his lot would be cast with the Whig party. Here again Trevelyan inserted partisanship where none existed. 'The young recruit', he says in his colourful way, 'went gaily to his post in the ranks of that party whose coming fortunes

[45] *LM*, i. 133.   [46] Ibid., i. 163.   [47] *CHE*, i. 31.

he was prepared loyally to follow, and the history of whose past he was destined eloquently, and perhaps imperishably, to record'.[48] The truth is more prosaic. Quite apart from Clapham's tradition of appealing to men of all parties (one corollary of which was that they accepted patronage with a fine impartiality from any), the Whigs could not offer the best prospects to political ambition, and the young Macaulay's early ambition was literary, rather than political.

The Whigs were an aristocratic party, knit together by a century or more of intermarriage, a 'cousinhood' as they were sometimes called, whose leaders were great landowners wielding their political influence through their electoral property in nomination boroughs. Some of the most prominent had a common memory of ancestral struggle with the Crown, but this had remained more a family tradition than a claim to popular leadership. There was some truth in the joke, made by one of the cousinhood, that Whigs, like poets, were born, not made.[49] Probably in Macaulay's youth they looked more like a clan than a political party because a Whig administration was becoming a distant memory. They had last held office in 1807. They had not wholeheartedly supported the war with France, and when peace came they viewed the problems it raised with incomprehension and distaste. Their protest over 'Peterloo' had been ineffectual. They failed to stop the Six Acts, or exploit the monarchy's embarrassment during the Queen's Trial in 1820. Not surprisingly, they came in for more abuse from radicals than the Tories did. In radical eyes, being a Tory was only an honest acknowledgement of the lure of office. But being a Whig was to profess some principles radicals professed, but to do nothing about them.

Of course, Whiggism was not only family connection. It was also a political outlook. It was pre-eminently an outlook acquired in the non-clerical universities of Scotland, where many young aristocrats were educated, and many without high connections like Henry Brougham, Francis Horner, Francis Jeffrey, and Sir James Mackintosh acquired the tone of mind we now

[48] Trevelyan, i. 130.
[49] G. W. E. Russell, *Collections and Recollections* (1903), 146. He adds, less plausibly, 'Macaulay was probably the only man who, being born outside the privileged enclosure, ever penetrated to its heart and assimilated its spirit'.

associate with the Scottish enlightenment. Its most notable literary expression was the *Edinburgh Review*. The *Edinburgh* helped to keep Whiggism intellectually alert and critical, but it could not put the party into office. Indeed, Whig theorists and men of letters often had either to give up hope of a political career, or else enter it on terms of humiliating dependence. The paradox of early nineteenth century Whiggism was that its political survival relied heavily on the nomination boroughs owned by Whig grandees. Some of these patrons, like the Duke of Devonshire, generously set aside personal connections for the party's sake, but such bounty was not something a young politician could depend on. And while the borough-owners in their opulent isolation remained indifferent to the coarse business of marshalling a political party, younger Tories like Huskisson and Peel absorbed the doctrines of the Scottish historians and economists to forge the economic policy which came to be called (by a later generation of historians) 'liberal Toryism'.

When he made his début as an Edinburgh reviewer, and began to meet prominent Whigs, Macaulay was more impressed by the writers than by the politicians. He visited Jeffrey at Craigcrook, his home in Edinburgh, and formed a friendship which was to last until the older man's death. Jeffrey was vastly impressed by Macaulay's talents, and wanted him as his successor in the editorship of the *Edinburgh*, and although Macaulay declined, there was no break in their relations. Jeffrey plainly gave the younger man the ungrudging praise so conspicuously wanting from Zachary. Sydney Smith too, though a more critical observer (it was he who called Macaulay 'a book in breeches') must have been a refreshing change from the serious clergy of the Clapham circle.

Nearer home, there were two House of Commons Whigs well known to the Macaulay family whose careers illustrated the hazards and sacrifices of politics in opposition. Sir James Mackintosh's career in some ways anticipated Macaulay's.[50] After a spectacular début as a political writer for the Foxite Whigs,

---

[50] R. J. Mackintosh's *Memoirs of the Life of the Rt. Hon. Sir James Mackintosh* (2 vols., 1836) is uncritical and poorly arranged. The latest biography is by P. O'Leary, *Sir James Mackintosh, the Whig Cicero* (Aberdeen 1989); but still the best portrait of 'the man of promise' is by H. L. Bulwer [Lord Dalling] in *Historical Characters* (2 vols., 1868).

he soon decided that the French Revolution was a bad thing, sought absolution from Burke, and accepted a legal appointment in India from Addington.[51] On his return he embarked upon a history of the revolution of 1688 which he never completed, and for which his transcriptions were bequeathed to Macaulay. His conversion to Burke's view of the Constitution as an 'entailed inheritance', to be respected and only gradually and reverently adapted to changing conditions was first outlined in a famous attack on Bentham's reform proposals, and it deserves credit as the first expression of the policy of piecemeal disenfranchisement pursued by Lord John Russell after 1820.[52] But he himself was not conspicuous on the reforming side in Parliament. When Macaulay first met him he was MP for the Duke of Devonshire's borough of Knaresborough, and a figure well-known to members of the Clapham Sect through his friendship with the Inglises. He was one of the few men from whom Macaulay admitted he learned something every time they met, but he was also a graphic example of the difficulty experienced by a man of slender means who tried to combine scholarship and the social round. Contemporaries remembered him as 'the man of promise' who never confirmed with any lasting work of literature the expectations which admirers formed from his conversation. Radicals looked on him as a turncoat, and James Mill wrote a long and clumsy polemic against him which has lost all its force because it seems so out of proportion to the meagre achievement of the man.[53] Macaulay deprecated this attack in a candid letter to its author;[54] but the frequency of his own references to Mackintosh's dilemma shows that he felt the same contrary loyalties himself. 'He fell between two stools. He attended too much to politics for a man engaged in a great literary work, and too much to literature for a man who aimed at a great influence in politics'.[55] His example showed that a man could achieve fame in one, but not in both.

[51] CPD, Lord Sidmouth to J. W. Croker, 26 June 1835. 'Absolution' was Sidmouth's word. Croker was consulting him for his article in *QR* liv. no. 107 (July 1835), 250–94.

[52] *ER*, xxxi. no. 61 (Dec. 1818), 165–203.

[53] [James Mill] *Fragment on Mackintosh* (1835).

[54] *LM*, iii. 151.   [55] Ibid., iv. 23, 264.

The other Whig exemplar who loomed large in Macaulay's youth was Henry Brougham.[56] He had a more impatient attitude than Mackintosh to aristocratic patronage. He wanted to be the leader of an educated liberal public, and he chafed at the fact that he, the most powerful orator among the opposition, could find a seat neither for a large town nor for his native county, but had to accept one for the tiny borough of Winchelsea from its patron, the Earl of Darlington. He had a wider vision of what the Whigs might do in politics than most of the grandees, and he had done more to revive the party's hopes of office than most House of Commons Whigs. But for all his capacity to inspire, he could not lead. He had what would surely now be called a depressive personality, periods of frenetic activity and gaiety, in which he thought he was carrying all before him, alternating with bouts of the blackest gloom, when he would retire to his castellated manor house in Westmorland and it would be given out that he was ill. Soon he would recover and return to the fray. He had a trenchant eloquence which made ministers quail, his witticisms were repeated throughout London society, and he had a personal magnetism which drew men of all sorts into his orbit. On the other hand, he was volatile and unreliable, his mind so engrossed in complex strategies, that he tended to overrate the number of people able or willing to follow his train of thought, and the still smaller number who would continue to give him credit when he changed his mind. He might captivate earnest philanthropists whose main test of a man's sincerity was that he should agree with them; hence the devotion of men like Zachary Macaulay and James Mill. But to the aristocratic Whigs, the unintellectual borough owners who inherited their politics with their land, he was an awkward ally, whom they regarded as one would a refractory horse, always ready to bolt out of course. Between these two was a substantial class of Whig writers and lawyers such as Jeffrey and Sydney Smith, who understood his arguments, appreciated his extraordinary gifts,

---

[56] The best political biography as far as it goes is still Chester New, *The Life of Henry Brougham to 1830* (Oxford 1961). R. Stewart's *Henry Brougham: His Public Career 1778–1868* (1986) uses none of the plentiful MS material. F. Hawes' *Henry Brougham* (1957) is the most penetrating psychological study, especially good on the relationship with T.B.M. (197–9). For the family background see M. W. Thomas, *A History of Brougham Hall and High Head Castle* (1992).

but totally mistrusted his judgement. Macaulay began by acting with his father in the first category but soon gravitated to the last.

Brougham's multifarious activities were all driven by political ambition. If he wrote a treatise on hydrostatics for the S.D.U.K., it was to show that he was leading the March of Mind. If he flattered Bentham, it was to gain converts to law reform among Bentham's followers. If he addressed Zachary Macaulay in the evangelical manner as 'My dear Friend', it was because he had shrewdly assessed the strength of the abolitionists' organization, which he was to exploit in 1830 when standing for Wilberforce's old constituency of Yorkshire.[57] He was all things to all men, and bothered very little about the consistency of appearing at anti-slavery meetings with evangelicals or at the council of London University with utilitarians. Even his old loyalties to the Whig leadership grew weaker. Convinced that he was in closer touch with public opinion than they, he offended some noble susceptibilities by urging Whig MPs to support Canning in 1827, and when Canning died, he declared that there had been 'a new casting of political sects', and that the old political labels of Loyalist and Jacobin, Whig and Tory were out of date. They would be replaced, he said, by 'two great divisions of the community . . . the *Liberal* and the *Illiberal*,'[58] and he was sure the former would predominate. With an orator's habit of mistaking applause for agreement, he expected to lead them, and in this scheme he saw Macaulay as a useful subordinate.

Macaulay's ambitions however, were more literary and historical than political. Such political views as he professed owed more to his historical reading than to his perception of contemporary political events. He first began to turn against the younger utilitarians when he realized their affinities with the English puritans and the French Jacobins.[59] His long review of Hallam presents an interpretation of English constitutional development since the Civil War before culminating in a demand for moderate reform of the representative system. As with Mackintosh, the scholar in him predominated over the activist.

[57] ZM, Brougham to Z. Macaulay, P/mark 2 July 1830, given with omissions in Knutsford, 454; and 15 July; 31 July; 4 Oct. 1830 (Knutsford, 456–7).

[58] ER, xlvi. no. 92 (Oct. 1827) 'The State of Parties', 431.

[59] ER, xlvi. no. 91 (June 1827) 'The Present Administration', 260–1.

So he did not share Brougham's political vision, and even though he had some sympathy with his educational plans, he remained critical of his literary pretensions and became resentful of his patronage. Resentment deepened into dislike as that patronage became more intrusive.

In 1826 Zachary Macaulay learned that his business had been ruined. The family did not face poverty at once, and wealthy friends helped to soften the first hardships, but the children's prospects were steadily curtailed. The girls faced the choice of domestic drudgery or marriage without a dowry. John had to look to preferment in the Church. Henry, who in 1824 had entered a counting house, was sent out to Sierra Leone to salvage what he could from the wreck of the family firm. Charles was to be apprenticed to a doctor cousin. Thomas himself had to face the prospect of becoming the mainstay of two ailing parents and his unmarried sisters, and as his earnings at the bar were negligible, that meant they depended on his Trinity fellowship, his writing, and any other post he could pick up. In May 1827 Brougham asked the new Lord Chancellor, Lyndhurst, to give his young friend one of the Commissioner-ships in Bankruptcy in his gift, and then told Zachary Macaulay what he had done.[60] A little more discretion on his part would have raised fewer hopes in the Macaulay household. Despite the poor economic prospects which made them eager, Thomas said that he would only accept the post while Canning was in power. But it had yet to be confirmed when Canning died in August. It was not officially granted until 4 January 1828, four days before Canning's successor Goderich resigned, and Wellington was sent for to form a ministry.[61] Macaulay was reconciled to accepting it on the grounds that it had been offered while there was no ministry in being,[62] but he held it through Wellington's ministry in which Lyndhurst was Lord Chancellor. He lost it when Wellington fell in November 1830, and Brougham failed to renew it when he succeeded Lyndhurst as Lord Chancellor. This became another cause of resentment between him and Macaulay and between Macaulay and his

---

[60] ZM, MS no. MY99. Selina Macaulay's Journal says this letter came on 4 May 1827, which would make Brougham's letter to Lyndhurst (Knutsford, 442) dated 2 May 1827.
[61] ZM, Selina Macaulay's Journal, 5 Jan. 1828.   [62] LM, i. 230.

father,[63] but the fact remains that Thomas was a Tory placeman before he became a Whig MP.

With legal preferment so unreliable, he naturally grew more anxious about his position on the *Edinburgh Review*. Jeffrey had the highest opinion of Macaulay's value to the review. But Brougham was jealous, contradicting what Macaulay wrote, and complaining that he was taking up too much space with his articles.[64] Jeffrey wanted to keep both men as contributors and his tact might have achieved some compromise, but in 1829 he became Dean of the Faculty of Advocates, and decided to give up the editorship. His successor was Macvey Napier, whose first number appeared in October 1829. Napier soon found he had a quarrel on his hands, or rather two, one between Macaulay and Brougham, the other in the form of Macaulay's attack on James Mill.

This, the most famous of Macaulay's polemics, has been much discussed by experts on utilitarianism and, as it played such a large part in his reflections on the nature of social science, by students of J. S. Mill. But Macaulay's own motives in the controversy have been relatively neglected. It is usually assumed that he wrote as a Whig and to defend Whiggism. One expert even claimed that in his successive attacks on the utilitarians Macaulay was drawing 'a definite line of demarcation' between them and the Whigs, as if he was already the established theorist of a united party.[65] But this is to credit the Whigs with more cohesion than they enjoyed, and it implies that the moderate programme of piecemeal reform which Macaulay shared with Mackintosh was exclusively Whig, whereas many liberal Tories (Croker included) would have subscribed to it too.

In any case I doubt whether Macaulay, a young lawyer treading warily in Whig company, only lately aware of the antagonisms below the surface courtesies, especially between Jeffrey and Sydney Smith on one side and Brougham on the other, was in a position to draw that 'line of demarcation'. His attack on James Mill and his followers made some shrewd political points, and I have described these in another book. But what we are concerned with here is what the controversy tells us about

---

[63] [Margaret Macaulay] *Recollections*, 62–5.
[64] Ibid., 55–6.   [65] Clive, 126.

Macaulay's evolution, not the wider reform movement. His early polemics, notwithstanding their hard aggression, are not political manifestos. They are too exclusively devoted to a single object of scorn to accommodate the tentative and provisional nature of political judgement, and their inexorable rhetorical momentum is not meant to give the reader much time to form his own opinions. Their object may be public, but their manner is highly personal. They choose targets which serve as proving-grounds for his own convictions. As polemics, they usually orig-inate in some personal feeling. The feeling gathers confidence and elaboration over a period, often making use of other men's arguments and observations. Then some vulnerable book or pam-phlet appears which offers the opportunity for a pulverizing dis-play of argument, rhetoric, sarcasm, mockery, and burlesque.

Macaulay's attacks on Mill and the utilitarians stand out among his polemical essays for two reasons. He did not want to reprint them, and the work reviewed was far from new. He had been familiar with James Mill's essays in his Cambridge days. What made him choose, nine years after its first publication and five after he had summarized its argument in his review of Mitford, to turn all the power of his ridicule upon the most famous of these essays?

Disillusionment was one factor. It was one thing to debate utilitarian ideas in the Cambridge Union among one's peers; quite another to encounter those ideas in the drab pages of a Benthamite review. Contradiction from men you respect is not half as disillusioning as agreement from men you despise. When Macaulay met the young friends of John Mill in the London Debating Society he was struck by the combination of the purit-anism he had come to dislike in the Commonwealth period, with the taste for abstract theorizing more reminiscent of the French Jacobins. At first he thought them formidable, and said so in his political article in June 1827. But by 1829 his tone had changed from fear to mockery. It is not hard to see why. From its first number, the *Westminster Review*, the utilitarians' periodical, had attacked the *Edinburgh* in articles which, from the abstraction of their style and the rigid logic of their argument, everyone knew to be James Mill's. But the *Edinburgh* did not deign to reply, leaving its radical rival to sink from its own aversion to the arts of pleasing its readers. The *Westminster*'s management lurched from crisis to crisis, and in February 1829 it was learned that the Mills, father and son, had quarrelled with the editor and seceded from the review.[66] Macaulay's first attack appeared the following month. This time the tone was loftily condescending. Some of Mill's admirers, said Macaulay, were 'men who have really read and thought much', but most were men 'whose attainments just suffice to elevate them from the insignificance of dunces to the dignity of bores'.

The political argument was fairly general. Mill's view was that as government is instituted to check men's propensity to plunder one another, only that form of government which reduces that propensity to a minimum is safe, and that is democracy. But the *Essay on Government* ended with the famous apostrophe of the 'middle rank' which 'gave to science, to art and to legislation their most distinguished ornaments'. So it was not clear what Mill advocated, a wide franchise giving the vote to the majority, or a restricted one which gave it to the best informed and most virtuous. Macaulay's sympathies were with a restricted franchise. He had already echoed Mill's praise of the middle rank in his article on London University and at the end of his review of Hallam. So what this part of his criticism amounted to was a challenge to the utilitarians to say whether they were democrats (in which case their premises of self-interest made them politically dangerous) or favoured a franchise more narrowly based upon property. It is not an anti-utilitarian argument. When Macaulay asked, 'If the interest of the middle rank be identical with that of the people, why should not the powers of government be entrusted to that rank?',[67] he was thinking of the franchise in a utilitarian sense. For if the middle rank are, by education and position, more competent than the less fortunate majority to judge what is best for the happiness of the community, might not entrusting power to a majority actually hinder the achievement of the general happiness?

The main thrust of Macaulay's first attack was not political but philosophical. He repudiated Mill's whole deductive method of enquiry. To start with, it claimed to rest on a universal law of self-interest which turned out on examination to be an identical

---

[66] Add. MSS. 34614, fo. 29; J. R. McCulloch to Macvey Napier, 16 Feb. 1829.
[67] *MW*, i. 315–16; Lively & Rees, 123.

proposition. It then went on to reach, by a spurious chain of logic, propositions which looked sound but were historically absurd. Macaulay had no difficulty in confuting Mill's general propositions by giving historical examples, and his final plea is that political science be based on the inductive method, by which every theory is patiently tested against the available facts. He calls this 'that noble Science of Politics' but he really means that politics should be based on the study of history. The crux of his objection to James Mill and his followers is that they want to reach their utopia by a short cut. They thought that the basic truths of morality, law, and social science could be taught in the form of simple, cogent nostrums, illustrated perhaps by the occasional homely example, but unburdened by the superfluous baggage of history, literature, and art, which they tended to regard as the characteristic occupations of a frivolous aristocracy. In their version of democracy there would be more stress on curbing the follies of the rulers than enlarging the pleasures of the ruled, and they saw the wider franchise as a device for keeping the rulers virtuous and public-spirited.

Macaulay's whole education had been an escape from the asceticism of the evangelical faith into the pleasures of classical scholarship and literature. He was not a hedonist, or at least no more than a half-hearted one. He became, as his father feared, an avid reader of novels, but when he records his addiction in his journal, he usually adds the word 'trash' as if to admit his error. He could write as severely on some arts (the theatre for instance) as his father could have wished, and was positively puritanical on eras like the Restoration when the arts seemed to ally with sensuality and vice. But more and more he favoured free choice and disliked authoritarianism and repression. He was too exact a scholar to want to see the studies he valued simplified, but something of his evangelical heritage survived in a belief that they should become more accessible. He was not a romantic, in revolt against the scientific discoveries of his age. The burden of his criticism of James Mill's method is that it was not scientific enough; it was deductive and a priori, when it should have been inductive and experimental. What made him doubt the whole utilitarian quest for devices to turn men's self-interest to the service of the general good was not that it was radical, but that it was facile. Mill's admirers were men who were 'delighted to be rescued from the sense of their own inferiority by some teacher who assures them that the studies they have neglected are of no value, puts five or six phrases into their mouths, lends them an odd number of the Westminster Review, and in a month transforms them into philosophers'.[68] What respect could such people have for their intellectual forebears if they believed that rational action rested on assent to a few bleak propositions set out in the manner of Euclid? How could they help sustain a complex, expanding society if they knew nothing of the trials through which it had emerged and thought nothing of discarding the experience of three thousand years?

He had found himself between two kinds of puritanism in the late 1820s. Hardly had he shed the religious version than he was confronted by the secular one. One led to the moral intolerance of his father and Hannah More; the other to the vulgar rationalism, the 'Jacobinism' one might call it, of the younger utilitarians. What historians have taken as his incipient Whiggism was really the expression of his refusal to embrace either of these alternatives. It was not the positive attraction of a political creed which made him a Whig, but a negative aversion to the two alternative dogmas; and the formative experiences which matured his opinions lay not in the field of party politics but in that of philanthropy and education.

In the early days of the movement for educational reform, evangelicals and secularist reformers had co-operated to instruct the poor. The Saints' wish that everyone should be able to read the scriptures coincided, for practical purposes, with the secularists' wish that no one, however poor, should be kept in ignorance of the laws governing his own betterment.[69] There were differences, but on the whole the alliance held at the level of elementary education. Higher up the pedagogic scale, differences became more marked. The S.D.U.K. had to avoid offending churchmen and would not publish works of 'controversial divinity' or political economy. Zachary Macaulay himself objected to a projected Life of Adam Smith because it must involve praise of David Hume.[70] When the founders of London University, in their anxiety not to offend either Church or Dissent, decided not to have a

---

[68] *MW*, i. 283; Lively & Rees, 99–100.
[69] ZM, Zachary Macaulay to Hannah More, 11 Sept. 1820.
[70] Brougham MSS., Zachary Macaulay to H. Brougham, 11 Aug. 1830.

Professor to teach the evidences of Christianity, the evangelicals were horrified. Wilberforce refused to co-operate, and Zachary Macaulay did so only after a reassurance that three of the clerical Professors would give Sunday instruction.[71]

His son's case for the university was much closer to James Mill's views and was purely utilitarian. He urged that the poor were advancing in literacy faster than were 'the lower part of the middling class', and that the political danger lay in the alteration of the relative conditions of the two. What was needed therefore was an improvement in the teaching available to the middle class. You could not 'unteach' the poor: they already held opinions hostile to the classes above them. So the best thing was to teach their superiors,

and, by increasing the knowledge, increase also the power of an extensive and important class,—a class which is as deeply interested as the peerage or the hierarchy in the prosperity and tranquillity of the country; a class which . . . though naturally hostile to oppression and profusion, is not likely to carry its zeal for reform to lengths inconsistent with the security of property and the maintenance of social order.[72]

This was very close indeed to the apostrophe of the middle class in James Mill's *Essay on Government*. The difference is that in Macaulay's version the sympathy for popular aspirations has almost disappeared. The whole stress is now (and would be still more in the attack on Mill two years later) on a heritage which might be lost rather than a utopia to be won. Macaulay's quiet rebellion against the evangelical outlook is much in evidence here.

The older generation of evangelicals thought of society as an organism which had phases of sickness and health corresponding with its spiritual state. Their solution to political radicalism was repentance for the great and powerful and Sunday schools for the poor. The latter would ensure, as Zachary Macaulay once put it, 'that at least there may not be any of them [the poor] who shall not have heard of God & Christ and Heaven & Hell and who shall not have had the call sounded in his ears to turn to God and flee from the wrath to come'. There is not much demo-

---

[71] Knutsford, 434–5, 451.
[72] *ER*, xlii, (Feb. 1826) repr. in J. Clive & T. Pinney, *Thomas Babington Macaulay: Selected Writings* (Chicago 1972), 6–7. Cf. also the review of Hallam, *CHE*, i. 215.

cratic feeling in this, but in his son's more utilitarian vision there is very little more. Rejecting the paternalist maxim that governments ought to 'train the people in the way in which they should go',[73] he offers the lower orders little more hope than that the free discussion conducted by their more educated leaders might filter down to them in the form of simple precepts of rational conduct. The 'wrath to come' was simply the consequence of their own ignorance. In this he resembles the hard-faced utilitarian conjured up by the romantic and Tory critics of the movement. But there is another side to his view of society which softens his utilitarianism and partially redeems it. He could not believe that the literature in which he had passed his happiest hours was ephemeral and not of value *sub specie aeternitatis*. Indeed, as the family's fortunes collapsed, literature was his only solace, and the hope of making a name for himself in it the nearest he could come to the idea of immortality. The evangelical view that human institutions were frail and temporary contrivances remained with him, but he always felt that great writing outlasted political arrangements. The result was that political revolution and the disruption it brought not merely to property but to literature and art and civilization generally, had more horrors for him than they ever had for his father. It is as if the loss of Christian optimism left an exaggerated fear of secular disaster, in which the tiny minority of educated individuals who appreciated the fragility of human achievement would be overwhelmed by a tide of popular ignorance and brutality. From the attack on Mill through the reform debates to his speech in 1842 urging the rejection of the Chartist petition, he wrote and spoke of universal suffrage as inseparable from the collapse of civilization.

The utilitarians, one might say, were optimists about the future of society. They might fear the economic stagnation of the stationary state, but in general they looked forward to an improvement of society through the spread of popular education. Macaulay sometimes echoes this optimism, in his assaults on Southey and Sadler, for instance. But these are public statements to establish his liberal credentials, which have the ring of a man shouting to keep his spirits up. In his imagination he was

---

[73] *CHE*, i. 245.

a pessimist whose escapes into the past reflected a constitutional aversion to the coarser, money-getting side of life and a preoccupation with images of decline and decay. They are not images of contemporary dislocation such as one finds in Dickens, for instance; of the human casualties of boom and slump, bank failure, brash speculators and demoralized clerks, petty provincial bullies and meek victims, debtors' prisons, poor-houses, and emigration. They are images of the classical world he knew best; or perhaps one should say of the Mediterranean world, so as to include the lands of the Bible. One striking image recurs in his writings, that of a ruined and decayed city, whose buildings are reverting to more primitive uses, and are discovered by some traveller from the new world. He was first captivated by it when, at sixteen, he read it in Sismondi's *La Littérature du Midi de l'Europe*.[74] He used it with variants in the Mitford review, and in the first attack on Mill. His first visit to Rome was in a sense a prolonged exploration of it, and he used it again in his review of Ranke (1840).[75] In all, it serves as a reminder of the fragility of civic life; in the Ranke, of cities newer but less enduring than Rome. In the Mill version he asks:

Is it possible that, in two or three hundred years, a few lean and half-naked fishermen may divide with owls and foxes the ruins of the greatest European cities—may wash their nets amidst the relics of her gigantic docks, and build their huts out of the capitals of her stately cathedrals?

The fishermen washing their nets is surely an echo of Ezekiel's curse upon Tyre.[76]

It would be hard to say if the attack on Mill had any appreciable effect on the Reform movement. It received only the feeblest answers in the *Westminster Review*, which I have described elsewhere. James Mill, deprived of his periodical, and plainly hurt by the articles, appealed unsuccessfully for help from Etienne Dumont, Bentham's Genevan editor-translator.[77] No one in the younger generation of the utilitarians replied, probably because

---

[74] *LM*, i. 78–9.
[75] *MW*, i. 179–80; Trinity MSS., MS. journal, 22 Nov. 1838; Trevelyan i. 458; *CHE*, iii. 209.
[76] *MW*, i. 314; Ezek. 26: 14.
[77] Dumont MSS, University of Geneva, 13 July 1829. TBM was called 'the empty-headed coxcomb, who only abuses what he does not understand'.

the ablest of them, John Mill, had already decided that his father's method of enquiry was faulty, and begun his own researches into the French Revolution which would confirm his belief in the narrowness of the old utilitarian outlook. That Macaulay hoped the attack on Mill would annoy Brougham seems likely. It certainly did. Brougham told Jeffrey that he felt 'more pain than I can well describe at a tone so disrespectful being taken in the E.R. towards one I so greatly esteem & one with whom I am really more connected in "all good works" than almost anybody else I could name'.[78] But he went on to insist that his own feelings were less important than the damage such attacks must do to the common cause.

In February 1830 Lord Lansdowne offered Macaulay the seat for Calne. It is not clear that in doing so he was consciously recruiting talent for the Whig party, and Trevelyan's assertion that it was because he was impressed by the articles on Mill rests on a family tradition of which I can find no confirmation. The seat was vacant because the sitting member, Abercromby, had been made Chief Baron of the Exchequer for Scotland, and because Lord Kerry, Lansdowne's heir, was a minor. The prospect of a parliamentary career for his son in such a safe seat made Lansdowne a very cool parliamentary reformer. He had joined Canning in 1827 with a clear conscience because he thought himself unpledged on the reform issue, and his conduct disgusted Grey.[79] He was prominent in the Anti-Slavery Society and had long known the Macaulays. His choice greatly annoyed Brougham, who thought the seat should have gone to his old comrade-in-arms Denman, a veteran Whig, hampered in his profession by royal prejudice and out of parliament, next to whom Macaulay was a novice.

Being MP for Calne was promotion for Macaulay, but it only intensified his dislike and suspicion of Brougham, who on his side had no intention of leaving the *Edinburgh Review* to the political direction of his former protégé. In July 1830 Brougham's triumphant return for Yorkshire gave him the euphoric feeling that he embodied the reforming aspirations of the industrial and commercial interests of the country, and

---

[78] Brougham MSS., 12 May [1829].
[79] A. Aspinall (ed.), *The Formation of Canning's Ministry* (Camden Soc, 3rd ser. vol. lix; 1937), 190–1, 271. Cf. E. A. Smith, *Lord Grey, 1764–1845* (Oxford, 1990), 243–9.

that the landed Whigs would now dance to his tune.[80] He announced his intention of proposing a comprehensive scheme of reform in the coming session, and to emphasize his leadership of liberal opinion he declared he would not take office. The news of the French Revolution of July was causing considerable excitement in Britain, giving encouragement to reformers of all shades. Brougham at once saw that it could be harnessed to the cause of reform, and when he heard that Macaulay had submitted an article on the subject, evidently felt that such an article should be written by the member for Yorkshire and not by Lord Lansdowne's nominee. He told Napier to countermand it and print his own instead. 'All our movements next session turn on that pivot', he told the editor, 'and I can trust no one but myself with it either in or out of Parl[iamen]t'. It might be different if the *Edinburgh* were not the mouthpiece of the party, 'but as it is, I and the party I lead, are really committed'.[81] To Macaulay this was the last straw. He looked on the *Edinburgh* as an arbiter of taste in literature and scholarship, and he knew his contributions had brought it widespread praise. If these were to be displaced at short notice by Brougham's hasty and rhetorical pieces, it would diminish both his reputation and the review's. He wrote to Napier—from Paris, whither he had gone armed with letters of introduction, including one from Brougham to Lafayette—that he would rather not contribute to the *Edinburgh* at all than do so at Brougham's dictation. Party politics had nothing to do with the matter: he had stayed with the review 'solely because I took pride and pleasure in it. It has now become a source of humiliation and mortification.'[82] He granted that Napier's position was more difficult. He even admitted that the loss of Brougham would damage the review more than his own retirement. But he accused Napier of bowing to Brougham's mere 'will and pleasure' by setting his own article aside. He could not see, he said, how any 'Whig manifesto about the late Revolution' could affect the coming session.[83] Perhaps the disagreement with Croker showed him.

[80] ZM, Brougham to Zachary Macaulay [p/m] 31 July 1830. For a very different version of Brougham's candidature, see Add. MSS. 34614, fo. 365, W. Empson to Macvey Napier, 24 July 1830.
[81] Add. MSS. 34614, fos. 383–4, 8 Sept. 1830.
[82] *LM*, i. 299 [16 Sept. 1830].   [83] Ibid., i. 309–10 [16 Oct. 1830].

4
Croker, Peel, and Party Loyalty

Sir Robert Peel had a peculiarity which is perhaps natural with men of very great talent who have not the creative faculty; he had a dangerous sympathy with the creations of others. There was always some person representing some theory or system exercising an influence over his mind.

DISRAELI, *Lord George Bentinck*

I

Croker's explanation of the origins and progress of the Reform Bill offered plenty of scope for abusing the Whigs, and as the Grey Ministry, 'that feeble but fatal conclave' as he called it,[1] broke up, its members were highly vulnerable to criticism. If they declared that they had always wanted moderate reform, they risked the reproaches of the radicals who had supported them through the crisis. If they supported the radical demands for further reform, they confirmed the Tory charge that they had opened a door which they could not shut. Croker harped continually on their capitulation to their radical allies, and not surprisingly they detested him. Many of his fellow Tories agreed with his political articles and valued him as a scourge of the Whigs. His correspondence is full of compliments on his various polemics, and they are by no means confined to members of his own circle. Yet the most damaging blow to his reputation was from a fellow Tory. Why did Disraeli, even before the crisis of 1846, portray him as Rigby?

I said earlier that *Coningsby* is primarily an attack upon Peel, and it is Croker's role in Peel's career which evidently called forth Disraeli's hostility. But Peel's aims are, to say the least, disputed, and Croker's have suffered misinterpretation in consequence. There are two sides to Peel. There is the man who is credited

[1] *QR*, liv, no. 107 (July 1835), 284.

with building up the Tory party until it took power in 1841, the first Prime Minister to be returned by a majority at a general election; and there is the man whose conversion to Corn Law repeal drove the same party on the rocks in 1846. The more Peel is credited with the Tory revival, the harder it is to understand his role in the split of 1846.[2] The traditional explanation, which took hold in the heyday of *laissez-faire*, but lasted well into the last century, was that Peel was a late convert to liberal economics, who regrettably failed to adjust his thinking to the more sluggish intelligence of his party, which rejected his policy and so consigned themselves to the political wilderness for twenty years. According to this view the débâcle of 1846 was caused by the conflict between a progressive cabinet and a reactionary rank and file, and whatever the truth of the economic argument, Peel's fault was that he 'betrayed' his party. Both Croker's biographers, Jennings and Brightfield, were influenced by this view, and both used it to portray their subject as a defender of Tory tradition, assuming that he ranged himself with his party.[3]

More recent students of Peel, carrying forward the scepticism which Namier had applied to political parties in the eighteenth century, have questioned whether Peel was interested in party at all. If they are right, and Peel pursued what Professor Gash called 'a governmental ethic' above party loyalties,[4] then the split of 1846 ought to be seen not as the effect of his belated conversion to liberalism, but rather as a contest between a traditional conception of executive government above 'faction', and a more modern view of party as a response to a new and more vigilant electorate. Other historians have presented Peel as actively hostile to the idea of party, as a minister who, had he lived, might have fashioned a strong bureaucratic monarchy on the European model.[5] The advantage of this more recent interpre-

---

[2] The late Dr Kitson Clark in his *Peel and the Conservative Party* (1929) committed himself so fully to the first side, that he never completed an explanation of the second.

[3] Jennings, iii, ch. 24; Brightfield, 431–6 ('The Tory party, by its very constituency, was pledged to the maintenance of the Corn Laws').

[4] N. Gash, 'Peel and the Party System' in *TRHS* (1951) 5th ser., i., 56.

[5] I. D. C. Newbould, 'Sir Robert Peel and the Conservative Party, 1832–41: A Study in Failure?' EHR (1983); A. Hawkins ' "Parliamentary Government" and Victorian Political Parties c.1830–80', ibid., (1989). Jonathan Parry, *The Rise and Fall of Liberal Government in Victorian Britain* (1993), ch. 7.

tation is not that it establishes Peel's own motives (which he seems not to have imparted even to his intimates) but that it replaces an anachronistic ideological conflict with a realistic political one. After all, the main problem which faced conservatives after 1832 was not how to reverse the verdict of the electorate, but how to preserve property and established institutions. Many, if not most of them, expected a social revolution to follow the political, and the very last thing they expected was that the new voters, enfranchised by Whig idealism and radical agitation, would turn out generally hostile to radicalism. But so it proved. By 1839 the Whigs had lost the English counties, and the electors in the large towns were not very radical. The new Toryism surged up from the shires and small market towns, and it took the politicians, men with their roots in the unreformed system who were used to thinking of such places as deferential and inarticulate, by surprise.

Croker broke with Peel over the Corn Laws in 1846, but the issues on which they agreed were far more numerous. Though Croker was eight years older, they entered political life about the same time, and Peel's first office, as Chief Secretary to Ireland, made him very dependent upon Croker's experience of Irish problems. They corresponded regularly from 1810 to 1846. Peel's side of the correspondence seems to have been destroyed, but Jennings quotes enough of it to indicate that Peel wrote in a more unguarded way to Croker than to anyone else except his wife.[6] Croker's letters to Peel are revealingly intimate and often funny, especially about the Court and the royal dukes. Read without Peel's replies they may well give the impression they seem to have made on Gash, that Croker offered a good deal of *gratuitous* advice.[7] But this is a little unfair. Peel's mastery of public business and his political acumen were legendary, but he had little general culture; or rather, he had cultural aspirations which his precocious political success had left undernourished, and he kept wanting to abandon politics to pursue them. One finds in his correspondence no striking literary and philosophical views

---

[6] Of the 620 holograph letters by Peel to Croker offered for sale at Christie's in July 1940, Jennings printed in full or in part only 73. The collection was described in the catalogue of the sale as 'probably the most voluminous and remarkable ever penned by any Prime Minister of Great Britain'.

[7] e.g., N. Gash, *Sir Robert Peel* (1972), 105.

such as enliven the study of Melbourne's career, for instance; no doubt because Melbourne had had long periods out of office in which to form them, whereas Peel, having held important and demanding offices from the outset of his career, had an outlook almost wholly shaped by politics. Peel's education also reminds one how insular the French revolutionary wars had made the English ruling classes. When he and Vesey Fitzgerald went with Croker to Paris after Waterloo, Croker noted sadly that neither had French enough to understand a line of a French play, and that Peel could not form a reply to the Duc de Berri who asked how long he proposed to stay in Paris.[8] It was natural for Peel to defer to Croker's judgement on many matters. Croker was constantly buying him books on French history for his library, exchanging opinions on pictures which came up for sale, and advising him about architects for his houses. This was no officious interference; it was friendly help to a very busy man to enable him to deal with the nation's affairs.

There is not much doubt that they were close friends. Croker once said that he loved Peel like a brother.[9] They paid regular visits to one another's houses. Croker was godfather to Peel's sailor son, William. They shared family problems. It was a friendship of complementary qualities and the two very different temperaments had, as it were, overlapping interests. Croker thought himself a misfit in politics and wanted to write history; but his historical studies gave him a deeper insight into politics than was common among politicians, and he could not suppress an urge to advise and correct them. Peel repeatedly announced his intention of retiring from politics, and sincerely hankered after the life of a country gentleman, but the only effect of this was to underline the fact that he was politically indispensable. Retirement, to be effective, would mean renouncing his political influence, and of course he finally achieved it only by destroying that influence altogether. Croker was loquacious. His mastery of words, his talent for coining the apt quotable phrase, his Irish love of puns (always underlined in his letters as if to ensure his

[8] CPD, Letter in Journal 16 July 1815; uncatalogued, given with omissions in Jennings, i. 61–75. See especially 63–4.

[9] Jennings, iii. 95, Lowther MSS, C. to Lowther, 14 Jan. 1835; Add. MSS. 40503, fos. 326–7, C. to Peel, 7 Mar. 1842.

reader grasped them) all suggest the sort of man who incautiously said too much, was too ready to express other men's thoughts for them, and so gave the impression of a meddler and a know-all. Peel was a strange mixture of public articulateness and private reserve. Unrivalled at setting out in parliament a piece of complex legislation, he was gauche and awkward in society and unskilled at forming an idea of the mood prevailing among colleagues and associates. His own huge capacity for work, which earned him the respect of professional politicians, blinded him to the motives not only of men who looked on politics as a pastime and parliament as a club, but also of those whose leading political views derived from party polemics or high theory. He was morally averse to the one, but he lacked the imaginative sympathy which might have enabled him to understand the other. When undecided he preferred silence to consultation, and in the political crises which brought men crowding into the clubs to exchange news, he often held aloof. Men complained of his coldness and formality, and he needed a confidant who would not be a rival. If such a person could also keep him informed about the movements of opinion and make useful suggestions as to how to act (suggestions which he was free to adopt or ignore) so much the better. Croker filled this role willingly. He knew their intimacy could be maintained only because he himself had retired from politics. Real rivalry would put an end to friendship. But he thought he could supply the advice and encouragement which Peel needed, and Peel did not discourage him.

There had been one breach in this friendship, which shows how intimate it was. During Canning's ministry in 1827 the two men found themselves on opposite sides. Peel joined Wellington and the seceders, Croker supported Canning. Though Peel agreed with Canning on every issue except Catholic emancipation, he objected to Croker's communications with Canning because he thought they must have conveyed information about himself which ought to have remained confidential.[10] On his side, Croker said that he had not initiated the contacts with Canning, but that once they were made, he had tried to use them to effect a

[10] Add. MSS. 40319, fos. 254–5, Peel to Croker (? Copy) 3 Oct. 1827; repr. in Jennings, ii. 375.

reconciliation between him and Peel.[11] Peel accepted the explanation and friendly relations were resumed.[12]

Peel in time realized that by joining Canning's opponents he had made a mistake. The split of 1827 had turned the Canningites almost into a separate party, like the Peelites twenty years later, and Peel urged that they should be re-admitted to the fold in 1828 when Wellington made his ministry. But the Duke was not the man to allay their sense of injured probity. When Huskisson offered his resignation, he accepted it quite readily, and that provided the signal for Palmerston, Lamb, and Grant to leave the ministry too. Peel remained, quite out of sympathy with most of the members of a government of which he was the mainstay. Had he joined Canning in 1827, he might have resigned with Huskisson and his friends in 1828. As it was, when it had become clear that Catholic emancipation would have to be granted, he first told the Duke that he would have to resign from the Cabinet, and then changed his mind and stayed in office to see the measure through the Commons.[13] This late rallying to the government earned him the distrust of those Tories who opposed Catholic emancipation, but it looked too opportunist to make him popular with liberal opinion. Grey's ministry absorbed the Canningites, who provided the political experience in a cabinet of novices. But Peel remained isolated, a reforming ex-Home Secretary, lukewarm in his opposition to parliamentary reform, but allied to and associated in the public mind with its more intransigent opponents. People thought him a liberal yoked against his better judgement with illiberal associates. He himself probably did not see the matter in such an ideological light. The lesson of the Wellington ministry, as he saw it, was not so much that it had been wrong-footed on reform, as that it had

[11] Add. MSS. 40319, fos. 256–7, C. to Peel, 4 Oct. 1827, Croker's letters to Canning are loyal to Peel, but he needed Canning's support if he was to be returned for Trinity: See Canning MSS, WYAS Leeds, Croker to Canning, 18 Aug. 1827.

[12] At least outwardly, but George IV's death prevented a further disagreement from becoming public. See NLS, Lockhart MSS 927, no. 48, fos. 68–70, Croker to Lockhart, 28 Mar. 1845. Peel had publicly disavowed in parliament an argument Croker had used, and Croker resolved not to remain in office. See PD, n.s. xxxiv. 183–90 [Croker]; and 195–203 [Peel] (28 Apr. 1830).

[13] Parker, Peel, ii. 54–6; Arbuthnot Journal, ii. 202, 206–7, 233, Peel's Memoirs, i. 282–94.

been too weakly manned in the Commons to be able to control events.[14]

After its fall, Peel seems to have hesitated between retirement from politics, or at least the independence of a backbencher, and an active bid for leadership. He was probably sincere about retirement, but he came to invoke it so often, especially when his political integrity was being questioned, that hardly anyone took him seriously. Leadership on the other hand very much depended on which men he was to lead. If the new ministry were to propose a moderate reform measure he could support, then his former colleagues would be an encumbrance. So he was cool about reuniting with the ultra-Tories because they had brought down the Wellington ministry, but at the same time he refused to pledge himself against the principle of parliamentary reform.[15] When the first Reform Bill was announced and turned out to be much more extensive than he had feared, he realized he must oppose it, but he did so coolly, in a manner which belied his own predictions of disaster.[16] As the bill was amended during its passage through the Commons, he realized that it had been made safe, and so deprecated a last ditch stand against it in the Lords. In May 1832, Grey was defeated in the Lords, and on failing to get the King's agreement to make peers, resigned, leaving the Tories to make a government. Peel refused to join it. His ostensible reason was that the reputation of public men would be damaged if he were required to support the reform he had originally opposed.[17] His real reason was that it would compromise his freedom of manœuvre. 'I see a great distinction', he told Goulburn, 'between *originating* a substantive measure of Reform, even as a reluctant Substitute for a worse measure, and the attempt to mitigate in a Committee the evil of a worse. The author of a substitute does assume if not the whole, at least a very serious share of the future responsibility of his own act. The mitigator in Committee is absolutely free from any responsibility'.[18] His refusal ensured the return of the Whigs and the passage of the

---

[14] N. Gash, *Mr Secretary Peel* (1961), 657.
[15] *Arbuthnot Journal*, ii. 415–16 [Mar. 1831]; Jennings ii. 116–17.
[16] Mrs Hardcastle, *Life of Lord Campbell*, i. 526; Jennings, ii. 151.
[17] Ibid., 261–2.
[18] Goulburn MSS., [undated but after 21 Dec. 1831]; Aspinall, *Three Diaries*, 253 [E. J. Littleton] 254–8 [Ellenborough].

Reform Bill and so estranged Peel from the Duke of Wellington and other leading Tories. But it also proved that no ministry which replaced the Whigs could do without him.

After the Reform Act was law, the Tories were at a low ebb. Peel is credited with the revival of the party after 1832 and he may have been willing to accept the credit. But the idea that he deliberately built the party up to achieve a victory at the polls is the invention of historians who have assumed that a two-party system was an inevitable development. It seems to me much more likely that Peel's main concern was the restoration of the exec-utive powers which the Reform Act had eroded. He had, after all, served his political apprenticeship in a period when the Crown chose ministers and when being associated with a party had been a disadvantage and a disqualification for office. A ris-ing politician needed patrons, and he needed associates, men with whom he could act and on whose abilities he could rely when in office, but he did not need followers. The time had gone by when cabinets had had to include owners of parliamentary boroughs, but that of governments returned by parliamentary majorities held together by party discipline had not yet dawned. Peel did not seek a party to lead. It would be more accurate to say that while enjoying his release from old political ties after November 1830, he found one thrust upon him.

Croker had deplored his friend's studied indifference to the efforts of their former colleagues to rally their forces, and he tried, as he told Hertford, to 'warm the cold caution of Peel into some degree of party heat'.[19] In this the wide scope of the first Reform Bill helped. Croker saw at once that it would polarize politics and that in the process Peel might be forced to follow the Canningites into the Whig camp. In an extraordinary letter he pointed to the flagging of the reforming impulse, and claimed that a bold opposition would defeat the bill. He then added the warning:

Two parties are now generated which never will die. *You* never could be more than the tail of one. You are, I hope, destined to be the victorious and, as to fame, impartial head of the other and I your humble '*vates*'.[20]

---

[19] CPC, Letterbook 25, fos. 48–50; Jennings, ii. 77–8.
[20] Add. MSS. 40320, fos. 175–6, 10 Apr. 1831; partly quoted in Brightfield, 106–7, 117.

By 'vates' he meant not merely a teacher, but a seer, a prophet, and the word indicates that it was part of Croker's strategy to stiffen Peel's resolve by stressing, with all the eloquence at his command, the revolutionary implications of Whig reforms. He may have had some effect, but when the crisis came a year later, in May 1832, Peel's cold caution was once again in command. Croker wrote him a long letter urging him to lead the ministry and rescue the King from the Whigs.

If Lord Grey returns see what must happen—the King enslaved, the House of Lords degraded, the bill passed—the Revolution, I may say consummated and what will be your consolation then? The poor and negative one that you have maintained an apparent consistency in not having touched even with a view to diverting it, the fatal instrument of mischief.[21]

But Peel was stubborn. He plainly thought that the Whig reform would present no such threat and that the Tories could not make a better bill themselves.

The two men drew different lessons from the reform crisis, and though their exchanges were cordial and their language was similar, one can detect signs of a divergence of practical aims. Neither had the least inclination to convert the masses to a new brand of conservatism. Both thought that the Reform Act had gravely weakened the power of the Crown and increased that of the House of Commons, that executive government itself had suffered by the change, and that there could be no question of co-operating with the radical critics of the ministry for the mere party purpose of turning it out. Peel justified his support of the government as 'protecting the authors of the evil from the work of their own hands'.[22] But he meant that in the process the levers of power must be preserved for use by more competent hands, and he knew that in offering such 'protection' he was gradually sapping the Whig government's authority. Croker by contrast thought that, as the authors of the evil, the Whigs had put themselves beyond the pale of political co-operation and even of polite society, and that Peel was therefore of more use in opposition than in government.

---

[21] Add. MSS. 40320, fos. 207–9, 11 May 1832, repr. in Jennings, ii. 177–80.
[22] Jennings, ii. 204.

So the dismissal of Melbourne in November 1834 came as a surprise. A month before, Croker had been assuring Peel that he ought to take a long holiday on the continent. 'I think your absence (with a good excuse) a public advantage', he said, and urged him to stay away till February.[23] Something in Peel's itinerary suggests that he himself thought there was less time to spare. Lord Hertford, who travelled slowly, savouring the local amenities, human and contrived, wrote ironically on 4 November from Milan:

Sir R. Peel passed thro' having I dare say in 48 hours fancied he had seen Milan[.] He is at this hour at Padua will be tomorrow at Venice and probably next day on his road to Rome to which he may perhaps devote half a week.[24]

Peel's return was still more rapid. The King's summons reached him on 25 November. He was back in London by 9 December. Croker was the first person he wrote to on his return.[25] Peel's first question when they met was whether Croker was still determined not to take office. Croker said he was. But further reflection made him pause. Peel had already had a refusal from Stanley and he would soon have another from Graham, the two Whigs whose resignations had begun the collapse of Grey's ministry. Without them, Peel told Croker, his would be 'only the Duke's old Cabinet'.[26] Croker had feared that the new ministry would be driven along like its predecessor by the reforming current. But the abstention of Stanley and Graham, which depressed Peel, made Croker more cheerful. It would at least be a Cabinet without Whigs. Croker decided to abandon 'retirement' and lend a hand. He would not join the ministry, but he would defend it as best he could in the *Quarterly*, and Peel's precarious position even moved Croker to the generous declaration that he would support him through thick and thin:

Me, you have not to persuade. With me *whatever is, is right*. When I tell you of adverse opinions, it is only to appraise you. As for *me*, whether I agree with you or not in the *abstract*, I am of *your opinion*

[23] Add. MSS. 40321, fos. 20–2, 12 Oct. 1834.
[24] Add. MSS. 60289, fos. 168–9. Hertford to Croker, 4 Nov. 1834.
[25] Jennings, ii. 248–9; Croker to Mrs Croker MS at CPC Box 21, Folder 14.
[26] Jennings, ii. 250; C. to Hertford, 11 Dec. 1834.

implicitly and unconditionally in the concrete, that is under existing circumstances.[27]

The first fruit of this co-operation was a defence of the famous Tamworth Manifesto, which by a curious lack of curiosity has acquired the status of a founding document of modern conservatism.

The Manifesto was Peel's address to his constituents, which became a government statement because it was approved by the Cabinet before publication. It aimed to reassure moderate opinion that the new ministry was not reactionary, that recent reforms would not be undone, that proved abuses and real grievances would continue to be redressed, but that prescriptive rights and established institutions would be respected.[28] Its tactical purpose was to gain the support of the Whigs by detaching them from their extreme radical allies; an urgent need, because the suddenness of Melbourne's dismissal had led many radical orators who, a few weeks before, had been vilifying ministers, to take care to appear with them at meetings called to protest at such a 'tyrannical' use of the prerogative. The Manifesto was designed to break this new-found unity.

Croker's review gives the Manifesto a much wider significance. It presents Peel as the last barrier against revolution. The Grey ministry, Croker said, had been relatively safe: one-third of its ministers after all had been Tories. But the Melbourne ministry, just dismissed, was a mere 'fortuitous concourse of atoms'.[29] It offered no prospect of stability and was the plaything of the radical extremists. So the issue was no longer between a Whig government and a Tory one, but between the maintenance of the constitution and its ruin. It is interesting that in reviewing what the historians have treated as a key party document, Croker asserted that the Reform Act had 'extinguished the constitutional utility of party'.[30] By this he meant that each MP instead of regulating his conduct by following the principles of a Fox or a Pitt (Croker might have said a Canning or a Perceval) was

[27] Add. MSS. 40321, fos. 90–1, 2 Feb. 1835.
[28] *Speeches by the Rt. Hon. Sir Robert Peel, Bar[one]t., during his Administration 1834–1835* and his *Address to the Elections of the Borough of Tamworth* (2nd edn., 1835) 1–9.
[29] QR, liii, no. 105 (Feb. 1835) 'Sir Robert Peel's Address', 270.
[30] Ibid., 269.

now obliged to obey public opinion, that is, something altogether more volatile and fickle. So Peel was not appealing for a fair trial as leader of a party, as his overture to Stanley had proved, but as a rallying point for all who favoured order; he would 'leave no man any resting-place between him and Mr O'Connell'. As for Stanley, by holding aloof he had neutralized himself politically, for where could he now look for colleagues, 'to the Cabinet which he had so recently quitted, or that which he had just declined to join?'[31]

Peel's reaction to this article is very interesting. He thought Croker had not made enough of the fact that the ministry had been brought into being by the King, and not by a vote in parliament. He said that the Tamworth address had been 'too much referred to necessities imposed by the Reform Bill'; it had actually arisen from the sudden change of ministers and 'the policy of aiding our friends at the election'. Finally he deprecated giving offence to what he called 'moderate men, not professing adherence to our politics', and he added: 'Remember Stanley's position, and that he will subscribe himself a Whig'.[32] It is clear from this letter that, despite the soothing reference to 'our politics', Peel would have liked a mixed ministry of Whigs and Tories; whereas Croker dreamed of a coalition of all the reliable forces of order, against a rising tide of anarchy.

The failure of the first Peel ministry made Croker relapse back into despair,[33] but he had at least come down from his prophetic mountain. He had committed the *Quarterly* to Peel's politics. Even after Peel had decided to resign, he assured him, 'I am resolved to think that whatever you shall do, is right'.[34] Intentionally or not, their private consultations thus acquired a public dimension. Peel, without compromising his own independence, acquired a fluent and vigorous apologist who was unusually free of editorial trammels. Murray's agreement of September 1832 that Croker should contribute up to four sheets each quarter (a sheet was sixteen pages) had been made in

[31] *QR*, liii, no. 105 (Feb. 1835) 'Sir Robert Peel's Address', 225.

[32] Jennings, ii. 256–7 (26 Jan. 1835). Peel may have been commenting on a draft, but the final version shows that if Croker changed anything in the light of Peel's criticisms, the changes did not alter the substance of the argument.

[33] Add. MSS. 40321, fos. 138–9, C. to Peel, 4 May 1835.

[34] Ibid., fos. 122–5, 29 Mar. 1835.

Lockhart's absence and without his knowledge. Lockhart later recognized that this was a slur on his editorial status, but at the time he must have been relieved.[35] He knew he was a stranger to the world of politics and the Tory split of 1827 had exposed his innocence. He had let Southey write a forceful attack on Catholic relief which had lost the *Quarterly* the approval of the Wellington ministry, and the premiership of Grey and the Whig's Reform Bill found the review without any political guide until Croker was brought in. Lockhart had welcomed his help, and he was generally content to let him write the political articles and, as he put it, 'interpret the talk of Downing Street in the dialect of Albemarle Street'.[36] But it did mean that he was never in complete control of his review. He often did not know what subject Croker would choose to write about, and Croker would deal directly with the printer, so that sometimes Lockhart had his first sight of the political article only when it was already in proof. John Murray II died in 1842 to be succeeded by his son John Murray III, but there was no change of policy. Of course, Lockhart and the Murrays both knew that, however good its contributions on subjects like art, architecture, science, travel, literary criticism, and theology, the *Quarterly* derived much of its reputation and authority from its connection with high political circles. They might worry that its politics would deter readers, especially if the politicians were not in office, but they knew that if Croker did not write the political articles (and he wrote much besides) someone else would have to be found to do them; and Croker knew that his connections were not easy to match.[37] Whenever there was disaffection in Albemarle Street, he took care to write from one of the great Tory houses, Drayton Manor, Stratfield Saye, Sudbourne, or Belvoir. That usually brought his editor and their common paymaster to heel.

Peel took a close interest in the *Quarterly*. He may not have suggested topics for articles, but he read them and criticized them. But he did not interfere with editorial policy, or invoke

---

[35] Brightfield, 404–5; Murray MSS, Lockhart to John Murray III, 28 Jan. 1857.
[36] CPC, Lockhart to Croker, 22 Oct. 1832 for his expression of gratitude, and 26 May 1845, for a retrospective view of the results.
[37] CPC, Lockhart to Croker, 26 May 1845 (Bound vol. iii. fo. 39), an interesting historical résumé of *QR*'s relationship with the politicians.

the interests of the parliamentary party as a way of influencing it. If he took Lockhart's advice over pensions for men of letters he made no conditions.[38] In any case, Lockhart did not approach Peel directly. Croker was always the intermediary. He would some-times tell Peel that Lockhart had asked for a political article in the next number, and sometimes Lockhart would be told that Peel or the ministry had asked for one.[39] But though many a polit-ical article was written with official encouragement, and after 1841 with information only ministers could command, the *Quarterly* was never formally an organ of Peel's. Croker chose informants he knew. He told Peel it was 'a kind of *direction post* to a large body of people, particularly in the Country', and he added that its chief use was 'to keep our friends in a right course and to furnish them with arguments in support of their opinions. I do not suppose that it makes converts, but it rallies friends'.[40] It is noticeable that Croker makes no mention of any obligation to *reflect* the views of the party. He might have been Peel's mouthpiece, but he was not answerable to any Carlton Club committee or whips' office. His relationship to the parlia-mentary party paralleled Peel's own; he would argue and expound, as Peel sought to lead and to rule, but on his own terms. So his position was at once powerful and vulnerable. People read his articles as a guide to Peel's views, which they often were, and he sought to express conservative interests, but he could not count on any support from fellow conservatives if he misjudged or misstated those interests, and it was not long before he was being vehemently accused of doing so.

Peel probably knew after 1835 that time was on his side. He knew he had won a great reputation for tenacity and courage and that respectable men deplored the way he had been brought down by a makeshift coalition of Whigs, radicals, and Irish. But he seems to have seen this less as a party defeat than as a symp-tom of the sort of politics he deplored and refused to imitate. It was O'Connell who created the first disciplined parliamentary

[38] Add. MSS. 40321, fos. 53–9 Croker to Peel 15 Jan. 1835; fos. 66–79 Lockhart to Croker 26 Jan. 1835. NLS, Lockhart MSS 928 fos. 20–3. Croker to Lockhart, 28 Jan. [1835].

[39] e.g. Add. MSS. 40321, fos. 301–2, C. to Peel, 9 Nov. 1838; fos. 427–8, to Peel, 25 Nov. 1840; NLS, (Lockhart) MS 927, no. 44 fo. 60, to Lockhart, 27 Apr. 1844.

[40] Add. MSS. 40502, fos. 326–7 20 Feb. 1842.

party. Radicals were the people who gave pledges to their constituents. Peel had his eye on a future ministry and did not want to tie his hands. When Lyndhurst tried to orchestrate a popular outcry against the Whigs' Municipal Corporations Bill and the Lords threatened to throw it out, Peel, mindful of his manifesto, thought his conduct factious and left town. His attitude to the Tory peers was so contemptuous that Croker had to appeal to him to return, asking him, 'Have you a right to leave your Army on the Beresina?'[41] It may not have been a flattering parallel, but it captured the fact that Peel was, like Napoleon, more concerned with his staff than with his soldiers. He had not had the support of Graham and Stanley, but he knew he would have it before long, and on his own terms, provided he led no premeditated party manœuvre which would put them off. Meanwhile, he deprecated 'all those who look on a party as a pack of hounds which must have blood'. He did not deny that some concessions to his followers must be made. 'It is important to keep a party in wind'. But he disliked being committed to a strategy concerted with the party in advance of a session, preferring instead occasional declarations of principle of the most general kind. These would be made 'in the manner we think *bona-fide* best calculated to serve, not party, but the public interests', and people could 'agree in them or dissent from them as they please'.[42] These were tactics which actually tended to retard the development of any two-party system. Though professing concern for stability and order, Peel was actually sapping and undermining the ministry of Melbourne. On the pretext of strengthening executive authority (saving the authors of the evil from the consequences of their own work) his refusal to formulate an opposition policy, and his baffling habit of alternately supporting and attacking ministers, were actually making it more difficult for the Whigs to govern. And all the while the pack of hounds at his back became harder and harder to restrain.

Croker, it is worth stressing, supported Peel against the party. In January 1836, when they discussed tactics for the following session he set out his conception of opposition and the role of

---

[41] Add. MSS. 40321, fos. 158–62 25 Aug. 1835. Peel's reply is in Jennings, ii. 282–4.
[42] Jennings, ii. 25–6 (10 Jan. 1835); 303–6 (12 Jan. 1836).

a leader. In his view, it was the Whigs who traditionally combined in groups and forced themselves into power: Tories never did.

The Whig power was the people against the Lords and the Crown. The Tories, who are for the Crown and Lords against the people, have in the latter no *audience*, much less an auxiliary [*sic*].

So a Tory opposition's aim should not be merely to drive out the Whigs:

Our friends wish for a division in hopes of driving the Government out. That is *their sole object*. Now, I am against any division with that mere object . . . If you shall be forced by circumstances to take the Government, let them at least not be of your creation. With this opinion you, of course, see that I arrive at the conclusion, move no spontaneous topic, no amendment which shall not be *forced*, upon you. I am quite aware that this will dissatisfy the *party*—so much the better, say I; for if our friends will be so mad as to consider the present struggle as a *party-matter* and to be guided by party practices and traditions, *their* measures will be more fatal to the monarchy than, but for their indiscretion, our enemies would be for a considerable time to come. In looking for *place* they may lose the *state* . . .[43]

This was the theory behind Peel's supposedly Fabian tactics in opposition. A House of Commons too obedient to the constituencies must have the effect of weakening executive authority. Any opposition which, for merely tactical reasons, forced a ministry's resignation, might savour victory in the short run, but it would weaken its own authority in the long. By acting with the radicals in opposition, the Whigs had been short-sighted and were now reaping the consequences in divided counsels and diminished power. A conservative opposition must be more responsible, not simply because an alliance with the radical critics of the Melbourne ministry would be unprincipled, but because Tories were under a greater obligation than the Whigs had been to respect the integrity of the Crown and its power to choose ministers. Peel's studied indifference to his supporters' clamour for active and demonstrative leadership had a very simple explanation. He did not want to be their nominee. It was not from a slavish obedience to Croker's theory. Peel looked

---

[43] Add. MSS. 40321, fos. 179–81; to Peel, 14 Jan. 1836.

forward to a united and efficient ministry. Croker looked backward to a balanced constitution unimpaired by radical change. But neither wanted to make party organization and discipline a means of acquiring power. Both knew that looking (and organizing) for place, they would lose the state.

Such altruism became harder to sustain as office drew closer. In the general election of 1837 Melbourne's majority fell from about sixty to twenty-four or less. The radicals suffered losses which Tories took as a sign that the country was returning to its senses, but which also raised the prospect that the government might be defeated on some colonial issue on which Tory and radical might coincide without compromising their respective positions on issues of domestic politics. Peel caused mounting frustration among the backbenchers by his refusal to exploit these issues. When for instance Lord Durham's mission to Canada in 1838 ended in illegality and disgrace, Melbourne's government faced a real prospect of defeat. Peel and Croker were quite well informed on Durham's errors.[44] Earlier, Croker had opened a cordial correspondence with Durham's chief critic Brougham, and on a visit to Paris became well aware, through the Whig arch-intriguer Ellice, of the English radicals' collusion with the French Canadian leader Papineau.[45] Peel could have framed a motion critical of the government's Canada policy in which radicals and Tory backbenchers might have joined to defeat the government. Instead, he proposed what was in effect a censure motion which the radicals could not support, and the government were saved.

The following year the crisis in Jamaica raised the same spectre. The Melbourne ministry's majority fell to five and it resigned. Peel was sent for and after discussing the disposal of offices raised the question of the dismissal of certain Ladies of the Bedchamber, nine of whom were wives or sisters of Whig peers.[46] The Queen refused to give up any of her ladies, and Peel resigned. Melbourne's cabinet returned for another few months of low vitality. The issue seems so trivial, that it is easy to believe

---

[44] Add. MSS. 40321, fos. 286–7 Croker to Peel, 1 July 1838. Cf. QR, lxvi, no. 121 (Jan. 1838) 'Canada' 249–72.

[45] Add. MSS. 40321, fos. 336–7 Croker to Peel, 30 Mar. 1839.

[46] CPD, F.R. Bonham to Croker, undated but giving a list of all the ladies of the Household with their political affiliations.

that Peel had been reluctant to take office, and now eagerly seized any excuse to retire. But another element, perhaps the vital one, was respect for the authority of the Crown. The ministerial press had presented Peel's demand over the bedchamber ladies as a rude bid to separate a young woman from her friends. What Peel wanted to uphold, characteristically, was an attribute of sovereignty, and this involved a distinction between the person and the office. He was annoyed that in the emotion generated by the episode the feelings of the Queen were being confused with the powers of the Crown.[47] To force the Whig ladies' dismissal, however, would have been to take a leaf out of the Whigs' book. So again, cold caution prevailed over action.

Croker was glad to see him in opposition for a little longer. 'I look with more fear than hope to a Tory ministry,'[48] he said. Tories would never take power by a party manœuvre:

They will come, when they do come, on leading principles of public policy, not by courting incongruous combinations, fomenting petty squabbles, or availing themselves of accidental embarrassments. Office is to them not even a secondary consideration: their first is the *country*,— the next their character . . .[49]

This sounds like the complacent opinion of a man safely outside the turmoil of party politics. But it was echoed by Peel in the famous declaration that he would not hold office by any 'servile tenure which would compel me to be the instrument of carrying other men's opinions into effect'.[50]

It was precisely the attitude which annoyed those professional party men who needed office and felt that, as the Whig ministry grew weaker and more perplexed, it was in their grasp. Croker certainly was sufficiently in touch with the rank and file to be aware of the feeling. On the appearance of one number, he received an ironic report from Alexander Grant, a regular member of Peel's shooting parties at Drayton, which warned of trouble to come:

---

[47] Jennings, ii. 343–5. Peel to Croker, no date, but plainly to offer materials for 'The Household and the Ministry'. QR, lxiv, no. 127 (June 1839), 232–83.
[48] Jennings, ii. 347.
[49] QR, lxv, no. 130 'The Privilege Question' (Mar. 1840), 600.
[50] *Speeches*, iii. 810–11.

The writer of that article in the Quarterly (whoever he may be) is at a terrible Discount at the Carlton Club: and the Horror of the Frondeurs is augmented by a strange conclusion to which they have come that the said writer is a confidential Friend of Sir Robert Peel's—and that, having been one of a conclave held at Drayton Manor in September last, he has only given words to the opinions of the Ex-Premier. They say that this Fabian Policy will dissolve the Party.[51]

There was a note of apprehension, a serious point behind this banter. A party more and more united, with a strong support in the press, a growing organization in the constituencies, and a higher morale and *esprit de corps* through its clubs, was apparently being held back by a leader who made a parade of his indifference to office. Croker was that leader's intimate counsellor, and Peel's views could be read in his articles in the *Quarterly Review*. Even in opposition Croker was thought to be the channel of Peel's opinions.

II

When Peel came to power in 1841 the party's disagreements became more acute. One might have thought that the Fabian policy would have lapsed with the victory it was supposed to produce, and that once in power, Peel would have recognized some obligations to the men whose efforts had put him there. But Peel notoriously never did. His party, or rather what he called 'the party with which he had the honour to associate', thought, with some justification, that the election of 1841 had been fought and won over the issues of agricultural protection and the defence of the Established Church. When the new ministry pursued an economic policy of tariff reduction, they became very restive. When it went further and offended Anglican opinion by concessions to dissenters and endowments to the Catholic Church in Ireland, they rebelled. By 1845 Peel's alienation of the party was complete. His conversion to total repeal of the Corn Laws only made the breach irreparable.

This story of the Tory split is a familiar one, and it would not be worth retelling here from Croker's point of view, if his

---

[51] CPD, A. Grant to Croker, 23 Nov. [1838]. Croker's endorsement, but *QR* file suggests it should be 1837.

own estrangement from Peel had merely followed the successive stages of the backbench rebellion. Both his biographers assumed that it did; that Croker was simply a more consistent conservative than Peel, and that his disillusionment 'caught the infection', in Brightfield's words, from the rest of the party, until 'the fatal blow fell without warning' in January 1846.[52] In fact, the story is much more complicated. Croker, with the support of Lockhart, put the *Quarterly* squarely behind Peel's policies, first on tariff reduction, then on industrial unrest and the Anti-Corn Law League, and finally on the Catholic Church in Ireland. If Peel risked breaking up the party on these issues, then Croker abetted him. Only at the final crisis over total repeal did he break away, and then it was because he thought Peel had betrayed him and the *Quarterly*. Only later, when Peel had taken with him numerous colleagues, did he realize that the party at large had irrevocably split. The uproar in the party over Peel's Irish policy had not in fact affected the review, which supported it from 1844, and it was this fact, which set the *Quarterly* at odds with the opinion of the bulk of the party, which provoked Disraeli's attack on Croker as Peel's *éminence grise* in *Coningsby*, published that year. Total repeal was the last straw: if Lockhart and Croker had supported that, the *Quarterly*'s credit with its readers would have been destroyed. Nevertheless, though repudiating Peel, and finding himself with Disraeli among the Protectionists, Croker never embraced Disraeli's view of party. For him the ruling antithesis was not Whig versus Tory, but revolution versus tradition, and he never accepted that Tories must learn to beat the Whigs at their own game in the new world of popular politics.

From the start of Peel's second ministry Croker took his part against the malcontents. His famous comment on the general election that 'all turns on the name of Sir Robert Peel' and that it was 'the first time . . . in our history that the people have chosen the first minister for the sovereign'[53] should not be taken as the admission of a popular mandate for Peel. On the contrary, he wanted to show that Peel's authority rested on 'the

<hr/>

[52] Brightfield, 431, 434.
[53] Add. MSS. 40485, fos. 232–5 Croker to Peel, 19/20 July 1841; partly quoted in Gash, 263; Stewart, 154.

Property, the Rank, the Education, the Established Religion of the Country'.[54] So he argued that in 1839 Melbourne, on finding he could not carry the Jamaica Bill, should have resigned or else dissolved parliament. Dissolution was 'an invitation from the Crown to the country to strengthen the hands of its servants, which never should be resorted to without some rational prospect of success'.[55] When the Whigs dissolved in 1841 they had no such prospect; still more objectionably, they had gone to the country on the issue of Corn Law repeal and cheap bread. *They* had dissolved unconstitutionally, and Peel had therefore been forced, after the elections, into the no-confidence motion, to remove a ministry obstinately unwilling to admit its incapacity. Croker did not think the conservative majority in the elections fettered Peel any more than Peel himself did. Before the election Croker quoted what he called 'the old Whig axiom', that 'parties are like snakes, of which it is the *tail* that moves the *head*'.[56] After his defeat in 1846 Peel said he would never again lead a party, and used exactly the same image.[57]

Croker's defence of the fiscal measures which by 1842 were provoking backbench criticism of Peel was not that they were consistent with what conservative candidates had declared at the elections the previous year, but that Peel had never given any pledges to justify their hopes. Besides reducing tariffs on a range of goods so as to suggest that free trade was a ruling principle, Peel modified the existing Corn Law, which adjusted the duty on imported corn according to a sliding scale. The new scale was supposed to make it easier to import foreign corn in times of scarcity without harming the British farmer. Peel was immediately accused by Sir Richard Vyvyan, a Cornish ultra-Tory and MP, of betraying his followers. Croker made Vyvyan's pamphlet the peg for his article on the new policies, writing to Peel direct for advice.[58]

Vyvyan accuses us of *bad faith* about corn tariff [*sic*] and Poor Law, against which, he says, the Conservatives pledged themselves at the elections &c. Now, pray, direct me to the most pithy indication of *your own* resolution *not* to pledge yourself on these points . . .[59]

---

[54] *QR*, lxviii, no. 135 (June 1841) 'The Budget and the Dissolution', 249–50.
[55] Ibid., no. 136 (Sept. 1841) 'The Old and New Ministries', 503.
[56] Ibid., no. 135, 240.   [57] Parker, *Peel*, iii.
[58] Add. MSS., 40513, fos. 185–7. Croker to Peel, 7 Aug. 1842.   [59] Ibid.

Peel obliged with various references, a copy of a speech, 'a sort of profession of faith, *before* the last General Election, and out of office', and the speech of 27 August 1841.[60] Croker quoted the last, in italics:

I still prefer the principle of a graduated duty, but if you ask me whether I bind myself to the maintenance of the existing law in all its details, and whether that is the condition on which the landed interest gives me their support, I say that, on that condition, I cannot accept their support.[61]

Croker added that the majority of ninety-one which concluded this debate was an endorsement of Peel's position.

This was to take a very high ground: Peel and Croker considered that the Prime Minister owed his position to his superior experience and judgement (aided of course by the fact that in office he had access to the best information). If his supporters could not accept that, he would resign, and they must take the consequences of their want of faith. Disraeli, and those who thought like him, would have retorted that Peel, knowing what a majority of his followers thought on protection, should have pledged himself to support it, if not before the elections, then once they were over and a majority secure.[62] The difference between his position and Croker's may seem trivial, but it is important. Croker was as concerned for the supremacy of the landed classes as any Tory county member. He thought Peel's new sliding scale offered 'the fairest promise of permanent protection to the farmer and permanent plenty to the people',[63] and that it was not in principle very different from the sliding scale devised in 1828 by Huskisson. He later maintained that Peel's close co-operation in the composition of the article (he saw it in proof and made several criticisms, and Graham, Peel's Home Secretary, said of the finished version, 'the case of the Government cannot be placed on stronger or safer ground')[64] amounted to a permanent commitment to a sliding scale. But if he had wanted to make sure Peel would be committed, it was surely unwise, in an article

[60] Jennings, iii. 386–7.
[61] *QR*, lxx, no. 140 [Sept. 1842] 'Policy of Sir Robert Peel' 509; *Speeches*, iii. 794; *PD*, 3rd. ser. vol. lix, col. 413 (27 Aug. 1841).
[62] R. Stewart, *The Foundation of the Conservative Party, 1830–1867* (1978), 154–65.
[63] *QR*, lxxi. no. 146, 528.   [64] Jennings, iii. 386–7, 389.

meant to soothe the protectionists' fears, to claim complete freedom of decision for the man who seemed to threaten them. Peel's mere preference for the sliding scale was, for supporters of aristocratic supremacy based upon the land, a rather frail safeguard, as events proved.

Croker's support for Peel's budget made many Tories restive, and Lockhart in particular worried about its effect on the circulation of the *Quarterly*.[65] Being in touch with writers of all political shades, Lockhart was more aware than Croker of new literary talent, as well as of a growing public appetite for articles (of the sort Macaulay was so good at writing in the *Edinburgh*) which treated literature and history in a non-political way, without the baleful implications which informed so much of Croker's literary criticism. Had he had more confidence in his judgement, he might have limited Croker's contributions to contemporary politics and the history of the French Revolution. But he was diffident, and his sense of being a cut above the hacks of Grub Street through his connections with high political circles compromised his editorial judgement. Croker by contrast was convinced that its politics sold the review, so that 'However bad our political articles may have been, our condition might have been worse if there had been none'.[66]

His view was tested in the course of 1842. Lockhart was very alarmed at developments in the industrial towns.[67] His view of the factory system, like Southey's, inclined to Tory paternalism, and he thought the *Quarterly* ought to show its sympathy for the poor. He had urged Croker to peg his political article on the Poor Law Commissioners' *Report on the Sanitary Condition of the Labouring Population*, 'a fearful volume' he called it, which dealt with 'the one real political Question—all else are vapid and worthless unless connected with it'.[68] Instead Croker had written the vindication of Peel's policy I have already quoted. When Murray and Lockhart ventured to suggest that something more 'consolatory' was needed, they got a lecture on which Peel himself could not have improved. Croker owned he had no sympathy for 'the Ashley school':

[65] CPC, Lockhart vol. ii. fo. 72 (15 Nov. 1841).
[66] NLS, Lockhart, MS 928, fos. 151–4, no. 121, 25 Jan. 1842 and fo. 155 no. 122, 26 Jan. 1842.
[67] CPC, Lockhart to Croker, vol. ii. fo. 88, 9 Sept. 1842.
[68] CPC, Lockhart to Croker, vol. ii. fo. 84, 23 July 1842.

It is a morbid school, a crazy school. They mistake, in a great measure, the disease; and they exaggerate what they don't mistake; and their remedies are all inflammatory; and they suppose that governments can make cripples walk, and the crooked straight, and the weak strong, that they can feed the hungry without labour, and so regulate, polish and oil the great machine of society that pain and sickness and sorrow, hunger, thirst and sweat may be abolished by act of parliament, that coal mines may become Elysian fields, and factories earthly paradises.

You yourself say that Governments must do something. What? or even of what kind? or, I will be satisfied if you will even say, in what *direction*?

Governments have no more power in these matters than the Captain of a ship has over the wind and waves . . .[69]

And he ended the letter with a veiled threat that if they could find a political writer to answer such questions he himself would 'most thankfully sing my *nunc dimittis*'.

Lockhart may not have been able to find another political writer, but he did find other literary contributors. Recalling Croker's savaging of Tennyson's first volume of poems, he sent the poet's second to John Sterling for review, though with a request that he should not draw attention to the earlier article.[70] When Croker hinted that he would like to review Macaulay's *Lays of Ancient Rome*, Lockhart told him he had sent the volume to Milman.[71] When he heard this, Croker exploded. Writing from Peel's house at Drayton, he sent in his resignation from the *Quarterly*. The ostensible reason was that Lockhart had, without consulting him, decided to bring out within a few days an extra number of the review, but it is plain that the real reason was the implied affront to his critical opinion of Tennyson and Macaulay. It is also clear that he did not intend his resignation to be accepted, for he explained to Lockhart that he had just been primed by Peel with a mass of information for an article on the Anti-Corn Law League, which could not possibly be done in time for the proposed extra number, and so would be published separately as a pamphlet. The letter was intended to remind the erring editor of Croker's political weight:

[69] Murray MSS, Croker to Lockhart, 10 Sept. 1842.
[70] Tuell, *Sterling*, 146–7.
[71] NLS, Lockhart MS 928, no. 29, fo. 40, C. to Lockhart 'K[ensington] P[alace] Sunday' end Oct./early Nov. 1842. CPC, Croker to Lockhart ii. fo. 93, 2 Nov. 1842.

It was only yesterday that my friend here [Peel] conveyed to me the urgent desire of a leading member of the Government, *enforced by his own*, that I should give in the next Quarterly an exposure of the complicity of the anti Corn Law League with the late riots and he put into my hands a very full and curious abstract of documents in proof of the fact. Instead of accompanying the party to *shoot*, I stayed at home to read and note these papers; and I promised that I would *today* write to you . . . to propose it to you for the Christmas number. My friend was against so long a delay, as the League were very active and required to be checked as soon as possible; on which I told him that you had resolved to bring out the Xmas number as early as the 16th December, which was full as soon as *I* could be ready with my share of the work, if you should accept my offer—and now it turns out that a number will be published within a week, of which of course he will scarcely credit that I knew nothing yesterday. What will he think of me, or at least what will he think of my influence with you, or your confidence in me? As however the case is urgent, and as it was clear that I could not accomplish the object, I have been obliged to recommend them to put the materials into the shape of a pamphlet and bring it out in their own time, which was their original alternative, if I should be unable to help them in the Quarterly. That alternative has been adopted, and the papers are gone back to town by this post. I think you will feel how very awkward all this must be to me individually . . .[72]

A more resolute editor might have called Croker's bluff, especially if he had wanted the *Quarterly* to voice rank and file conservative opinion. Lockhart was not so resolute, and it must be admitted that what Croker presented to him was the prospect of the loss of his contact direct with the Prime Minister and Cabinet. He wrote a conciliatory reply, explaining the editorial reasons for the new number (which was however abandoned) and hoping that Croker would continue his connection.[73] Croker did, and his next contribution was the very paper on the League, which showed the *Quarterly* to be more closely in the counsels of ministers than any previous article.

It was an excoriating attack. The League's leaders were charged with 'the old Jacobin spirit of enmity to our existing institutions', conduct the more heinous since many of them had been made magistrates, and even been knighted, by the Whigs.[74]

---

[72] NLS, Lockhart MS 927 no. 35, fos. 47–8, 20 Nov. 1842, Copy in CPC, Box 23.
[73] CPC, Box 23, 22 Nov. 1842.
[74] *QR*, lxxi, no. 141 (Dec. 1842) 'Anti-Corn Law Agitation', 244–5.

Historians of the last generation have tended to make a simple distinction between the League and the Chartists. The Chartists are supposed to have been working class, and so forerunners of socialism. The League were leaders of the industrial bourgeoisie and therefore grinders of the faces of the poor. To Croker such a distinction would have been meaningless. In an earlier article of 1839 he had noted that John Frost, leader of the abortive Newport Rising, had been made a magistrate by Lord John Russell when Home Secretary;[75] and just as that article accused the Whig government of, in effect, encouraging disorder and sedition, so the attack on the League played heavily on the way the 'Russell magistrates' had borrowed from the Paris revolutionaries of July 1830 the notion of turning out their workers in what came to be called the Plug Plot. This showed, Croker declared, that their boasted philanthropy was bogus. Their ruling motive was gain:

Revolutionary feelings and projects have mixed and will continue to mix themselves up with it; but the first and great object of the League was and is the LOWERING OF WAGES.[76]

This article, reprinted at Peel's recommendation as a pamphlet, had a powerful effect in sobering the extreme rhetoric of Cobden and his colleagues, and this was due to the fact that it had been written with ministerial help. Details of the northern magistracy were supplied by Graham and the Home Office.[77] The claim that the League wanted to lower wages came from Peel himself.

Croker was now in a stronger position to impose his views on the *Quarterly* in the other area where Peel's government faced backbench criticism, Ireland and the Irish Church. Here again, what is striking is that he used his authority to swing the review behind Peel, in defiance of traditional, backbench conservative opinion. The *Quarterly's* tradition of supporting the Established Church had recovered from the dissensions of Catholic Emancipation, and the Whig administrations' scant sympathy for

---

[75] QR, lxv, no. 129 (Dec. 1839) 'Conduct of Ministers—Seditious Meetings', 284.

[76] Ibid., lxxi, no. 141, 311–12.

[77] Jennings, ii. 388–391, N. McCord, *The Anti-Corn Law League* (1958) 125–131.

the Church had throughout the 1830s enabled Tories to raise the alarm that their Church was in danger. Nowhere was the danger more acute than in Ireland, where the Whig assault on the revenues of the Church had become bogged down in the controversy of 'appropriation', and this issue, about how the appropriated revenues might be applied, may be deemed a landmark in the Whigs' decline. Having stemmed Whig advances there, many Tories wanted to pass to the offensive and construct a coherent alliance between Church and party. A conspicuous expression of this wish was the Oxford Movement, with which many Tories such as Gladstone identified, and which at first seemed to indicate a revival of strength in the Established Church. The movement however perplexed Lockhart and the *Quarterly*. On the one hand he was alarmed at the sceptical tendencies of German theological scholarship which he, like Pusey, feared would lead to atheism.[78] On the other hand the Romanizing tendencies of the Tractarians compromised the conservative defence of the Church in Ireland, where a revived Catholic nationalism not only weakened the Union but led to a new danger, ultramontanism. What was wanted was a *via media*, a Protestant, episcopalian orthodoxy which, without showing sympathy for the scepticism lurking in Dissent, would still stop short of Catholicism and ultramontanism. Early in 1839 Lockhart went up to Balliol, his old college, to find out what moderate men thought of the Tractarians. He came away much encouraged by the new stirring of theological activity which they had fostered, very impressed by their scholarly productions, but convinced that they must be kept 'from going beyond the principles of our own Reformation.'[79] One result of this visit was the recruitment of a Fellow of Exeter College, William Sewell, to review Gladstone's book on *The State in its Relations with the Church*.[80] Sewell was to become famous as the founder of Radley and notorious for publicly burning a copy of James Anthony Froude's *Nemesis of Faith* in Exeter College hall. In 1840 he spent the summer in Ireland, from which, Lockhart was relieved to report, he 'returned with his mind considerably cleared of the most

---

[78] CPC, Lockhart Letters vol. ii. fo. 17, Lockhart to Croker, 21 Jan. 1839; fo. 29, 1 Nov. 1839.
[79] CPC, Lockhart Letters vol. ii. fo. 18, 4 Feb. 1839.
[80] *QR*, lxv, no. x, Dec. 1839, 97–153.

perilous of the Pusey views by his observation of the Popish system as there reduced to Practice'.[81] Sewell now wrote a series of articles on Ireland which were violently anti-Catholic and helped confirm the *Quarterly*'s general stand against O'Connell and against the repeal of the Union.[82] He also began to write more critically of the Tractarians.

When therefore Peel, after the fiasco of the trial of O'Connell, turned to a policy of conciliating the Catholic hierarchy, Lockhart and the *Quarterly* management faced a serious dilemma. Were they to stand by Peel or by the Church? Croker was in favour of the proposed grant to the Catholic seminary of Maynooth, which for him was only a first instalment of the larger project he had always advocated, that government should pay the Catholic priesthood.[83] But most of the *Quarterly*'s clerical readership would have opposed the grant and been horrified at the idea of endowing the Catholic priesthood. Were Lockhart and Murray to keep their oldest and most valuable contributor, or their most numerous and loyal readers? Croker, conscious of the strength of his position, set out the government's policy as being 'to permit, if not to make an endowment for the priests' (which was to become the Charitable Bequests Act) and to 'try to reconcile the papists to the government'. The policy coincided with the views he had held for forty years, but he admitted the *Quarterly* had never adopted them. He went on

What is it to do now? Is it to abandon politics, or to stick to the old Ascendancy line or to adopt *my old* and *Peel's new* views? You and your proprietor must decide this question. If you wish to go on with the Government, I may be of some use to you; if you should think that the interests of the Review lead the other way, you will not want able hands to enforce that doctrine which has been indeed the staple of the Review.[84]

The following month Lockhart agreed to put the *Quarterly* behind Peel's policy and asked Croker to write the article on the Charitable Bequests Act.[85] Later in the year Croker wrote a fifty-

[81] CPC, Lockhart Letters vol. ii. fo. 46, 13 Oct. 1840.
[82] 'Romanism in Ireland' in *QR*, lxvii, no. 139 (Dec. 1840), 117–71, and 'Romish priests in Ireland' in lxvii, no. 140 (Mar. 1841), 541–95.
[83] *QR*, lxxvi, no. 151 (June 1845), 276.
[84] NLS, Lockhart MS 927, no. 42, fos. 57–8, 28 Feb. 1844.
[85] CPC, Lockhart letters ii. fo. 152, L. to Croker, 4 Mar. 1844.

page defence of the Maynooth Grant in the *Quarterly* for June 1845.[86]

The issue of agricultural protection, relatively quiet in parliament since 1842, stirred again early in 1845, when Peel's budget proposed to extend the period of the income tax and in return made reductions in the tariffs on a further range of imported goods. The interests of agriculture were ignored. For the writers on the *Quarterly* the alarm was raised by an ambiguous overture from Gladstone. Having just resigned from office over the Maynooth grant (which he would nevertheless support in the Commons) Gladstone's tortuous intellect turned, as it always did when he was relieved of political duties, to advocacy, and he proposed to Lockhart that he would write for the *Quarterly* a defence of the 1842 budget. As Croker had written such a defence at the time, this could only mean a new exposition from a free trade rather than a protectionist viewpoint.[87] Moreover Gladstone's religious tergiversations made his judgement suspect. Croker and Lockhart thought he was making a bid to take over the *Quarterly*. Croker was later to call him 'a cross between Machiavelli and Loyola'.[88] But his intervention did raise the issue whether the *Quarterly* ought not, for its own prosperity, to turn with the tide, and Croker saw quite clearly that in a conflict between profit and principle, it was the proprietor's right to opt for profit. 'The Review is *his* landed interest and he should consider how it is to be most productively tilled—"*quo sidere*" under what auspices?' Alternatively, he might keep it in 'its ancient station at the head of what may be left of the ancient Tory party'. Able writers could be found to support either course: the question was, 'which will Murray think safest for his permanent interests, *stare super antiquas vias*, or to float with the surface-stream into mesmerism, Germanism, Puseyism, free tradism, Young Englandism and eventually Whiggism, Jacobinism, Chartism and, to use Prospero's alliteration, the *abysm* of all things!'[89] Once again, both editor and publisher agreed with their political mentor. They may well have felt that, having offended

---

[86] *QR*, lxxvi, no. 151, 247–98.
[87] It was presumably this article which Gladstone later published as a pamphlet *Remarks upon Recent Commercial Legislation* (1845).
[88] NLS, Lockhart MS 927, no. 59, fos. 88–9, 25 Jan. 1846.
[89] NLS, Lockhart, MS 927, no. 47, fos. 65–7, 20 Feb. 1845.

many of their readers once, with support for the Maynooth grant, they must not do so again by advocating free trade. But on Maynooth, at least it could be said that the higher Anglican clergy were divided. So were the Tractarians.[90] Croker was not alone in thinking it a transient agitation, quickly roused but soon forgotten. The grant to extend a Catholic seminary had angered Protestant opinion, but it was not so momentous in its political implications as the Charitable Bequests Act, which had attracted much less criticism. Free trade and the Corn Laws, by contrast, seemed to present a clear-cut issue. Its applications seemed immediate and palpable; it divided parties; it ranged class against class; and the *Quarterly*'s line was clearly stated and fresh in its readers' minds. So Croker's opinion prevailed in Albemarle Street. Unfortunately, it was to bring direct conflict with Peel and his government.

It is not easy to understand a crisis in which all the participants seem to be on a disastrous collision course, and some writers simplify the issues by taking sides and attributing personal blame—to Peel for not consulting his supporters, to Disraeli for being driven by personal spite, to the country gentlemen for being unable to see outside their economic interests, and so on. Almost the only sources historians have not considered in connection with the great schism of 1846 are those I have been using in this narrative, and though these concern only Croker's relations with the *Quarterly* on the one hand and with the ministry on the other, they do enable us to discriminate between the elements which were amenable to discussion and agreement and those which were not. Among the men I have been considering, there was a personal conflict taking place inside a larger political one, which exacerbated and prolonged it. There was a personal misunderstanding between Peel and Croker which the resources of civilization might have resolved amicably, and even in public was conducted with decorum.[91] But this coincided with a political conflict which the traditional constitutional conventions were too weak to contain or control. It was the *Quarterly Review* and its readership which connected the two, turning the personal disagreement into a political estrangement.

---

[90] CPC, Lockhart to Croker vol. iii, fo. 35A, 17 May 1845.
[91] cf. Gash, *Sir Robert Peel*, 609 where they are called 'savage attacks'.

Before the Maynooth debates there was no open breach between Croker and Peel, but each must have been aware of the gulf between them. Croker regarded the landowning aristocracy as the foundation of true conservatism, the class whose wealth was least volatile and most devoted, through the multifarious duties of landownership, to the public good. Their education being liberal and not mercantile reinforced a responsible attitude to their political duties. They were the heart of the English parliamentary system, the chief cause of the country's immunity from revolution. Protection for landed wealth was the just expression of society's gratitude for these benefits. Free trade, the triumph of the commercial spirit, would undermine them and lead to revolution. By contrast Peel's outlook, however refined by privilege, was firmly based on industry and commerce, and for all Croker's earlier assertions that he led a cabinet which represented the landed interest, his record reflected his sympathies. In social status a landowner and a local notable, by official habit he was a metropolitan administrator. His political life had given him close understanding of the world of banking and trade. He understood, much more readily than Croker, the idiom of political economy, and his success in finance increased his reputation with the classes who risked their capital in commerce. To an inherited sympathy with the new wealth he added a dash of moral puritanism quite absent in his friend. He did not see why landed wealth should be shielded from the laws of the market nor, more impatiently, why policies based on long experience of those laws should be denied by a confederacy of idle squires living on their rents.[92] What gives his attitudes in the repeal crisis an air of rigid obstinacy is that he came dangerously close to thinking political principle identical with fiscal orthodoxy. One could express the divergence in the abstract language of political theory by saying that Croker's conservatism was based on a conception of society that was historical and organic, and Peel's on one that was utilitarian and mechanistic. In political terms, the contrast is more stark. Croker idealized the landed proprietor as the bulwark of political stability and Peel looked on him with suspicion as an obstacle to progress and social justice. Croker's conception

---

[92] Parker, *Peel*, iii. 324.

played down the frivolous side of aristocratic life; Peel's, more fatally, played down its political power.

The larger conflict was between Peel and his followers over their respective shares in the making of policy. Peel, like many other politicians whose formative experiences in politics were of the unreformed constitution, assumed that ministries broke up from internal weaknesses and not from 'backbench revolts'.[93] So for instance, according to this view, Wellington would not have found the Ultras a serious threat to his government if he had managed to keep in the Canningites. Even the Crown's authority could not make up for the disunity of a Cabinet. In 1841 he had deliberately formed a Cabinet on which he could rely. He treated his Chancellor of the Exchequer like a clerk, presenting the budgets himself. His Home Secretary Graham referred all important decisions to him, so that Greville could write of them as political partners.[94] His close supervision of all his government's legislation, and his refusal to accept amendments in committee provoked the charge of arrogance. His reply was that people 'like a certain degree of obstinacy and presumption in a minister. They abuse him for dictation and arrogance, but they like being governed'.[95] Another result was that his parliamentary supporters held him responsible for everything the government did which they disliked. The two devices which in a modern parliamentary system head off such discontent are first, a prior agreement with one's supporters on general principles of policy, and second, a cabinet reshuffle to placate and absorb the dissentients. Neither was available in the system that emerged from the first Reform Act. MPs were too independent-minded to take kindly to a party programme, and Ministers were still formally chosen by the Crown, which in practice meant that cabinets reflected a Prime Minister's preference rather than the views of his supporters in the Commons. It would in any case have been hard to judge what those views were and how strongly they were felt. If Peel had a programme of legislation

[93] The phrase is Stewart's (*Foundation of the Conservative Party*, 187–95) but it is, strictly speaking, misleading, since it implies a clear division between a 'frontbench' and its supporters, which did not yet exist. Had it existed, Peel might have been more accurate in his expectations of success.

[94] Greville, v. 190, 202.

[95] Parker, *Peel*, iii. 270 (to Hardinge, 24 Mar. 1845).

it could hardly be revealed to the electorate and was only offered
piecemeal to his supporters rather as a doctor gives unpleasant
medicine to a patient to see how much he can take. Whereas
Melbourne had preferred (despite the urgings of his apothecary
Russell) to leave the patient alone, Peel had a number of remedies to prescribe. The result was that his government had to face
a series of protests, as the successive doses were administered.
His difficulties were increased by the fact that the patient had
a much stronger conviction about what was good for him.
To abandon a threadbare metaphor, Conservative MPs who
thought the elections of 1841 were a vindication of their
opposition to Whig attacks on the Church and the land were
soon disillusioned by a leader who met their protests not with
concession but with threats of resignation. What made this an
effective weapon was that, if carried out, it would bring a Whig
ministry and the dissolution of the party. It would cease to be
effective at the point where those alternatives had come to seem
no worse than the policies Peel insisted on pursuing. By the
third reading of the Maynooth Bill, on 21 April 1845, 149 Conservatives, a bare majority of the parliamentary party, thought
that point had been reached, and voted against the bill.[96]

In the early years of the Ministry, Croker had supported
Peel's view of the party's obligation to obey. In 1843 he had
assured the *Quarterly*'s readers that Peel's government was
committed to agricultural protection, in an article which carried
a rebuke to Young England, for creating distrust in 'the only statesmen in whom the great Conservative body has any confidence,
or can have any hope'.[97] The Maynooth debates made him realize that backbench discontent was more deeply rooted. He
urged on Graham the need to placate the country gentlemen.
Their 'turn of mind', he told him, was 'towards immediate
and tangible interests rather than prospective, circuitous, and
consequential advantages'.[98] In other words, they were not to be
bought off with arguments about national prosperity when they
saw interests traditionally hostile favoured and their own livelihood threatened. Graham gave the official reply that, if the
country gentlemen overthrew the government they would live

---

[96] *PD*, 3rd. ser. vol. lxxx, cols. 750–3, Apr. 1845.
[97] *QR*, lxxii, no. 144 (Sept. 1843) 'Policy of Ministers', 554–7.
[98] *CPD*, uncatalogued MSS, partly in Jennings, iii. 30.

to regret it, and passed the letter on to Peel.[99] Knowing that Croker had invested part of the Hertford legacy in a small farm in Gloucestershire, Peel commented, 'Croker has about 100 acres of land and is infected with the agricultural contagion'.[100] It is clear, however, that Croker realized, what Peel seems to have ignored, that the Maynooth protests were symptoms of a more formidable revolt. 'The question is not Maynooth', he told Lockhart a few days before the vote on the third reading, 'the question is what you and I have lately been foreseeing, want of confidence in Peel'. He went on:

The relief bill, the currency, the antiprotectionist policy, tariffs, Canada corn, timber and sugar duties and expending the *whole* surplus [from the income tax] in uncalled for and partial remissions of taxation. This is the real cause of the serious part of the present turmoil, in which the religious principle has no formidable share.[101]

After the vote he wrote direct to the Prime Minister, warning him, in effect, that his fiscal policy had increased his difficulties on Maynooth.

As to the majority of the *Tories* who have voted against you, I am satisfied that *they* would have voted £50,000 to Maynooth and £200,000 for an actual endowment if it had not been for the Timber Duties, Tariff, Canada Corn Bill and the giving up of your *whole* surplus to the manufacturing interest, which appears to them a strong symptom of Anti-protective policy and frightens them about Corn.[102]

Peel's reply was a defiant assertion that he enjoyed the support of the really influential in the House of Commons and that those who opposed him did so from interested motives. He noted the fact that some of his critics were responding to constituency pressure as if it were a matter for reproach. But he said he was determined to carry the bill and professed himself indifferent to the consequences 'as far as they concern me and my position'. He said nothing of the corn tariff, and nothing about his party.[103] Still there was no open breach. Croker accepted Graham's help

---

[99] CPD, uncatalogued MSS, partly in Jennings, iii. 31.
[100] BL, Graham MSS, 23 Mar. 1845. It was actually 336 acres. Add. MSS. 40518, fos. 300–1. Croker to Peel, 13 Nov. 1842.
[101] NLS, Lockhart MS 927 no. 50, fos. 74–5, 15 Apr. 1845.
[102] Add. MSS. 40565, fos. 7–8, 20 Apr. 1845.
[103] Ibid., fos. 9–10 (2 Apr. 1845) repr. with variants Jennings, iii. 32.

with his summer article on Maynooth.[104] In August Peel asked
him to Drayton. Croker admitted that he had had a bout of
deafness which made him a social liability, and the visit was
deferred.[105] Perhaps Peel had intended to give his friend a
confidential hint of his changing views. But in an exchange of
letters in late August, when a wet summer and the potato blight
were already causing alarm about the food supply, Croker gave
his opinion that the country gentlemen were 'the only support that
a government can rely on' and Peel gave a warily non-committal
reply. Croker was quite right, he said, about 'the importance in
a moral and social point of view of the Agricultural interests but'
and he added what may have been meant as a warning shot:

the question at issue is, what will conduce to the real welfare of that
interest. I believe the maintenance, if possible the steady increase of
Commercial prosperity absolutely essential to it.

I should shudder at the recurrence of such a winter and spring as
those of 1841–2.[106]

This was well short of a change of mind, and Croker was not
too alarmed. He knew that the free trade doctrine was gaining
ground. He wanted to give up writing political articles for the
Quarterly. But he was convinced Peel was committed to the Corn
Law of 1842, and he thought the alliance between the government and its conservative supporters more likely to be broken
by Peel's resignation than by any backbench revolt. 'I fear Peel's
disgust more than anything else' he had told Lockhart in March,[107]
and in November he admitted wistfully, 'I wish he would by a
little more *Toryism* enable us to give him a more effective support'.[108] He had no premonition of an impending political crisis.

Peel was quite well aware of the strength of protectionist
feeling in the party and he may have contemplated its gradual
conversion to total repeal, supported by a general and palpable
improvement in the economy.[109] But events forced his hand. By
October 1845 it was clear that the failure of the potato crop was

---

[104] CPD, Graham to Croker, 24 May. 1845.
[105] BM, Add. MSS. 40572, fos. 196–8 (19 Aug. 1845).
[106] Add. MSS. 40573, fos. 158–9, Croker to Peel, 29 Aug. 1845; fos. 160–1.
[107] NLS, Lockhart MS 927 no. 48 fos. 60–70, 28 Mar. 1845.
[108] Ibid., no. 57A, fo. 85, 4 Nov. 1845.
[109] Parker, *Peel*, iii. 272–3, 325.

complete and some alteration in the Corn Laws would be necessary. Even then, though favouring complete repeal himself, he
might have preferred to repeat the strategy of 1831, letting the
Whigs propose the radical measure, and keeping his freedom to
amend it as it went through parliament. But on 22 November
Lord John Russell issued the famous Edinburgh letter calling
for total repeal, which weakened Peel's position.[110] He could not
persuade the whole Cabinet to agree with him, and he could not
hope to carry the measure through parliament with a divided
Cabinet. In May 1832 he had refused to join a Wellington ministry to pass a Reform Bill because adopting a measure he had
opposed would discredit public men. He now met the same argument from his Cabinet colleagues. Goulburn told him that if he
altered his previous views on corn, he would prejudice his own
and his colleagues' characters 'as public men'.[111] He decided to
resign, but not before *The Times* had announced that the out-
going ministers had decided on repeal. Peel might have salvaged
party unity had his successor been able to form a government,
but Russell failed, and gave up his commission. On 20 December
the Queen asked Peel to resume office and suggested he take time
to consult his colleagues. Peel replied that he did not need it, that
he would have greater authority if he accepted straightaway. As
in December 1834, the royal command was enough. He said he
felt like a man restored to life.[112]

In the heyday of free trade, it was easy to present Peel, in the
struggle that ensued, as a heroic figure fighting for the truth against
the malign forces of bigotry within his own party, and Croker
has suffered by contrast. Peel's editors, Cardwell and Stanhope,
made no mention of him, but their residuary legatee, C. S. Parker,
had before him Jennings' account of the last exchange between
Peel and Croker. Parker was a mere compiler of documents
he did not always understand or accurately transcribe, and he
attempted irony. Croker loved Peel, he wrote, 'But he loved the
Corn laws more, and sacrificed to them a friendship of seven-
and-thirty years'.[113] This misses the point even of the letters
Jennings had quoted, to say nothing of the numerous letters from
Croker to Peel of which Parker was then custodian. Croker's main

---

[110] *Peel Memoirs*, ii. 175–9.   [111] Ibid., 201; Gash, *Sir Robert Peel*, 547.
[112] *Memoirs*, ii. 249, 251–2.   [113] Parker, *Peel*, iii. 374.

concern was the integrity of the landed interest as 'the only solid foundation on which any Government can be formed in this country'. The Corn Laws were a secondary consideration.[114] But the political activity of the League had made them a symbol of the landed interest's power, and the *Quarterly* in 1842 had defended them, as modified by Peel, in an article which he had approved. Though this could not be a binding commitment for a politician, Peel had not revealed his own change of mind, and even when the *Quarterly* had warned him of the state of mind among his supporters, he had kept his own views from them. They, by contrast, had changed theirs to support him on Maynooth and his Irish policy. All their relations with him, indeed, suggested reciprocal trust, and as they were thought to be in his counsels they felt they were entitled to his confidence. Instead, the first intimation Croker had had that the Cabinet was contemplating another change in the Corn Laws was a newspaper report in the wake of Russell's *Edinburgh* letter. He had written to Peel asking his advice, but warning him, that if he was not in a position to answer, the *Quarterly* would stick to its old policy. Peel did not reply.[115] When Peel resigned, therefore, and even before he had announced his conversion to total repeal, Croker's old fear of the dissolution of the party seemed to have been realized. While Russell was making his fumbling efforts at forming a government, Croker was expecting a dissolution of parliament and had assured the *Quarterly*'s readers that they could trust Peel in the event of his returning to power.[116] The catastrophe was not repeal but Peel's resignation. Reaffirming his support for 'the sliding scale and our doctrines of 1841–2', Croker asked:

And has it all been in vain? And is the great Conservative Party dissolved? And are the Landed interests, and ultimately the aristocracy and the Monarchy, to be handed over to the fierce democracy of the League?[117]

He meant that these would be the effects of a Russell ministry acting in harmony with the League. He little expected that when

---

[114] Jennings, iii. 67.   [115] CPC, Box 23, Folder 10, repr. Jennings, iii. 36–7.
[116] *QR*, lxxvii, no. 153 'Ministerial Resignations' (Dec. 1845), 320.
[117] Add. MSS. 40581, fos. 126–9, 17 Dec. 1845. Copy in CPC, Box 23, Folder 10. Jennings (iii. 39) seems to have printed this copy dated 16 Dec.

Peel returned to power he would adopt the very policy which the Whigs had been too divided to propose. The protectionists in parliament had been to some extent forewarned, and were ready to act. Croker by contrast had deprecated their unrest, feeling that they should be loyal to Peel. Now for the first time he experienced their sense of betrayal, with the extra pang that, unlike them, he had suffered it at the hands of a friend. His confidence that a minister who had co-operated with the *Quarterly* would not let it down turned out to be hopelessly unreal.

The conflict which followed when parliament met in January has often been described. What made it irreparably bitter was the fact that it was a clash between two ideas of constitutional propriety, neither of which quite corresponded to the facts of the case. Peel, thinking that Russell's failure to form a ministry gave him a free hand to choose total repeal, acted as if the Crown's choice raised him above the party battle and provided him with as strong a mandate as he needed to carry it through parliament. His Cabinet, after two resignations, was united as it had not been in November. His colleagues were buoyed up with their leader's sense of the righteousness of their cause and the superiority of their information. Peel knew he faced a task persuading some of his party, but he had a poor opinion of their capacity and motivation and was convinced he had the intellect of the House on his side. He forgot that his first ministry had, even with the Crown support, never had a majority, and that his second had been made possible by a victory at the polls which produced a majority with a much more united outlook even than the combination which had brought him down in 1835. Even after the first debates of the session showed the protectionists in his own party were much angrier than he expected, he thought they would 'return to their old standard'.[118]

On their side, there were some equally fallacious expectations. The protectionists wanted to avenge themselves on Peel for a long series of humiliations, but personal feelings would hardly account for their tenacity and organization, which so surprised the ministry. Their anger was based on a very justifiable feeling that Peel had betrayed them, that he had echoed their opinions in order to get into power, only to abandon them once there.

[118] Parker, *Peel*, iii. 309.

Disraeli put it memorably when he called Peel 'a great Parliamentary middleman . . . who bamboozles one party and plunders the other, till, having obtained a position to which he is not entitled, he cries out, "Let us have no party questions, but fixity of tenure" '.[119] The betrayal was not merely over protection, but also the defence of the Established Church. Nine years of successful resistance to Whiggism and Radicalism had in 1841 brought a victory at the polls, creating an expectation that their leader would consolidate their gains, not squander them in concessions to free trade and Irish discontent. They felt they were a political party, representing the most stable elements in society and politics, and they expected their leader to reflect that feeling. But this implied the modern doctrine, that the government should be drawn from the majority party and reflect its views. As Disraeli put it:

There are always men ready to form a government; and if the noble lord [Russell] had formed one, and the country would not support free trade, that would not show that his principles were wrong; but it would show . . . that the nation was not ripe for those opinions, or that it was against them. This is a legitimate thing, but it is not a legitimate trial of the principles of free trade against the principle of protection if a Parliament, the majority of which are elected to support protection, be gained over to free trade by the arts of the very individual whom they were elected to support in an opposite career. It is not fair to the people of England.[120]

In the event, the protectionists overrated the magnetic pull of their own grievances. They did not expect to form a government by themselves, but they did expect to attract to their cause those of Peel's colleagues known to favour protection or to have qualms about repealing the Corn Laws. In fact the protectionist principles of these men proved weaker than their respect for power. The split that occurred was not between free traders and protectionists, but between backbenchers and official men. The official men stayed with Peel because they thought free trade from him would be less damaging than free trade from Russell. If Peel was complacent in thinking that his Tory critics would return to their

---

[119] J. E. Kebbel (ed.) *Selected Speeches of the Rt. Hon. the Earl of Beaconsfield* (2 vols. 1882) i. 94.
[120] Ibid., i. 109.

allegiance, they on their side were naïve in thinking his colleagues would desert theirs. Conservatism split into a Peelite front bench without a party, and a protectionist party without an experienced front bench. Disraeli's theory of party was not realized for a generation. The protectionists' main gain was negative: they had driven Peel into the wilderness, exiled by his own view that leading a party was a form of servitude.

This development turned Croker into an advocate of an organized Tory party. In the 1830s he had been prepared to admit that the two parties of Whigs and Tories corresponded very approximately to opposing impulses or temperaments in human behaviour; that people who valued stability and order gravitated to the Tories, and those who wanted change and innovation to the Whigs.[121] But he was far from seeing that these contrary tendencies needed to be channelled into formal organization, with electoral agents, party whips, and central funds supervised by the parliamentary party. All these things were alien to the Tory tradition and made for weak executive government. So at first, he backed Peel against the party. The crisis of 1845–6 made him realize what a sacrifice he had made to personal friendship. But it was too late. Peel with his experienced colleagues, in alliance with the landed interest, would have made a formidable barrier against revolution. But Peel had shattered that larger Conservative interest. The party to which Croker was to give his allegiance was only a fragment of that interest.

Did Croker then agree with Disraeli's view? Did the victim become a convert? Not quite. Croker's position is actually a judicious one, midway between Peel's and Disraeli's. Peel's explanation of his failure to warn his followers of his conversion to total repeal was that he was doing something he knew to be to their advantage; that it was hard to impart commercially sensitive information to a large and numerous party; and that the time had passed when a minister could learn his party's intentions by consulting 'the Marquess of Hertford and the Duke of Rutland and the Earl of Lonsdale'.[122] It may be no coincidence that in naming the three leading borough patrons of the unreformed system he was also naming Croker's friends. But the excuses would not have satisfied the average Peelite, let alone

---

[121] Brougham MSS, Croker to Brougham, 14 Mar. 1839; repr. Jennings, ii. 352–4.
[122] *Peel Memoirs*, iii. 322–3.

any protectionist. There were various ways of communicating with one's parliamentary party being developed in the reform era—through whips' offices, through the clubs and the press—which Peel conspicuously failed to use. But more seriously, his defence makes the egoistic assumption that the formulation and alteration of policy was his alone.

Both Croker and Disraeli would have questioned this. Disraeli's conception of the relations of a leader with his party is rather too dependent on his own case. He thought a political party put its leader into power, and he in turn rewarded its members with office according to their contributions to the common victory. His work as a journalist had made him acutely aware of the party battle as a contest of arguments, put across to the voting public with rhetorical skill, and there is a journalist's frustration in his charge against Peel, of using Whig arguments to advance Whig policies, when he should have observed 'the demarcation between parties' and made use of his own. The constitutional case for parties which he makes is however one which might be supported by liberals or conservatives. It is that, if a leader is raised to power by means of the opinions of one party, but once in power adopts the policies of his erstwhile opponents; if, as Peel did, he rises to power on Tory principles but governs by Whig ones; then he exercises power without the wholesome check of a parliamentary opposition and so in defiance of the section of public opinion which he was taken to represent.[123]

Croker's idea of party also owes much to his disillusionment with Peel. Even Chatham, he says, broke down 'from the overweening and, as we believe, insane arrogance of standing absolutely alone.' A leader guides his party with his superior tact and judgement, and the party makes sure that his policy is made acceptable. But no party is the mere tool of its leader.

A Party is a kind of republic, of which the leader is only President—owing to his party the same or indeed rather stricter allegiance than his party to him, and that allegiance should be in direct proportion with the eminence to which the confidence of the party may have raised him . . . A Party raises a man, or, which is nearly the same thing, affords him the footing and the force by which he raises himself, to great political distinction; the Sovereign in consequence raises him to power. What would be thought of the Minister who, *on any pretence whatsoever,* should turn against the Sovereign the power so confided? And are not gratitude and fidelity due at least equally to the Party as to the Sovereign —for the Party has been the earlier and the greater benefactor?[124]

What if such a leader, raised to power by a party which trusted him, came to disagree with his supporters? Croker's reply is that he should retire and, since it involved his individual conscience, scrupulously refrain from involving others in his decision. Peel had not only changed his mind. He had invited others to follow him in an enterprise he had admitted would break up the government, and then declared his determination never again to take office. Croker thought that for consistency's sake he should retire from parliament altogether, and that until he did, there was no prospect of a reconciliation of protectionists and conservative free traders. But reconciliation foundered on fundamental differences of policy. Protectionists were too hostile to free trade, Peelites too wedded to it, to co-operate. By the time the elections of 1847 gave Russell's government a small majority, while still leaving it dependent on the co-operation of the Peelites, Croker realized that reconciliation was hopeless.[125]

III

Peel's defeat over Irish Coercion in June 1846 was a surprise, and its significance took some time to sink in. We can now see that in various ways it was the end of an era. But the *Quarterly* writers were staunch upholders of principles which, they thought, remained unchanged by party fortunes. When a Tory MP, Sir Robert Gardiner, protested against one of Croker's articles against Peel he was told that the *Quarterly* thought that the two parties represented the principles of 'maintenance' and 'change', but that change ought to come from the Whigs, not the Tories; that Peel should have resigned when he saw that the Corn Laws were threatened and that he had conceded repeal from fear of the League, which would not scruple to attack the Church, the Lords, and even the Crown. 'Which of the great institutions under which we have lived may be the next for attack we do not

---

[124] QR, lxxiii, no. 156. 'Close of Sir Robert Peel's Administration' (Sept. 1846), 566–7.
[125] QR, Sept. 1847 'Parliamentary Prospects', 541–78.

pretend to conjecture.'[126] This was in the review's tradition, and it presumably had Croker's approval, as well as John Murray's. What was new was the defeatism, the expectation that, now the floodgates were open to liberalism, the prospect was one of successive retreats before the demands of democracy.

Whether Lockhart really believed it is hard to say. He was certainly pessimistic about the political prospects of conservatism, but as a son of the manse he was more worried about the progress of scepticism than of revolution. For Croker the most instructive period of modern times was the great French Revolution. For Lockhart it was Scotland in the seventeenth century.[127] Both men feared revolution and liberal principles, but for Croker the answer was a political and constitutional one, whereas Lockhart inclined (when he ventured a political opinion) to a more whiggish view that the disruptive forces were subtly allied to cultural change, and might be softened by concession and transformed by education. Croker's response to some radical slander was to draw up a direct refutation from an authority like Lord Sidmouth or the Duke of Wellington and trumpet it in the *Quarterly* with appropriate italics. Lockhart's was the more conciliatory and more positive one of sympathizing with new grievances and recruiting new writers who understood them. No one expected Croker even to have read Carlyle, but Lockhart appreciated his outlook and recognized his genius.[128]

So the conservative schism of 1846 affected Lockhart much less than it did Croker. Lockhart had always chafed at the review's being linked with the temporary expedients of a parliamentary party, and only his early dependence on the publisher and his diffidence in his own political judgement had led him to acquiesce in it.[129] He was an observer, an analyst, but not a persuader or an inspirer. When Peel came to power in 1841, Lockhart had feared that John Murray II's agreement with Croker would lead the review into supporting measures alien to its traditions, as indeed it did.[130] By 1842 he had been convinced

---

[126] CPC, Lockhart to General Sir Robert Gardiner, 22 Apr. 1846 vol. iii, fo. 88. The protest was against Croker's Postscript to 'The Oregon Question', *QR*, lxxviiii, no. 154 (Mar. 1845), 603–11.

[127] e.g. Murray MSS, Lockhart to J. Murray III, 3 Feb. 1846.

[128] Lang, *Lockhart*, ii. 234–239.

[129] Murray MSS, Lockhart to J. Murray II, 12 Oct. 1840.

[130] Ibid., to J. Murray II, 9 Nov. 1841.

that Peel was the only barrier against a Whig-radical administration, and he swallowed the fiscal measures of 1842 and the
premier's coolness over factory reform.[131] He could hardly, four
years later, claim he had been right and Croker wrong, because
he himself had agreed, and it was Croker who, as Peel's apos-
tasy unfolded, had to sacrifice an old friendship to the traditions
of the *Quarterly*. But Lockhart had in effect been vindicated:
following Peel had been shown to be a fatal error. Croker's
position in fact had been more gravely compromised than
Lockhart's. Croker's 1832 deal with Murray had restored the review's traditional stance of defending conservative politics; but
in 1846, for the first time in its history, it faced the prospect of
becoming the organ of an opposition with little prospect of office.
The purpose of Croker's role had been reduced if not destroyed.
Lockhart however had always seen the review as the organ of
an educated and openminded conservatism, and that ideal was
as reasonable in 1846 as it had been in 1832. To justify his
old role on the *Quarterly*, Croker had to open a political correspondence with Lord Stanley, the future Earl of Derby, a
man whose political importance he had mocked in 1835, who
would, as Peel had reminded Croker, 'subscribe himself a Whig',
and whose claim to lead the Protectionists was due to a rather
late conversion, and was contradicted by much else in his
record.[132] Croker soon found Stanley was even more pessimistic
than he was himself about the prospect of the Protectionists.
Lockhart by contrast had shed his political trammels and could
exercise his editorial functions freely, conscious that there was
no ministerial manifesto to be tucked into the last sheets of every
number. He was closer to the new proprietor, the third John
Murray, than he had ever been to his father. He did not question Croker's better judgement in political matters, or assert his
own, but he was certainly aware that his hold over the review
had grown firmer. The old high Tory anti-Jacobin stance of
Gifford was, he knew, quite outmoded. So the *Quarterly*
approached the Year of Revolutions less an organ of a parliamentary party or of the party of government than it had ever
been.

---

[131] Murray MSS, Lockhart to J. Murray II, 12 Aug. 1842.
[132] Derby MSS, Croker to Stanley, 20 Feb. 1847; Jennings, iii. 103–5.

5

Macaulay Joins the Whigs

A man is not bound to be a politician any more than he is
bound to be a soldier; and there are perfectly honourable
ways of quitting both politics and the military profession.
But neither in the one way of life, nor in the other, is any
man entitled to take all the sweet and leave all the sour.
MACAULAY on Sir William Temple

We left Macaulay on the threshold of the House of Commons
but quarrelling with the Whig Lord Chancellor over his attempt
to control the *Edinburgh Review*. Now we must look at his short
political career so as to understand its bearings upon the *History
of England*.

Grey's government was only partly Whig. He had not been
chosen as Prime Minister because he led a united party. What
made him suitable was that he had held aloof from the squabbles
of 1827 and it was so long since he had held office that no
one could connect him with any strong political line which
might alienate possible colleagues.[1] When in 1828 Canning's
followers left the Wellington ministry they created a shortage of
ministerial talent in the House of Commons which dogged the
Duke until his resignation in November 1830. One proposal for
strengthening the ministry was the inclusion of Grey, but this
would always have foundered on the personal prejudices of
George IV. So it was William IV's accession which ended Grey's
long wait for office, but he had been such an irresolute leader
with such a repugnance for associating his party with popular
causes, that what commended him was less his Whig past than
his recent neutrality. Not surprisingly, the team he put together
lacked unity. Those in it with strong views about reform lacked
experience of Cabinet discipline. Those who had that experience

---

[1] E. A. Smith, *Lord Grey, 1764–1845* (Oxford, 1990), 245–58.

were not enthusiastic about reform. Even the aristocratic Whig element were divided on the issue, Lansdowne and Carlisle being moderate, Grey and Holland more committed. The man who had done most to force the issue on the public in the months before Wellington's resignation was Brougham, but far from commanding the party as he had boasted, he found he was 'muzzled' by being made Lord Chancellor. Possibly the most radical minister on the reform issue was Durham, Grey's son-in-law, but he also proved one of the most divisive members of the government. Two of the most efficient offices, the Home and Foreign Office, were held by Melbourne and Palmerston, former followers of Canning. It was a heterogeneous government, and Grey's blend of arrogance and despondency did not make for decisive leadership or evoke loyal co-operation from his subordinates.[2]

Even so, a unity of purpose might have been achieved if the bold strategy which launched the first Reform Bill had been persisted in. Grey's isolation between 1827 and 1830 had lulled the friends of Wellington into a false security that the new premier had lived down his reformist past. The radical groups, long accustomed to tiny minorities for their reform proposals and inclined, from the mid-twenties, to despair of rousing public opinion behind them, did not expect much from a Grey government. So when the measure was announced, at the end of February, it took everyone by surprise. The Tory opposition, scarcely believing Grey would undermine his order and flattered by reports of the new ministers' dissensions, were quite unprepared for so far-reaching a measure.[3] The radicals could hardly believe their luck.[4] Those who now assert that the Reform Bills aimed to consolidate and stabilize the political system tend to forget the fact that the first bill was so extreme that the ministers' hope of carrying it in committee had to be abandoned, and a dissolution became inevitable. But an appeal to the country could be construed as an appeal against the Commons, and that threw doubt on the stabilizing character of the reform. Moderate Whigs and Tories, growing alarmed at popular threats and mob violence, needed

---

[2] cf. Rosslyn's remark to Croker, 28 Jan. 1831; Jennings, ii. 104.

[3] Jennings, ii. 108–9; Aspinall, *Three Diaries*, 13–14.

[4] e.g. G. Wallas, *Life of Francis Place* (1898), 257 sq.; but see also M. G. Brock, *The Great Reform Act* (1973), 148 *et seq*.

persuading that the measure did not threaten them, and would not be convinced if it seemed that the Ministry was being driven by popular demonstrations in a direction it had not chosen. So by dissolving, the Grey government acquired a set of opponents it could never convince and a set of supporters it could never really absorb. Tories thought the reform proposed could never be a final settlement, but must lead to further democratic changes. Radicals thought that it was too modest, but supported it because it would facilitate those changes. A more resolute leadership might have sought to ally Whiggism with either moderate Toryism or moderate radicalism. In fact Grey's government did neither. It acquiesced in an alliance with the Radicals which lasted as long as the fate of the Reform Bill remained in the balance. Whigs could restrain radicals with the argument that, without them, no bill of any sort would be possible. Radicals, knowing that what the Whigs were offering was more extensive than anything they might have achieved by themselves, gave the Grey ministry what they regarded as only conditional support. But as soon as the bill was law, the alliance fell apart.

There was very little disposition for Whig and radical to sink their differences in a common set of policies. If there had been, the Victorian liberal party might have been born a generation earlier. But both sides harboured suspicions which were hard to live down. The Whigs in opposition had received more abuse from their radical critics than from Tories. There were social divisions which meant that if a Whig found an ally in a radical he lost caste. A deep conviction ran through the radical movement that political parties were no more than aristocratic confederacies for distributing the spoils of office, pensions, places, and sinecures, among relatives and their dependants, and that the doctrinal, or as we would say, ideological differences between Whig and Tory were quite trivial. Hence the longevity of their archaic names: they preserved the notion that the connections they described were deep-rooted yet frivolous. Even the followers of James Mill, who had some claim to have thought more deeply and systematically about politics than the rabble-rousing radical demagogues of Tory mythology, were very reluctant to abandon the radical suspicion of party and organize their efforts in parliament, and when J. S. Mill tried to capture their distinctive outlook with the name Philosophic Radical, it did not catch on.[5] The term was too radical for most of the supporters of Melbourne and Russell, and too intellectual for most radicals. 'Whig', therefore, as a label for moderate reformers gained a new lease of life. A term which covered aristocratic Whigs like Holland and Russell as well as moderate radicals such as Charles Buller or Henry Warburton is almost too elastic for definition, but the fact remains that in the era of reform it was not superseded by the name 'liberal'.

Of the younger Whigs Macaulay stands out as an intellect as powerful in abstract argument as in historical learning, and admirers have been very naturally inclined to credit him with a coherent Whig philosophy. In fact, his arguments were not of the sort that translate readily into legislative measures. Those were laid down by professional politicians like Russell and Althorp. Macaulay supported them in grand language and with a wealth of historical illustration, but if one asks where on the political spectrum his speeches place him, one would have to say that he wavers between the radical demands of shorter parliaments and the ballot (which had been in the recommendations of the Committee of Four which drafted the first proposals, but not in the bills themselves), and the very Burkean theme that the constitution, though like 'all the proudest works of human power and wisdom' liable to decay, still contained 'the means of self-reparation'.[6] His speeches were consistent with the sketch of constitutional reform with which he closed his essay on Hallam.[7] He would have agreed with many moderate radicals who thought that the worst fault of the representative system was its exclusion of the 'intelligence and virtue' of the middling orders from the constitution, but who were too worried about the security of property and the fragility of credit to want a really popular franchise. To this he added a shrewd historical argument about the dangers, in a time of popular unrest, of a polarization of opinion which would threaten the moderate centre. It is this theme that has led one scholar to propose a new term for Macaulay's politics and to call him a 'Trimmer', a term which has the merit of questioning the traditional assumption that he was a Whig in the fullest sense.[8] It seems to imply however that Macaulay never

[5] See my *Philosophic Radicals*, 2–3.
[6] *Speeches*, 81.   [7] CHE, i. 214–16.
[8] J. Hamburger, *Macaulay and the Whig Tradition* (Chicago and London, 1976).

resolved the tensions between radical principle and Whig allegiance, but kept up a balancing act between them till the end of
his life. This surely overrates his interest in day-to-day politics.
Most of us, who only take an intermittent interest in politics,
now approving change, now alarmed at it, are trimmers in this
sense; but this reflects detachment rather than commitment. If
he trimmed, or in other words, oscillated between supporting
radical measures and defending ancient institutions, it is unlikely
to have been from a determined policy, decided early and followed consistently. It is more likely that even on his début he
was uncertain, that he lacked the skill of reading a political
situation, and that his emphatic manner concealed a diffidence
about his fitness for a world which at close quarters he found
increasingly distasteful. His oratory was ornate but impractical:
it lacked the grasp of detail that proclaimed the future minister.
Gradually, as his experience clarified his aims, he realized that
he was not one of nature's politicians, and his early insistence
on his independence was replaced by a recognition that a
moderate Whiggism was the political creed which answered his
outlook best.

Of course, when Grey's government replaced Wellington's,
its members' bickerings were forgotten in the novel experience
of office and the pleasures of patronage. Lord Chancellor
Brougham was able to give Zachary Macaulay a place on the
Charity Commission, and his son John a church living.[9] Thomas
lost his old post but gained another, on the Board of Control,
of which he soon became Secretary. This did not ensure his
loyalty. Even before the Reform Bill was passed, he had formed
a low view of the capacity of ministers and admitted feeling
ashamed at having to support such a government.

'The weakness, dulness, cowardice, and tergiversation of the ministers—
those I mean who sit in the House of Commons,—have begun to disgust their most devoted friends . . . It is no business of mine whether
[they] stand or fall.'[10]

---

[9] ZM, Selina Macaulay's Journal, 8 Dec. 1830 [for the Church living]; 3 June
1833 [for Zachary's Commissionership]. The living was worth £400 p.a., the
Commissionership £800.
[10] *LM*, ii. 87–8.

But this hardly guaranteed his support of the ministry. Under the Grants, the Board of Control was almost a Claphamite concern, and the pull of family allegiance to the anti-slavery cause was strong enough to make Macaulay vote against the government on the issue of negro apprenticeship.[11] He offered twice to resign an office which was an important source of income, but the offers were refused. He knew he was lucky to have been excused the normal consequences of disloyalty and, as he put it, 'saved both my honor and my place',[12] but he had seen that it was a symptom of the government's weakness, and he made no secret of his wish to be free of politics in the event of its defeat.

The key to Macaulay's loyalty was personal affection, and the Whig ministry did not, at this stage, arouse much of his affection. Late in 1831 he said he would never serve in a ministry headed by Brougham. In May 1832 he said that if the Whigs abandoned the Reform Bill he would no longer follow them.[13] To his patron Lord Lansdowne, he expressed great respect, but this did not prevent him declaring in the reform debates that sitting for a nomination borough was liable to 'pervert the principles and break the spirit of men formed to be the glory of their country'.[14] He may have been thinking of Brougham or Mackintosh, or even describing himself, 'wearing the badge, though not feeling the chain of servitude', but it explains why he soon became MP for Leeds.

Even the great Whig mansion Holland House did not captivate him. He was undoubtedly flattered to find himself in the same circle as wits like Sydney Smith, Alvanley and Luttrell, and 'Conversation' Sharp, poets like Rogers and Moore, not to mention politicians and lawyers who formed living links with the party of Fox, Burke, and Sheridan. Yet he was plainly shocked at the laxity of Whig society, especially by its loose morals and its irreligion. Lady Holland had never heard of the parable of the talents, and was described in one of his strings of sharp

---

[11] *LM*, ii. 262. For the political background, see I. Gross, 'The Abolition of Negro Slavery and British Parliamentary Politics 1832–3', *Historical Journal* xxiii., no. 1 (1980), 63–85.

[12] *LM*, ii. 279. Althorp agreed with him. See Aspinall, *Three Early Nineteenth Century Diaries* (1952), 330.

[13] [Margaret Macaulay] *Recollections*, 96.

[14] *Speeches*, 72, cf. Greville ii. 225.

antitheses as 'a great lady ... ill-natured and good-natured, sceptical and superstitious, afraid of ghosts and not of God,— would not for the world begin a journey on a Friday morning, and thought nothing of running away from her husband.'[15] One might think from the amusing descriptions of Whig society which he sent his sisters that the son of Clapham had been seduced by the worldly cynicism of his aristocratic hosts. One of Macaulay's most quoted remarks comes in his review of Moore's *Life of Byron*: 'We know no spectacle so ridiculous as the British public in one of its periodical fits of morality'. Hardly anyone remembers the next paragraph:

It is clear that those vices which destroy domestic happiness ought to be as much as possible repressed. It is equally clear that they cannot be repressed by penal legislation. It is therefore right and desirable that public opinion should be directed against them. But it should be directed against them uniformly, steadily and temperately, not by sudden fits and starts. There should be one weight and one measure.[16]

The homily which follows is a good example of how the evangelical, on the threshold of the *beau monde*, found a halfway house at once rational and severe in the morality of utilitarianism. Macaulay remained both socially and politically detached, family loyalty retaining its priority in his private life, intellectual and moral conviction holding him back from enjoying the rough and tumble of politics.

The ambivalence of his Whiggism in the year he left for India is well illustrated in his review of a young historian whom he might well have seen as a rival. Lord Mahon had published a *History of the War of Spanish Succession* in which he severely criticized the Tories for concluding the Peace of Utrecht. Mahon was a Tory. He had sat in Parliament for Wootton Bassett, till it was disenfranchised in Schedule A of the Reform Act. But his ancestors had been Whigs, and the first Earl Stanhope (Mahon was to become the fifth Earl) was a hero of the war against Louis XIV as well as a bulwark of the Hanoverian succession. It was natural therefore for Mahon, in defence of his family, to contrast the belligerent Whiggism of his ancestor with the Francophile pacifism of the party in the era of Fox and Grey,

[15] *LM*, ii. 22, 254.   [16] *CHE*, i. 315–16.

and to note ironically how the meaning of the terms Whig and Tory had in a century become inverted.[17] Macaulay's review, in contrast to those he gave Southey and Sadler, is strikingly gentle. A committed Whig might have defended the record of the Whigs as a party. Macaulay explicitly says that though he prefers them to their rivals, he does not feel bound to 'defend all the measures of our favourite party',[18] because politics involve compromises, whereas the historian is or ought to be concerned with truth. So he agrees that the Tories were right to negotiate the Treaty of Utrecht, because peace was good for the state; and such defence of the Whigs as he does make is really a defence of his own empiricist conception of the March of Mind. He insists that, as society is 'constantly advancing in knowledge', and 'a boy from the National Schools reads and spells better than half of the knights of the shire in the October Club', so, 'though a Tory may now be very like what a Whig was a hundred and twenty years ago, the Whig is as much in advance of the Tories as ever'. He evades Mahon's implied charge that the modern Whigs had forgotten that their predecessors had waged a successful war against tyranny, by shifting attention from party politics to social progress, and his argument is worth quoting more fully because it provides a mark against which we can measure his evolution into a moderate Whig.

The absolute position of the parties has been altered; the relative position remains unchanged. Through the whole of that great movement, which began before these party-names existed, and which will continue after they have become obsolete, through the whole of that great movement of which the Charter of John, the institution of the House of Commons, the extinction of villanage, the separation of the see of Rome, the expulsion of the Stuarts, the reform of the Representative System, are successive stages, there have been, under some name or other, two sets of men, those who were the wisest among their contemporaries, and those who gloried in being no wiser than their great grandfathers. It is delightful to think, that, in due time, the last of those who straggle in the rear of the great march will occupy the place now occupied by the advanced guard.[19]

---

[17] See A. Newman, *The Stanhopes of Chevening*. The historian's father was a Tory, but his grandfather had been nicknamed 'Citizen Stanhope' for his sympathies with the French Revolution.

[18] *CHE*, ii. 91.   [19] *CHE*, ii. 88–9.

Macaulay here shows little of the regard for Whiggism as a family heirloom which one might find in the work of a Whig like Lord John Russell. Instead he turns the argument into a picturesque version of the utilitarian theory of progress. The movement he celebrates actually antedates the rise of party and makes contemporary party names seem trivial.

There were also social obstacles to his assimilation to the Whig party. Aristocratic society especially valued good conversation, and conversation presupposes a willingness to let others talk, whatever the topic. Macaulay engaged in few of the pursuits which provide small talk, and was too prudish to enjoy gossip. When a subject came up on which he had views, he tended to engage in a monologue which, in its learning and force of eloquence, left an audience stunned and bewildered. Chivalrous though he might be with society women like Lady Holland, and playfully patient with the questionings of young women like his sisters, he was among men something of an intellectual bully. In their company, he undoubtedly enjoyed talking people down, confuting them with recondite references, and reducing them to silence.[20] It is of course hard to be certain how anything so intangible as a social manner affects a man's reputation, but in Macaulay's case we have the observations of an acute judge, the diarist Charles Greville. When Greville first saw Macaulay at Holland House, he set him down as 'some obscure man of letters or of medicine, perhaps a cholera doctor'; but when he heard his name, he nearly fell off his chair.[21] Greville was always generous in recording Macaulay's extraordinary learning and fluency, but as he came to know him better, he became more critical. In November 1833, for instance, recording Sydney Smith's *mot* already quoted, he added his own view that he was not 'agreeable': his talk was too copious.

It is more than society requires, and not exactly of the kind; his figure, face, voice, and manner are all bad; he astonishes and instructs, he

[20] In his journal of his visit to Rome he records meeting Lord Caernarvon and talking politics 'in which I thought that I had the upper hand, [19 Nov. 1838, fo. 129]; later he records meeting Goulburn when he came aboard the steamer bound for Marseilles, and putting him down 'on electoral committees' [fo. 334].

[21] Greville, ii. 248–9. Similar observations were made by Mrs Brookfield, see [Charles and Frances Brookfield] *Mrs Brookfield and Her Circle*, 2 vols. (1902) ii. 377; and by Sydney Smith, *Letters*, ii. 741.

sometimes entertains, seldom amuses, and still seldomer pleases. He wants variety, elasticity, gracefulness; his is a roaring torrent, and not a meandering stream of talk . . . I believe we would all of us have been glad to exchange some of his sense for some more of Sydney Smith's nonsense.[22]

Other Whig diners-out agreed. He was 'too much a holder-forth'. Melbourne once said wearily that he wished he could be as cocksure of anything 'as Macaulay is of every thing'.[23]

Social graces are not always essential to a successful political career, as we have seen in the case of Peel, but Macaulay also lacked another quality, political ambition. This may seem an odd assertion, in the light of the shortage of talent on the government benches after 1832 and the Macaulay family's economic plight, but it is borne out by the letters. Financial hardship such as usually sharpens a man's desire for office and promotion had come to him quite late in life, after he had developed his other, literary ambition. He realized that he was unusual in this, and described himself as the only *parvenu* he had ever heard of who preferred 'the exercise of the intellect and the affections' to worldly success.[24] He was excited by the drama of politics but its routine bored him. Even when he described the dramatic moments, as in the letter to Ellis describing the scene in the House of Commons on 22 March 1831 when the first Reform Bill had been passed by one vote, he dealt only with the surface appearances and ignored their immediate political significance.[25] How the crisis will be viewed by Ellis's son when he is eighty excites Macaulay more than what may happen next. The key question— what can the reformers do with a majority in the Commons of only one vote?—is not considered. The stuff of politics, the details of cabinet decisions, party conflict and the play of personalities which provide the foreground for the true political operator are hardly touched on in his letters.

When the excitement of being lionized had palled, he thought of retiring to his writing. 'If I were to leave public life tomorrow,' he told his sister Hannah in June 1833, 'I declare that, except for the vexation which it might give you and one or two others,

---

[22] Ibid., ii. 419. Greville was later a little more charitable, iv. 437–8.
[23] *Journal of Thomas Moore*, ed. Wilfrid S. Dowden (Newark, N.J., 6 vols, 1983–91), v. 2072. D. Cecil, *Lord Melbourne* (1954), 276.
[24] LM, ii. 276.   [25] LM, ii. 9–11.

the event would not be in the slightest degree painful to me'.[26] Two months later, he realized that he could not consult only his comfort and that of his sisters. His father was finally bankrupt and he was the sole breadwinner. He could not make money from legal practice, in which he had never so much as broken even, and his reviewing made him only £200 a year. So when the chance arose of becoming Law Member of the Governor-General's Council in India, he could hardly have refused it. Indeed his letters give the distinct impression that he asked for it.[27] It offered security to himself as well as to his family. But it also offered a chance to be away from England in the approaching political upheaval. His dilemma was set out with great candour in a letter of 17 August 1833:

If I remain in office, I shall, I fear, lose my political character. If I go out, and engage in opposition, I shall break most of the private ties which I have formed during the last three years.

It is worth noting that he dates these ties not from his début in the *Edinburgh* in 1825, but from his acceptance of Calne in 1830, and he calls them private as if they involved no political bond. He went on:

If I could escape from these impending disasters, I should wish to do so. By accepting the post which is likely to be offered me, I escape for a short time from the contests of faction here. When I return I find things settled,—parties formed into new combinations,—new questions under discussion. I shall then be able, without the scandal of a violent separation, and without exposing myself to the charge of inconsistency, to take my own line. In the mean time I shall save my family from distress. I shall return with a competence honestly earned . . . and able to act on all public questions without even a temptation to deviate from the strict line of duty.[28]

Macaulay went to India to escape from politics. He was not so Whig as to want to take part in the 'contests of faction' which would break up the Grey ministry, but neither was he so radical

---

[26] *LM*, ii. 258.

[27] At i. 320–2 Trevelyan prints a letter of TBM to Hannah dated 5 Dec. 1833, in which he uses passages from four letters of other dates, 31 Oct., 22 Nov., 26 Nov., and 6 Dec. 1833 [*LM*, ii. 328–9, 343–4, 355]. This conveys the impression that TBM learned of the appointment as a bolt from the blue.

[28] *LM*, ii. 300–1.

as to want to blame the Whig leadership. It was not the line of a committed Whig, or even of an adopted one. He calculated that with a salary of £10,000 a year, he could put by £5,000 annually, saving it 'with the accruing interest'.

I may therefore hope to return to England at only thirty-nine, in the full vigour of life, with a fortune of thirty thousand pounds.

He went out to India with the fixed aim of staying just so long as it took him to gain his independence. He left England a radical of the left of centre, in whose political principles the utilitarian theory of progress loomed larger than party loyalty to the Whigs.

In one way Macaulay's aim to be far away from the political battles at Westminster was fulfilled. He went out to India as if to a prolonged exile, taking with him a very reluctant younger sister and a large library of European classics.[29] Once in Calcutta he set up house with Hannah, kept aloof from society, saved money, read voraciously in his favourite authors (using successive readings as a way of counting the passage of time) and took no interest in native life beyond what was forced on his attention by his official duties. He admitted that he yearned for England as Ulysses had for Ithaca, adding of his Indian routine, 'I shall leave nothing that I shall ever remember with regret'.[30] Not surprisingly, he has been accused of learning nothing from the experience.[31] Probably India made a deeper impact on him than this allows, but as usual with Macaulay the new impressions had to percolate through layers of literature and literary associations before reaching an outlet much later in his writing. Meanwhile, deprived of the familiar *old* impressions so essential to his emotional life, he tried as much as he could to keep the new world at arm's length, by immersing himself in official routine. It is noticeable that the event which brought him nearest to collapse was not political but domestic, when Hannah's engagement to Trevelyan threatened to deprive him of the last fragment of home life which he had hoped would assuage his

[29] ZM, Hannah Macaulay to Frances Macaulay [Feb. 1834] from the *Asia*.
[30] *LM*, iii. 203.
[31] Eric Stokes, 'Macaulay: the Indian years 1834–1838' in *Review of English Literature* Issue no. 4 (1960) 41–50. Stokes may have been echoing Bagehot, *Literary Studies* (Everyman edn. 1920) ii. 202.

exile. His distress was exacerbated, but not provoked, by the news of his sister Margaret's death, which caused him so much grief that the Trevelyans had to cut short their honeymoon to comfort him.[32] Many men under the impact of bereavement would have seized the chance of travelling to distract their mind. Macaulay retreated deeper into his favourite books, later crediting them with saving his reason.[33]

Macaulay's revulsion against the Orient, his determination not to succumb to its enervating effect, had the curious effect of making him more utilitarian. This may not be so surprising. The attack on Mill's *Government* is essentially an attack upon abstract theory and a vindication of experience. We cannot, the argument runs, establish a true science of politics unless we first gather all the relevant facts, suspending or abandoning our hypotheses as new information is discovered. Deduction from a few assumed principles of human nature will not do: we have to go into the real world and observe how human beings actually behave. Macaulay called this the inductive method, but probably the impulse behind it was a realization that the utilitarians' ideal of social science threatened his own, culturally much richer sense of history. When he went to the Board of Control, however, he realized that Mill's *History* (and not the essay on *Government*) was the required reading for administrators of India.[34] He tried to square this with his earlier criticism of Mill by claiming that the *History* abandoned the deductive method and adopted his own prescription, but this is not convincing.[35] Mill's *History* was a scissors-and-paste performance stiffened by pure utilitarian dogma. Mill repudiated as reliable evidence the firsthand observations of travellers in India, ridiculed the scholars who translated its indigenous literature, and claimed to be more objective because he had *not* visited the country whose laws and government he analysed. His book, whatever its original purpose, turned out to be well-suited to the outlook of those top British administrators who went out to India determined not

[32] *LM*, iii. 99–107, 129. TBM told Margaret of his distress at Hannah's engagement before he received the news of Margaret's death. The debt to literature he confided to T. F. Ellis, 8 Feb. 1835.

[33] *LM*, iii. 158.

[34] Stokes, *The English Utilitarians and India* (Oxford, 1959), 52.

[35] *CHE*, i. 225–6.

to stay long. Macaulay's adoption of the utilitarian idiom in some (though not all) of his writings in India is therefore not surprising. It matched and justified his self-induced insulation from the world around him. Before his departure he had decided that India's past was irrelevant to its government. 'We interrogate the past in vain. General rules are useless where the whole is one vast exception.'[36] It may even be that, once there, he deliberately made his utilitarianism more uncompromising in order to keep the Indian world away from the things he loved, making his remark about leaving nothing he would remember with regret a self-fulfilling prophecy.

At any rate, it is remarkable how readily he agreed with the authoritarian aspect of the creed. To Bentham and James Mill, British military success in India offered an opportunity for rational planning not possible in Europe, and the principle of utility legitimized this dominance, since it condoned the right of an advanced culture, whose progress in science and philosophy involved a superior grasp of consequences, to rule over peoples still groping about in barbarism and superstition. As Clive puts it, 'the happiness of the greatest number of Indians mattered more than their freedom'.[37] 'A simple form of arbitrary government', James Mill had declared, 'tempered by European honour and European intelligence, is the only form which is now fit for Hindustan'.[38] Macaulay echoed this. 'We know that India cannot have a free Government. But she may have the next best thing—a firm and impartial despotism'.[39]

It is well known that in the controversy between the Orientalists and the Anglicizers, Macaulay threw his weight behind the latter. And here the Burkean Whig in him disappears altogether. The dispute over the money set aside for education by the 1813 Charter Act was a repetition of the arguments of Montesquieu and Burke on the one hand and Bentham and James Mill on the other. The Orientalists like H. H. Wilson and John Tytler wanted the money spent on the teaching of native languages, especially Sanskrit. The Anglicizers Trevelyan and Macaulay thought this obscurantist; spending money on

---

[36] *Speeches*, 139.   [37] Ibid., 311.
[38] Quoted in Stokes, *English Utilitarians*, 65–6.
[39] C. K. Dharker (ed.), *Lord Macaulay's Legislative Minutes* (Madras, 1946), 180.

teaching Sanskrit would enhance its literature and so propagate a false morality and erroneous science. Only the use of English could emancipate the native mind from the tyranny of the past. Macaulay put the case with his usual force.

The question now before us is simply whether, when it is in our power to teach this language [English], we shall teach languages in which, by universal confession, there are no books on any subject which deserve to be compared to our own; whether, when we can teach European science, we shall teach systems which, by universal confession, whenever they differ from those of Europe, differ for the worse; and whether, when we can patronise sound Philosophy and true History, we shall countenance, at the public expense, medical doctrines which would disgrace an English Farrier—Astronomy, which would move laughter in girls at an English boarding school—History, abounding with kings thirty foot high, and reigns thirty thousand years long—and Geography, made up of seas of treacle and seas of butter.

The historical analogy he drew was even less tolerant: it was the civilizing mission of the Tsars of Russia. 'The languages of Europe civilized Russia. I cannot doubt that they will do for the Hindoo what they have done for the Tartar'.[40] Surely a very un-Whiggish tribute to the policy of Nicholas I, but quite in line with the interventionist, intolerant spirit of utilitarian thought on India.

Between his official duties and his escapist reading in the Latin and Greek classics, Macaulay had little time to attend to political developments at home, news of which in any case arrived in Calcutta four months late. He seems to have thought with many radicals that the Reform Act had dealt the Tories a mortal blow, and that the gathering force of reformist opinion would sweep the Whigs along in a policy of further reform, which would include shorter parliaments, the ballot and the reform of the House of Lords. He told James Mill that while he disliked tampering with ancient institutions he would go along with their reform if the public mind demanded it.[41] At the same time, he seems to have wanted to stay out of politics. He had decided to write a *History of England*. He had written some of the *Lays of Ancient*

[40] Quoted in G. O. Trevelyan, *The Competition Wallah* (2nd edn. 1866), 323–4; repr. in J. Clive & T. Pinney (eds), *T. B. Macaulay: Selected Writings* (Chicago, 1972), 242, 244.
[41] *LM*, iii. 150–1.

Rome. Literary fame seemed to him (as it always had) purer, longer-lasting, more genuinely beneficial than political power, especially when that involved long hours, boring committees, and mediocre oratory. What would Burke not have written if he had given up politics, or Cicero if he had not written all those speeches?[42]

When he returned home in June 1838 he was not prepared for some of the political changes, which he took in rather slowly. From India, he had advised Spring-Rice to 'stick to the *Centre Gauche*', that is, the part of the Whig-radical alliance represented by moderate radicals like Charles Buller and Henry Warburton.[43] He had not registered that by the time he left India this party was almost extinct, its losses at the general election of 1837 never to be recovered. By July 1838 he realized that the philosophic radicals, who ten years earlier had looked like becoming an English Jacobin party, were now reduced 'to Grote and his wife'. He still assured Greville (who records the conversation) that he was as much a radical as ever, but he spoke like a man valuing his independence, as if politics concerned him only indirectly. He told the poet Moore he was 'bound to no party'.[44]

He left England for Rome in October, and while in Florence he received an offer from Melbourne of the office of Judge Advocate. But he refused to be drawn back into politics, recording in his journal:

The offer did not strike me as even tempting. The money I do not want. I have little but I have enough. The Right Honble before my name is a bauble which it would be far, very far indeed, beneath me to care about. The power is nothing. As an independent member of parliament I should have infinitely greater power. Nay, as I am, I have far greater power. I can now write what I chuse: and what I write may produce considerable effect on the public mind. In office I must necessarily be under restraint. If indeed I had a cabinet office, I should be able to do something in support of my own view of government. But a man in office and out of the cabinet is a mere slave: I have felt the bitterness of that slavery once. Though I hardly knew where to turn for a morsel of bread, my spirit rose against the intolerable thraldom. I was

[42] *LM*, iii. 159.   [43] *LM*, iii. 74 [11 Aug. 1834].
[44] Greville, IV.77; *Journal of Thomas Moore*, v. 1984.

mutinous; and once actually resigned. I then went to India to get independence: and I have got it, and I will keep it . . .[45]

There is no hint here that his service in one Whig ministry incurred any loyalty to its successor, or that taking Cabinet office might demand agreement in some common policy. But as so often with Macaulay the vehemence of the language betrays an inner unease. He told Melbourne that he would serve in parliament and not take any subordinate office, but he must have known that this might be read as a bid for something higher. As he wandered round Roman antiquities he found time for apprehensive reflections on the Whig government's difficulties. If there were a coalition, he reflected, 'I would rather be with the Whigs in opposition than in power'.[46] In Naples he talked with Frederick Lamb, Lord Melbourne's brother, and was relieved to hear that the government had weathered the crisis in Canada.[47] After his return to England in February, he began in earnest the *History of England*, thinking the political barometer set fair, and it was not till the Bedchamber crisis in May that he was drawn back into politics. When the ministry had fallen and been reinstated, he consented to stand for Edinburgh, and in his speech to the electors made his first public declaration of his allegiance to Whiggism. 'I entered public life as a Whig; and a Whig I am determined to remain'.[48] But it was a Whiggism he was careful to qualify. He was still radical enough to support the ballot and shorter parliaments, though he was against lowering the franchise below £10. And he made it clear that his was not a Whiggism of doctrine, not even that of Locke; that he followed no statesman, not even Fox. His was a Whiggism, in effect, of progress.

. . . when I look back on our history, I can discern a great party which has, through many generations, preserved its identity; a party often depressed, never extinguished; a party which, though often tainted with the faults of the age, has always been in advance of the age; a party which, though guilty of many errors and some crimes, has the glory of having established our civil and religious liberties on a firm foundation; and of that party I am proud to be a member . . .[49]

[45] TCM Journal, fos. 94–5, 10 Nov. 1838.
[46] Ibid., fo. 143 [20 Nov. 1838].   [47] Ibid., fo. 319.
[48] *Speeches*, 182.   [49] Ibid., 183.

If we compare the list of this party's achievements which follows with that given in the review of Mahon, we find it is more modern but also more extensive in scope. Macaulay's 'party' begins with Elizabeth; it defeats Charles I over ship-money; it 'effects' the Revolution of 1688 and the Act of Union with Scotland; it maintains the Hanoverians 'against the hostility of the Church and of the landed aristocracy of England'; it opposes the wars with America and France; it gives political rights to Dissenters and 'by unparalleled sacrifices and exertions' to Roman Catholics; it abolishes the slave trade and colonial slavery, reforms the House of Commons, extends popular education and mitigates the penal code. For two centuries it seems to have embraced every advance in human happiness and all good men and true, until Macaulay approaches his own time and then, with a certain unavoidable bathos, identifies it with the party of Melbourne and Russell:

I see them now hard pressed, struggling with difficulties, but still fighting the good fight. At their head I see men who have inherited the spirit and the virtues, as well as the blood, of old champions and martyrs of freedom. To those men I propose to attach myself.[50]

So at last the projector of a still nebulous *History of England* joined a party whose leaders had declared the Reform Act a final settlement, were in the process of suppressing the Chartists, and held their precarious majority through the stubbornness of a young queen and the forbearance of Peel.

He had meant to stay out of office, but the Melbourne ministry in its last years was too much in need of talent for this resolution to last. He joined it in September 1839 as Secretary for War, and after a few weeks of work decided that he liked it, and that it did him good. 'I became too mere a bookworm in India and on my voyage home,' he told Ellis, adding, 'It may be that some months of hard official and parliamentary work may make my studies more nourishing.'[51] This is certainly what happened. He was glad to be out of office when the Melbourne ministry fell in August 1841, but the taste of office, working on the experience in India, seems to have made him more and more impatient of the ideologue and radical in politics. He had only

[50] *Speeches*, 184.   [51] *LM*, iii. 321.

just joined the Cabinet when the outbreak occurred known as
the Newport Rising, and having seen the Chartist movement
in its most violent phase as a minister, he was not disposed to
sympathize with its aims when in opposition. His main objection
was to universal suffrage, which he called the 'essence' of the
Charter.

If you withhold that, it matters not very much what else you grant. If
you grant that, it matters not at all what else you withhold. If you grant
that, the country is lost.[52]

Even the more moderate Anti-Corn Law League, which many
radicals joined from a hatred of the landed aristocracy, struck
him as too fanatical, its effect being a polarization of the argument into total repealers and total protectionists to the disadvantage of moderate, dispassionate debate.

Even in Edinburgh, the city which he once said had done 'more
for the human mind during the last hundred years than Italy,
Spain and Portugal together during the last two hundred',[53]
Macaulay encountered fanaticism from two sets of extremists in
the dispute which led to the Disruption of 1843. If he supported
the Scottish established church, he displeased the would-be
seceders. If he supported grants to the Catholics in Ireland, he
displeased the conservatives in the Kirk. He took a stubborn stand
on his right to follow his own judgement which is reminiscent
of Burke's rebuke to the electors of Bristol.

The demands of the liberals, heated as they are by religious fanaticism,
are such as I will not comply with. I will not vote for the abolition of
the Churches now established in this island, and I will support any
well-digested plan for establishing the Catholic Church in Ireland.[54]

The whole uproar disgusted him. 'No combination of statesmen', he told Napier, 'is a match for a general combination
of fools.' He added (a sentence Trevelyan omitted): 'The place
[Edinburgh] is in a foam with all sorts of fanaticism, political
and religious; and I am neither fit nor desirous to represent
men out of their wits. So much the better. My history will go
on faster'.[55] When he was defeated at the general election of 1847
he compared himself to a manumitted slave.

[52] *Speeches*, 200.   [53] *LM*, v. 27.
[54] *LM*, iv. 161.   [55] Ibid., 164.

He was by this time a rather conservative Whig. India had given him the experience of advising the rulers of a great empire, and the confidence that he could master the intricacies of legislation and present them in a compelling form. Cabinet office had given greater substance to his reputation as a parliamentary orator: he had successfully presented the business of a department of state to a House of Commons not too kindly disposed to the government. Neither of these experiences involved activities to which he wanted to devote his life; but they deepened his appreciation of the burdens of executive responsibility and made him more sceptical of the value of abstract theory. He no longer felt himself a spectator; he had actually been a participant in the political process. He had learned to admire men engaged in arduous administrative tasks, and to have a sense of the 'greyness' of political decision, a recognition of the fact that in politics there is seldom any clear distinction to be made between black wickedness and white rectitude, but that men in power must make choices between a greater evil and a less. This sense is almost wholly lacking in early political essays such as that on Machiavelli, but is powerfully expressed in his essay on Warren Hastings (1841). One feels too that the experience of personal bereavement and loss gave him a wider sympathy with human failure. The wounding review so characteristic of his earlier work becomes much more rare. The moralistic dismissals of whole societies and generations which disfigure, for instance, his 'Hallam' give way to a more discriminating sense of human variety and idiosyncrasy.

His liberalism ceased to be doctrinaire; so much so, indeed, that one hesitates to call it liberalism. One might think from his letters from India that he kept his official business and his classical reading in separate compartments, but even in 1835, one senses the man of affairs lending a robust realism to the work of the classical scholar. A long account of the character of Socrates in Plato's dialogues written to Ellis, for instance, closes with the judgement: 'the more I read of Socrates, the less I wonder that they poisoned him'.[56] After his return, his disillusionment with radical politics appears in many of his judgements on men he had once admired. Reading Bowring's life of Bentham

---

[56] *LM*, iii. 141.

for instance in 1849, he shows what a long way he had come from the views of Charles Austin. 'Trash—by a trashy man and about a trashy man. How Bentham ever imposed on me I cannot now understand'.[57] When Wordsworth's *Prelude* was published a few months after the poet's death, Macaulay had his own explanation of why the publication had been so long delayed. It is emphatic and may cause Wordsworth scholars unease, but it is interesting as an example of how Macaulay had come to regard English Jacobinism:

The plain truth is that he wrote it when he was a Jacobin and was ashamed to print it after he became an exciseman. He goes all the lengths of Thelwall and Tom Paine; and the poem ends with loud vauntings of his own incorruptible integrity—vauntings which he might well shrink from publishing when he had become an electioneering agent of the Lowthers.[58]

He was quite aware of the change in his own sentiments. He told his nephew

You call me a liberal, but I don't know that in these days I deserve the name. I am opposed to the abolition of standing armies. I am opposed to the abrogation of capital punishment. I am opposed to the destruction of the National Church. In short, I am in favour of war, hanging and Church establishments.[59]

In the decade which saw the publication of the first two volumes of the *History of England*, Macaulay professed a Whiggism of a very conservative cast, neither partisan nor doctrinaire. But what was Whiggism in 1848? Lord John Russell's late and opportunist advocacy of repeal did not in the end strengthen traditional Whiggism with an accession of popular support. Macaulay was to have been in the abortive Russell Cabinet of December 1845, but he was not sorry that it broke up, and he had considerable respect for Peel. But Peel's conversion only split his party into Protectionists and Peelites, and the latter refused to join Russell after Peel's fall. The result was that Whiggism could never claim free trade as its popular cause, just as in the 1830s it had failed to exploit its initiative in parliamentary reform. The Whig party to which Macaulay had attached himself in 1839, was in

[57] TCM Journal, vol. ii, fo. 110 [21 Oct. 1849].
[58] *LM*, v. 118.   [59] Trevelyan, ii. 142.

terminal decline a decade later. By 1856 a critic of the *History of England* could write that the Whigs who took so much space in the book 'are now only to be found in a few noble houses, where the name is hereditary, and in a few provincial towns, where the old politicians hold by their own factions, unmoved by the general motion of the world. Pure Whiggism is perhaps scarcely strong enough to keep a periodical afloat, or force a pamphlet into a second edition'.[60] Almost the only Whig element in the *History* was his debt to Burke, as we shall see.

I have already said that this debt was one he shared with his old enemy, Croker. Party allegiances aside, they had much in common. Why then did they continue bitter antagonists? One reason, of course was that each man had hurt and humiliated the other. But, supposing some kindly mutual friend with diplomatic gifts, like Dean Milman, had tried to persuade them to put old resentments aside, one senses that he would have had more success with Croker than with Macaulay. Croker was more tolerant, not just of moral laxity such as he knew in Lords Lowther and Hertford, but also of different political opinions. No man had had a greater dislike of Burdett and Brougham in their radical prime, but both men became his friends in later life. Brougham even became a contributor to the *Quarterly*. Croker was not touchy about his own publications, tolerating and even inviting heavy editing from Lockhart, from an awareness of his own prolixity and over-censoriousness.[61] By contrast, Macaulay was a great hater, and his hatreds, far from being part of the hearty give and take of political life as his nephew claimed, were nurtured in private and often recall the passionate vindictiveness of an introverted child. His journals, which are most copious for the periods when he lived alone, are full of snap judgements on men he scarcely knew. As a member of the Athenaeum, for instance, he must have known that Theodore Hook had amused and entertained his friends in a place which from its popularity came to be known as 'Hook's Corner'. But Macaulay disapproved of what he called 'levity', and when Hook's old friend Barham wrote his life, Macaulay described it in his journal as 'the life of a blackguard layman who had some wit, by a blackguard parson who has none'.[62] Judgements like this, superficially clever, actually betray great loneliness. He had attained a certain gruff sociability in his official contacts, but the small change of political discussion bored him, and he kept no record of his political career save his own speeches. His emotional life centred on his family and his childhood. His happiest moments were re-creations of a lost childhood, much of his favourite reading a reminder of it. Clouds across that sunny time—bankruptcy for instance—he held in particular horror. People who had marred his happiness in his youth—Baptist Noel, George Stephen, John Moultrie—were never forgiven. Croker and Brougham joined this list, one may conjecture, because they had each overshadowed an otherwise spectacular début; they had shattered his youthful idealism, and what he later learned of their lives enabled Macaulay to create a private portrait of each, to hang in his imaginary gallery of villains.

So matters might have remained, had it not happened that in the 1840s the old antagonism flared up again. In June 1842 Croker, at Lockhart's request, reviewed Fanny Burney's *Diary and Letters* in the *Quarterly*. Lockhart feared that her description of the court life of George III would be used by liberal writers as an excuse to abuse 'Courts and Kings'.[63] Croker's review was long and severe, the main burden of his criticism being that Fanny Burney's account of her activities was egotistical and tedious. But he also mentioned the fact that her novel *Evelina* was not written, as gossip had it, when she was seventeen but when she was twenty-five.[64] Macaulay reviewed the same work in the *Edinburgh* in January 1843. He did not deny that *Evelina* was not the work of a girl of seventeen, but he condemned Croker for looking up the parish records to prove it. He said this act was 'merely a speck in the life of one who got a good place by playing the spy or a courtesan in his youth, and a good legacy by turning parasite to a whole seraglio of courtesans in his old age'. Napier refused to print this sentence, and what appeared in print was the assertion that this 'truly chivalrous exploit' of searching a parish register 'to hurt an old lady with having concealed her age' was 'reserved for a bad writer of our own time,

[62] Trinity MSS, July, i, fos. 435–6, 9 Dec. 1848.
[63] Murray MSS, Lockhart to J. Murray II, 19 May 1842.
[64] *QR*, lxx, no. 140 (June 1842), 254.

whose spite she had provoked by not furnishing him with materials for a worthless edition of Boswell's Life of Johnson, some sheets of which our readers have doubtless seen round parcels of better books.'[65] It was in the letter to Napier insisting on the inclusion of this passage that Macaulay gave the full list of Croker's supposed moral failings, which G. O. Trevelyan printed in the *Life*.[66] It happened that Lockhart saw what he called Macaulay's 'effusion of bile' when he had just sent the *Lays of Ancient Rome* to Milman for review, and Milman had written a highly complimentary first paragraph which Lockhart, out of regard for Croker, now felt obliged to omit.[67] The review as printed starts rather abruptly.

Soon after this Macaulay published his *Critical and Historical Essays* in three volumes. He omitted his attacks on James Mill and the utilitarians, but included his review of Croker's *Boswell*. An odd decision, for Mill, though dead, had been kind to him, but Croker had not, and was alive. So he set aside the most effective polemic he ever wrote, and reprinted a vindictive essay, half of which he was to repudiate later with a more maturely considered essay on Dr Johnson.[68] Even that might not have provoked the busy reviewer. But in November 1844 Murray proposed to reissue the Boswell in a single volume, and Croker agreed to do it. That meant reconsidering Macaulay's charges. 'In all points of history and learning I hesitate not to say that he was wrong', Croker told Murray, 'but there were a few—not more than half a dozen I am sure—in which he was right—those I would correct'.[69] The edition had to compete with other work—the *Quarterly*'s internal debate over Maynooth, the schism in the Tory party, the final crisis over the repeal of the Corn Laws—and it was not finished until late 1847. The work for it cannot but have revived memories of the conflict sixteen years before.

[65] *LM*, iv. 89 n.; *ER*, lxxvi, no. 154, 537. Macaulay did not reprint the article in *CHE*; it is in the Everyman edn. of the *Critical and Historical Essays*, 2 vols. (1907), ii. 563–612.

[66] *LM*, iv. 89, cited above, p. 20.

[67] Murray MSS, Lockhart to J. Murray, 25 Jan. 1843; Lang's *Lockhart*, ii. 214–16.

[68] Lady Trevelyan (ed.) *Collected Works* (1866) vol. vii, 324–56.

[69] Murray MSS, J. Murray III to Croker, 21 Nov. 1844; Croker to J. Murray, 16 Jan. 1845.

But that had taken place when parties were sharply divided. Now they were hardly distinguishable. Peel was praised by Whigs and reviled by Tories, but his successor Lord John Russell had to cast about for a policy which would keep his radical followers without offending Peel's. Just as the political antagonism in Parliament was running out of steam, Croker's and Macaulay's rivalry revived. What political content could it still have? Ostensibly, the argument in its later stages was more historical than political, but plainly the differences were still great. So let us now look at their non-political concerns, their aims as men of letters, so that we can understand the final battle. Mill once said that all differences of opinion were, when analysed, differences of method, and this may provide our key.

6

Croker as Historian: The Moralist under Siege

It is the radical vice of a certain acute mind that it really is cursed *nil admirari*, and therefore I must try, as far as possible, to keep it at work in such affairs as French politics and French memoirs.

J. G. LOCKHART to H. H. MILMAN

I

Some modern historians give the impression that Macaulay's method is more remote from contemporary practice than Croker's. Every schoolboy knows, or is told on authority, that 'the whig interpretation of history' is something very primitive and outmoded; and even academic historians would consider that Macaulay's aim to write a lively narrative puts him beyond the pale of respect. Croker, on the other hand, is evidently a writer who respects evidence, never underrates the complexity of issues, and conveys a strong sense of the gravity and difficulty of the whole enterprise. Herbert Butterfield himself, who was the chief critic of the whig interpretation, declared that Croker's importance lay in the fact that he 'had so much of the specialised outlook of the technical historian', and that his Tory prejudices were overridden by 'a certain scientific passion'. He brought us 'one stage nearer the world of modern scholarship'.[1] One could add that he was a great collector of primary materials. His articles are long and reassuringly clogged with references. On this view, Macaulay is a popular historian; Croker is a historian's historian.

The only serious attempt in print to consider Croker as a historian was published nearly thirty years ago by a pupil of

---

[1] H. Butterfield, *George III and the Historians* (1957), 119, 120.

Butterfield, Dr Hedva Ben-Israel. Her *English Historians on the French Revolution* is a very full survey of English writing from Burke to Acton, and it treats Croker as primarily a historian of France. To do this in the proper academic manner she sought to make a distinction between his political views and his scholarship. For instance, she tried to show that while in domestic politics Croker might have been a Tory and a follower of Burke, in his study of the French Revolution he actually undermined and refuted the conclusions of his mentor.[2] The book was given a long review in the *Times Literary Supplement*, by the late Richard Cobb. Cobb poured scorn on the enterprise of studying the work of three generations of English historians whose insularity, timidity, and complacency ensured that everything they published would be hopelessly inaccurate and amateur. But even he made an exception for Croker, describing the account of him as 'by far the best study' in the book (and it included a fine study of Carlyle). He praised Croker's knowledge of the sources and especially the fact that he gathered 'the finest collection of printed material in existence' (meaning the pamphlet collections Croker acquired and presented to the British Museum). With all these virtues, however, Croker resembled his countrymen in leaving no major work. He was 'a mere seeker after *curia* [*sic*], a collector of autographs, rather than a historian, a man who 'was always going to write a general history of the Revolution' but never completed it. In short, compared to the other 'dull dogs' who, writing 'with their slippers on about events that, far from moving them, left them with mixed feelings of moral superiority, disquiet and tempered languid indignation', Croker's achievement stood out only because he left materials which would eventually contribute to 'the future of revolutionary studies'.[3]

What then was Croker's contribution to historical understanding? Was he a man struggling to escape from the compromises of politics into a purer world of scholarship where issues and authorities could be assessed without bias? Or was he, for all his prodigious literary output, only a dilettante, spreading his talent over so wide a range that he could be no more than

---

[2] H. Ben-Israel, *English Historians on the French Revolution* (Cambridge, 1968), 177.

[3] *TLS*, 28 Nov. 1968, 1325–7, reprinted with variants in Cobb's *Tour de France* (1976), 35–44. I quote from the original.

an unusually assiduous collector of books and pamphlets and historic relics?

I have already mentioned his political debt to Burke, and it seems to me futile to argue that Burke's influence was something Croker had in his historical work to resist or overcome. 'History issues from the Romantic School', Lord Acton once said, 'it hails from Burke . . . as emancipation from the Quakers'.[4] He meant that Burke taught a whole generation to value tradition, giving men and women living in an age in which traditional institutions were under fierce attack, reasons for valuing them, for studying their origins and seeking ways of preserving them. Croker made no secret of his admiration for Burke as a guide to understanding the French Revolution. As late as 1848 he told Brougham that Burke's revolutionary writings seemed to him more admirable every time he read them.[5] He was not unusual in this. The Murray circle included a number of men who felt the need to understand and preserve the past: Isaac D'Israeli, a repentant Jacobin who became a compendious authority on the English Civil War; Francis Douce whom D'Israeli was instrumental in persuading to give his collections of medieval manuscripts and incunabula to the Bodleian Library; Francis Palgrave, Jewish like D'Israeli but a convert to Christianity, and one of the first advocates of the systematic arrangement and publication of the public records; and Sharon Turner, the first historian of Anglo-Saxon England.[6]

Croker shared their concerns. He played his part in preserving records, and was an unusual kind of collector, as we shall see. But he was more restlessly active and practical than the other members of the Murray circle, who have by contrast an air of nostalgia and escapism. Croker's taste in literature was Augustan and classical. He took much from Burke. He looked up with awe to kings.[7] He revered aristocracy as 'the Corinthian capital of polished society'. He had a low view of 'sophisters, economists and calculators', at least in the role of legislators.

---

[4] Quoted by H. Butterfield, *Man on his Past* (Cambridge, 1955), 70.

[5] Brougham MSS, 4 Sept. 1848.

[6] For the elder D'Israeli, see James Ogden, *Isaac D'Israeli* (Oxford, 1969); for Douce, see *The Douce Legacy: an Exhibition to Commemorate the 150th anniversary of the bequest of Francis Douce (1757–1834)* ed. Oxford, Bodleian Library, 1984.

[7] Murray MSS, Croker to J. Murray, 18 Sept. 1816; quoted by Jennings, i. 95.

He echoed Burke's dislike of abstract theory, adding an experienced administrator's distrust of 'patent-office models of the good society'.[8] There were other Burkean themes which are obvious in Croker's interpretation of the French Revolution, which I shall come to later. But one general theme is worth particular notice, because if Croker adapted it, it was to be a liability in his historical work.

Acton's associating Burke with 'the Romantic School' is an early indication of the common assumption that Burke inspired 'the revolt against the eighteenth century' and was therefore the father of the political counter-revolution, whose artistic expression is to be seen in the cult of nature, the return of reverence for the Church and the ages of faith, and the beginnings of an interest in the historic past for its own sake. It is not often noticed how suspicious Burke was of history as a guide. In one of his pamphlets he notes that Louis XVI was 'a diligent reader of history', but, he adds, 'the very lamp of prudence blinded him'.[9] In the *Reflections* he warns that we are liable to draw the wrong lessons from history. It can instruct, but it can also be 'the means of keeping alive, or reviving dissensions and animosities, and adding fuel to civil fury'. It is interesting to note this peculiarly Irish insight being made decades before the rise of Catholic nationalism. Burke goes on:

History consists, for the greater part, of the miseries brought upon the world by pride, ambition, avarice, revenge, lust, sedition, hypocrisy, ungoverned zeal, and all the train of disorderly appetites, which shake the public with the same

> —'troublous storms that toss
> The private state, and render life unsweet'.

These vices are the *causes* of those storms. Religion, morals, laws, prerogatives, privileges, liberties, rights of men, are the *pretexts*. The pretexts are always found in some specious appearance of a real good.[10]

We must look behind the pretexts at the vices: 'wise men will apply their remedies to vices, not to names'. What Burke meant

---

[8] In one of his reviews he says of the French reformer Turgot, 'The plausibility of reducing the art of administration to a system raised Turgot to office, and its impracticability drove him from it'. *QR*, xxvi, no. 51 (Oct. 1921), 231.
[9] *Letters on a Regicide Peace*, II. Works (Oxford, World's Classics edn.) vi. 207.
[10] *Works*, op. cit., iv. 155.

of course was that vices recur in different forms and guises. In illustration, he mentions the Massacre of St Bartholomew in which the vices of cruelty and 'ungoverned zeal' had assumed the guise of a good (religious orthodoxy) in a manner every modern Frenchman would deplore. But he reminds them that a recent play about the Massacre, shown in a theatre close to where the National Assembly was sitting, presented 'the Cardinal of Lorraine in his robes of function, ordering the general slaughter'. In this way, cruelty and intolerance were revived, but turned against the Church. So the portrayal of a historical example of fanaticism was no surety against the revival of the vice. 'You are terrifying yourself with ghosts and apparitions', Burke tells the French, 'while your house is the haunt of robbers'.[11] Yet what is good advice for the moralist might be rather restrictive for the historian, especially the historian of parliamentary government, nine-tenths of whose material must consist of the records of conflict entered into by people without either the time or the inducement to make a nice distinction between vices and names, causes and pretexts. How can a severe scrutiny of virtue and vice make sense of a system which adjusts rival claims to have correctly interpreted the public good in a spirit of compromise and with an eye to expediency? In adopting Burke's conviction that the French Revolution was a shameless overturning of the moral order, any historian who attempted to explain the phenomenon would direct his attention primarily, if not exclusively, to the ethical motivation of the leading actors, treating the formulated political aims as a screen of pretexts not to be taken at their face value. I have no documentary proof that Croker consciously followed Burke in this, but his identification with Burke's views was close enough to make it seem very likely. To the modern reader the striking feature of his historical writing is his attention to the moral intentions and failings of individuals; he passes through the film of argument and ideology and searches for the motive of the agent. He is the historian as censor; invariably informed and precise, but not always just, and sometimes flagrantly unfair. The objection to seeing him as a scientific or technical historian is that the respect for evidence is constantly being vitiated by imputations of motive.

[11] *Works*, op. cit., iv. 157.

II

In his historical work Croker was both editor and critic. Few modern historians attempt to combine both functions, and in Croker's case it would be hard to say whether the editor in him gave the edge to the critic, or whether it was critical exposure of the careless editing of others which led him to try his hand himself. If an editor's duty is to preserve the records of the past, checking their accuracy and where necessary correcting their errors, it is the very essence of conservatism. Croker's editions aimed to preserve evidence where possible, but they are not monuments of scholarly erudition. Probably he did not take his editing as seriously as his criticism. His first four editions seem to have been done rapidly and he did not put his name to them. Taken together, they suggest an amateur working out his method as he goes along. The first is an edition of the journal kept by a French ambassador in London in 1626.[12] The text is rather meagre and the notes ludicrously out of proportion to their occasion. The second and third are two sets of eighteenth century letters by two ladies, Mary Lepel, Lady Hervey, and Henrietta Howard, Countess of Suffolk, and the notes are more unobtrusive. These two works mark the start of Croker's deepening fascination with eighteenth century politics and literature.[13] Already he was exploring the personalities of the circle round Alexander Pope, and planning the edition of his poems which was unfinished at his death. The fourth edition is a trilogy of French royal memoirs in translation and with notes, and seems to have been Croker's first contribution to the history of the French Revolution.[14]

The edition of Boswell's *Johnson*, the first to which he put his name, was a more ambitious project, but even here he worked fast, and with more limited resources and a much more limited

[12] *Memoirs of the Embassy of the Marshal de Bassompierre to the Court of England in 1626, translated with notes.* (London, 1819).

[13] *Letters of Mary Lepel, Lady Hervey, with a Memoir and Illustrative Notes* (1821). These were Lady Hervey's letters to the Revd Edmund Morris from 1742 to 1778. *Letters to and from Henrietta, Countess of Suffolk, and her second husband, the Hon. George Berkeley; from 1712 to 1767, with Historical, Biographical and Explanatory Notes, in two volumes* (1824).

[14] *Royal Memoirs of the French Revolution . . . with Historical and Biographical notes by the Translator* (1823).

ambition than a modern editor would have. He worked by himself and aimed to serve the ordinary intelligent reader. He did not seek to improve on the existing text, but to gather together all the information he could find about Johnson and Boswell from those who had known them, before it was too late. He also thought he was entitled to interpolate other writers' records of Johnson in Boswell's text,[15] and he included the *Tour to the Hebrides* because he thought the only reason Boswell had published it as a separate book was that he had made a prior contract with another printer. He did make some enquiries after the MSS in the possession of Boswell's descendants, but after a discouraging response from the family and some misleading advice from Scott,[16] he decided not to persevere. (When one thinks of the burning of the MS of Byron's *Memoirs* in Murray's drawing-room, it may be just as well that Croker did *not* discover the Boswell papers in the late 1820s.) His task was not, after all, to explain Boswell's motives and methods, but to provide a sort of biographical compendium of Dr Johnson. The edition is now remembered, if at all, for Macaulay's critique, which gives a misleading impression of its faults, for in spite of his claim that he had 'smashed' it, it sold out and later editions held the field until George Birkbeck Hill's edition in 1887. Hill records Gladstone saying of his work: 'You have succeeded in doing what Macaulay attempted to do and failed—You have suppressed Croker'.[17] Hill's text certainly replaced Croker's, but Gladstone's compliment is inaccurate. Macaulay's aim was to discredit Croker's scholarship. He made no comment on the text. Indeed, the crude and erroneous portraits of Johnson and Boswell with which he tried to make his list of Croker's supposed blunders more palatable to his readers, show how thoughtlessly he had read the biography itself.[18]

---

[15] Jennings, ii. 25.

[16] Ibid., 32. 'I do not think there is anything to be had at Auchinleck'. For the effect of this advice see, David Buchanan, *The Treasure of Auchinleck: The Story of the Boswell Papers* (1975), 23.

[17] Lucy Crump (ed.), *Letters of George Birkbeck Hill* (1906), 197.

[18] For Hill's comments on Macaulay's portraits of Johnson and Boswell see his *Dr. Johnson, His Friends and his Critics* (1878), 97–145 and 160–99. Hill was also rebuffed at Auchinleck. A recent verdict on Macaulay's essay is J.C.D. Clark, *Samuel Johnson: Literature, Religion and English Cultural Politics from the Restoration to Romanticism* (1994), 245–9.

The social constraints on strict textual scholarship are also illustrated in Croker's last major editorial undertaking. The existence of the manuscript of Lord Hervey's *Memoirs of the Reign of George II* was no secret, but its author had asked that it should not be published till after the death of George III. By then, parts of the original had been deleted by his descendants, although another copy had been made and presented to the Prince Regent. Croker's qualifications as an editor presumably rested on his earlier edition of the letters of Lady Hervey, and when he received the commission, he wanted to compare the mutilated original with the copy. By then it was in the possession of the Duke of Wellington, as George IV's executor. The Duke promised to look for it, but without result.[19] Croker's edition is therefore based on the original, imperfect MS. Even if he had seen the copy, however, he might have been too inhibited to publish it. Hervey's modern editor, Romney Sedgwick, did see both MSS, and his statement that he had edited them 'without regard to considerations of decency or of dullness' reads like an implied rebuke of his predecessor's inhibitions.[20] But Croker's position was more delicate. He was divided between what he saw as his editorial duty of veracity and a desire not to offend good taste or the feelings of the Hervey family. He explained his editorial problem to Murray:

It is a nice matter to say how far an editor is authorised to go either in omission or substitution. As to omission, no doubt all that would shock the modern reader would be better omitted, but, at the same time, we must recollect that even coarseness and violence are parts of the evidence, and are characteristic both of the writer and his personages to whom we have no right to assign a character of a more polite or delicate taste and sentiments than they have really made for themselves. The inclination of my mind is that as much should be preserved of these objectionable passages as would serve to show the characters of the parties—but that the *frequent recurrence* of violent and coarse language should be avoided; and that all indelicacy and nastiness should be either omitted or replaced by more decorous equivalents . . .[21]

---

[19] Wellington MSS, Duke to Croker (draft) 21 Apr. 1847.

[20] R. Sedgwick (ed.) *Lord Hervey's Memoirs* (1931), xiii. Sedgwick went on to imply that Croker had a hand in reviewing his own edition in the *Quarterly*. The review was actually by Lockhart.

[21] Murray MSS, 28 Mar. 1847.

To his readers he explained that he had here and there replaced indelicate expressions with 'a more decent equivalent', but as eighteenth century conversation was coarse, a more thorough purification would have been 'an unpardonable distortion—indeed, a falsification of my materials'.[22] This was the positive side of Burke's legacy, the preservation of evidence of past history in as accessible a form as was compatible with historical truth and literary decorum.

The negative side of Croker's writings, his literary and historical criticism, arouses much more feeling. It took its tone from the dark days in which the *Quarterly* was founded. Gifford, its first editor, was both a scholar and a powerful writer of polemic. He wanted the journal to be a guardian of established values, and to have the permanent appeal of solid worth. 'We are read', he wrote in 1812, 'by at least 50,000 people of that class whose opinions it is most important to render favourable, and whose judgements it is most expedient to set right. Our sale is at least 6,000, and I know of no pamphlet that would sell 100; besides pamphlets are thrown aside, reviews are permanent, and the variety of their contents attracts those who would never dream of opening a pamphlet.'[23] It was critical, but it was also a permanent record: Croker kept to this tradition. His very first article in the new venture sets a tone he never wholly abandoned, one of critical vigilance for popular error.

The customers of the circulating library are so numerous, and so easily imposed upon, that it is of the utmost importance to the public, that its weights and measures should be subject to the inspection of a strict literary police, and the standard of its morality and sentiment kept as pure as the nature of things will admit.[24]

This conception of a literary police, interpreted to include any writer whose work seemed to weaken or discredit traditional institutions, was the keynote of the *Quarterly*'s policy under Gifford. It was the literary equivalent of the political siege mentality generated by war and blockade, and it persisted in a dilute form under Lockhart's editorship. Lockhart's politics were, as we have seen, staunchly Tory. But he was not financially

---

[22] *Memoirs of the Reign of George II* by John, Lord Hervey 2 vols. (1848) i. xii.
[23] Brightfield, 164.
[24] *QR*, ii. no. 3. (Aug. 1809) Maria Edgeworth's 'Tales of Fashionable Life' (146).

independent and he had too close a knowledge of the world of struggling men and women writers to be able to relish fierce literary feuds. He would often try to soften the asperity of an article from a knowledge of the circumstances of its victim. He did not really hate Whigs and he was more than a little envious of the success of the *Edinburgh* under his rival Napier.

The *Edinburgh* in contrast was begun as a literary adventure and a speculation against the prevailing political climate.[25] It was not deliberately democratic; indeed it was suspicious of radicalism and radical leaders, and very aware that its appeal was to a fastidious and propertied readership. But it liked to show its heterodoxy by choosing its own targets, rather than identifying with particular opposition causes. Hence Brougham's failure to control the review for his own ends. Francis Jeffrey was too aware of the fluctuating fortunes of the Whig party in parliament, to want to take his orders from any of its leaders, preferring instead to appeal to a wide range of liberal opinion. His successor, Macvey Napier, had been editor of the *Encyclopaedia Britannica*, and so had served his apprenticeship as a popularizer. The *Edinburgh*'s criticism was therefore leavened with more entertainment and it had in general a lightness of touch which one does not often find in the *Quarterly*. The governing classes may have read the *Quarterly* out of duty tinged with a certain masochistic relish; but a wider range of people, from within the political establishment as well as outside it, must have read the *Edinburgh* for instruction and pleasure. Now Croker and Macaulay each represented an extreme version of the traditions of their respective reviews, Croker the ideal of a literary police allowing his readers only so much enjoyment as that sterner duty permitted, Macaulay the tradition of the essay on a literary or historical topic, which descended to critical severity only when he felt like administering a drubbing to some figure he disliked.[26]

Quite early in his career as a reviewer Macaulay ceased to write on politics and contributed essays which often had only the most casual connection with the work reviewed. He knew that his articles had swelled the *Edinburgh*'s sales, and he was able to make a bargain with Napier. On his departure for India he asked

[25] J. Clive, *Scotch Reviewers: The Edinburgh Review 1802–1815* (1957).
[26] Ibid., 52.

to be paid in books, and when he had begun the *History of England* in earnest, he insisted that the books he reviewed should be on subjects which would advance it.[27] He kept the rule so closely that a tolerably consecutive History has been compiled from Macaulay's essays, which gives us some idea of what the *History* might have been like if it had been completed in the time originally planned.[28]

Croker's contributions to the *Quarterly* were, for reasons I have already suggested, prompted by a quite different set of considerations. There was no single literary scheme to which all else was subordinated. One might think, from the list of his articles, that they point to a grand design, of which his *Essays on the Early History of the French Revolution* is the only fragment. But this seems unlikely. There was certainly a guiding doctrine, a pessimistic conservatism which took its most persuasive examples from the French Revolution; and there was a consistent style and manner of presentation with which readers of Croker can soon become familiar, so that they can pick any volume of the *Quarterly* between 1809 and 1854 and identify his work from internal evidence alone. Macaulay, picking up a number in the English Reading Room in Rome, guessed at Croker's article, quite correctly as we now know.[29] But the range of Croker's subject-matter is very wide, suggesting a fluent writer of *pièces d'occasion*, willing to try his hand rather like a barrister getting up a brief, on any subject that happened to be called for in any quarter. Once he had a topic and enough factual information to illustrate his argument, he wrote very rapidly and trenchantly. He often salted the censure with his own brand of humour. Sending Lockhart his review of Fanny Kemble's Journal in 1835, for instance, he told him that he thought it contained the best joke he had ever made, adding, 'but even *that* if it displeases you shall cut out and that you may be at liberty to do so I shall not even hint what it is'.[30] Perhaps Lockhart did cut it out: it is certainly hard to find, but nothing is more elusive to one age than what another thinks funny. What cannot be doubted is

---

[27] *LM*, ii. 352, iv. 17.
[28] *The History of England in the Eighteenth Century* ed. Peter Rowland, Folio Society (1980).
[29] It was Croker's review of Lister's *Clarendon*, *QR*, lxxii, no. 125 (Oct. 1838).
[30] NLS, Lockhart MS 1927, no. 17, fos. 22–3, 10 June 1835.

Croker's intellectual energy and versatility. Well into his seventies, he wrote vigorous, clear arguments of great length. He was sixty-nine when he wrote the eighty-page review of Macaulay, seventy-two when he began his last attack on Lord Holland's *Memoirs*.

Some contributors to the reviews, like Croker and Brougham, wrote so much that they could not be sure afterwards which pieces were theirs. In Croker's case authorship is further complicated by the fact that he often reworked other writers' contributions. It would be idle to deny that he was capable of hackwork. It is much harder to say which articles represent his best work, because our own specialized studies make us pick out those on the topics which most interest us. Students of literature, for instance, remember Croker chiefly for his critique of Keats, a short and actually rather unrepresentative trifle made notorious by a line of Byron.[31] But his main work is plainly both historical and political. He seldom discusses politics without a framework of history or pushes history so far back in time as to make it irrelevant to his politics. I cannot hope to summarize his whole output as a reviewer on historical topics, but they seem to me to fall into three groups, corresponding to three roles which he assumed in his reviewing. He wrote as a prophet, a polemicist, and a critical historian.

He sounded the prophetic note in periods of political crisis when he thought he must warn his readers of the likely course events would take. It is clear that these predictions rested on a theory that events in the modern world unfolded according to a pattern, illustrated by seventeenth century England, late eighteenth century France, and contemporary Britain. It was a secular theory, not an eschatology such as propounded by Croker's Irvingite friend Henry Drummond, but it was certainly meant to make men, and especially politicians, pause and take heed of what he called 'the awful lessons' of history.

What were these lessons? Croker thought, with Burke, that societies were the products of a long process of historic growth, and were held together by traditional ties of habit and convention. They did not originate with any affirmation of natural rights or abstract principles, and appeals to such principles had the

---

[31] *QR*, xix, no. 37 (Apr. 1818) 'Keats's *Endymion*', 204–8.

effect of breaking asunder traditional ties and returning society to barbarism.[32] Societies advanced by a steady adherence to time-honoured procedures, not by appeals to return to a mythical past or by sudden reformations. 'Though enthusiasm may win a battle, it is only the material interests of mankind that can keep the field'.[33] Societies had a finite supply of talent and virtue, and the stability of this supply depended on the security of property, the hard-won surplus of which made possible the leisure which made for upright conduct and public service. Even in democratic governments power would gravitate to a minority of the experienced and able: constitutions were the devices which prevented those minorities from becoming self-interested and oligarchic. But constitutions (and here Croker reflects the eighteenth century experience of weak governments starved of funds by subjects jealous of the central power) however deep their origins in the past, prove delicate and fragile when subjected to rapid political change. They depend on 'fidelity', the fidelity of colleagues in a common enterprise, and fidelity to the other experiences of previous generations, which have been passed down in conventional beliefs and established forms of business. Neither is proof against the operation of self-interest.

That was why change usually originated inside the ruling groups. There was no such thing as a spontaneous popular revolt. Revolutions were always started by minorities, especially by disaffected critics from within the ruling group, who questioned the traditional rules of their society.[34] Croker may not have had much direct experience of the great centres of industry, but he knew London and Paris, and he was less apprehensive of the mass of humble people wholly occupied in the business of living than of the newer classes of restless, irresponsible writers and publicists who provoked the masses into unrest and violence. Just as in rural Ireland he blamed violence on the Catholic priests rather than the peasants, so in the great cities he thought those responsible for riot and revolution were the philosophers and writers and their admirers among the middle classes—journalists, petty clerks, provincial attorneys and the like. Once started by the writers and orators, revolutions brought to prominence

[32] *QR*, lxxxv, no. 169 (June 1849) 'Democracy', 286.
[33] *QR*, lxii, no. 124 (June 1838) 'Life of Wilberforce', 238.
[34] *QR*, liii, no. 106 (Apr. 1835), 555. 'Fisher Ames' Essays'.

people who in stable times would remain obscure.[35] These had neither the inherited outlook to assume leadership nor the political experience to foresee the effects of what they did. Their chief quality was 'audacity': their political role was to accelerate disruption and violence.[36] Once started by 'the impulse of theoretic change', the cycle of revolution will tend to run its course till all constitutional checks are discredited, and authority must be restored by a strong man, a Cromwell or a Napoleon, who reminds an exhausted society of the fact, which civility and its established rules tend to conceal, that authority rests in the last resort on force.[37] But this sort of rule is sterile. The seeds of constitutionalism have to be sown again afresh, but this time in a soil exhausted by misuse. The great virtue of the English constitution to Croker lay in the fact that it had taken account of these lessons in the course of the seventeenth century. The impending danger after 1815 was due to the fact that the lessons of French history since 1789 had not been learned so well.[38]

What made this gloomy theory plausible in an age of reform was that, like many deterministic theories, its terms could be tacitly adjusted to accommodate actual experience, and in this flexible form it fitted Croker's temperamental pessimism too well to be abandoned. He was prepared to admit that the onset of democracy might be delayed for a time, and that its effects might be milder in England than they had been in France, but that a democratic revolution would come eventually he had no doubt. He acquired the reputation of a rather tedious and predictable Jeremiah because he did not mind sounding a discordant note just when his friends were growing more cheerful. In May 1835, when Peel's short ministry had given a check to the so-called 'movement party', Croker told him 'we shall never get right without a convulsion', and announced that 'the republican principle must have a trial'.[39] When Lyndhurst and the Tory peers

[35] *QR*, xv, no. 30 (July 1816) 'Chateaubriand', 435.

[36] *QR*, liii, no. 106, (Apr. 1835), 554–5. 'An audacity of which respectable men are in every way incapable—an audacity which is compounded by hatred of *rank* which it cannot attain—of envy of *character* which it does not possess—of contempt of *law* whose control is irksome.'

[37] *Essays on the Early Period of the French Revolution* (1857), 311.

[38] *QR*, xlvii, no. 93 (Mar. 1832) 'Revolutions of 1640 & 1830' by Croker & Lockhart.

[39] Add. MSS. 40321, fos. 138–9. To Peel, 4 May 1835.

were successfully drawing the teeth of the radical Municipal Corporations Bill, Croker was still more gloomy. 'Nothing can do us any good, and every step will be, therefore, chargeable with having done mischief. Whether we advance or retreat or stand still, the avalanche will equally crush us'.[40] Peel's second ministry had provided five years of comparative optimism, but at its close the worst fears returned, and in 1851, when for the first time since 1846 the Conservatives seemed on the brink of power, Croker declared that in the previous ten years 'Government has been carried on only by expedients and concessions and I fear that the advent of the Conservatives, which seems close at hand, will only accelerate *the Republic*'.[41]

In his prime, however, Croker did not stand idly by prophesying doom while radical opinion made its strides through society. He believed in hitting vigorously back. He was active in helping to direct the Tory press against radical journalists in the years after Waterloo. He was friendly with Peter Street, who edited the *Courier*, and may have channelled official information to other sympathetic editors. His friend Theodore Hook edited the Tory satirical paper *John Bull* and there are clear signs that they co-operated over the crisis of the Queen's Trial.[42] Not much evidence has survived in his papers of this side of his literary career. There are gaps in Hook's letters to him which do not look accidental. A furious letter from a relative, Stanley Lees Giffard, who edited the *Standard*, written in June 1832 and reproaching the Tory party for neglecting the journalists who wrote for it, partly explains why. How could he be expected to write accurately about the politicians he defended, Giffard asked, when he could meet so few and by the rest was 'shamed as a beggar, dreaded as a spy'?[43] The low status of journalists meant that records were either not made or not kept. So this side of Croker's literary activity has to be inferred from fragments.

But even in his contributions to the *Quarterly*, where he wrote for a more fastidious audience and at greater leisure, his

---

[40] Add. MSS. 40321, fos. 158–62, 25 Aug. 1835. Peel's reply is in Jennings, ii. 282–4. For the effect of the Lords' amendments, see my *Philosophic Radicals*, 273–91.
[41] Wellington MSS, 24 Mar. 1851.
[42] Hook–Croker Letters, Regenstein Library, University of Chicago, 1820 but otherwise undated, fos. 1–7.
[43] CPD, 11 June 1832.

motive was still ultimately political. The modern reader is likely
to find these articles too unremittingly fault-finding, but Croker
thought such an approach was a moral duty. 'I can safely assert',
he told Lockhart in 1835, 'that I never in my life said one word
more of censure than I thought absolutely just and necessary. I
may have been wrong—but I declare I have always been sincere,
my only leaning from the straight upright of duty having been
in the direction of favour'.[44] The reason for this unbending censoriousness was his belief (as remote from modern attitudes as
it could possibly be) that the literary world was peopled by half-
lettered charlatans who were filling the bookshops with trash,
and that a critic's duty was to expose them. Even in his time,
the expansion of the reading public might have made this seem
like a task doomed to failure. It might have suited the *Quarterly*
under Gifford, but one would have expected Lockhart, with his
wider sympathies and his cosmopolitanism, to have abandoned
it. But in fact Lockhart, although he nudged him more into historical and political topics, shared Croker's conception of the duty
of a critic. If Murray worried that the *Quarterly*'s circulation was
falling and he was losing money, they told him that he was being
penny wise and pound foolish, that it stood for quality in a world
of deteriorating standards, and that more than any other periodical it represented 'the feeling and opinion and taste of a higher
order of society'.[45] Their tone accordingly assumed that they were
writing on behalf of the educated and well-connected, and had
a duty to take their part against their critics and traducers.
Towards established reputations they tended to be deferential;
towards new writers they were rather condescending, often
treating them as upstarts and *arrivistes*. 'Do favour us with the
flagellation of some literary quack', Lockhart asks in August
1832;[46] and ten years later when the two men had come to understand one another better, he sends Madden's *United Irishmen*
for possible review, adding, 'Perhaps it merits no notice whatever unless as a specimen of the vast impertinence with which
such fellows these days fling themselves into *History*'.[47] Both men

---

[44] NLS, Lockhart MS 927, no. 7, fos. 22–3, 10 June 1835.
[45] CPC, Lockhart to Croker [undated, but before 12 Jan. 1835] in Lockhart Letters
vol. i, 115.
[46] Ibid., i. fo. 63, 14 Aug. 1832.   [47] Ibid., vol. ii, fo. 86, 11 Aug. 1842.

felt they were guardians of traditional literary standards no less than of traditional institutions.

Croker's critical method probably owes more to his forensic training as a lawyer than to any other discipline. He often writes as if persuading a jury to return a verdict of guilty, and however learned he became in the historical sources, that preoccupation still shows in his phraseology. He likes to set out a charge, and he then proceeds with great acuteness and clarity, through the stages of a complicated argument, to prove the charge and condemn the unfortunate author in question. The argument is laced with a good deal of personal comment on the writer's veracity, taste, and even integrity. Some of these articles are bound to seem inordinately tedious and often gratuitously cruel, unless one appreciates what Croker is aiming at. Brightfield, who did more than any other scholar to identify and assess Croker's critical work, patiently examined most of his important literary targets from Godwin and Leigh Hunt to Fanny Burney and Lord Holland. But his main concern was to justify Croker's charges, not to understand the political motives which kept leading him into such controversies, and his defence is one-sided. I hope after my account of Croker's politics, that we may be in a better position to appreciate those motives. The essential point to bear in mind in reading Croker's criticism is that he was defending what he conceived as polite taste in literature and traditional standards in politics, from the misunderstanding and misrepresentations of those who only knew them from the outside. He was writing for a tiny, élite readership. His severity may seem dated, but it is in fact still common in the journalism of small communities where the readers are few. What has changed is not that people have grown kinder, but that readerships of such national periodicals have grown too large and anonymous for their writers to be certain what sort of people they are addressing.

A good example of Croker's prosecuting-counsel style is his review of Sir Nathaniel Wraxall's *Historical Memoirs of His Own Time*. Wraxall was a garrulous MP who had seen service in India, followed by a little diplomatic experience in Germany, and he ended his short parliamentary career as a follower of Pitt in 1794. His book was exactly the sort of work a man on the margin of political society might write for money and embellish with borrowed anecdotes and unverified gossip to secure a larger sale.

Croker's central objection is that Wraxall writes with pretensions to knowledge that he does not possess, like a man reading a clock and knowing 'nothing of the principles that regulate the machine'.[48] So he undertakes to prove the worthlessness of his recollections:

What he advances on his own evidence is generally not worth knowing, and what he gives on the authority of others he generally contrives to render suspicious either by his manner of relating, or by not quoting his authority when he might, or by quoting authority which is notoriously incredible.[49]

There follows a witty exposure of Wraxall's errors in dates and facts and his inaccurate retailing of anecdotes. The most serious charge Wraxall had made was that the Princess of Württemburg had been murdered, with the connivance of her husband, by Catherine II of Russia. For this he was later sued, by Count Worontzov, Wraxall's alleged source, in the King's Bench. Found guilty, he was fined £500 and sentenced to six months in prison. The Count however pleaded for clemency; the Prince Regent intervened, the fine was waived, the sentence halved, and Wraxall bounced back to the life of a gossip about town. The *Memoirs* were reprinted and more concocted. Croker's closing remarks in his review were confirmed by these events. He had predicted that the book would have a longer life than it deserved because the public appetite for gossip was growing, and he quoted Junius: 'Trifles float and are preserved—while what is solid and valuable sinks to the bottom, and is lost forever'.[50] That expresses the anxiety which informs both his editing and his criticism. He hovers, discreet and curious, in the ante-rooms of power, privy to transactions he may not reveal but qualified to scotch rumours and innuendoes he knows to be false. He worries that a knowledge of what really happened will be lost for ever, and that falsehoods will float by their own buoyancy and be preserved. His only comfort is that he can record the truth for posterity. The *Quarterly* would be his arena for critical combat and for public instruction: the darker secrets would be left in manuscript.

---

[48] *QR*, xiii, no. 25 (Apr. 1815), 201.
[49] Ibid., 193.   [50] Ibid., 215.

Wraxall lived until 1831 and his effect upon the writing of history lay in the future, but Croker was equally concerned with the memoirs of men no longer alive which he feared would work their way, errors and all, into the accepted histories. A good example of his method here is his work on Horace Walpole. It was this which Butterfield praised for its modernity, but he was primarily concerned to criticize Namier and his followers, and he forgot to practise what he had preached in his own essay on *The Whig Interpretation of History*. He wanted to use Croker to show that Namier was not as original as his admirers claimed, and in order to do this he misstated Croker's situation and his aims.

Walpole was a much more important witness than Wraxall. The son of the great First Minister, he knew personally most of the leading politicians of the Pelham era which followed his father's fall. Though a political career was open to him, he chose instead the life of a wealthy dilettante, keeping a seat in the House of Commons as his window on the political world, but devoting most of his time to building the gothic fantasy of Strawberry Hill, filling it with historical curiosities, investigating such historical episodes as took his fancy, and describing his life and the society he knew to a wide range of correspondents. Croker was one of the first, outside the circle of Walpole's intimates, to edit some of the correspondence (to the first Marquess of Hertford, the father of his patron) and but for his other avocations he might have become the editor of Walpole's *Reminiscences*. He admitted that he liked 'that tea-table kind of history', but he shrank (as well he might) from the task of annotating the letters.[51] Clearly they would be more demanding than those of Lady Hervey, and Croker, having some claim to being a good judge in such matters, looked jealously at the work of the various editors of the letters as they appeared.

It was one thing, however, to leave vivid materials for history, quite another to try to write it. It soon became clear that Horace Walpole had crossed the boundary between observer and historian, and when his *Memoirs of the Last Ten Years of the Reign of George II* appeared in 1822, edited by Lord Holland, Croker saw that something more serious than gossip was at issue, and

[51] Brightfield, 309–10.

warned his readers that he must be severe. The work belonged 'rather to history than to memoirs' and in it Walpole had disfigured and traduced historical events and characters 'with all the malignity of political party and of private enmities.' It would have been easy, he continues, to have written 'what is called an *entertaining article* out of such a book', by selecting 'the very passages which we the most deplore', but 'truth and justice' call for an examination not of 'what may amuse a cursory reader, but what may do justice to public character, and to historical truth'.[52] The reader, chastened by this admonition, is then given an account of the origin of the manuscript, a sympathetic treatment of Lord Holland's problems as editor, and a long exposure of Walpole's slanders and falsifications. Croker shows that Walpole's dislike of the Pelhams was due, not as he had claimed to their part in his father's fall, but to the fact that they had failed to give Horace, already the possessor of a large sinecure income, the reversion to a further sinecure enjoyed by his elder brother; that the charge of Jacobitism made in 1753 against the tutors of the young Prince of Wales, the future George III, was aggravated by the circulation of a document fabricated by Walpole himself, a fact he later suppressed; and that his claim that political pressures had frustrated efforts, his own included, to save Admiral Byng from execution in 1757, was completely without foundation. The argument is not light reading. Each stage is illustrated by direct quotations from the evidence, and in these there is much use of italics to mark the words the reader has to notice, but the exposition is clear and convincing. The proof of Walpole's errors is drawn from his own works, together with a few others in print, such as the *Memoirs of Lord Waldegrave* and Coxe's *Life of Sir Robert Walpole*. It is assumed that we know the background events, such as the death of Frederick, Prince of Wales, and what Byng was court-martialled for. Croker gives page references to quotations as if inviting the reader to check each assertion for himself. No concession is made to gossip.[53] Walpole had, Croker claims, confused history with

---

[52] *QR*, xxvii, no. 53 (Apr. 1822), 179.

[53] One of Walpole's anti-clerical sneers was against Archbishop Secker, and in a footnote, Croker gives an extract from one of Secker's sermons on 'Idle Words' directed against slander, which accurately describes the process by which idle tittle-tattle works its way by thoughtless repetition into being taken for historical truth. See 187.

memoirs, and instead of describing only the motives of those he knew, he pretended to give the notices of his antagonists which he could not possibly have known, so giving the *Memoirs* the character of a party pamphlet. The article ends with a warning to readers to treat warily the evidence of a witness who 'has been, we may almost say, *convicted* of all the arts of calumny, misrepresentation and falsehood'.[54]

This advice, however just from a scholarly or ethical viewpoint, was to prove an awkward self-denying ordinance. As other collections of Walpole's letters were uncovered and edited, notably the long series to his friend Horace Mann, and those to the Countess of Ossory, it became clear that he was not just a gossip but an acute and sympathetic observer and a letter-writer of genius. And there were writers who would work this material into a misleading caricature with less scruple than Croker and a good deal more skill. In 1833 Lockhart sent Croker a copy of the *Edinburgh Review* containing Macaulay's essay on Walpole. 'Pray read this paper', he wrote, 'before you settle to do one in the Q.R. on the same subject and consider whether it would be *infra dig* and doing Tom too much honour'. Croker evidently thought it would be and bided his time. Macaulay was ostensibly reviewing the first two volumes of the letters to Horace Mann, but the essay hardly mentions them. It is a brilliant evocation of Horace Walpole's inconsistencies, built around a central paradox, that he was serious about trifles and frivolous about large matters, which then rather abruptly leads into a narrative of his father's last years in power.[55] Somehow Croker managed to restrain himself from cutting it to shreds. He may have had other things on his mind. The reform crisis seems to have driven him back to his French Revolutionary studies, and it was not until Peel's second ministry was firmly in the saddle and the Corn Laws (as Croker thought) secure, that he returned to Walpole. When he did, it was to review the next two volumes of the letters to Mann.

Unlike Macaulay's essay this is a review, but it is one in which Croker struggles to blend the severe criteria of historical accuracy with his own admiration for Walpole as a writer and man

---

[54] Ibid., 183, 215.
[55] *ER*, Oct. 1833, repr. *CHE*, i. 98–145.

of taste. He admires the indefatigable letter-writer, whose style was 'sparkling but cold, like icicles in the sunshine', and who adapted his manner and his news with delicate tact to a wide variety of correspondents. He compares him to Madame de Sévigné and says we have to thank him for 'the greatest mass of amusement and information that epistolary literature has ever bestowed upon England, or indeed the world'. He admits that Walpole had a 'precarious' temper and was volatile and capricious in his friendships, but he insists that we have to take the faults along with the virtues. Even his malice towards political associates is condoned. 'To look to Walpole for strict accuracy and impartiality would be to expect from a harlequin the gait and garb of an undertaker'.[56] To the assertion of 'our northern contemporary'—meaning of course the *Edinburgh* and Macaulay—that Walpole's affectations were so many masks concealing the real man, Croker suggests that he was in fact that type of eccentric whose amiable qualities arc shown to a narrow circle of intimates, while his harsher ones are 'prominently and permanently exhibited to the world at large'.[57] He admits that the letters read as if intended for eventual publication, having too much 'prepared wit, laborious ease, and studied familiarity' but then

it cannot be denied that ease, wit and pleasantry were indigenous to his mind, and that whatever of art and effort he may have employed, was only to polish and perfect those natural qualities.[58]

(Was that a rebuke to Macaulay the conversational bruiser?) As he goes on, with only the occasional squeeze of lemon, it is clear that Croker admires in Walpole's life many of the activities he pursued himself. Strawberry Hill is described with the eye of the architectural amateur who advised Peel on the rebuilding of Drayton and got Decimus Burton to design the Athenaeum and later his own Alverbank:

The delightful work grew on his hands, the toy-villa gradually assumed the mingled features of a cloister and a castle, and of course

---

[56] *QR*, lxxii, no. 144 (Sept. 1843), 525. He wrote three other articles on Walpole's letters, a review of the last two volumes of letters to Mann, in lxxiv, no. 148 (Oct. 1844), 395–416; and the letters to the Countess of Ossory in lxxxiii; no. 165 (June 1848), 110–127.
[57] *QR*, lxxii, no. 144, 526.   [58] Ibid., 534–5.

there ensued great incongruities between the works of his original ignorance and those of his tardy and never very perfect knowledge. But he made for himself a very enjoyable and interesting villa, and created for his country a noble and characteristic style.[59]

Strawberry Hill's contents had been auctioned the previous year, and Croker regretted that some of the curiosities had not been bought for the nation and that for instance Cardinal Wolsey's hat had not been put in an appropriate setting in Hampton Court. These things had a serious historical value for Croker, and the collector in him did not like to see them dispersed. But above all what he delighted in most of all was Walpole's wit, which he quoted to show that 'no man under all his air of levity had a sounder judgment, when his own wayward prejudice and passion did not disturb it'.[60]

One wonders if Lockhart was relieved to have an article from Croker which was an essay rather than an extended critique, and whether he would not secretly have preferred the sort of sketch Macaulay had written. Probably not, given his political loyalties, but even from an editor's viewpoint the advantage was not all on Macaulay's side. Macaulay's essay is more brilliantly written and more quotable. But what Croker tells us, though it calls for more attention, is actually more absorbing. One is carried along by Macaulay's pace, but he is like a guide to a historic site who talks so cleverly that one pays more attention to his turn of phrase and his jokes than to the items he is supposed to be pointing out. Croker's style is more discursive, and the prose is constantly interrupted with illustrations and quotations; but the reader is allowed to make up his own mind, the elements of a portrait are there for him to form for himself, and he is told where to look if he wants to know more. Macaulay writes as if afraid of taxing his reader's patience. He knows exactly what Walpole stood for, he is satisfied with the editorial standards of the letters before him, and he is bent on pressing all the information into a picture of a dilettante, all insincerity and affectation. Objects are used as symbols to illustrate the basic antithesis: strenuous frivolity versus languid public service.

After the labours of the print-shop and the auction-room, [Walpole] unbent his mind in the House of Commons. And, having indulged in

[59] *QR*, lxxii, no. 144, 536.   [60] Ibid., 541.

the recreation of making laws, he returned to more important pursuits, to researches after Queen Mary's comb, Wolsey's red hat, the pipe which Van Tromp smoked during his last sea-fight, and the spur which King William struck into the flank of Sorrel.[61]

Croker by contrast sees these objects in the context of Walpole's life:

a gouty old bachelor of large income, refined taste, and literary habits, incapable of out-of-door amusements, and weaned from the busy world, could not have imagined for himself a more rational enjoyment than the making his whole residence a gallery of curiosities—through which he might stroll, alone to enjoy, or with company to communicate, all the varied recollections connected with so many objects of art and so many relics of history. It was not, and such things can never be, the creation of a great mind . . . but it was an assemblage in which the most enlarged intellect might find abundant matter, not merely of curiosity, but of contemplation . . . [62]

Yet Macaulay's essay is often quoted (even with a rueful affection by Walpole's Yale editors) while Croker's is forgotten. A caricature is usually more memorable than a portrait from life.

Croker's enjoyment of the letters did not soften his criticism of Walpole's *Memoirs of the Reign of George III*. One might have thought that a fuller appreciation of Walpole the letter-writer, collector, and amateur architect would have produced a kindlier and more rounded estimate of the memoir-writer, setting his shortcomings in that role in the wider perspective of his long and varied life. Instead, the *Memoirs of George III* (December 1845) bring out again the counsel for the prosecution. The article is notable for Croker's exposure of Walpole's claim that Bute remained the secret influence in George III's counsels even after his formal dismissal, and for a forceful defence of the King against the charge of indolence and inactivity.[63] Its tone is consistently critical. Croker argues, as he did before, but this time with further evidence from the letters, that the driving motive behind Walpole's abuse of Bute, Jenkinson, Henry Fox, Lord Grenville, and even friends like Conway and Thomas Pitt, was his selfish concern for his sinecures, and the morbid feelings that generated.[64] Croker is very insistent on the critic's duty to expose such slander

---

[61] CHE, i. 100.   [62] QR, lxxii, no. 144, 537–8.
[63] QR, lxxvii, no. 153, 282–5.   [64] Ibid., 293.

and distortion in detail. Walpole's 'pertinacious attempts to poison history require that *at each successive attempt* the antidote should be administered'.[65] Already it had affected the historians writing about the period. He instances Lord Mahon's use of the *Memoirs* in his *History of England* and he criticizes him for saying explicitly that he would not trust Walpole as a guide to men's motives, but then tacitly adopting many of his opinions. The *Memoirs*, Croker snorts, 'are little else than an apocryphal chronicle of *motives*'. That is what memoirs are all about; they are one man's story of his own acts and how they are affected by others, whose reasons for acting can only be tentatively inferred; but if the narrator himself suffers from a 'self-interested malignity working on a cynical temper' as Walpole did, even those inferences will be wrong. Only with a clear idea of the motives activating the *other* parties to a transaction can one say whether the memoirist's account of it is just. So without going so far as to assert that Walpole's *Memoirs* have no historical value, Croker argues 'that their value is much less than their mischief', since few readers are going to have the means or the time to check one account against another, while 'the public will greedily swallow the potion so suited to the general appetite for scandal, without attempting to distinguish the ingredients'.[66]

Looking back from this to the review of September 1843 of the letters to Mann, it seems clear that, though Croker *could* compose an agreeable literary portrait of a man he admired, he still felt that historical truth called for something more severe, and that no agreeable traits or talents, moral, literary, or aesthetic, ought to be allowed to excuse the crime of poisoning history. His criticism of Mahon suggests that he was much more interested in correcting a lapse from historical truth in a memoir or in the work of a fellow-historian than in composing a more accurate account himself. At one point in the critique of the *Memoirs of George III*, Croker compares the work of the historical critic with that of a restorer of pictures.

Walpole is like any other prejudiced witness: though there may be a predominance of falsehood and a general discolouration, there will yet be, in a long and varied narration, a considerable portion of voluntary

---

[65] *QR*, lxxvii, no. 153, 274.   [66] Ibid., 276.

or involuntary truth. The art of using such a witness to advantage is a minute study of the admitted facts, a general balancing of the antagonist testimonies, and a conscientious sifting of the evidence in each minute portion of the case, so as finally to discriminate between the real colour of the transaction and the partial colour of the narrative. It ought to be something like restoring an old picture which has been painted over: you must wash off the whole varnish, and then proceed with great care and caution to remove the supposititious touches from the original ground. You will probably find there some elemental traces, more or less slight, of the surcharge which you have removed— but you will also frequently find that the manufacturer, by way of producing an effect after his own taste, has made gratuitous additions of which he had no ground whatsoever.[67]

The passage is very revealing. It shows Croker's central preoccupation and his strongest instinct, was the preservation of a record. The record, like the picture, acquires accretions which cover and conceal the original. The historian, like the restorer, must return as far as possible to the original. Croker's theory of art was mimetic. Accuracy in representation was what he looked for, and his fascination with the records of his time extended to the work of painters. He wanted Lawrence to add to his portrait of Canning in the Commons details of the other ministers sitting on the benches behind him. When he saw David's famous painting of the murdered Marat in his bath, he thought it must be 'by someone who did not know that Marat was near sixty'.[68] In comparing the historian's with the restorer's task, he was surely thinking of his own editing of a text. But the analogy is misleading. It presupposes an accurate picture to start with. If all the witnesses to a historic episode, however well-placed to observe what happened, are partial and prejudiced, how can we be sure what was 'the real colour of the transaction', what really happened? What did the historian do when the eye-witnesses to an event could not agree? Earlier in his edition of *French Royal Memoirs*, he had noted of the various firsthand accounts of the Flight to Varennes, 'that agreeing in the main, all the

[67] Ibid., 275.
[68] Add. MSS. 40607, fos. 239–40, C. to Peel, (n.d. 1836). He was actually nearer fifty, but David's treatment was avowedly hagiographical, not only foreshortening his face but concealing the skin disease which Marat was treating. Cf. Anita Brookner's *David*, at 113–15.

witnesses contradict one another in the most wonderful way, on facts, which they all witnessed and which none had any interest in altering'.[69] If an accurate account of what happened can only be achieved by a laborious compilation from a range of expensive works by people with the requisite education and leisure, is not a generally accurate history (let alone a popular one) likely to be impossible to achieve? Croker's suspicion of the popular appetite for sensation and scandal in high places seems to imply that the historian must be a kind of compiler, either of original documents with minimal commentary, or else of a story derived from highly confidential sources treated with the caution which we now give 'classified' information. It would be easy to see in this a political motive. A Tory historian, one might think, would naturally favour a conception of history which effectively shielded the governing classes from popular scrutiny. But mere political animus would not explain why, for instance, it is a fellow Tory, Mahon, whom Croker criticizes for naïvely swallowing Walpole's slanders. There are other factors which show that we are dealing with an ingrained critical mentality and not just an inveterate political prejudice, and it is this mentality which explains why Croker left no work of synthesis either of the English history he knew so intimately or of the French Revolution on which he was probably the best informed English writer of his time.

It is obvious that Burke's advice to apply remedies 'to vices, not to names' will lead the historian who observes it to concentrate on the lives of those who leave records of their personal life and these will tend to be the educated and the influential. History then will be largely a record of high politics diversified with fashionable gossip. This was the sort of material Croker knew best in his editorial work, and reading his articles on eighteenth century memoirs and biographies one feels that he could have written a history of high politics from the Revolution to the reign of George IV had he wanted to. Macaulay planned such a history and had to abridge it, but at least he left a magnificent fragment. There is no record that Croker got further than an anecdotal history book for the nursery, which Mackintosh described as 'wickedly contrived to instil slavery into the minds of

---

[69] Add. MSS. 40321, fos. 184–7. Croker to Peel, 5 Apr. 1836.

children'.[70] Tory high politics for infants, in fact. But why no adult narrative?

Croker certainly had his own interpretation of his age, which might have provided the conceptual framework for a general history. But he had used this interpretation in an ambivalent way, partly as scholarly editor and partly as political polemicist. Had he really retired from politics in 1832 his studies might have acquired perspective and proportion as the political scene receded and its emotions cooled. Instead, he decided to leave office and still continue to write for the political cause in retirement. We have seen one half of the result: as a political commentator he was so buried in the past that he became more and more out of touch, quite unable to grasp why his readers did not share his perception of the dangers which threatened them. But as a student of the historic past, he could not shed the habits of the polemicist. He idealized the aristocratic world before 1789, and he wanted to believe that it was safer, better governed, and more civilized than the world which had superseded it, because if it had not been, all his political polemics would have been in vain. So he defended the institutions of the old regime from their critics and detractors with a strange blend of scholarship and abuse. As the scholarship became deeper and more assured the abuse became shriller and more trivial. Isolation from the political scene really seems to have intensified the critical habit, but narrowed its scope. In applying Burke's dictum, he had taken so literally the duty to correct vices that he ignored the names altogether.

Reading Croker's historical work one is repeatedly struck by the fact that his moral sympathies are most often with people in authority, and his moral censures directed at the memoirists and historians who misrepresent them. But there is a whole world of ordinary, obscure but not necessarily inarticulate people, who administer local institutions, man the professions, own factories and workshops, print the books and newspapers, run the shops, and generally make up the body of what is called society, which is left undescribed. It is not that he did not know of this society, or pretended that it did not exist. The editor of Boswell could

---

[70] Add. MSS. 52442, fos. 38; Mackintosh to his wife, 29 Apr. 1817. The book was *Stories Selected from the History of England, from the Conquest to the Revolution. For Children.* (1817).

hardly do that. But it did not interest him as a historical critic. Again, he was well aware, in his political articles, of the efforts of economists, statisticians, and philosophers to describe and explain the dynamics of this society, which was evidently challenging the old order and in places supplanting it, on both sides of the Channel. But he did not assimilate their work to his historical studies.

Two convictions confirmed this critical habit of mind. He distrusted the imagination. 'I prefer an ounce of fact to a ton of imagination', he once told Peel.[71] One could say his sensibility was pre-romantic, or at least prosaic:

> A primrose by a river's brim
> A yellow primrose was to him
> And it was nothing more . . .

His preference for written evidence over imaginative projections of what it might have felt like to live in past periods (which is not unlike the utilitarians' dislike of works of imagination as fictions and therefore false) made him very reluctant to convey an impression of a character or a place in a graphic verbal sketch. Neither had he much time for that deliberate exposure to and imaginative saturation in unusual scenes and ways of life, by which historians of the next generation like Michelet, Lamartine, Carlyle, and Macaulay tried to achieve a vividness and realism in their descriptions. No one was more precise about reconstructing events where they occurred. 'I have the bump of locality very strong', he told Brougham, 'and my satisfaction in reading of any event is enhanced, to a degree that I believe is uncommon, by giving it not in fancy but in fact "a local habitation".'[72] Not in fancy but in fact; in other words, he distrusted scene-painters who invented the local colour for dramatic effect. Topographical detail was a check on the accuracy of men's recollections, not an aid to the imagination of later readers. He would have thought sympathy for the actors an idle and sentimental activity, much less important than a patient sifting and comparison of documentary evidence, and less honest than an admission that, for some areas of history, no evidence has survived.

---

[71] Add. MSS. 40321, fos. 142–5.   [72] Brougham MSS, 10 Aug. 1855.

He also distrusted narrative, especially the sort which tried to give historical events the pace and excitement of fiction. One of the ways in which the middle classes reconciled themselves to an aristocratic political system was by devouring novels purporting to describe the world of their social superiors. They gratified their growing taste for history with the novels of Scott and his imitators. One would not have expected Croker to have had much sympathy for the novels of the first genre, the 'silver fork' school. Macaulay and his sisters, in contrast, devoured them, delightedly counting the number of duels fought by men, swoonings suffered by women and so on.[73] To the end of his life Macaulay was a compulsive reader of novels. He read them while dressing, at meals, in bed, even walking in the streets, and he was a connoisseur of the well-constructed plot, with consequences I shall later explore. Croker moved the other way. His early reviews of the Waverley novels deprecate the mixing up of fictitious characters with real ones.[74] The year after his son's death, he reviewed Galt's *Annals of the Parish*, but he admitted to its publisher that it caused him pain: 'a small matter affects me, a slight touch of pathos is now a full dose, and I cannot bear to see a tragedy'.[75] Thereafter he concentrated on history, biography, and politics, bringing to them a much more intense concern for human motivation than such literature can normally satisfy, and developing for novels a real distaste. In one review he admitted that he had never finished *Nicholas Nickleby*.[76] I am inclined to think he was sincere in saying that he had never read *Coningsby*. As if to prove it, he added that he had never read any of Theodore Hook's novels either, though some of them had been written under his roof.[77] It is this immunity to the lure of fiction which marks him out from those historians, like Macaulay, who were affected by it. Croker was quite capable of reconstructing the different elements of an episode, but he was too conscious of the gaps in the evidence, the weakness of witnesses, and the general untidiness and loose-endedness of human affairs ever to aspire to writing an absorbing or enthralling story himself. He talked of being a prophet, and he had, as we saw, a general view of the movement of European

[73] Trevelyan, i. 123–4.   [74] *QR*, xi, no. 22 (July 1814), 377.
[75] NLS, MS 4715, fos. 1–2 to William Blackwood 25 Mar. [1821].
[76] *QR*, lxxvii, no. 142.   [77] Jennings, iii. 304.

history, but when he came to study a character or an event, the analytical moralist took over and he saw only what Burke called 'the dust and powder of individuality'. This preference for studies on a small scale is particularly important when we consider his work on the French Revolution.

III

Croker was thirty-four when he first visited France, and he went better equipped than most Englishmen who went when peace came. He spoke good French, and had gleaned a good knowledge of the events of the Revolution from *émigrés*, like General Dumouriez, whose portrait he cherished. Very early on, he had acquired an exact topographical knowledge of revolutionary Paris. Unlike the carpet-slippered English historians of Cobb's strictures, he met and interrogated many survivors of the Revolution. He corresponded with and interviewed Mme de Genlis, the governess to the family of Philippe Égalité, which may account for the prominence he gave to the ambitions of the Orleanist branch of the royal family in the fall of the Monarchy.[78] He was particularly interested in people who had known Robespierre.[79] He may have met Robespierre's surviving sister, Charlotte, and he certainly tracked down her will. On his first visit, before Napoleon's Hundred Days, he met Colin, the printer who had published Marat's works and whose collection of pamphlets he bought. Through him it seems, he met Marat's sister, in 1837.[80] Not many of Croker's letters to his wife have survived, but those that have suggest that when away from home he wrote to her every day. The two letters describing Mlle Marat in her squalid sixth-floor apartment in the Rue de la Barillerie, are very detailed, and they show him first recording and then editing the experience. In the first he vividly describes the tiny creature, 'like a dwarf scarecrow', with her meagre clothing and bright intelligent eyes, looking exactly like her brother's 'best portraits' (not, apparently, David's) and talking with fervent revolutionary enthusiasm (for she was, she said, the daughter of an *homme de lettres*) of books and portraits, and of other survivors of the Jacobin party,

[78] CPD, C. to Mme de Genlis (copies endorsed by him) 28 Dec. 1821, 7 Jan. 1822.
[79] CPC, Lowther to Croker 16 Jan. [1820]; 24 Jan. [1820].
[80] Jennings, iii. 316–17.

condemning those who sought to come to terms with the July Monarchy, but confident that her republican principles would triumph in the end. Croker listens, fascinated, not daring to ask about Charlotte Corday, but gratefully accepting a specimen of Marat's handwriting instead of a signature, and finally asking if he might call again. 'Yes, by all means', is the reply, 'come and dispute with me. You have your principles, I have mine . . . arguing will change neither—but it will pass the time'.[81] The next day Croker writes home again, more reflectively, placing the experience in a wider framework. It was, he says, 'like a glimpse into the infernal regions and an association with spectres which had, as I thought, long vanished from the earth'. He explains why he had to inflict 'this phantasmagoria' on his wife:

In spite of Charlotte Corday—of his apotheosis in the Pantheon and of his final exit through l'égout de Montmartre, Marat was alive before me. The effect these persons and scenes have on me is exceedingly like what I feel at an historical tragedy. When I look at the *actual scene* of the event—the very walls that echoed to the cries—the very pavement that ran with the blood—I can fancy the actors—but, in Mlle Marat's case, I had not only the scene but *almost* the actor himself— for her lodging is opposite the Palais whither and whence he was carried by the people to and from a mock trial and a real triumph—and opposite to the Conciergerie, one of the chief scenes of the September Massacres, the dungeon of the Queen and the short prison of all the victims of the reign of terror. And there *she* sits, the fierce old woman, looking down on all these localities—*justifying* the terrible scenes they witnessed and *prophecying* [sic] their revival.[82]

When three years later he heard she was dying, Croker sent 'the fierce old woman' some money to relieve her wants. 'It might seem mighty odd', he told Peel, 'that I, of all men in the world, should be paying a *tribute to [the] memory of Marat*—for after all, if it were not for that accursed name, my charity would never have found its way into the miserable sizième of the Rue de la Barillerie, such is the magical interest which great crimes create even in minds which fully appreciate their villainy'.[83]

It is as if, when describing his revolutionary interests to his friends, Croker had to justify a bad habit, like gambling or going

---

to the races. He loved going to France, and he went as often as his means allowed, but he went like a man visiting an old friend who has just recovered from a bout of insanity, half expecting a relapse. He did not rough it like a modern scholar, but travelled like an English gentleman. He liked to stay at the Hotel Meurice in the Rue de Rivoli.[84] Sometimes he went with Lowther, once at least with Hertford. The 1837 visit was with Sir Alexander Grant in a new steam yacht. They enjoyed the social life of the capital, and Croker renewed old political acquaintances such as Pozzo di Borgo and Madame de Lieven, besides meeting many other English visitors. Historical researches, those descents into 'the infernal regions', even if they were the main purpose of the visit, had to be fitted into this social programme. He later claimed for his researches 'something of the accuracy of contemporaries, the diligence of enquirers, and the impartiality of historians, all combined', and it is worth noting that the historians come last.[85] There were no great repositories of public archives where a scholar might immerse himself for weeks. Croker had to find such information as he needed by personal enquiry and the help of friends. So, for instance, Lowther, who good-naturedly let himself be sent on errands for Croker's enquiries, reported to him that a certain singer had been a surgeon's apprentice and had dressed Robespierre's wounds just before his execution; and later in London he reports that a French lady from Charlotte Corday's village has evidence that can throw light on her motives for assassinating Marat.[86] Croker had to apply his own judgement in sifting such suggestions, and there must have been many other avenues of enquiry closed to him for political and social reasons. It is not surprising that he came to value the printed official sources which were least liable to unconscious or deliberate falsification. His purchases are not those of an amateur or dilettante, picking a choice item here and there. He bought whole sets and series: a complete Voltaire; all Grimm's *Correspondence*, the whole *Moniteur*, all the *Histoire Parlementaire*, and so on. They were works of reference but they

---

[84] Add. MSS. 40321, fos. 420–1, to Peel, 4 Aug. 1840. It was opposite the site of the *manège* where the Constituant & Legislative Assemblies sat. (*Essays*, 554, note).

[85] *Essays*, 562.

[86] CPC, Box 12, Folder (1), Lowther to Croker, n.d. 1821; 26 Jan. 1836.

do not necessarily prove that Croker wanted to do something more ambitious than his reviewing. The pamphlet collections were certainly bought for the use of future historians. Croker seems to have recognized that he could not hope to catalogue them all himself, and he sold them to the British Museum hoping that they could. Hence his irritation with Panizzi, the Museum's Librarian, when he found that the catalogue was not far advanced.[87] More purchases followed that from Colin. In the 1830s he was buying from a royalist bookseller in the Palais Royal called Dantu.[88] From 1837 he seems to have relied on an English (or Irish) contact living in Paris called Francis Moore, who accompanied him on the visit to Mlle Marat, and was willing to follow up some of Croker's requests from England.

In 1821 Croker told Madame de Genlis of his hope, if his health allowed, of completing a shadowy project which sounds like a history of the French Revolution. In a later letter, he refers to 'that horrible *chasm* in human affairs called the French Revolution'.[89] In the next decade many people thought he was going to write some such work, and before Peel's premiership drew him back into active conservative politics, his reviewing suggests he was more concerned with works relating to the French Revolution than with anything else. Peel, himself a collector of books on the Revolution, urged him to write a History of the Reign of Terror, not 'a pompous, philosophical history, but a mixture of biography facts and gossip: a diary of what really took place, with the best authenticated likenesses of the actors'.[90] Croker replied that he would try, and added that he thought he might do it better than a Frenchman could.[91] The result was an essay on Robespierre, written at the seaside 'without any book save the *Liste des Condamnés*'.[92] He thought he would follow it up with studies of Marat and Madame Roland, but these were never completed. In 1838 Peel suggested (what any student of the French Revolution soon finds he needs) a Revolutionary Encyclopaedia, by which he meant a biographical dictionary of

[87] Jennings, ii. 285; NLS, Lockhart MS 927, Croker to Lockhart, 19 Mar. 1841.
[88] CPC, Lowther to J.W.C., 26 & 28 Nov. 1835.
[89] CPD, Croker to Mme de Genlis, 3 Dec. 1821; 7 Jan. 1822.
[90] Jennings, ii. 277, ca. 6 June 1835.
[91] Add. MSS. 40321, fos. 148–51, Croker to Peel, 7 June 1835.
[92] Jennings, ii. 285; Add. MSS., 40321, fos. 165–172, 7 Oct. 1835.

the leading figures, along with accounts of the things readers find
hard to understand, like the Commune, the Sections, and the many
places where important events took place. How useful it would
be, Peel said, 'to turn to the letter J. and the word *Jacobins*,
and find all that is recorded or can be preserved as to localities
and details'.[93] Croker's reaction to this is revealingly unhelpful.
He said that such an Encyclopaedia was impracticable because
there were too few subjects and they would overlap; as he put
it, 'the heads too few for the dictionary form and they so complicated with each other as not to be kept distinct', a laconic
judgement which probably indicates his distrust not so much
of analysis (which with him was an ingrained habit) as of generalization and the misleading labels and slogans of popular
discussion.[94]

The same distrust of generalization marks his attitude to
the earliest histories of the French Revolution. When the popular narrative histories of the Revolution began to appear in the
1820s, he read them with the critical eye of a man already well
acquainted with the sources and irritated by their evident misuse. Nearly all historians who have gone beyond the secondary
authorities and handled primary sources experience this irritation,
and it must be admitted that it does not presuppose vast and compendious learning. When a scholar finds that a document which
he has discovered and painstakingly transcribed for its novelty
or importance, has been either ignored or else misunderstood
by some hasty writer bent on telling a story, he is likely to have
a feeling of honesty frustrated and diligence undervalued. There
is a connoisseurship in scholarship just as there is in the appreciation of wine or vintage cars. If you have acquired it, you are
annoyed and dissatisfied with its counterfeit. Croker felt this about
narrative history but he was not content with a modern scholar's
condescending shrug. He thought the errors, as he saw them, must
be exposed, and his censure fell on political allies and enemies
alike.

Archibald Alison was a Scottish lawyer who started publishing
a *History of Europe* in 1833. Its twenty volumes appeared at
the rate of one every eighteen months, and some at least were
dictated, in time spared from the law, to an amanuensis. Of course

---

[93] Jennings, ii. 336.   [94] Add. MSS. 40321, fos. 301–2, 9 Nov. 1838.

they sold very well. Alison shared Croker's view that the French Revolution was a disaster and that the first Reform Act threatened a similar revolution in Britain, and he looked to the *Quarterly* for a puff.[95] But Croker refused him. He thought the work 'a mere compilation'.

Now the history of *past* times must necessarily be a compilation, but the history of a man's own time ought to be something more. I looked in vain for a single instance in which Alison searched beyond some well known predecessor, Thiers or Mignet, or Lacretelle and so forth. I cannot find that he has consulted any collection of the publications of the day (not even Gurwood!!!) where after all the real truth is to be only found. In short it is a miserable humbug instead of a history.[96]

But Lockhart was anxious to please Alison, and when Croker included a hostile note in an article in 1843 he protested. Alison was 'a good old Tory', an old acquaintance, and 'the Sheriff of my county whom I meet often whenever I go to Scotland'.[97] Croker was however inexorable, and replied with chapter and verse. Giving as an example the topographical details in Alison's account of the execution of Louis XVI, he showed that an error in the first edition had been compounded by a 'correction' in the third. 'So you see', he wrote triumphantly, 'Mr Alison's tardy amendment is not only erroneous in itself, but is at variance with the context on which it has been sowed: and I think you will now agree with me that of the two the *first* edition with its *omissio veri* is less disgraceful to the historian than the *suggestio* or rather *suggestiones falsi* of the third.'[98] Alison never got his review, Croker arguing that he was lucky enough to escape a fuller exposure. But the result was predictable. Alison attributed the *Quarterly*'s silence to Croker's jealousy at the success of a rival narrative.[99]

Croker showed less forbearance towards the writers of the earliest French narratives of the Revolution, Mignet and Thiers. François Mignet and Adolphe Thiers were close friends. Both

[95] NLS, Lockhart MS 927, no. 46, fos. 53, 54. Croker to Lockhart, 4 Jan. 1844.
[96] Brougham MSS, Croker to Brougham, 25 Sept. 1842. Gurwood was the editor of Wellington's *Despatches*.
[97] CPC, Lockhart Letters, ii. fo. 138, 6 Dec. 1843.
[98] NLS, Lockhart MS 927, no. 41, fos. 55–6, 8 Jan. 1844.
[99] A. Alison, *Some Account of My Life and Writings* 2 vols. (Edinburgh & London, 1883) i. 316–18; ii. 235–6.

were from Provence, and they had come to Paris after the Restoration to make their fortunes in the law. But the law had to be supplemented with journalism and journalism led to the writing of history. Both men were strong liberals, but in the France of Charles X they could hardly abuse the monarchy. Their interpretation of the Revolution was cautious and equivocal. Mignet's work was spare and abstract. His verdict on the Revolution was that it had brought 'transient excesses alongside lasting benefits'.[100] Thiers' exposition was more colourful and he was a more vivid writer. His newspaper *Le National* had played a large part in the overthrow of Charles X and the legend grew that the July Revolution had been made by journalists, a legend that seemed to be confirmed when Thiers came to political prominence under Louis Philippe.[101]

Croker was not the only English writer who thought the two historians had used historical argument to serve their political ambition. Even Carlyle and Mill were shocked at the way their histories palliated the atrocities of the Revolution of 1789.[102] Croker went further, relating the bias in interpretation to the political careers of the two men. He told Brougham that he had started Mignet's History 'with a strong prepossession in his favour, (having heard it praised by good judges) but as I went on I was astonished at the audacious falsehoods and partiality that pervaded it—and, even now, I never look into it without wonder how anything so dry can be so deceptive'. Brougham had evidently, like so many of Croker's friends, advised clemency, but as with Alison, Croker thought that would be a moral capitulation. 'Can there by any doubt', he asked,

that [Mignet] and Thiers were employed to do the *job* of whitewashing the Revolution each in his own line—Mignet as sketcher—Thiers as Dutch painter—has not Mignet's rise in the world been like Thiers's the result of his labour in this vocation both in the history and in the *National*? What else has he ever done? What can I praise him for?[103]

[100] Quoted by N. Hampson, 'The French Revolution and its Historians' in G. F. A. Best (ed.) *'The Permanent Revolution'* (1989) 215. For a good survey of the liberal interpretation of the Revolution, see S. Mellon, *The Political Uses of History* (Stanford, Calif., 1958), ch. 1.

[101] J. P. T. Bury & R. P. Tombs, *Thiers, 1797–1877* (1986), ch. 2.

[102] A. Carlyle (ed.). *Letters of Thomas Carlyle to J. S. Mill, John Sterling and Robert Browning* (1923), 34 (12 Jan. 1833); J. S. Mill, *Collected Works*, ed. J. A. Robson et al., vol. xii., 139 (2 Feb. 1833).

[103] Brougham MSS, 17 Aug. 1845.

Probably Brougham's reply would have made little difference. Croker had already had a full account of Thiers' career from Francis Moore. 'This man', Moore wrote, 'is so universally detested, I am assured it would be an excellent speculation to publish a counter-history, exposing all the falsehoods and exaggerations which appear in his work on the French Revolution'.[104] Croker's assault appeared in the *Quarterly* for September 1845. It is nothing less than an attempt to show that the careers of both men, but especially Thiers', were prefigured in their historical writing; that Thiers was an Orleanist before 1830, so anticipating the result of the July Revolution; but that under the July Monarchy which made him a minister, he had written warmly of the Consulate and of Bonaparte, 'not in fact from any love of Bonaparte's principles or memory, but to electrify France with a galvanic exhibition of his false glory' in order to boost his following in opposition to the pacific foreign policy of Guizot. He then gave a close examination of Thiers' account of the French Revolution up to July 1789 (there was not room for more) designed to show that 'every line betrays a fraudulent spirit, and every page some perversion of fact'.[105]

In manner and ambition the attack on Thiers anticipates some of the features of the critique of Macaulay. It sets out to demolish Thiers' credit as a historian, and this aim is so interwoven with a dislike of Thiers' politics that it is hard to see how any reader of Croker could maintain that he kept his historical scholarship and his political prejudices separate, or even that the strong political feeling which he put into his articles on English politics gave way to calm objectivity when he dealt with French history. But I am less concerned with the charges against Thiers than with Croker's method. I noticed that when he dealt with English memoirs he had difficulty putting the critical habit aside. Even with Walpole, whom he admired, he could not help finding fault with the editors' defective methods, their ignorance, and their stupidity. One might have thought that in considering French history he could, as a foreigner, have stood a little aloof from the spectacle and treated it with the detachment of an outsider. But that was hard for him. He thought French society was

[104] CPD, Francis Moore to Croker, 30 July 1845.
[105] *Essays on the Early Period of the French Revolution* (1857), 26–7. Oddly enough, Macaulay agreed with him. *LM*, iii. 354.

deeply tainted with the revolutionary spirit, and his revulsion was always finding vent in his letters and his articles. In a letter to Peel, for instance, he says, 'There is nothing which a Frenchman will not believe if he sees it in print, except the Bible'.[106] Noting in a review how Frenchmen in the Revolution were preoccupied with humanity and education, he cannot resist adding, 'The erection of a thousand scaffolds testified the love of the former, and the destruction of every kind of discipline proved the anxiety for the latter'.[107] So his criticism, though always acute, is very often quite disproportionate to its object.

His major essays on the French Revolution are lengthy reviews. They usually originate in an attempt at proving a memoir-writer wrong, unless indeed he or she is on the side of monarchy. They do not choose a particular area or period; they state a case against some piece of retrospective error, and they prove the charge with a wealth of quotation and rather more moral imputation than seems appropriate, to a modern reader at least. Croker plainly enjoyed exposing falsehood, and if he had chosen to recast his reviews in the form of essays, they would probably have been uncharacteristically bland. On the other hand they carry a greater weight of information than most reviews, and it must have been this consideration that made him gather up the best of them in book form. The eight studies that make up his book *Essays in the Early Period of the French Revolution* were drawn from ten reviews in the *Quarterly* and from his own edition of *Royal Memoirs*. They appear in the book in chronological order of subject, so as to cover the history of the Revolution from 1789 to 1794, but they still read as reviews. What gives them unity is the moral urgency of the criticism. Croker seems to be urging his readers not to let the first French Revolution, as it receded into the past, come to seem less frightful, barbarous, and dislocating than it really was. In our time we have supped so full of horrors that cautionary writing of this sort has migrated from the era of Marat and Danton to that of Hitler and Stalin. The sense that certain crimes must not be forgotten or condoned remains, but when reading Croker now, we are likely to feel a certain impatience that he could be so upset

---

[106] Add. MSS. 40321, fos. 205–6 [Oct. 1837 'Friday'].
[107] *Essays*, op. cit., 77.

at what at most was only a dress rehearsal or prologue to modern barbarism. The first essay is the attack on Thiers. The second is a defence of Marie Antoinette against the slurs cast on her character before and after the Revolution, and it awkwardly combines a review which Croker wrote in 1823 of the *Memoirs of Madame*, with another, of Lord Holland's *Foreign Reminiscences*, which he wrote thirty years later. The fourth is a review of P. L. Roederer's *Chronique de Cinquante Jours* covering the period from 20 June to 10 August 1792 (between the first and the second attack on the Tuileries which effectively ended the French monarchy), which he wrote in 1836. Here as much space is taken up with aspersions on Roederer's honesty as with the story he had to tell. A modern reader is used to seeing the historical exposition (whether of narrative or argument) in the text and the criticism of sources in the footnotes, and so is likely to find this distracting, though it is fair to say that it is never obscure. But Croker cannot tell a story. A good example is the third essay on the Flight to Varennes. It begins with a very accurate and clear account of the Tuilleries and the escape route out of Paris, but after that all the drama and suspense drain away, as Croker stops to consider why each participant took one course rather than another, and seems to be more impressed by the discrepancies in their recollections than by the tremendous consequences of their failure.

The best of the studies and the most famous was that on Robespierre, originally written, as we saw, away from his library, but extended in the last decade of his life to double its original length.[108] This is the nearest Croker came to composing a portrait of one of the revolutionary leaders, and it seems that what spurred him on was the meagreness of the biographical materials and the attempts of subsequent historians to supply their own. Keeping strictly to the printed documents, he peppers his text with derisive comments on the embellishments of Thiers and Lamartine. 'Nothing is more remarkable or embarrassing than the neglect of dates in all those works which are called *Histories*

---

[108] Both J. M. Thompson (*Robespierre*, 2nd edn. 1939, xxxi) and G. Rudé (*Robespierre: Portrait of a Revolutionary Democrat*, 1975, 68) quote the fuller version of 1857. Few historians before Dr Ben-Israel seem to have noticed the difference between the review of 1835 and the 1857 essay. *English Historians*, ch. 10.

of the French Revolution',[109] he says acidly, and as if to high-
light their negligence, he offers his observations as a series of
problems which future historians might solve.[110] This unwonted
modesty and the single-minded concentration on the only reliable sources are what make the essay so impressive, even today.
The central theme is expository rather than critical. Because
Robespierre had been made the scapegoat for the Reign of Terror
by his opponents and by French opinion since, Croker relishes
the task of unpeeling layer after layer of unjustified blame
and revealing the real facts underneath. He does not dogmatize
about the man, however. He frankly admits it when the evidence is lacking and only tentative theories are possible. But he
conveys with something like respect the cold clarity of
Robespierre's intellect. Robespierre was the only advocate of
Louis XVI's execution, Croker notes, who clearly saw that the
issue was not one of legality but of state policy.[111] He also
cuts through the horrors of the Terror to calculate, with actuarial
precision, that the number of monthly victims of the guillotine
increased when Robespierre absented himself from the Committee of Public Safety. The Terror did not end with his fall. His
enemies had every intention of using its machinery for further
massacre and what they objected to was his clemency, not his
cruelty. He even suggests that Robespierre may have ensured his
own downfall by expressing contempt for the mummeries of
the Cult of Reason and advocating that France return to the recognition of a Supreme Being.[112]

The fact that Croker extended and elaborated the original
review article and in the process jettisoned some of the more
obtrusive devices of his reviewing style makes the essay on
Robespierre more like a conventional piece of historical writing
than most of Croker's work. For that reason, it seems fair to
take it as an example of the limitations of his method. Croker
grasped the source of Robespierre's power. He saw that by the
very regulation which prevented members of the National
Assembly from sitting in the Legislative which replaced it,
Robespierre was forced to make the Jacobin Club his sounding-
board, and that it was there that he became an embodiment

---

[109] *Essays*, op. cit., 368.   [110] Ibid., 303.
[111] Ibid., 363–4.   [112] Ibid., 409–10, 420.

of the popular will. '*His force was the* PEOPLE *itself*. He was really their child and champion, the incarnate type of *Public Opinion*.'[113] But he treats Robespierre as the leader of an extra-parliamentary opposition,[114] stirring up popular opinion in the capital, but without a seat in parliament. To the peculiarities of Robespierre's education and especially to the source of his political ideas, he is indifferent. He dismisses, probably correctly, the claim that Robespierre met Rousseau at the end of the latter's life, but denying the encounter, he also denies the influence and so misses altogether Robespierre's fatal debt to the theory of the general will.[115] He has no psychological insight into Robespierre's motives; indeed he says a man's motives are usu-ally inscrutable, and Robespierre's especially so.[116] But lacking an imaginative perception of the sort of man he was, he can convey none of the drama of the climax to the Terror. The struggle between the Gironde and the Jacobins becomes a mere fight between two sorts of ruffian, one cowardly and equivocating, the other single-minded and ruthless, but Croker does not con-sider the rival constitutional doctrines in the struggle, or the social backgrounds of the rival parties and their supporters. So for all his accuracy about dates and places, a reader gets almost no idea of the nature of the psychological or social forces which drove the Revolution into extremes of popular violence after 10 August 1792 nor why Robespierre became the person who articulated and guided the popular will.

His treatment of the Terror illustrates the difference between close familiarity with sources and a just perspective on events. It was a Tory article of faith that the war against revolutionary France had been provoked by the French themselves. Only the Whigs blamed Pitt for British intervention. But the war created great food shortages and hardship in Paris, and popular feel-ing vented itself on refractory clergy, royalist aristocrats, and émigrés' families who were thought to be only waiting for a chance to betray the Revolution to its enemies outside. Croker hardly notices the effect of foreign intervention on popular opin-ion in Paris.[117] For him violence and atrocity unfold as the logical

---

[113] Ibid., 398.   [114] Ibid., 368.   [115] Ibid., 309.   [116] Ibid., 373.
[117] He quotes Robespierre on 'the Duke of York—Mr Pitt, and all the tyrants who are in arms against us' and adds that the reference 'seems at first sight too absurd for serious notice'. *Essays*, op. cit., 407.

consequence of the destruction of legitimate authority, not as the political expression of an economic necessity. Obedience is the norm. Untune that string, he seems to say, and see what discord follows. That the Jacobin dictatorship had a hungry and resentful constituency to satisfy does not seem to have struck him as an important factor.

These shortcomings seem obvious now, but one has to remember that the same sort of view of the French Revolution had many faithful followers in Britain during Croker's lifetime, whose apprehensions were refreshed in 1830 and 1848 by further outbursts of 'the red fool-fury of the Seine'. Tories shared it with Whigs. Both were agreed that the French Revolution provided an argument against radical reform, by illustrating how unrestrained democracy led infallibly to confiscation of property and mob rule. But Tories tended to trace disaster from the earliest assaults on the monarchy. Whigs inclined to an argument in favour of moderate reform, the 'safety-valve' argument, that timely concessions would have averted the violence which was caused by a policy of no concessions, or concessions made too late to appease the demand. We have seen Macaulay use this argument, 'reform that you may preserve', in the debates of 1831. Applied to the French Revolution, it implied that sweeping changes had been needed to preserve monarchy and the old order and that these, originating in a general agreement amongst the political classes, had from unforeseen circumstances been allowed to swing out of control. This view at least had the merit of provoking the question how it was that the early promise of moderate reform had been frustrated. It granted that many men of large property and moderate opinions could have sincerely supported the original aims of the Revolution, and it led to an assessment of the different types of revolutionary leader who came to prominence after 1791, without in any way condoning the violence which led to the Terror.

Croker's view was more uncompromisingly hostile to the Revolution from its start. He agreed with Burke that there had been an ancient constitution in France which might have been revived, 'the outworks and the walls' which might have been built upon. But he was not prepared to admit any faults in the monarchy, and like Burke he traced its fall from the march of Parisian women to Versailles in early October 1789. The

King's arrest at Varennes was for him the pivotal event of the Revolution.[118] Thereafter chaos and violence were assured. Instead of allowing that the Revolution began with a period of constructive administrative and constitutional reform, he claims that fear of popular violence had been the ruling motive all along, from the Reveillon riots of April 1789 up to the Terror. Between the violence of the mob and the sufferings of the royal family, we hear very little of constitutional reform. Of course a series of critical reviews strung together in chronological order cannot be judged by the criteria one might apply to a general history. But there is surely something absurd in claiming that a moderate and pacific impulse to reform nevertheless produced the horrors and bloodshed of the Terror. If the path to orderly change was so plain, why did it lead to such anarchy? At the centre of Croker's account there is a sharp contradiction, between a blind complacency about the political health of the old order and an alert horror at the violence of the revolutionaries. It was only a little caricatured by Carlyle when he said that in explaining the Revolution Tories always claimed 'the universal insurrectionary abrogation of law and custom was managed in a most unlawful, uncustomary manner'.[119]

Carlyle and Mill both directed their criticism at Alison, whose broad, unreflective narrative was vulnerable. Croker was better informed, ventured less into general theories, and was severe on those who did. His attention to detail commands respect, but its remorselessly close focus makes the reader long for a more distant perspective which he never gets. There are few general views, of the country, the city, or of this or that institution to make the detail more intelligible and interesting. His method was better at negation than affirmation, but the negation was, no less than Alison's work, guided by a political message which younger readers and writers found more and more quaint. Having placed monarchy above criticism he could never have admitted that Marie Antoinette was anything less than a martyred saint, or Louis XVI anything worse than badly advised. He could never have understood the outlook of the leaders of the aristocratic revolt any more than he could set aside his distrust of Whig aristocrats like Russell. Nothing would have persuaded him to re-read Rousseau in the hope of understanding the outlook of Robespierre or Saint-Just. For him the Revolution remained a recent warning, because what had happened in France would, he thought, be replicated stage by stage in England. 'These things', he exclaims of the guillotined victims of the Committee of Public Safety, 'happened in our own time —thousands are still living who saw them'; and the sentence written in 1835 is retained in the revision of 1856.[120] Just as he was acute and efficient in dealing with everyday problems, but fearful and foreboding about the larger movements of his time, so in his historical researches he allowed new evidence to alter his perception of smaller matters, while his wider convictions about the imminence of revolution remained the same. Pessimism marked both the closer and the longer perspective, and it was a pessimism which survived the collapse of parliamentary radicalism and the Chartist movement and the emergence of England as the most stable country in Europe.

Later generations however, who had not known the war but only the order and prosperity which followed, wanted to understand the French Revolution less as a political lesson than as a process which belonged to a world removed from their own. They certainly did not want to apologize for the Terror and the Jacobin dictatorship: that would be the achievement of French academic historians of the Third Republic. But they wanted to be released from the intolerable association of mob rule and terror with progressive politics. A defence of the French Revolution as a democratic movement would not be acceptable. That was implicitly admitted by John Mill when he abandoned his idea of writing a radical history of the Revolution and passed on the task to Carlyle. But even Carlyle's vision of the 'smoke-and-flame conflagration' as he called it, was made acceptable to the Victorian public by being set in a framework of an avenging Providence; so that radicals could hardly derive much comfort from his picture of revolutionaries fulfilling a pre-ordained role of destruction, and moderate reformers had to swallow a good deal of abuse of the 'froth philosophy' of the Age of Reason and the futility of 'parliamentary eloquence'. Carlyle

---

[120] QR, liv, no. 108 (July 1835), 564; Essays, op. cit., 386.

allowed a generation of English readers oppressed by the French Revolution as politics to contemplate it as a work of art. But he did very little to further its study as a historical phenomenon because he said little to link it, and indeed much to separate it, from their everyday political conceptions.

Did Croker do more? I come back to my original question about those modern historians who have felt, without defining it very precisely, that he is a forerunner and in some sense an ally. Some features of Croker's historical writing do indeed seem to anticipate the methods of the modern academic historian. He was a close reader of original sources, and he always preferred the first-hand evidence of eye-witnesses to accounts based on rumour and hearsay, however vivid. He was very sceptical of the veracity of writers of memoirs and of historians who derived their conceptions of a period from them. He thought narratives of events inherently flawed, being compiled from recollections which were seldom verified from other evidence, and often made in response to pressures which favoured self-deception, evasion of responsibility, and sensationalism. Finally, he distrusted imaginative evocations of events and situations as akin to fiction, and disapproved of vivid narratives such as those by Thiers and Michelet for pandering to the debased taste of the general public. History was too serious a matter to be subjected to popular judgement. All these attitudes are to be found among professional historians today. Yet in Croker's case all are consequences of his political outlook and none is the product of any academic discipline. He went to the sources because he was a lawyer and an official, which also accounts for his stress on accuracy and consistency. He disliked memoirists and narrative historians not only because they falsified facts, but because their falsifications brought traditional authority into disrepute. He disliked the wider reading public in the same spirit and for the same reasons that he distrusted a wider suffrage. He thought the establishment of historical truth was an arcane proceeding to be conducted like an official inquiry, by informed people shielded if possible from the passions and interests of the ignorant rabble.

All this shows, not that Croker is a forerunner of the modern historian, but that he reached a comparable scepticism by a different route. Modern historians feel obliged to acknowledge their authorities—in footnotes, bibliographies, and so on—but in return for this trouble, they are privileged to withhold their own opinions; and the smaller their subject and the shorter the period they study, the more innocent such discretion will seem to their readers. The opinions may nevertheless be there, prejudicing the conclusions. Hundreds of history students of my generation thought Namier's studies of eighteenth century politics the acme of scholarly objectivity. Much later it transpired that his nostalgia for the landed aristocracy of eighteenth century England was the obverse of his contempt for the liberal and revolutionary intelligentsia of his own day. Croker does not parade his social prejudices, but he does make it clear that the events and actions he described carry moral lessons for his readers. The moral censure leaves little room for any consideration of social movements and the 'impersonal forces' underlying events. Indeed Croker would have thought 'the social interpretation' of the French revolution an elaborate apology for violence and crime.

In one crucial respect, his method marks him out from that of modern historians. We are now sharply aware of the dangers of anachronism, the imposing of our own values upon those of the past, and the insistence that we should judge the past in its own terms is derived from the idealist doctrine of the romantic era. In fact we now carry it into the realms of unreason, to the extent that some accounts of modern times make it seem that the human race has made no progress at all. Croker did not want to study the past for its own sake. He wanted to study it for its lessons for the present. Those lessons were nearly all negative. He did not deny that there had been improvements in the conditions of life. But he was too anxious about social order to want to make them, as Macaulay did, a central theme. Instead he wanted to keep alive a sense of the fragility of the social fabric, and to do this he stressed the factors which threatened it. Despite his own rise to respectability and affluence he remained the anxious, restless, rootless immigrant, who found a kind of luxury in the indulgence of pessimism, in using his sharp powers of observation and analysis to remind the ruling classes he admired and served how insecure the foundations of their authority were and how powerful the forces ranged against them. Hence the periodic donning of the garb of prophet. Croker was too self-conscious, too various in his interests, and too analytical to engage for long in jeremiads, but he certainly thought his study of the past enabled him to see further into the future than other men, and that his mission was to tell the politicians what he saw. He was part of 'the high tide of prophecy' now associated with Marx. He had however no talent for synthesis, no interest outside Britain and France, no great taste for abstract theory. With a little more *esprit de système* he might have been the English de Maistre. As it was, all his writing was critical, and all his critical acumen devoted to discrediting the interpreters. The last and greatest of these was Macaulay, but even there, Croker's critical bent was so habitual and his hatred of what he called 'embroidered sentimentalities' so deep-rooted, that he failed to see how much was deception and how much art.

7

Macaulay's Craftsmanship: Opening up the Narrative

What labour it is to make a tolerable book, and how little
readers know how much trouble the ordering of the parts
has cost the writer!
MACAULAY'S JOURNAL, 6 February 1854

I

Croker was not a historian by choice, but a critic whose method
conspired with his politics to sharpen his expertise in eighteenth
century history, both English and French. One could say the
historian in him developed out of the political critic, political events
in which he had an interest becoming history as they receded
into the past. Macaulay by contrast aimed to be a historian
from his late twenties, and politics were an interruption, at first
embraced with enthusiasm, but persevered in from duty and finally
abandoned with relief. His intentions as a historian are often taken
to have been openly political, but this common view is hard to
sustain in the light of his short political career, and the fact is
that his ideas about how history should be written were formed
before he went into politics. I have already questioned the received
opinion that his political career was that of an ardent and committed Whig. I now want to ask what his youthful conception
of the historian's task was, and how much of it survived his political experiences.

Macaulay himself may have encouraged the idea that his aims
as a historian, once formed, underwent little change. In 1841 he
told the essayist Leigh Hunt that when 'a young fellow' he had
been familiar with contemporary writing, but 'I was on a sudden
plunged into politics. I then went to India. Since my return I have
been engaged in politics again. My notions of contemporary

literature are what they were in 1828'.[1] It is worth asking what was special about 1828. As watersheds in his career one might have thought 1829, the year he attacked James Mill, or 1830, the year he entered parliament, would have been more appropriate. But Macaulay's memory was literary and the landmarks in his development were also literary. In 1828 he had been considering a history of England in the seventeenth century for the S.D.U.K.; he had written the essay simply called *History*; and this had been followed by the long review of Hallam's *Constitutional History* which had begun the rift with Brougham.[2] It was a year of speculation and projection, and the chronology suggests that the project for the S.D.U.K. provoked the reflections about conventional histories, classical models, and modern needs which make up the essay on history, while the Hallam review provided an occasion for estimating whether the ideas about historical writing for a modern readership could be combined with exact scholarly standards, as well as a sketch for a history of England from 1760, where Hallam stopped, until his own day. Plainly Macaulay was thinking about *a* history. Indeed, these early reflections on history are so intensely felt and raise so many questions about the historians' task that they can hardly fail to be read as a prospectus of some kind for the *History of England*. They also help explain his early disenchantment with political life, and why he was to call it 'that closely watched slavery which is mocked with the name of power'.[3] Reading them one is again struck by the fact that Macaulay was not one of those politicians whose education culminates predictably in a political career. Rather, politics was a spring frost which delayed the flowering of his literary ambition. The question for us is, how much these early plans were followed out in the *History of England*. Did Macaulay on his return from India take up his youthful scheme unaltered, or did he adapt it in the light of his experience of politics?

Macaulay's essay on history is his only extended statement of his views about the historian's task. But he did not reprint it,

---

[1] *LM*, iii. 367.
[2] Ibid., i. 322; *MW* i. 233–81; *CHE*, i. 113, 216. Selina Macaulay found the 'History' essay 'in some parts rather abstruse': it was read aloud on 2 Feb. 1828 (Selina Macaulay's journal, unfol., Huntington Lib.).
[3] *CHE*, iii. 2.

and it seems more likely that this was because he thought it too crude than because he repudiated it altogether. Three features of it are relevant to his mature work.

The first is that Macaulay's literary models are largely classical: Herodotus, Thucydides, and Xenophon from the Greeks; Livy, Sallust, and Tacitus from the Romans. It is noticeable that he does not mention any writers of the Whig tradition, such as might have been formative influences on the founders of the *Edinburgh Review*, like William Robertson, Adam Smith, and John Millar. The only modern writers mentioned at any length are rather anti-Whig: David Hume, whose *History of England* set out to undermine certain whiggish doctrines, and William Mitford, a Tory whose *History of Greece* was intended to protect his countrymen from the contagion of classical republican ideas during the period of the French Revolution. But even these two are said to have the modern vice of 'distorting narrative into conformity with a theory'.[4] Macaulay is not making a party-political point here. He is explaining why historical writing has become so abstract and impersonal in his own time. Hume and Mitford were polemicists in a century which had developed the generalizing habit at the expense of the imagination. How had this habit been formed? Macaulay explains why the great classical models of historical writing had come to be superseded. The Roman Empire had collapsed in the terrible scourge of the barbarian invasions, but the chaos which followed had at least ensured that the culture which emerged had linguistic variety. 'It cost Europe a thousand years of barbarism to escape the fate of China'.[5] Scientific progress had been encouraged in a Europe united as 'a great federal community' by 'the easy ties of international law and a common religion', and the historians of this era of scientific and philosophical advance had been more interested in the features common to states than those which distinguished them from one another. Hence the general truths had occupied them more than the local details. Macaulay mentions no examples here, but it seems that he has in mind the historiography of writers like Robertson and Millar, whose concern was general trends, 'the progress of the human mind', studied from the comfort of a university chair. But it is noticeable that

---

[4] *MW*, i. 272.   [5] Ibid., i. 268.

Macaulay is impatient of its bland liberalism. He wants the historian to be wider in his sympathies and more curious about life as lived by ordinary men and women. He wants him to have a wider appeal.

This brings us to the second feature, a rather romantic one, Macaulay's claim that the major changes that have taken place in the history of mankind have been 'noiseless revolutions'.

The circumstances which have most influence on the happiness of mankind, the changes of manners and morals, the transition of communities from poverty to wealth, from knowledge to ignorance, from ferocity to humanity—these are, for the most part, noiseless revolutions. Their progress is rarely indicated by what historians are pleased to call important events. They are not achieved by armies, or enacted by senates. They are sanctioned by no treaties, and recorded in no archives. They are carried on in every school, in every church, behind ten thousand counters, at ten thousand firesides. The upper current of society presents no certain criterion by which we can judge of the direction in which the undercurrent flows. We read of defeats and victories. But we know that nations may be miserable amidst victories and prosperous amidst defeats. We read of the fall of wise ministers and of the rise of profligate favourites. But we must remember how small a proportion the good and evil effected by a single statesman can bear to the good or evil of a great social system.[6]

One could find similar assertions in other European writers of the same period. In France, there was a feeling that the revolutionary and Napoleonic era had produced such tremendous changes, accelerating the process of learning from the past and widening the relevance of its lessons, that the old histories had become stale and trite.[7] In Britain, political changes had been less shattering, and all classes had rallied to the defence of traditional institutions in a way which makes Croker's conservatism less extravagant than has been supposed. But even in Britain, it was a stock radical theme, that the common people who made the wealth should have a place in the history books alongside the great names that spent or squandered it. Macaulay shared this radical impatience with traditional political history, but his

[6] Ibid., i. 275.

[7] S. Mellon, *The Political Uses of History* (Stanford, Calif., 1958) ch. 2. Namier once said that in times of political disillusionment, men yearn for 'symphonies not arias'. 'The Biography of Ordinary Men' in *Crossroads of Power* (1962) 2.

stress is more cosmopolitan than democratic. What he objects
to in the traditional historical writing about kings and queens
and their courts is not its omission of the common man but its
indifference to the national culture. In the great federal community which was Europe, the 'balance of moral and intellectual
influence' between the nations was 'far more important than the
balance of political power.'[8] He is more interested in the differences between nations than the antagonisms of classes within one
nation, and when he urges the historian to pay less attention
to 'the surface of affairs' and more to 'the mighty and various
organisation which lies deep below',[9] he is really thinking of the
changes wrought by unsophisticated people which usually leave
their mark in literature. This is amplified in the essay on John
Dryden written in the same year. As people become more critical, the conventional forms ossify and are replaced by new
and more popular ones. 'The few great works of imagination
which appear in a critical age are, almost without exception,
the works of uneducated men.'[10] He instances Bunyan, Burns,
and the plays of Shakespeare. These were revolutions in literature and taste, not upheavals in society.

   The third notable feature of the essay is that in conveying vividly
and memorably these noiseless revolutions in society, Macaulay
recommends that the historian take a lesson from the master of
'historical romance' Sir Walter Scott.

At Lincoln Cathedral there is a beautiful painted window, which was
made by an apprentice out of the pieces of glass which had been rejected
by his master. It is so far superior to every other in the church, that,
according to the tradition, the vanquished artist killed himself from
mortification. Sir Walter Scott, in the same manner, has used those fragments of truth which historians have scornfully thrown behind them
in a manner which may well excite their envy. He has constructed out
of their gleanings works which, even considered as histories, are
scarcely less valuable than theirs. But a truly great historian would reclaim
those materials which the novelist has appropriated. The history of the
government, and the history of the people, would be exhibited in
that mode in which alone they can be exhibited justly, in inseparable
conjunction and intermixture.[11]

---

[8] *MW*, i. 268–9.   [9] Ibid., i. 275.
[10] Ibid., i. 202.   [11] Ibid., i. 278.

This passage, and others like it, have encouraged the idea that Macaulay set out to copy Scott's narrative method, and Macaulay's famous remark that he hoped his *History* would 'for a few days supersede the last fashionable novel on the tables of young ladies'[12] is often quoted as proof of this influence. One eminent critic, George Levine, deciding that by 'supersede' Macaulay meant 'replace' and not 'dislodge', has even claimed that he set out 'to create a work like a novel'.[13] This would seem rather an absurd claim, but for the fact that, in the course of the nineteenth century, novelists did attempt to set their plots in wider social and historical contexts, often carefully researched, so that, while the *History of England* might seem to owe little to *Rob Roy*, it does seem to have more affinities with *Vanity Fair*. One might think this was due to the fact that Macaulay and Thackeray were responding to the same changes in the Victorian readership. But for Levine, the literary inspiration is all. The social detail of Macaulay's *History of England* derives, he says, from 'the realistic aesthetic of the mid-century novel'.[14]

A close reading of the essay *History* however shows that Macaulay was rather careful to distinguish between the methods of the novelist and the historian. What he wants the historian to do is to 'reclaim those materials which the novelist has appropriated'. The point is made again, with a sharper antithesis, in *Hallam*. 'Good histories, in the proper sense of the word, we have not. But we have good historical romances, and good historical essays.' The novelist, he goes on, has taken over the historian's duty 'to call up our ancestors before us with all their peculiarities of language, manners, and garb, to show us over their houses, to seat us at their tables, to rummage their old-fashioned wardrobes, to explain the uses of their ponderous furniture';[15] whereas the duty of generalizing, tracing causes and effects and drawing out 'general lessons of moral and political wisdom' has passed to another class of writers. Who are they? One feels that Macaulay might have named the political economists, but he does not. But it is plain that what he likes in Hallam is the fact that he brings a critical eye and greater

---

[12] *LM*, iv. 15.

[13] G. Levine, *The Boundaries of Fiction: Carlyle, Macaulay, Newman* (Princeton N.J., 1968), 118.

[14] Ibid., 121.   [15] *CHE*, i. 113–14.

documentary evidence to the same periods portrayed in fiction by Scott. What is needed for the reclamation is that such scholarly accuracy should be blended with an accessible and vivid style. In his later review of Mackintosh he finds, amongst some careless writing, a passage with 'the diligence, the accuracy, and the judgment of Hallam, united to the vivacity and the colouring of Southey'.[16] These remarks suggest a man looking out for examples to help define and confirm his own historiographical conception in which accuracy and vividness would be combined. But in the essay on *History* already it is plain he thinks his conception more truthful than what currently passes for historical writing, because it would bridge the gap between the daily preoccupations of ordinary people and the inflated claims to fame of monarchs, ministers, and generals. Since revolutions in literary and artistic taste precede the political changes and to a large extent shape them, it is the conventional mode of writing history that is false, indeed fictitious.

In *History* Macaulay writes of the novelist in a spirit of rivalry rather than of imitation, as if the prospect of writing a volume for the S.D.U.K. presented a challenge, that of making a history which was truly popular. He was probably thinking of the readership yet to be enfranchised, a group still the object of apprehension and alarm; certainly not of the complacent and prosperous voter who had seen off the Chartists twenty years later. To the ordinary intelligent reader the obvious difference between the novelist's and the historian's task is that the one invents a story to tell and the other tells one which actually happened. Macaulay asks why a true story should not be as interesting as a fiction. 'He who can invent a story, and tell it well, will also be able to tell, in an interesting manner, a story which he has not invented'.[17] Of course, he cannot include every detail, any more than a painter does. He must select the characteristic features, 'such parts of the truth as most nearly produce the effect of the whole'.[18] But the picture he conveys is more instructive than fiction. We go to novels, Macaulay argues, to confirm our expectations of human nature. They tell us nothing new. In fact we think less of them if they offer characters in actions which we find implausible. History, on the contrary, offers us information

---

[16] *MW*, i. 279.   [17] *MW*, i. 240.   [18] Ibid., i. 242.

that is unexpected. That is its attraction. 'Hence it is . . . that what is called the romantic part of history is in fact the least romantic. It is delightful as history, because it contradicts our previous notions of human nature, and of the connection of causes and effects. It is, on that very account, shocking and incongruous in fiction. In fiction, the principles are given, to find the facts: in history, the facts are given, to find the principles; and the writer who does not explain the phenomena as well as state them performs only one half of his office.'[19]

Of course Macaulay wanted history to convey the truth, but the parallel with the fine arts enables him to see more truth in a clever caricature than in a representational painting. He sees that the caricature can convey the required message with more economy. 'An outline scrawled with a pen, which seizes the marked features of a countenance, will give a much stronger idea of it than a bad painting in oils. Yet the worst painting in oils that ever hung at Somerset House resembles the original in many more particulars.' Warming to the comparison with painting, he says the historian must observe the rules of perspective like the landscape painter.

History has its foreground and its background: and it is principally in the management of its perspective that one artist differs from another. Some events must be represented on a large scale, others diminished; the great majority will be lost in the dimness of the horizon; and a general idea of their joint effect will be given by a few slight touches.[20]

To Macaulay the master of this technique is not a novelist, but a historian, Thucydides.

There is a second difference between novelist and historian which is particularly relevant to those who think Macaulay's taste for fiction diminishes his seriousness as a historian. The novelist can succeed by telling only a story. Provided his characters are plausible, he need not concern himself with 'background'; social and historical detail can be assumed rather than elaborately described. If the stress is on the story, in fact, too many of these details are liable to be distracting. Scott held the balance in novels like *Old Mortality* and *The Heart of Midlothian*; but to the extent that, for instance, Henry Morton or Jeanie Deans

<hr>

[19] Ibid., i. 244.   [20] Ibid., i. 242.

hold the interest of the reader, the historical scenery is only a device for creating the illusion that they really lived.[21] Real historic characters in Scott's novels, like the Young Pretender or the Duke of Argyle may exercise a remote and unexplored influence over the lives of the fictitious characters, but they do not need to be carefully or faithfully drawn, because the centre of attention is the fictitious narrative. In contrast, the historian as narrator has much less freedom. He cannot fabricate a plot, and in the material he uses, the historic characters traditionally credited with most influence and power will normally loom much larger than the common people. Every historian who attempts to tell 'the story' finds his curiosity gravitating to wielders of power because they tend to leave the fullest records.

To this familiar problem, Macaulay's argument in the essay on history adds a further, modern difficulty which he shares with other historians who came to maturity after the revolutionary wars. His theory of 'noiseless revolutions' commits him to the view that the major changes in the historic past are social and cultural rather than political, and this means (at least in the way he formulates the problem in 1828) that while he must feel sceptical about the significance traditionally given to battles and treaties, he must look for the major changes in areas and types of evidence until then regarded as too humble for 'the dignity of history'.[22] Whether he is aware of it or not, Macaulay is in effect demanding that his ideal historian-artist should take up a vast canvas, and attempt on it a landscape in which there will be room for a huge variety of people and incidents. He seems to be envisaging a history on the scale of Tolstoy's *War and Peace* or Hugo's *Les Misérables*, a generation in advance of those works, and with the extra handicap that he must describe only what really happened and people who actually lived. There *is* a parallel with the historical novel as it developed by the mid-nineteenth century, but the difference between them is crucial. It was well expressed by Firth, 'Instead of using facts of history to make fiction seem true, as a novelist does, he uses fiction to

---

[21] I am aware that Jeanie Deans is based on a real character, Helen Walker, but my point is that Scott's version of her character is his own invention. See John Sutherland, *The Life of Walter Scott: A Critical Biography* (Oxford, 1995), 211–19.

[22] *CHE*, iii. 18.

make historical events seem more real and less remote'.[23] The novelists were to use history to make fictional events seem more plausible. Macaulay wants to use the methods of fiction and, one might add, drama, to help his readers see actual events more vividly.

It is noticeable in the 1828 essay that, in proposing to describe the events of the past with, so to speak, a cast of thousands, Macaulay has little use for theory, whether in the form of a philosophy of history or of laws of social development, both of which have offered historians ways of passing rapidly over long periods or summarizing as general trends the activities of large numbers of individuals. It is true that he has a breezy confidence in the progress of society. But he seems reluctant to assign this to any one set of causes. His reasons are more literary than philosophical. He wants to hold the reader's attention. He grants that history is philosophy teaching by example, but he adds that 'what the philosophy gains in soundness and depth the examples generally lose in vividness'; and one of the precepts his perfect historian must observe is that he 'possess sufficient self-command to abstain from casting his facts in the mould of his hypothesis'.[24] At the end of the essay, after a glowing evocation of how English history might be written in the new way, Macaulay says that such a history would convey instruction 'of a vivid and practical character. It would be received by the imagination as well as by the reason. It would be not merely traced on the mind, but branded on to it.'[25] In other words, the more vividly the events are described the more memorable would be the lessons taught. The whole conception is infused with a confidence in the power of literary art applied to historic fact. He is still a little naïve about the colourfulness and allure of what survives in historic documents: no inkling here of what the Age of Chivalry would be reduced to on the long road from Scott and Tennyson to Stubbs and Tout. He is also still inclined to sentimentalize the life of ordinary people and to exaggerate their capacity to sustain an interest in the history of past societies. But he is, as always, acute on the shortcomings of contemporary history as literature, and his knowledge of European languages

---

[23] C. Firth, *Commentary on Macaulay's History of England* (ed. Godrey Davies, 1938), 110–11.

[24] *MW*, i. 233.   [25] Ibid., i. 280.

already gives him access to the literatures of Europe and a range of cultural reference which does not come easily to the archive-based historian. He knew that a new readership had come into being which demanded a richer, more colourful and less parochial idea of its past, and he knew he could supply it.

In relegating theory to a secondary role in historical explanation, one which follows a narrative of events, Macaulay anticipated his own critique of James Mill's *a priori* method the following year. It is entirely characteristic of his mind that he should first object to theory on literary and rhetorical grounds, and only later broaden his objection into an attack on deduction as a method in the social sciences. His real allegiance is to art; to science he pays only lip-service. It is as if he felt intuitively that if the historian approached the past too possessed by his theory, his narrative would lose its immediacy and dramatic suspense, the reader would be given a general sense of what was likely to happen next, and all his interest in the characters in the story would be dissipated. But Macaulay was quite capable of writing polemic soon after in a contrary sense. When John Mill read Macaulay's attack on his father's deductive method he saw at once that it could not apply to political economy. The economist's method was to assume certain propensities of human nature as if they were universal, not because any political economist thought they really were so, but because abstracting a general propensity from particular situations was the only way the science could proceed.[26] Macaulay not only failed to square his defence of induction with political economy: in his polemic against Southey in January 1830, he used the economists' arguments against Southey's pessimistic assessment of industrialism. To the poet's sensitive forebodings about the deteriorating conditions of work, he opposed his own confidence in 'those general laws which it has pleased [the Supreme Being] to establish in the physical and in the moral world'. He went on: 'We rely on the natural tendency of the human intellect to truth, and on the natural tendency of society to improvement.'[27] Admirers of Macaulay have been reluctant to call such oscillations by the right name, but it is surely time to do so. In these early articles in the *Edinburgh* he is essentially a rhetorician. He has the

---

[26] *Collected Works*, ed. J. A. Robson et al., iv. 321–2.   [27] *CHE*, i. 265.

debater's want of scruple about where his arguments come from, and he is a master at burlesquing and misrepresenting those of his opponents. What he adds from his own store is based on his prodigious memory. From the attack on Mill to that on Gladstone, his stock weapon is a *reductio ad absurdum* backed with an intimidating array of examples, imaginary or historical. The opponent's position is first described, not always accurately but very clearly and forcefully; then it is examined for its practical implications, and usually it is parodied and ridiculed, with contrary examples piling up to indicate that the bulk of mankind simply could not go on as they do if the views in question gained currency. The critic implies that he represents the solid commonsense of the majority, and as separate instances of folly are held up for him, the reader is likely to enjoy the mockery. But the enjoyment ends with the performance. Taken together, the polemical articles leave a rather confused picture of Macaulay's general outlook and an uneasy sense that the enemy's positions have not been taken, so much as impetuously overrun; that one has been witnessing a spectacular display of fireworks, but not a real conflict. Though Macaulay ridicules the utilitarian, he remains a utilitarian. Though he mocks Southey's sentimentality, he remains, under the hard mockery, very much a sentimentalist. He actually resembles his own account, in the essay on Southey, of the way Burke thought and wrote: 'His reason, like a spirit in the service of an enchanter, though spell-bound, was still mighty. It did whatever work his passions and his imagination might impose'.[28] The only completely consistent position for so restlessly rhetorical a talent is the avoidance of controversy altogether. And this is why I now need to qualify the picture I gave of Macaulay's strictly political development in Chapter 5. Outwardly he undergoes a swing to the right. Inwardly it is more like a growing taste for tranquillity, a flagging of the aggressive urge, a softening of censoriousness, what John Burrow calls 'a voice modulating from strident to sonorous'.[29]

The important point is that for Macaulay literature was always a more urgent and absorbing activity than politics, and

[28] Ibid., 219.
[29] J. W. Burrow, *A Liberal Descent: Victorian Historians and the English Past* (Cambridge, 1981), 38.

those who think that he subordinated his writing to his political loyalties misunderstand his original purpose. There can be no doubt that after 1832 his politics became more moderate: that is, the oscillations between radical hostility to aristocratic government and Burkean fears of disorder become less extreme. But he never became so absorbed in politics as to allow it, consciously at least, to dominate his inner life, even though he did become a liberal minister and spoke for his government in that role. He continued to cherish his vision of a new form of historical writing, and if he was diffident about his capacity to realize it, he became more and more convinced that a political career would be fatal to it. What he proposed to write would transcend the temporary and superficial concerns of contemporary conflict. It would have a wide appeal, but its argument would rest on accurate scholarship, presenting events as they occurred, and undistorted by political or philosophical preconceptions. It would be inductive in its method, in the sense that all knowledge solidly gained was gained that way. But readers would be so brought into the presence of the people and events of the past that they could, like contemporary spectators, draw their own conclusions. They would not be led by the nose to adopt this or that theory, whether of human nature or of social change. Instead, they would see unfolded the process which had made them what they were, as they might on a great panoramic canvas painted by a master hand.

II

Macaulay's political career both sustained and threatened this ideal. In one sense his reputation was political. It was parliament which had given him a station from which he could look down on the hacks of Grub Street who lived by their pens, as if he did not do the same. It also gave him the respectability and the contacts which he valued and which his father's misfortunes had once threatened to take away altogether. He would have liked most of all to be an MP of independent means like Grote or Milnes. But he needed a salary, and that meant office, and with it the drudgery and the compromises of carrying legislation through parliament, tasks of which he had seen enough in his short career to realize that they spelt an end to his independence and his literary hopes. Even the lucrative Indian exile was not security enough, for it marked him out as ministerial material. He must eventually be invited to join a ministry, and then how could he, with his record as orator and administrator, refuse? Some colourful rhetoric against a parliamentary career shows his awareness of this. Addison and Gibbon had been almost silent members of parliament, yet had achieved more enduring fame than their more vocal contemporaries. Listing the parliamentary orators of Gibbon's day, he asked, 'Who would give the worst chapter of the Decline and Fall for all that is extant of their eloquence?'[30] He calls political office an 'intolerable thraldom' to which he would never submit.[31] But he knew some political role was inevitable, and he tried to have it on his own terms. Did he succeed? Did the original vision survive his contact with politics?

In the narrow party sense of politics, it did. Macaulay never wrote as an apologist for the Whig *party*. It is commonly held that he extended and popularized an existing Whig tradition of historical writing, but even this needs qualification. There was a Whig historical tradition, of which Macaulay was well aware, but it was ambivalent and widely scorned, and he did not identify with it. It was primarily Foxite, and at its core was a contractualist interpretation of the Revolution of 1688, according to which the Whigs were essentially the party which opposed monarchy and sought to preserve and extend the power of parliament. George III's treatment of the Whig leadership in the first decades of his reign had given a new lease of life to the notion of a royal plot against the constitution, and in Macaulay's youth Whigs had found solace for their long exclusion from power in the belief that William Pitt and his followers had given way to the monarch's plans for arbitrary rule in order to keep themselves in office. A theory which is three parts jealousy and one part fact is hard to treat seriously as an interpretation of history, and it would be easy to present Foxite Whiggism as essentially the collective grievance of a coterie of borough-owners united more by marriage and social habit than by philosophical conviction. But there *is* a thin pamphlet literature contending rather

---

[30] *LM*, iii. 220; cf. *CHE*, ii. 431. 'It is not by accuracy or profundity that men become the masters of great assemblies'.

[31] Journal, 10 Nov. 1838, fos. 94–5.

feebly against some powerful critics. Most notable of these was Hume's *History of England*, with its open scepticism about the contractual theory of government and its chivalrous sympathy for the House of Stuart.[32] Hume was supported by a Scottish lawyer, Sir John Dalrymple, whose transcriptions of the correspondence of Barillon, Louis XIV's ambassador at the courts of Charles II and James II, seemed to throw discredit on the first Whigs, the Exclusionists, who had opposed the succession of James to his brother's throne.[33] Fox himself was convinced that Dalrymple's work involved forgery, and at the Peace of Amiens, he sought the permission of the First Consul to consult the originals. This unwonted excursion into historical scholarship did nothing for his reputation as a reliable politician, and the *History of James II* remained unfinished. But in any case, at his death Fox was a leader only of a fragment of the Whig party. The majority had followed Burke in his denial that there was any similarity between the English Revolution of 1688 and the French of 1789. Croker was not alone in his reverence for Burke as an interpreter of the 1688 Revolution. In the Holland House circle there was no more fervent admirer of Burke than Sir James Mackintosh, and it is to his influence on Macaulay that we must look for any sign of conversion to the Whig historical outlook.

Macaulay did not enter Holland House till 1831, and by then he had already written the long review of Hallam, which if it did nothing else would show that he did not merely take up the task where Mackintosh had left off. Hallam is often taken as Macaulay's predecessor in the Whig tradition, and Macaulay's review as a confirmation of this. Actually Hallam was an independent gentleman without political connections, and by 1828 his views were very moderate indeed. He approved of the transfer of the seats of the corrupt boroughs Penryn and East Retford to industrial cities, but he was appalled at the sweeping nature of the Reform Bill when it was announced, and thought it would upset the balance of the constitution.[34] He ended the

[32] The fullest study is by Duncan Forbes, *Hume's Philosophical Politics* (1975); especially chs. 5 and 8. See also, Burrow, *A Liberal Descent*, op. cit., 25–35.

[33] *Memoirs of Great Britain and Ireland*, 2 vols. (1771–73).

[34] He corresponded with both Macaulay and Croker. Hallam MSS, Ch.Ch. vol. 16, fos. 49–52, 192, 126, 322.

Constitutional History in 1760 with the death of George II, so these opinions may not have been apparent to his reviewer. What Macaulay cannot have missed however was Hallam's distaste for what he called 'the unstable prejudices of the multitude'.[35] The review attacks Hallam's interpretation of the Civil War and Commonwealth, and if its estimate of Cromwell is a good deal less ardent in praise of Puritanism than the essay on Milton, it is severe on Hallam's excuses for the Stuarts, calls the reign of Charles II 'that wild and monstrous harlequinade' and has nothing good to say of the early leaders of the Whig party. Party strife, says Macaulay, always leads to 'an indifference to the general welfare and honour of the State'. He denies any credit is due to the makers of the Glorious Revolution:

Through the whole transaction no commanding talents were displayed by any Englishman; no extraordinary risks were run; no sacrifices were made for the deliverance of the nation, except the sacrifice which Churchill made of honour, and Anne of natural affection.[36]

The review ends with a sweeping interpretation of English politics since 1760 which is in effect an argument for the radical reform which would enfranchise 'the whole of the middle class, that brave, honest and sound-hearted class, which is as anxious for the maintenance of order and the security of property, as it is hostile to corruption and oppression'.[37] Macaulay may have been thinking of his own projected history of the seventeenth century for the S.D.U.K., but he turned the review into a radical polemic.

Six years later, Macaulay reviewed Mackintosh's unfinished fragment *A History of the Revolution in England, in 1688*. By this time he was familiar with the conversation at Holland House, and could write with a proper reverence of 'Mr Fox' and with real affection for Mackintosh.[38] Indeed, in the original

[35] *Constitutional History*, iii. 230, quoted by Timothy Lang, *The Victorians and the Stuart Heritage: Interpretations of a Discordant Past* (Cambridge, 1995), 48–9. Macaulay recorded Hallam's glee at the Melbourne Ministry's resignation on 7 May 1839. 'He talked of the utter downfall of the Whigs. They will never, he sᵈ, hold up their heads again. They are dead men,—buried etc. I listened and disbelieved him.' (*Journal*, i. fo. 387).

[36] *CHE*, i. 190, 197, 202.   [37] Ibid., 215.

[38] *CHE*, ii. 201–2. To Hannah he mentioned Fox's *History* as one of 'the books written by public men of note' which were 'generally rated at more than their real value'. *LM*, ii. 288.

review he was so severe on Mackintosh's biographer Wallace, that he received a challenge (from which he was luckily extricated) on his return from India. But his view of the Revolution of 1688, though much more favourable than in the Hallam, was still the bi-partisan view, of Mackintosh and of Burke. Macaulay agreed that James II had offended both parties, and that the coalition which offered William III the throne could not have survived had William not been above party. The Revolution, Macaulay insisted, made sure that 'doctrines favourable to public liberty' were thereafter shared by the Whigs in power and by their Tory opponents.[39] There is not much Whig party-feeling in this review of Mackintosh. Macaulay's treatment of party is quite compatible with his private resolve to go to India to escape party contention. In fact, there is a weariness about his account of 'the flux and reflux' of the strife of party during the period 1660–1688 which suggests that he was glad to be out of politics altogether.

He went quite determined to retain some literary interests as a refuge from his legal work. He took a library of Greek, Latin, Spanish, French, and Italian classics. On arriving in Calcutta, he sent home his article on Mackintosh, but he also began what were to become the *Lays of Ancient Rome*. This illustrates a dual allegiance, utilitarian and romantic. The jurist who was to compile a legal code in his office hours, wrote heroic songs of Republican Rome in the manner of Scott when he relaxed.

The article on Mackintosh contains a passage on James Mill's *History of British India* which proclaims Macaulay's reforming credentials. He did not apologize for his attack on Mill's *Essay on Government*. He repeated his view that its method was wrong. But he said that in the *History* Mill had used a different method, with eminent ability and success.

We know no writer who takes so much pleasure in the truly useful, noble, and philosophical employment of tracing the progress of sound opinions from their embryo state to their full maturity. He eagerly culls from old despatches and minutes every expression in which he can discern the imperfect germ of any great truth which has since been fully developed. He never fails to bestow praise on those who, though far from coming up to his standard of perfection, yet rose in a small degree

[39] *CHE*, ii. 265, 277.

above the common level of their contemporaries. It is thus that the annals of past times ought to be written. It is thus, especially, that the annals of our own country ought to be written.

In the passage which follows we read a brief preview of the *History of England*, a sketch of the various struggles between progressives and their opponents, from Domesday Book to the Reform Bill which, Macaulay declares, makes English history the story of the change in 'the moral, the intellectual, and physical state of the inhabitants of our own island', rendering them 'the greatest and most highly civilized people that ever the world saw'.[40] What is odd about this passage is not its novelty, for it is characteristic of Macaulay's eloquence, but its apparent derivation from the doctrinaire puritanism of Mill. I said in Chapter 5 that his stay in India made Macaulay stress the authoritarian, interventionist aspect of utilitarian doctrine. Perhaps as interesting, and certainly less explored, is the impact of Mill's *History* on Macaulay the historian.

Mill's *History of British India* is a forgotten classic, and what helped it into oblivion was the success of the grand narrative style which Macaulay first perfected. So it seems on the face of it highly improbable that Macaulay owed Mill anything at all. Even late Victorian historians of the utilitarian movement were hardly aware of Mill's major work, though it underpinned much of the social thought of his more famous son. Leslie Stephen ignored it, and the great French positivist historian Élie Halévy seriously underrated the whole Scottish tradition of philosophical history of which James Mill was the last major exponent.[41] Mill was faithful to his Scottish predecessors in holding that all societies advance through a series of progressively more civilized states. His contribution was the assertion that each state was marked out from its predecessor by a more complete recognition and application of the principle of utility. He had no patience with the

[40] Ibid., 226–7.
[41] L. Stephen, *The English Utilitarians* 3 vols. (1900) ii. 23–4; E. Halévy, *The Growth of Philosophic Radicalism*, trans. Mary Morris (London, 1928). I sought to correct this in my selections from James Mill's *History of British India* (Chicago and London, 1975). For my complaint about Halévy, see my 'L'Utilitarisme et le liberalisme anglais au début du XIXe siècle' in Mulligan K. and Roth, R. *Regards sur Bentham*, vol. 4 of *Recherches et Rencontres: Publications de la Faculté des lettres de Genève* (Geneva, 1993), 39–58.

errors of past epochs, no inclination to study them for their own sake, and so his approach is the very antithesis of the romantic nostalgia which prefers the past to the present. Mill was very severe on those admirers of oriental cultures (notably Burke) who pointed to great architecture and intricate craftsmanship as signs of an advanced civilization, for, he said, the test of worth was the degree to which any artistic achievement was directed to the happiness of mankind. 'Exactly in proportion as Utility is the object of every pursuit, may we regard a nation as civilized. Exactly in proportion as its ingenuity is wasted on contemptible or mischievous subjects, though it may be, in itself, an ingenuity of no ordinary kind, the nation may be denominated barbarous'.[42] So, for instance, it was no great credit to the Hindus that they had invented the game of chess, for they can only have been seeking to relieve 'the pain of idleness'.[43] Mill is quite clear why Samarkand was a fine city: 'the streets were paved, and water was conveyed into the city by leaden pipes'.[44] He uses utility as a two-edged tool. Various instances of technological backwardness prove the Hindus to be at a very low level of civilization, that of the Chaldeans or Babylonians in the Old Testament. But if they do show some ingenuity, as in astronomy, or fine weaving, or great poetry, then he denies that these are essential to an advanced civilization.

For Mill the main failing of British administration in India was the idea that the inhabitants should be governed by their own legal traditions, for this meant that the resources of an advanced culture were being devoted to fostering and perpetuating the worst faults of a backward one. Hence his hostility to Sir William Jones and his followers the Orientalists. Jones is the villain of Mill's *History of British India* hardly less than James II is of Macaulay's *History of England*. Mill was not at all impressed, as posterity has been, with Jones's philological learning, and the affinities which Jones saw between Sanskrit and European languages left him cold. He thought the richness of Sanskrit, which delighted Jones, was actually a defect, since 'a perfect philosophical language would have one word for each object, and no more'.[45] As for poetry, that was essentially the

---

[42] James Mill, *History of British India* 3 vols. (1817), i. 432.
[43] Ibid., i. 360.   [44] Ibid., i. 626–7.   [45] Ibid., i. 391.

expression of a primitive society, since 'men feel before they speculate'. So Jones's translations from Sanskrit did nothing to prove the Orientalists' case for patronizing the native languages.

We have seen that in his official work, Macaulay subscribed to this doctrine, and that nothing in his experience in India led him to question it. But in another sense he was (without perhaps being aware of the debt) the inheritor of a tradition to which Jones had largely contributed. In Germany, Jones's work had had a huge appeal.[46] There, philological research was not inhibited, as it was in Britain, by an abstract theory of perception; indeed the idea that a language was the authentic record, dating from before formal historical writing, of a people's life, even of a national soul, had an obvious political appeal. In Britain, political unification followed by imperial success made the linguistic minorities eager to adopt the metropolitan culture. Scots like the Mills and Macaulays sank their provincial loyalties in a common unity. Macaulay takes pride in the achievements of the English, not the British. In Germany, political disunity and disintegration made men like Herder and Friedrich Schlegel hanker after a deeper unity, in which a common language had a stronger appeal than laws made for them and boundaries imposed upon them by foreign conquerors. Hence Jones's work had more significance for German scholars than it had in England.

Macaulay was aware of German influences both in poetry and classical scholarship. It was in response to German models that Scott was led to compile his *Minstrelsy of the Scottish Border*, and in so far as he was an admirer of Scott, Macaulay was certainly touched by the themes of cultural nationalism. But his enthusiasm for Scott was, as we saw in the essay on *History*, tempered by a scholarly purpose. If the *Lays of Ancient Rome* take their inspiration from Scott's work with popular poetry, their academic content is indebted to the historian Barthold Niebuhr.[47] The great medieval epic, the *Niebelungenlied*, as Macaulay noted, was for Niebuhr what the border ballads were for Scott; but whereas Scott freely adapted and embroidered the

---

[46] H. Aarsleff, *The Study of Language in England 1788–1860* (Princeton, N.J., 1967). See ch. 4, esp. 141.

[47] See H. R. Trevor-Roper's *The Romantic Movement and the Study of History* (1961). Macaulay did not borrow from Scott's metres: he claimed his verse was based on the Saturnian measure. *Lays of Ancient Rome*, (1870 edn.), 19 note.

legends for a popular readership in such poems as *Marmion* and *The Lay of the Last Minstrel*, Niebuhr used the German poem to develop a serious scholarly hypothesis about Roman history.[48] He suggested that earlier books of Livy's *History* took the form they did because they had been transcribed from oral poetry which, unlike the *Niebelungenlied*, had not survived. Niebuhr's *History of Rome* was translated by two of Macaulay's Trinity contemporaries, J. C. Hare and Connop Thirlwall, and published in that important year, 1828. Macaulay's *Lays* are a working out of Niebuhr's hypothesis, an attempt to reconstruct for English readers the ballads which it held Livy had rendered into prose narratives before they were irretrievably lost.

Taken together, as scholarship and as poetry, the *Lays of Ancient Rome* illustrate very well Macaulay's dual allegiance. On the one hand they embody the utilitarian view of the historic function of poetry. If, as men progressed in scientific knowledge, they made 'better theories and worse poems', because poetry was the characteristic expression of a pre-scientific age, then all a modern poet could hope to produce was an imitation of the literature which had come down from ages when princes took advice from seers and soothsayers, and bards were expected to record their heroic deeds in verse. On the other hand the *Lays* show that popular culture is worth recovering. The prose passages which introduce each poem are full of scholarly references and parallels with other literatures to prove that the idiom used and the moral conveyed are historically appropriate. The poetry glows with a feeling of popular patriotism, and a sense of the unity of Roman culture secured by wise laws and popular institutions. 'Virginia', for example, is offered as a song composed to stir up plebeian feeling against the Decemvirs, and plebeian sufferings in Rome are compared with those of the Irish Catholics between 1792 and 1829. The popular revolt which produced the Licinian laws is described as if the latter were a Roman Reform Act:

The results of this great change were singularly happy and glorious. Two centuries of prosperity, harmony and victory followed the reconciliation of the orders. Men who remembered Rome engaged in

[48] See H. R. Trevor-Roper's *The Romantic Movement and the Study of History* (1961), 11.

waging petty wars almost within sight of the Capitol lived to see her mistress of Italy.[49]

Popular participation brings national strength. Roman patriotism is a forerunner of and model for English patriotism.

As his view of the European past matured, Macaulay tended to give national character a greater influence over events than he would ever give theological dogma or political principles. In the first chapter of the *History of England* surveying the state of the realm at the close of the Tudor period, he abruptly reminds the reader that the Reformation was not only a revolt of the laity against the clergy, 'but also an insurrection of all branches of the great German race against an alien domination'. He goes on:

It is a most significant circumstance that no large society of which the tongue is not Teutonic has ever turned Protestant, and that, wherever language derived from that of ancient Rome is spoken, the religion of modern Rome to this day prevails.[50]

Throughout the *History* indeed, there runs a vibrant pride in national culture which is very un-utilitarian.

Cultural nationalism of this kind is often accompanied, in the nineteenth century, by an anti-rationalist, anti-scientific message. A people knows instinctively what is best, without the contrivances of planners or the predictions of science. Macaulay was too much a utilitarian to take this line. He agreed with Mill on the benefits of paving and lead pipes. But he elaborated the conception of 'the noble science of politics' with which he had closed his attack on Mill's *Essay on Government*. There, induction is presented as a prolonged study of 'the present state of the world' as well as 'the history of past ages' which must be undertaken before any general laws can be formulated. But in the long, book-length essay which he wrote on Bacon towards the end of his stay in India, he explains that the inductive method is everyone's way of interpreting nature. By it 'the schoolboy learns that a cloudy day is the best for catching trout', and the mechanic gathers much more knowledge than the philosopher.[51] What Bacon did was to describe more accurately than any previous writer the only reliable way of reaching truth, and the implication

[49] Ibid., 115–16.   [50] *HE*, i. 59.   [51] *CHE*, ii. 406, 415.

is that by doing so he spread a widening beam of dry light which practical men have trusted much more than the fitful flashes of revelation or the abstractions of academic theorizing.

The Bacon essay is in fact Macaulay's farewell to theory. Against the theorist's contempt of the useful arts it celebrates the common sense of the ordinary man. Macaulay pours scorn on Plato, not James Mill this time; but the scorn is for the same propensity castigated in the attack eight years earlier, for making theory so important that practical knowledge of the properties of phenomena was devalued and despised, with disastrous effects upon such important sciences as medicine. By contrast, Bacon taught men to solve what was practicable. 'The aim of the Platonic philosophy was to raise us far above vulgar wants. The aim of the Baconian philosophy was to supply our vulgar wants'.[52] Philosophers have taught men to subdue suffering by contemplating higher things, and have assumed that men can be compensated for the shortcomings of reality by the creation of imaginary societies where no such faults exist; but 'an acre in Middlesex is better than a principality in Utopia'.[53] All this does not make Macaulay less utilitarian—he says that the two key words of Bacon's doctrine are Utility and Progress[54]—but it founds his utilitarianism on technological advance rather than abstract speculation, and gives more credit to the contriving intelligence of the artisan than the high-flown speculations of the theorist. His famous list of the inventions and improvements we owe to Bacon is often cited as an expression of mid-Victorian philistinism.[55] It is more likely to be a bookish man's belated but excited recognition of the immense technological advantages enjoyed by the British in India. But the most interesting thing for our purpose is that it is an elaborate working out of the idea of 'noiseless revolutions' in the 1828 essay on History. From 1837 on, Macaulay had a firm conception, much more realistic than the Tory nostalgia for a vanished golden age, but also much more popular and democratic than the unpalatable and dry dogmas of political economy and Benthamite jurisprudence, of the real motor of progress. Its operation is discernible long before the

---

[52] *CHE*, ii. 395.   [53] Ibid., 396.   [54] Ibid., 357.

[55] By Matthew Arnold, in *Essays Literary and Critical* (Everyman edn.) 172; by Leslie Stephen in *Hours in a Library* 3 vols. (1899), ii. 355, and even by J. Clive, *Macaulay*, 484–9.

eighteenth century. It need not be attributed to the influence of particular scientists or engineers or philosophers. It cannot be precisely dated, to this invention or that discovery. It slumbers with the rude forefathers of the hamlet, until it is awoken and diffused by the right political conditions. No glib formula or learned term can describe it. It must be conveyed cumulatively through a mass of details, giving pictures of men and women doing unselfconsciously what posterity will later give some plausibly misleading label. To use that label in advance would be to replace the spontaneous action of innumerable wills with the determinism of a single process.

Macaulay composed the Bacon essay with a great deal of care, and one can only speculate on how he squared its argument with the compilation of the legal code which was his official work. In his references to his Indian sojourn, there are two dominant themes, securing financial independence, and doing a mass of reading which would serve as the groundwork for a great work of history. Establishing a legal reputation seems to have played little or no part in his plans. When he returned he was careful to tell Napier, when the question arose of reviewing the code in the *Edinburgh*, that he did not want his name associated with the work.[56] Perhaps he did not want to have a reputation in jurisprudence, lest it affect his independence.

Given his negative attitude to his Indian experience, it is not easy to assess its effect upon his *History*. The problem is made more difficult by his reticence. He kept his ideas about the writing of history to himself, making no converts and seeking no exchanges of opinion with other writers. Outside his family he had few intimate friends who shared his thoughts. T. F. Ellis was one, William Empson another, but both men were admirers, hardly candid critics. Criticizing Macaulay was in any case liable to provoke a volcanic lava-flow of evidence, example, and counter-criticism which would engulf and silence the critic. Napier, as editor of the *Edinburgh*, received regular notices of Macaulay's intentions, but no confidences and a good deal of advice. With all these men Macaulay was fairly reserved about his literary ambitions. There are no loud lamentations about the pains of the creative process such as we find in the letters of

---

[56] *LM*, iii. 252.

Carlyle. Perhaps if Margaret Cropper had lived, the case would have been different. She was, as her *Recollections* of her brother show, not only an avid listener, but tenacious enough to ask him for his reasons for thinking this or that, and she had a good ear for his peculiar turns of phrase. What she recorded was more acute than the notes made by her sister Hannah. Macaulay's letters to Margaret in his early months in India have a boyish gusto and enjoyment which are not, I think, found in his other correspondence. But her early death turned him in on himself, and if Hannah and her husband remained close to him, providing the admiring audience he needed, they left no record of what they heard. His emotional dependence on Hannah Trevelyan (for his other sisters, Frances and Selina, were never as close) in fact entails a major biographical loss, since living near her meant that long letters were unnecessary. Nor do Macaulay's political associations yield much more evidence. His boredom with politics, his sense that it was all so much time taken from his reading and writing, are amply illustrated by the fact that entry into parliament, or Cabinet office, which for many people would be the occasion for keeping a journal, was with him the occasion for giving one up. We have his journal for his visit to Italy from October 1838 to May 1839 when he began the *History* in earnest, a single entry for 1840, and then again from November 1848, when he had completed the first two volumes of the *History*, until his death.[57] For the actual writing of the first part, therefore, we are in the dark.

With any other writer that would mean a bleak prospect, but what we do have—a few letters, the Italian journal, and four major essays—is so rich and idiosyncratic that it may be enough for our purposes. After all, from 1828, Macaulay's main purpose, though distracted and delayed by political and administrative duties, was relatively fixed, and from 1841 he was free to develop it in the manner he had sketched thirteen years earlier. Novel events and experiences might have enriched, but they do not seem to have fundamentally altered the original conception. In any case, the experiences of a man who was accustomed to reading on his walks are likely to have had a somewhat delayed effect. They would have had to compete with and penetrate

[57] TCM, hereafter Journal.

through layer upon layer of literary images stored in that extraordinary memory; so that their impact, unnoticed or unrecorded at the time, becomes plain only much later, when they emerge, to illustrate some literary or historical observation in a letter or an article.

We need to bear in mind this process of maturing the vintage when we consider Macaulay's journal of his visit to Italy. It is remarkable as the work of a forceful talker who, being alone, has to talk to himself. It does not have the eager enjoyment of new sights so noticeable in his letters from India to Margaret Cropper. He is no Ruskin, registering impressions in all their texture and colour with an unrefracting eye. One has the feeling of a storing away of experience for future use, like a thrifty housewife bottling summer fruit for winter puddings. In Florence his hotel has a courtyard 'adorned with orange trees and marble statues'. He is immediately reminded of Goethe's poetry and that reminds him of his own reputation. 'I never look at the statues without thinking of poor Mignon.

> Und marmorbilder stehn und sehn mich an
> Was hat man dir, du armes kind gethan?

I know no two lines in the world which I would sooner have written than those'.[58] His guide in Rome is an English Catholic called Colyar, who takes him to the newly-excavated tomb of a Roman baker on which there is an ambiguous description. Macaulay comments:

'Strange city. Once sovereign of the world—where news now consists in the discovery of the buried tomb of a tradesman who has been dead at least fifteen hundred years. The question whether *apparet* is the short for apparitor is to them what the Licinian Rogations & the Agrarian laws were to their fathers—what the Catholic Bill and the Reform Bill have been to us. Yet, to indulge in a sort of reflection which I often fall into here, the day may come when London, then dwindled to the dimensions of the parish of St Martins and, supported in its decay by the expenditure of wealthy Patagonians and New Zealanders may have no more important questions to decide than the arrangement of "Afflictions sore long time I bore" on the gravestone of the wife of some baker in Houndsditch.'[59]

---

[58] Journal, i. fo. 33. I retain TBM's spelling.   [59] Ibid., fo. 143.

He reads a great deal, and his comments on his reading suggest
that this is more important to him than the Englishmen he meets,
whom he does not always recognize. He begins by following the
lead of Gibbon; but by the end of his stay he is reading Ranke's
History of the Popes. His early judgements are often very
Gibbonian. He finds the Latin of the Roman Mass barbarous:
it would have been 'unintelligible, a mere gibberish to every one
of the great masters of the Latin tongue'.[60] In Pius VII's gallery
of inscriptions he notes the inferiority of the Christian ones to
the pagan, and comments, 'You see at a glance that the Xtns
were never up in the world till the arts were down'.[61] But Gibbon
of course had resented Christianity for supplanting paganism and
weakening the Empire. To Macaulay this is a stale dispute. The
Roman Empire has now been eclipsed by the British, and what
interests him as a lapsed evangelical, is how the Roman Church
has, despite the decline of its capital city to a quarter of its ancient
size, still retained its vitality and authority. At first his comments
are what one might expect of a radical Protestant with fresh
memories of India. He calls the Papal government 'Brahminical'.
'Corruption infects all the public offices. Old women above,—
liars and cheats below,—that is the Papal administration'.[62] But
the longer he stays in Rome the less satisfactory this interpretation seems. The grandeur and antiquity of the Papacy fascinate
him. He goes frequently to St Peter's where he attends High Mass
on Christmas Day, and pronounces it finer than William IV's
coronation.[63] On his last visit he can hardly tear himself away.
'I ambled about quite sadly. I could not have believed that it could
have pained me so much to part from stone and mortar. It is a
glorious place!'[64]

Both his rejection of the idea of a theocratic state and his explanation of its continued vitality were worked up in reviews.
At the close of his stay in Rome, he met Gladstone in St Peter's,
and the two men seem to have liked each other, in spite of their
different politics.[65] But Gladstone was at this stage one of the

---

[60] Journal, i. fo. 33, fos. 85–6.   [61] Ibid., fo. 153.
[62] Ibid., fos. 184, 186. He used the same phrase in a letter to Frances. *LM*,
iii. 269.
[63] Ibid., fo. 268.   [64] Ibid., fos. 286–7.
[65] Trevelyan, ii. 468; H. C. G. Matthew (ed.) *Gladstone Diaries*, 14 vols,
(Oxford, 1968–94), ii. 539.

High Anglicans who took the *Tracts for the Times* and hankered after a revived political role and a stricter doctrinal discipline for the Church of England. When, on his return to London, Macaulay read a copy of Gladstone's book *The State in its Relations with the Church*, he swooped upon it to review it: 'a capital Shrovetide cock to throw at'.[66] The review is famous for a line which Gladstone was never allowed to forget (but which Macaulay seems to have added as an afterthought) describing him as 'the rising hope of those stern and unbending Tories who follow, reluctantly and mutinously, a leader [Peel], whose experience and eloquence are indispensable to them, but whose cautious temper and moderate opinions they abhor'.[67] But the tone, unlike that of Macaulay's earlier reviews, was designed to persuade or at least overwhelm, not to humiliate. Whether or not Macaulay knew that Gladstone was powerfully attracted to the ideal of a confessional state, he could enjoy driving a wedge between the young man's Toryism and the more moderate views of his leader.

His case is essentially the conventional liberal one, that the state, however it came into being, functions to protect property and life, and that to add to this non-doctrinal, ethically neutral function the additional duty of propagating religious truth is bound to cause strife.[68] Law and order were every subject's concern but religious opinion was his private affair. Governments which tried to legislate on religious questions were almost always wrong.[69] Gladstone's earnest but futile effort 'to keep as far in the rear of the general progress as possible'[70] by proposing religious tests for political office, is shown to have made just enough concession to the modern world to make his position inconsistent. So he had opposed the grant to Maynooth on the grounds that a government professing one religious truth should not pay men to teach another, but saw nothing wrong in the government in India professing one faith yet tolerating paganism among its subjects. India for Macaulay is the test case for religious toleration, for even if its British rulers were far in advance of their native subjects in 'moral science', and it was very easy to believe that the conversion of the latter even to dark

---

[66] Journal, i. fo. 362.   [67] *CHE*, ii. 430.
[68] Ibid., 437.   [69] Ibid., 452.   [70] Ibid., 466.

age Christianity would abstractly considered be an improvement, yet attempting it 'would inevitably destroy our empire, and, with our empire, the best chance of spreading Christianity among the natives.'[71] Later he says, 'Christian instruction given by individuals and voluntary societies may do much good. Given by the Government it would do unmixed harm.'[72] Gladstone had, along with the early Tractarians, upheld the supremacy of the minority Protestant Church in Ireland. So quite consistently, he deplored the position of the Scottish Kirk under the Union. Macaulay was scathing, accusing him of wanting the Irish problem and O'Connell's agitation replicated north of the Tweed.

Surely it would be amusing, if it were not melancholy, to see a man of virtue and abilities unsatisfied with the calamities which one Church, constituted on false principles, has brought upon the empire, and repining that Scotland is not in the same state with Ireland, that no Scottish agitator is raising rent and putting county members in and out, that no Presbyterian association is dividing supreme power with the Government, that no meetings of precursors and repealers are covering the side of the Calton Hill, that twenty-five thousand troops are not required to maintain order on the north of the Tweed, that the anniversary of the Battle of Bothwell Bridge is not regularly celebrated by insult, riot and murder.

Scotland had flourished, and was content with the Union, says Macaulay, because at the Union 'the true ends of government alone were kept in sight. The nations are one because the Churches are two'.[73]

It is a powerful review, combining trenchant argument with a mass of illustration delivered with a sardonic wit.[74] Its main thrust, and the point to which all the illustrations—from

[71] *CHE*, ii. 470.

[72] Ibid., 498. Compare his remarks to Zachary in October 1836 . . . 'If our plans of education are followed up, there will not be a single idolater among the respectable classes in Bengal thirty years hence.' *LM*, iii. 193.

[73] *CHE*, ii. 471–2. The Precursor Society was O'Connell's attempt to secure 'justice to Ireland', failing which he would demand repeal of the Union. O. MacDonagh, *The Emancipist: Daniel O'Connell 1830–47* (New York, 1989), 176–8.

[74] Dr P. Butler finds it witty but superficial. *Gladstone: Church, State and Tractarianism* (Oxford, 1982), 87. No recent biographer of Gladstone makes any serious attempt to assess the effect of Macaulay's review on Gladstone's political convictions, an illustration of my complaint in Ch. 1, p. 4. For the best assessment the most helpful guide is Gladstone's own, in *Gleanings*, vii. 105–15.

Christian theology and Church history, including some pointed mockery of Tractarian Oxford—are all subordinated, is that a man in Gladstone's position has to choose. He can either be a Protestant and embrace with all the Protestant communion the right of private judgement, or he can be a Romanist, embrace authority and abandon private judgement.

There are two intelligible and consistent courses which may be followed with respect to the exercise of private judgment; the course of the Romanist, who interdicts private judgment because of its inevitable inconveniences; and the course of the Protestant, who permits private judgment in spite of its inevitable inconveniences . . . The Romanist produces repose by means of stupefaction. The Protestant encourages activity, though he knows that where there is much activity there will be some aberration. Mr Gladstone wishes for the unity of the fifteenth century with the active and searching spirit of the sixteenth. He might as well wish to be in two places at once.[75]

Macaulay's implication is of course that a man of Gladstone's abilities ought to be on the Protestant side. Whatever the faults of the Church of England, what mattered most was not that it was or was not apostolic, but that it was open-minded and tolerant.

Macaulay's essay on Ranke's *Popes*, which appeared in October 1840, shows the other side. It extends an entry he made in his journal at Christmas 1838. Then he wrote of the ceremony in St Peter's:

The bearing of the performers, the incomparable beauty of the edifice, made the sight a very fine one. And the immense antiquity of the Papal dignity which can certainly boast of a far longer, clear, known, and uninterrupted succession than any other dignity in the world, and which links together the two great ages of human civilization, adds to the interest. Our modern feudal kings are mere upstarts compared with the succession in regular order—not to be sure of Peter but of Sylvester and Leo the Great.[76]

It was of course precisely this feeling which drew some Tractarians to Rome, an awe for the continuity of a hallowed

---

[75] *CHE*, ii. 476.

[76] Journal, i. fos. 267–8. TBM meant Sylvester I, Bishop of Rome 314–35; and Leo I 'the Great' who became Pope in 440. To have admitted St Peter would have conceded the continuity of the Apostolic Succession.

sacerdotal imperium. No such admission was allowed to soften the attack on Gladstone's views of the apostolic succession. In the review of Ranke the passage is elaborated:

The proudest houses are but of yesterday, when compared with the line of the Supreme Pontiffs. That line we trace back in an unbroken series, from the Pope who crowned Napoleon in the nineteenth century to the Pope who crowned Pepin in the eighth; and far beyond the time of Pepin the august dynasty extends, till it is lost in the twilight of fable. The republic of Venice was modern when compared with the Papacy; and the republic of Venice is gone, and the Papacy remains. The Papacy remains, not in decay, not a mere antique, but full of life and youthful vigour . . . Nor do we see any sign which indicates that the term of her long dominion is approaching. She saw the commencement of all the governments and of all the ecclesiastical establishments that now exist in the world; and we feel no assurance that she is not destined to see the end of them all. She was great and respected before the Saxon had set foot on Britain, before the Frank had passed the Rhine, when Grecian eloquence still flourished at Antioch, when idols were still worshipped in the temple of Mecca. And she may still exist in undiminished vigour when some traveller from New Zealand shall, in the midst of a vast solitude, take his stand on a broken arch of London Bridge to sketch the ruins of St Paul's.[77]

Here is a reversal of Gibbon's 'triumph of barbarism and religion'. Macaulay sees a triumph of religion in spite of civilization and the progress of knowledge. For the Papacy had survived four great revolts of the human intellect against her. She had suppressed the Albigenses, the Wycliffites and Hussites, and she had withstood the Reformation. This third crisis was severe, but it ended with Protestantism weak and divided, its churches merely national establishments; whereas the Catholics of the Counter-Reformation were united and militant over Eastern Europe and the New World. Protestantism might have been more friendly to an expanding commerce and industrial invention, but this was not a religious victory. 'The stronger our conviction that reason and scripture were decidedly on the side of Protestantism, the greater is the reluctant admiration with which we regard that system of tactics against which reason and scripture were employed in vain'.[78] Even the last great crisis, of eighteenth century rationalism, had done more harm to

Protestantism than to Catholicism. The Catholic Church had more influence in 1840 than it had had in the time of Voltaire and the *Encyclopaedia*. Protestantism was still confined to the areas it had won by 1648. 'Catholic communities have, since that time, become infidel and become Catholic again; but none has become Protestant'.[79]

Why was this? Macaulay's explanation is that Protestantism was divided. Catholics fought Protestants, but Protestants also fought each other. National churches had no motive for seeking converts abroad. But the main reason (one the son of Clapham knew too well) was that the Catholic Church knew 'how to deal with enthusiasts'. Enthusiasts in Protestant churches, unlettered men who were suddenly touched by the message of the Gospel and moved by it to preach, found themselves excluded from the establishment.

For a man thus minded, there is within the pale of the establishment no place. He has been at no college; he cannot construe a Greek author or write a Latin theme; and he is told that, if he remains in the communion of the Church, he must do so as a hearer, and that, if he is resolved to be a teacher, he must begin by being a schismatic. His choice is soon made. He harangues on Tower Hill or in Smithfield. A congregation is formed. A license is obtained. A plain brick building, with a desk and benches, is run up, and named Ebenezer or Bethel. In a few weeks the Church has lost for ever a hundred families, not one of which entertained the least scruple about her articles, her liturgy, her government, or her ceremonies.[80]

But Rome takes such a man and makes him a friar, and at no cost to the church or the clergy he works for her glory. 'In this way the Church of Rome unites in herself all the strength of the establishment, and all the strength of dissent'. In fact, Protestantism creates secession.

Place Ignatius Loyola at Oxford. He is certain to become the head of a formidable secession. Place John Wesley at Rome. He is certain to be the first General of a new society devoted to the interests and honour of the Church.[81]

It is primarily for its subtle policy with enthusiasts that Macaulay calls the Catholic church 'the very masterpiece of human wisdom'.[82]

[79] Ibid., 254.   [80] Ibid., 240.   [81] Ibid., 240–1.   [82] Ibid., 237.

The article on Ranke caused a flutter in Catholic circles, but it marks no rapprochement with Rome on Macaulay's part. In fact, taken together with the essay on Gladstone, it shows how rhetorical his method was. When attacking Gladstone, he allows none of his victim's 'Romanist' sympathies a hearing. In his praise of the toughness and tenacity of the Papacy, on the other hand, the intellectual strength of Protestantism, so proudly expounded in the Gladstone review, is deliberately masked and underplayed. Why the contrast? It looks as if Macaulay was setting out the issues of a debate which would lend drama to his *History*. His Indian experience gave an imperial dimension to a growing interest in the eighteenth century, and he was moving steadily away from his boyhood interest in the Puritans and the Civil War. Whig writers had concentrated heavily on the Revolution of 1688, but only Mackintosh had carried the research beyond the insular concerns of Englishmen and studied foreign archives, notably in Holland. Macaulay may not have seen Mackintosh's papers until his return from India: a letter to Napier of July 1838 speaks of them as if he had not yet registered their value.[83] They are likely to have anchored his conception round about the period of the Revolution, but while in Rome, he was still undecided:

Where am I to begin? I cannot plunge slapdash into the middle of events and characters. I cannot on the other hand write a whole history of the reign of James II as a preface to the history of William [III]. And if I did [,] a history of Charles II would still be equally necessary as a preface to that of the reign of James II . . . But after much consideration I think I can manage by the help of an introductory chapter or two to glide imperceptibly into the full current of my narrative. I am more and more in love with the subject. I really think that posterity will not willingly let my book die.[84]

The last sentence is particularly interesting. Macaulay seems to be echoing, if not exactly quoting, Milton's famous hope 'that by labour and intent study . . . joined with the strong propensity of nature, I might perhaps leave something so written to after-times, as they should not willingly let it die'.[85] If he was thinking

---

[83] *LM*, iii. 252.   [84] Journal, i. fos. 248–9.
[85] *Complete Prose Works of John Milton* ed. Don M. Wolfe, vol. i. (1953), 810. Macaulay would have known the quotation from Johnson's 'Milton' in the *Lives of the Poets*.

of Milton, it suggests that he hoped he might be capable of writing a prose-epic.

Macaulay could never have written a conventional history with terminal dates but his visit to Rome and the reading to which it gave rise ensured that what he wrote would have a central dramatic motif. The Revolution of 1688 would be shown to have come at a pivotal moment in international affairs, when, the European balance between Catholic and Protestant being even, the issue of the conflict in Britain would determine on to which side her weight would be thrown. In the opening chapter of the *History* Macaulay made clear the historic significance of the choice he had put before Gladstone. The Church of Rome might have favoured science and civilization in the middle ages, but in the past three centuries 'to stunt the growth of the human mind has been her chief object'. The present state of Europe proved it:

The loveliest and most fertile provinces in Europe have, under her rule, been sunk in poverty, in political servitude, and in intellectual torpor, while Protestant countries, once proverbial for sterility and barbarism, have been turned by skill and industry into gardens, and can boast of a long list of heroes and statesmen, philosophers and poets ... Whoever passes in Germany from a Roman Catholic to a Protestant principality, in Switzerland from a Roman Catholic to a Protestant canton, in Ireland from a Roman Catholic to a Protestant county, finds that he has passed from a lower to a higher grade of civilisation.[86]

If the two creeds had each these very different long-term effects, then the struggle against James II could be shown to be not merely a domestic political dispute, but a struggle which had repercussions for all Europe.

Macaulay had only worked for a few weeks on the *History* when he was invited to stand for Edinburgh in May 1839. In October he joined the Cabinet as Secretary for War. His articles slowed to a trickle, and the *History* was set aside. When he took it up again in November 1841 he spoke of it as a new start.[87] In one sense it was, for even the brief experience as a minister had changed his views. He had feared a life in parliament impaired a man's faculties. In fact, official work absorbed him. The first effect of this was that he began to see that there was a difference between political science and political skill.

[86] *HE*, i. 44. · [87] *LM*, iv. 15.

As so often with Macaulay a historical essay becomes a vehicle for the reappraisal, or at least for a rhetorical reordering of his impressions. Reflecting on his Indian experiences, he seems to have realized that the missing ingredient in the British public's perception of its Indian empire was an appreciation of the multifarious labours of individuals. British rule could hardly have been achieved, as Mill implied, by the mere pressure of an advanced civilization upon one less advanced. Mill's *History* was the classic example of the facts cast in the mould of a hypothesis, and it conveys very little sense of the experience of the soldier and the administrator, men learning to discharge novel duties in a cruel climate with either irrelevant training or no training at all. To supply the deficiency Macaulay chose to tell the story of two men who had gone out to India as mere boys, and achieved fame in ways no one at home could have anticipated, Clive the soldier and Warren Hastings the diplomat and administrator.

The essay on Clive purports to be a review of the first biography by Sir John Malcolm, but it is actually a blend of the work of Mill which Macaulay thought too dull and too severe on Clive, and the ornate narratives of Robert Orme, Clive's friend and historiographer, whose volumes he found 'minute even to tediousness'. Macaulay turns Clive's career into the story of how a handful of Englishmen belonging to 'a trading company, separated from India by fifteen thousand miles of sea, and possessing in India only a few acres for purposes of commerce, would, in less than a hundred years, spread its empire from Cape Comorin to the eternal snow of the Himalayas'.[88] To make it easier for his readers he uses European parallels: the deputies of the Mogul who, as his authority collapsed, set up for themselves, are compared to the princes of the Holy Roman Empire. The native names and titles are used sparingly. Clive is presented (against Mill's charges of duplicity and greed) as a hero, 'the very opposite of a knave, bold even to temerity, sincere even to indiscretion, hearty in friendship, open in enmity'.[89] It is the native powers with whom Clive has to deal who show cunning, duplicity, and guile.[90] So in the end Clive's faults and errors are balanced by his achievements, which outshine those of Rome.

---

[88] *CHE*, iii. 122.   [89] Ibid., 149.
[90] Surajah Dowla behaves 'with all the faithlessness of an Indian statesman . . .' Op. cit., 150.

Such an extent of cultivated territory, such an amount of revenue, such a multitude of subjects, was never added to the dominion of Rome by the most successful proconsul. Nor were such wealthy spoils ever borne under arches of triumph, down the Sacred Way, and through the crowded Forum, to the threshold of Tarpeian Jove. The fame of those who subdued Antiochus and Tigranes grows dim when compared with the splendour of the exploits which the young English adventurer achieved at the head of an army not equal in numbers to one half of a Roman legion.[91]

Macaulay knew its tone was popular; he called it 'flashy'.[92] The article was finished a month after he joined the Cabinet.

The essay on Warren Hastings was the first product of his escape from politics after the fall of the Melbourne ministry. Formally a review of Gleig's biography, it actually summarizes Hastings's achievement and supplies the narrative line so conspicuously lacking in Mill's *History of British India*. Mill, concerned to show Hastings as the great delinquent of a monopolist company, conveys very little of the strategic problems Hastings faced as the only man who might have co-ordinated the scattered British authorities in India. Nor is he very good even at a straightforward story. For instance, he gives a long account of the rise of Hyder Ali, the ruler of Mysore who was the greatest threat to British dominion in the South of India. It is fourteen pages long, and it confuses the reader with strange names and complex genealogies, weighing him down with dutifully recorded details of no great relevance to central events. Macaulay's account, using the same information, is by contrast a marvellous exercise in dramatic climax. The general background is rapidly sketched, the smaller details are spared, the main outlines of the career of an obscure adventurer graphically described, then the figure is named. It is worth giving in full, because it is a device used very effectively in the *History of England*.

About thirty years before this time, a Mahommedan soldier had begun to distinguish himself in the wars of Southern India. His education had been neglected; his extraction was humble. His father had been a petty officer of revenue; his grandfather a wandering dervise. But though thus meanly descended, though ignorant even of the alphabet, the

---

[91] Ibid., 205.   [92] *LM*, iii. 344.

adventurer had no sooner been placed at the head of a body of troops than he approved himself a man born for conquest and command. Among the crowd of chiefs who were struggling for a share of India, none could compare with him in the qualities of the captain and the statesman. He became a general; he became a sovereign. Out of the fragments of old principalities, which had gone to pieces in the general wreck, he formed for himself a great, compact, and vigorous empire. That empire he ruled with the ability, severity, and vigilance of Lewis the Eleventh. Licentious in his pleasures, implacable in his revenge, he had yet enlargement of mind enough to perceive how much the prosperity of subjects adds to the strength of governments. He was an oppressor; but he had at least the merit of protecting his people against all oppression except his own. He was now in extreme old age, but his intellect was as clear, and his spirit as high, as in the prime of manhood. Such was the great Hyder Ali, the founder of the Mahommedan kingdom of Mysore, and the most formidable enemy with whom the English conquerors of India have ever had to contend.[93]

But the important feature of the portrait of Hastings is that Macaulay, steering between the polemics of Burke and the theory of Mill, conveys an idea of the lonely grandeur of political responsibility, and the sense that in politics there is seldom any clear distinction between wickedness and virtue, but that men in power must make choices between a greater evil and a less. This is almost wholly lacking in the early essays on political figures. What particularly draws Macaulay to Hastings is that he had none of the advantages of European statesmen. As Clive was a self-taught soldier, Hastings was a self-taught administrator, and moreover one who produced an administrative and judicial system out of chaos.

The just fame of Hastings rises still higher, when we reflect that he was not bred a statesman; that he was sent from school to a countinghouse, and that he was employed during the prime of his manhood as a commercial agent, far from all intellectual society.

Nor must we forget that all, or almost all, to whom, when placed at the head of affairs, he could apply for assistance, were persons who owed as little as himself, or less than himself, to education. A minister in Europe finds himself, on the first day on which he commences his functions, surrounded by experienced public servants, the depositories

[93] *CHE*, iii. 394.

of official traditions. Hastings had no such help. His own reflection, his own energy, were to supply the place of all Downing Street and Somerset House. Having had no facilities for learning, he was forced to teach. He had first to form himself, and then to form his instruments; and this not in a single department, but in all the departments of the administration.[94]

Here Macaulay, surely for the first time, describes a politician from the vantage point of an insider. It is ministerial experience which gives the portrait of Hastings its grainy realism.

By the time he started the *History of England*, then, Macaulay was a liberal imperialist in all but name. He subscribed to the political economy of his time, and to the utilitarian morality which underpinned it. He was less secular-minded than the Mills, father and son. He saw utilitarianism as doctrinally rigid and insensitive to culture and so disliked the name, but he agreed that the morality of an action lay in its consequences. It followed from this that the most admirable type of character was self-reliant, open-minded, provident, and frugal. The difficulty, for an evangelical upbringing, was reconciling this secular morality with the Christian ideal of altruism and the Christian mission. Utilitarians and evangelicals might agree on the general aim of educating our Indian subjects, but on the aim of converting them they would have to part company. Macaulay decided that the best hope for Christianity in India was that the natives would be persuaded by a just and tolerant government to look with kindly respect on its preferred religion. 'A firm and impartial despotism' would by its impartiality raise its subjects out of abject submission into self-reliance, and one effect of this might be the spread of Christianity, but that could not be the main aim. If then conversion was implicitly abandoned, what gave Protestant Christianity any claim to be superior to any other form of Christianity? Catholicism had been more successful than Protestantism in the New World. It could not have been Protestantism which had spread to the Empire of Asia. In Europe it had generated strife, and its theology, however learned and refined, could never be a 'progressive science';[95] so that it could claim no direct credit for the inexorable progress of reason, with its concomitants of inventiveness and practical contrivance,

---

[94] Ibid., 417–18.   [95] *CHE*, iii. 211.

which underlay the success of European dominion in the East. But one could say that its influence was indirect. Among its adherents there was general agreement on the principle of private judgement, and where that principle had been allowed to shape laws and institutions, free enquiry had penetrated all areas of a society's life. In that indirect sense it underlay the success of the progressive nations of Europe.

In this way, Macaulay embraced a kind of dualism, which is to be found in the work of other liberal Victorians, like that other jurist with experience of India, Sir Henry Maine. The civilized world was divided into stationary and progressive, stagnant and dynamic states, and after long struggle the latter were in the ascendant. But go back two centuries and you find that the struggle was more even, and the issue more in doubt. Then it was Catholic against Calvinist. In England it became monarchist against parliamentarian, Tory against Whig. But these were mere local and transient manifestations of a more fundamental struggle, between stationary and progressive politics. Party labels, like religious sectarianism, only gave a polemical twist to a person's true historic destiny, and were therefore unreliable guides. It did not matter, for instance, whether Gladstone was a Whig or a Tory, a High Churchman or an evangelical. What mattered was that his efforts should be harnessed to the cause of progress, and that he should realize that Rome represented its antithesis. This is why the Ranke and Gladstone essays are a good guide (in the absence of explicit evidence from the author himself) to the aim of the *History of England*. It was part of Macaulay's art, as we have seen, that he should not give his readers advance notice of his aim, but there is no doubt that the *History* was shaped by such a conception. When the first two volumes had been published, a reader wrote to him objecting that certain passages in it were too gross to be read aloud to his daughters. He replied, with some asperity, that his book was not written for 'female boarding schools'. He added:

I open a school for men: I teach the causes of national prosperity and decay: and the particular time about which I write is a time when profligacy, having been compelled during some years to wear the mask of hypocrisy, had just thrown that mask away, and stood forth with a brazen impudence of which there is scarcely any other example in any modern society. How is it possible to treat a subject like mine without inserting a few paragraphs . . . which it would be better that a young lady should not read aloud?[96]

Not many readers of the *History of England* open it expecting a 'school for men' which would teach 'the causes of national prosperity and decay'. Croker, for one, thought its purpose altogether more frivolous. So it is time, before I consider Croker's critique, to try and gather together the main elements of Macaulay's method.

III

Macaulay does not seem to have made very careful plans for the completion of the *History of England*. He had, as we have seen, projected theories and interpretations of the period from 1688 down to his own day, but he was vague how long it would take him, and kept changing the date at which he thought the work could come to a close. In 1838 he thought he might end it in 1830. By 1841 he thought he would end with the death of Anne in 1714.[97] The readers of the *History* were told he intended to go down to a time 'within the memory of men still living'.[98] In the end, he barely reached the close of William III's reign.

In a sense, a man who sets out to tell a story, especially if he is popularizing one already familiar to a restricted readership, need not have a very elaborate plan. The chronological sequence gives him the main direction, and he can determine the amount of information he must acquire by the form of narrative he chooses. Macaulay's later essays seem to have been in large part exercises in narrative technique, rather than critical reviews of evidence such as we find in Croker's articles. But it was one thing to trace the rise of the Elder Pitt or the career of Robert Clive in a manner that would 'take' with the readers of a review. It was another to write the history of a whole society, or describe those 'noiseless revolutions' which ten years before he had almost claimed as the real determinants of the more famous events. Political experience may well have increased his scepticism about the primacy of social history, as it impressed upon his mind the impact of political institutions and the forms by which decisions which affect large numbers are actually made.

[96] *LM*, v. 42.   [97] *CHE*, iii. 252, 382.   [98] *HE*, i. 9.

Another problem making the *History* a much more complex undertaking was that it was to be a national story set in an international setting. That would mean not merely that foreign archives would have to be consulted, but also that Scotland and Ireland would have to be brought into the picture of a progressively more united nation. The fact that Macaulay had Scottish origins and represented Edinburgh in parliament does not seem to have made him very well informed about Scottish history. In November 1841 he had to ask Napier what were the best sources for the 1688 revolution and the reign of William III in Scotland.[99] His first visit to Ireland was in August 1849 after the appearance of the first two volumes of the *History*. It is a proof of his integrity that he did not take refuge, as a modern historian would, in a preliminary demarcation of his 'field', but went to considerable lengths to describe in detail matters which are merely referred to in passing in his essays. But such scruples delayed the completion of the *History*. In fact, from 1841 until the heart attack in 1852 which shortened his life, he seems to have felt quite confident that he could combine writing with membership of parliament, the social round, and a good deal of foreign travel.

So it would be easy to present Macaulay's method as rather casual, and to forget the talents which he brought to his task. Those talents are so extraordinary that they make diligence, perseverance, and careful planning look like the trademarks of lesser men. There was first of all his prodigious memory, which enabled him to recall whole works *verbatim*; not just works which he had deliberately memorized like *Paradise Lost*, but details most people are content to look up in encyclopaedias and biographical dictionaries, dates recalled accurately to the month and day, satirical poems lying long forgotten in obscure newspapers, and phrases from pamphlets, sermons, and speeches perused or heard only once. There are many stories about Macaulay's feats of memory, but not much attention has been given to his use of it as a daily resource. He could retain, and recall with great ease, a huge range of factual illustrations and examples which ordinary people are obliged to record in notes or marshal with card indexes and computer data-bases. Indeed, his mind seems

---

[99] *LM*, iv. 15.

in many ways to anticipate the computer. There are times when he seems to revel in the advantage his memory gave him. Reviewing Leigh Hunt's edition of *Restoration Dramatists*, for example, he shows in two highly-condensed paragraphs, recalling the plots and characters of each play, how Wycherley's plots were plagiarized from Calderon, Shakespeare, Molière, and Racine and how they were always morally debased in the process. The demonstration has the ruthless precision of a practised marksman.[100] Another example is the short passage in 'Warren Hastings' where he sets out his reasons for believing Philip Francis was the author of the *Letters of Junius*.[101] One cannot be sure of this, but the fluency of the demonstration suggests that Macaulay was writing, not from notes, but from a copious memory. It was this which would enable him in the *History* to write out swiftly and confidently a summary of a debate, or describe the phases of a political crisis, without losing the thread of his argument or arresting the pace of his prose. Croker by contrast, in his critical writings, always gives the reader the impression that he is shuffling through a considerable library to make the smallest point.

A well-filled storehouse demands systematic arrangement if it is to yield its contents to an enquirer, and it often strikes a reader of Macaulay that he was particularly fond of arranging his experience on a scale of merit, as if the very copiousness of his information demanded it. This seems to have been a confirmed habit, because one also finds it in his journals and letters. Versailles is an inferior Castle Howard: 'The churches of Boston and Louth rank with Cathedrals of the second class'.[102] In literature the marks are, as might be expected, awarded with greater precision. Macaulay is not quite like the Oxford don who marked *The Prelude* as 'beta double plus with alpha passages' but something of that spirit informs many of his judgements. Had Wycherley, we are told in the essay just cited, written poetry, 'he would have been nearly as far below Tate and Blackmore as Tate and Blackmore are below Dryden'.[103] It is as if such classification was an essential device for marshalling the vast stores in Macaulay's memory.

---

[100] *CHE*, iii. 287–90. The same assertion is condensed in the *History*, ch. 3; [*HE*, i. 310].

[101] *CHE*, iii. 361–3.　　[102] Journal, i. fo. 358; *LM*, v. 218.

[103] *CHE*, iii. 274. TBM liked this formula. 'The Mandragola . . . is superior to the best of Goldoni, and inferior only to the best of Molière'.

The second asset was his great facility with languages. He read and re-read the Greek and Latin classics, and his familiarity with them made him a vigilant critic of other men's errors in relation to the world of classical antiquity. Accuracy in those two literatures, as we see from his critique of Croker's *Boswell*, was for him a touchstone of scholarly accuracy in general, and he often wrote as if he thought a man who was untrained in classical authors could not be trusted in his assertions on any other matter. His critical outlook therefore has the flavour of a humanist scholar of the Renaissance, and he revered men like Casaubon and Bentley for the philological knowledge which enabled them to elucidate a corrupt text which had baffled previous scholars. Bentley's 'supernatural sagacity' in showing how all the combined learning of Christ Church had misread the letters of Phalaris remained for him one of the high points of European scholarship.[104] He says more gently in the third chapter of the *History of England* that the college's 'stock of Attic learning' would in his own time be equalled 'by several youths at every great public school',[105] but the remark is not merely another assertion of the progress which his own age had made. It implies—and the passages which follow reinforce the point—that the classical authors provide models of perfection for every subsequent generation, and are a universal standard of literacy and scholarly taste. So he notices the want of classical attainments in the oddest places. 'All true Etonians will hear with concern that their illustrious schoolfellow is guilty of making the first syllable in *labenti* short'.[106] The illustrious schoolfellow is the elder Pitt. Again, he says of Frederick of Prussia's admiration of Voltaire, that he could never have praised the Frenchman's *Charles XII* if he had known Thucydides or Tacitus in the original.[107]

Of course, his classical grounding gave Macaulay much easier access to other European languages. He read quite fluently in French, Italian, and Spanish literature. German came later, followed by Dutch. In his range of reading, Macaulay was truly, in Tennyson's phrase, 'heir to all the ages and the foremost files of time'. But his classical preferences set a boundary to his sympathies. He preferred the Augustan age when French writers

---

[104] Munby, '*Macaulay's Library*' 25; *CHE*, iii. 102–5.   [105] *HE*, i. 304.
[106] *CHE*, ii. 150.   [107] *CHE*, (Everyman edn. 1967), ii. 127.

shamed their English contemporaries by a closer adherence to ancient models.

> Still green with bays each ancient Altar stands,
> Above the reach of sacriligeous hands; . . .
> See from each clime the learn'd their incense bring!
> Hear, *in all tongues* consenting Pæans ring!

Macaulay would have had reservations about Pope's politics, but he agreed with the poetic message of the *Essay on Criticism*.[108] Writers of any stature must start with the ancient classics. 'Tis not that Homer nods, but that we dream'. However closely he followed the events of his own time, however ardently he wished to bring his *History* down to the memories of men still living, in his imaginative life he recurred to the age of Molière and Racine, Dryden and Pope. Culturally, his rebellion against evangelicalism involved no more than a shift away from the Puritanism of Milton and Bunyan towards the wits who opposed Walpole; but he could never decide how far to go with the writers of late Stuart England in their reaction to the morality of the Commonwealth. The classicist in him approved their elegance and wit, the puritan in him was repelled by their hedonism and impiety. For contemporary writers by contrast he had little respect: he thought in 1850 that the previous twenty-five years had produced 'hardly a volume that will be remembered in 1900'.[109]

It is not that Macaulay was insular or parochial. It is rather that his cosmopolitan learning gave him a classical and literary rather than a political conception of Europe. He sincerely thought that at least Western Europe was one country, and whereas a political analyst would see stages of development and types of institution as separating one nation from another, he tended to see a family of nations inheriting and transmitting a common culture. The emphasis becomes more plain if we recall Croker in Paris after Waterloo. Despite his interest in the French classical theatre which meant so little to Peel and Fitzgerald, Croker's primary interest was political. A hierarchical order had first been disrupted in France, which was, accordingly, the crucible in which the problem of social stability would be decided, not only for Frenchmen, but for all Europe.

---

[108] cf. *MW*, i. 132 'On the Athenian Orators'.   [109] *LM*, v. 99.

France and its politics accordingly absorbed him, and he never went beyond the Alps. Croker, it is fair to say, would have agreed in condemning what Macaulay called 'that Chinese cast of mind, that stupid contempt for everything beyond the walls of his celestial empire'[110] which besets the monoglot. But Croker's outlook had been shaped by political crisis. Macaulay's had not. His enjoyment of the literary landmarks of European culture, each providing a centre from which to explore the history of individual countries, transcended the intricacies of politics and rendered them, in the long run, ephemeral. Croker was inclined to censure any literature he thought subversive, whatever its aesthetic merits. Macaulay was inclined to stress those merits whatever their political tendency. Both men feared disorder; but Croker thought it arose out of popular envy which in his own time had taken the form of a demand for an extended suffrage which must be hostile to property. Macaulay thought disorder stemmed from ignorance, which would threaten property no less, but which could at least be combated by education. One of the fears in his speech on the Charter in May 1842 was that, as things stood, if universal suffrage were granted, knowledge would be 'borne down by ignorance'.[111] Croker's message to his readers was bleakly pessimistic, to expect chaos but resist its onset as long as they could, by clinging to tradition. Macaulay's habit was also to look back to past achievements, but his message was more positive, that the chaos could be averted and the people taught how to value their heritage.

Here I come, not without trepidation, to Macaulay's third quality, his style. After his death, when the horror of revolution seemed to have receded, and the educated classes acquired confidence enough both to resist the masses and to dispense with aristocratic patronage, there was a general reaction against Macaulay as a writer. It was expressed most memorably by Matthew Arnold who coined the term 'Macaulayese'. The external characteristic of this style was 'a hard metallic movement with nothing of the soft play of life', its internal 'a perpetual semblance of hitting the right nail on the head without the reality'. Macaulay's

---

[110] 'The London University' in *Selected Writings* ed. J. Clive and T. Pinney (Chicago and London, 1972), 23.
[111] *Speeches*, 267.

rhetoric was for Arnold a phase in intellectual life which educated people outgrew: it was a style 'pre-eminently fitted to give pleasure to all who are *beginning* to feel enjoyment in the things of the mind'.[112] Arnold's target seems to have been Macaulay's essays and of those mainly the literary and critical aspect. But it is clear that Macaulay not only looked on them as ephemeral (reprinting them only reluctantly in self-defence against a pirated American edition), but regarded them (at least those after 1835) as preparatory exercises for a more ambitious work, the *History*. They 'took' with the public, which encouraged him, but his sights were set higher. He wanted to rival Gibbon, and it is by comparing him with Gibbon that we can form an idea of the change he brought about in English historical writing.

There is no extended discussion of Gibbon in Macaulay's work, but enough references to him to suggest a conscious rivalry.[113] He respected Gibbon's classical scholarship. He shared his opinion of the early Church, though he thought he wrote 'like a man who had received some personal injury from Christianity and wished to be avenged on it and all its professors'.[114] But he called Gibbon's style 'rank', by which he meant that it was affected and over-elaborate, characteristics which Macaulay always associated with a coterie culture out of touch with the national mood.[115] Gibbon disliked repeating proper names and was fond of the device grammarians call 'elegant variation', often to the reader's confusion. Macaulay preferred to repeat proper names for the sake of clarity. Gibbon had a fastidious distaste for 'low' words, preferring a polite paraphrase. His Gothic chiefs do not come home drunk after a feast, they return 'in the fearless confidence of intoxication from one of their nocturnal festivals'.[116] Gibbon's prose style betrays an adolescence spent abroad speaking French; he never absorbed the English writers who were Macaulay's delight. Macaulay always thought the King James Bible the foundation of good prose and among eighteenth century writers he copied the colloquial vigour of Swift and Defoe and the purity of Addison.[117] His short sentences are not as

---

[112] Quoted by G. S. Fraser, 'Macaulay's Style as an Essayist' in *Rev. of English Literature*, i. 4, 15–16.

[113] *LM*, iii. 220.   [114] Journal, i. fo. 245, 22 Dec. 1838.

[115] *LM*, iii. 178.   [116] Ch. xix. J. B. Bury ed. (1926), ii. 300; Cf. *HE*, i. 199.

[117] *LM*, iv. 27–8.

subtle as Gibbon's but they carry a heavier freight of fact. No one can deny it is a very graphic prose. The reader knows exactly who is talking, who is doing what and when. When Macaulay describes a battle one has a clear idea of the terrain, the numbers involved, and even the strategy: in Gibbon battles are mere rumbles of Latinate rhetoric, no more revealing than the sound of distant gunfire.

Macaulay's is not a complete emancipation, it is true. He keeps some of the pointed antitheses, the sardonic observation and many phrases which are very Gibbonian. He favours some circumlocutions like Gibbon, but from primness, not pomposity. Monk's troopers drink too much of the wealthy Londoners' wine, and they are 'sometimes seen in a condition not very honourable either to their religious or to their military character'.[118] But any one who turns from the *Decline and Fall* to the *History of England* is at once struck by two differences. Macaulay respects the domestic virtues, and in particular is always more chivalrous to women than Gibbon. There is none of what Sainte-Beuve called 'une obscenité érudite et froide', no sneers that feminine emotions are the natural soil of religious superstition, no affected incredulity when women prove vigorous rulers, no glee at violated Christian maidens.[119] On the contrary, the *History of England* has memorable portraits of three heroic and tragic women, Alice Lisle, Elizabeth Gaunt, and William's Queen, Mary. Macaulay had no time for Gibbon's irony, not only because he had himself suffered no personal injury from Christianity and so did not share the central paradox of the *Decline and Fall*, but also because a sustained irony would have been fatal to his design. Gibbon did not, strictly speaking, write a narrative history so much as an ironic commentary on narratives which as he proceeds become steadily more unreliable. He was too aware of the fragmentary nature of his evidence to attempt more, and the irony expresses his sense that political disorder and literary decline go hand in hand. Irony presupposes two sorts of reader, a naïve one who understands the literal sense of the words, and a more sophisticated one who appreciates their hidden meaning. It is the characteristic weapon of the writer under

---

[118] *HE*, i. 120.
[119] *Decline and Fall* i. 325–6 (on Zenobia); ii. 124–5 (on Diocletian's Christian Empress); iii. 342–3 (on virgins).

censorship, the cautious and even timid controversialist, who
wants to satisfy both the educated few and the unthinking many
or the government they obey. When he is accused of a subversive meaning, he can appeal to the literal one, implying that the
hidden meaning is his accuser's, not his own. There are examples of such a defence in Gibbon's *Vindication*.[120] But Macaulay
was not a timid controversialist, and he certainly did not want
to write for a minority of readers. Moreover, his message is
optimistic: rise and expansion, not decline and fall. To reach a
wide audience he needed to fashion a prose that was forthright,
accessible, and unambiguous. Irony would be an obstacle, and
Gibbon's stance as amused commentator on human futility would
not do. A popular history must engage the reader's emotions:
he must feel sympathy with the characters and participate in their
actions. To help him do this, the historian must feel and share
them first, and write while the emotions were still vivid.

Macaulay was a born story-teller, but in the *History* he
had to widen his skill from biography to social history. In both
his method draws on drama. Though he was brought up to consider theatres as dens of vice, and did not enter one till he was
in his twenties, he had a very strong sense of theatre. He was
thoroughly versed in dramatic literature from Aeschylus to
Sheridan, and he had a tendency to treat the stage (perhaps because he knew it mainly from books) as a substitute for real life.
Any event, in his life or in past lives, tended in his hands to
be cast in a dramatic form. His first visit to Holland House was
described in sham-Shakespearean blank verse to amuse his
sisters.[121] He adored play-acting with small children. Whenever
he had to tell a story his language became more histrionic. There
is an amusing example in his letters. When Leigh Hunt offered
Napier an article on some chatty subject, Napier replied stiffly
that he would accept one if it was written 'in an amusing but
gentlemanlike style'. Hunt took this phrase as a slur on his social
position and appealed to Macaulay. To soothe him, Macaulay
assured him that Napier often turned down work by distinguished
men, by Lord Brougham, by an eminent diplomatist (meaning
Henry Bulwer), and by Carlyle. But when he passed on to Napier

---

[120] *Vindication* (Oxford repr. 1961), 67–8.
[121] *LM*, ii. 24–5; and 253–4 (a letter which Trevelyan mutilated because 'too thickly
strewn with personal allusions' ii. 192–3).

what he had told Hunt, he could not resist dramatizing the editor's ruthlessness: 'I knew', he told him, 'that you had not scrupled to hack and hew articles on foreign politics which had been concocted in the hotels of ambassadors and had received the *imprimatur* of Secretaries of State'.[122] In the essays are many examples of this dramatizing habit. In the Ranke essay religious rivalries are summed up in a stage-direction from *Hamlet*.[123] His account of Voltaire's quarrel with Frederick of Prussia (in an essay he admitted was superficial, and which he did not reprint) reads like the prose sketch of a play.[124] One feels Macaulay was only one step away from setting it out in a succession of scenes in dialogue.

The construction of imaginary dialogues between characters became in time an inseparable part of Macaulay's method of understanding a period. The well-known conversation recorded by his sister Margaret in 1831, usually cited to illustrate Macaulay's tendency to confuse history with fiction, is actually more interesting as a record of this habit. After describing how he associated historic places with the people who had frequented them in the past, he added: 'The conversations which I compose between great people of the time are long, and sufficiently animated: in the style, if not with the merits of Sir Walter Scott's'.[125] In the essays he often casts an episode in the form of a conversation, as in his account in the essay on Sir William Temple of the dispute between Boyle and Bentley. The same method is used in the *History*, but the dialogues are larger disputes about national issues. We cannot illustrate this for the first two volumes, because we have no journal, but we have one for the third volume onwards, and there what is striking is the casual confidence with which he studies different kinds of material, in between social engagements, in order to construct the narrative. On 28 July 1849, for instance, he 'turns over' three volumes of newspapers and tracts and finds 'some curious things which will be of direct service'. Evidently this is desultory reading, for he comments that its chief advantage is that 'the mind is transported back a century and a half, & gets familiar with

---

[122] *LM*, iv. 10–13.
[123] *CHE*, iii. 233.   [124] *CHE*, (Everyman edn, 1967), ii. 149–57.
[125] Margaret Macaulay's *Recollections*, 36–7; quoted in G. O. Trevelyan i. 703.

the ways of thinking & with the habits of a past generation'.[126]
The next day he walks about town, visits the Athenaeum, has
a City appointment with his broker, then starts again in the British
Museum. He writes:

Read and extracted there till near five. I find a growing pleasure in this
employment. The reign of Wm III, so mysterious to me a few weeks
ago, is beginning to take a clear form. I begin to see the men and understand their difficulties and jealousies.[127]

He could read on different levels simultaneously, mainstream biography for the men and their disputes and pamphlet ephemera
for the colourful detail, and all the time the great capacious
memory was shaping the information into a drama of great complexity as well as great clarity, where the figures move with appropriate impedimenta through a vividly described landscape.

Macaulay's sense of theatre is very much in evidence here. A
great deal of the interest of a complex episode like a military
campaign depends on a careful setting of the scene, and major
judgements on the character and purpose of the actors can
be conveyed in this way, without any heavy-handed moralizing.
In Chapter 5, for instance, two executions, of Argyle and of
Monmouth, follow quickly upon one another and offer a contrast between heroic puritanism and cavalier folly. The passage
describing Argyle sleeping like a child before his execution conveys a pathos notably absent in the account of Monmouth's
behaviour. These set pieces seem intended to illustrate the comparison of the historian and the painter which Macaulay made
in the essay on *History*. Like Croker, he wanted painters to record
historic occasions, and he gave a list of historical subjects to
the painter Sir George Hayter.[128] The difference was that for
Croker they were mere records done with the greatest possible
accuracy; for Macaulay the subjects also carried a great emotional charge.

Macaulay also shared Croker's concern with topographical
detail, but again, where Croker studied street plans and measured
buildings to discredit other men's narratives, Macaulay used
them to clarify his own narrative and help it to convey a mood.
When William III lands at Torbay we are reminded of the later

---

[126] Journal, ii. fo. 42. [127] Ibid., fo. 46. [128] *LM*, iii. 258.

prosperity of 'a great watering place'—Torquay is not named—
'to which strangers are attracted . . . by the Italian softness of the
air'[129] . . . and so on. The details are irrelevant to William's
progress, but point obliquely to the long-term effects of his
arrival. They create a mood of cheerful expectancy. By contrast,
James II is portrayed after 1689 in an Ireland barely emerging
from tribal barbarism where the sun never shines. When he
travels to Dublin from Cork (where the Torbay motif is reversed
and present prosperity cited to contrast with the squalor of the
city in 1689) he passes through 'an untilled and unpeopled
desert'.[130] So too with the Scottish Highlands. When Macaulay
comes to describe the massacre of Glencoe in Chapter 18 he first
gives an account of the valley designed to make the reader feel
that no events in such a setting can be judged by the standards
of civilized men. In Gaelic, we are told, the name means 'Glen
of Weeping; and in truth that pass is the most dreary and
melancholy of all the Scottish passes, the very Valley of the
Shadow of Death'.[131]

A taste for drama, a histrionic gift, and an eye for the picturesque in landscape and pageantry account for some of the richness of the narrative, but there is another ingredient. Besides what
he would have called 'the court, the senate and the camp',
Macaulay manages to give a vivid picture of the lives of ordinary
people without political office or influence. Part of the *History*'s
popularity was evidently due to readers sensing that this was
a story with which they could identify. His journal for May
1849 records his pleasure at receiving a letter from a group in
Dukinfield near Manchester who had heard the *History* read aloud
to them and thanked him 'for having written a history which
working men can understand'.[132] One might think this popularity
was a response to a more democratic interpretation, as was the
case in France with the work of contemporaries like Thiers and
Michelet. There are hints in his letters, which echo the attacks
on exponents of 'the dignity of history' which appear in the essays,
and suggest that he intended to deal with social change in a way
never before tried. He told Lady Holland for example, in a letter
describing what he considered 'the real materials of history' that

[129] *HE*, ii. 75.   [130] *HE*, ii. 345.   [131] *HE*, iii. 63.
[132] Trevelyan, ii. 173; Journal, ii. fos. 5–6, 7 May 1849.

he had 'found more historical information in a small receipt-book than in a folio of diplomatic correspondence'.[133] The disparagement of 'diplomatic correspondence' sounds very radical, but while it is possible that Macaulay was being mildly provocative of a lady famous for her snobbery, there is not much evidence that he carried radical or democratic feeling into the *History*. It may be that the events of the 1840s, working upon his short ministerial experience, made him more tolerant of official correspondence as well as more disillusioned with popular aspirations. There are several echoes of Chartism and the Revolutions of 1848 in the *History of England*. When in the famous third chapter he comes (last of all) to the state of the poor, he says:

In those times philanthropists did not yet regard it as a sacred duty, nor had demagogues yet found it a lucrative trade, to talk and write about the distress of the labourer.[134]

Although he has great sympathy for the poor who joined Monmouth's rebellion or were butchered in the Bloody Assizes, he has none for their judgement.

The charge which may with justice be brought against the common people is, not that they are inconstant, but that they almost invariably choose their favourite so ill that their constancy is a vice and not a virtue.[135]

Throughout the *History* there is a corresponding stress upon the way the Revolution was conducted according to precedent and in a spirit of the strictest constitutional propriety. Yet neither of these features seems to have affected the book's popularity.

The reason, I believe, lies in Macaulay's political detachment. Once out of politics, he wrote to please himself. Released from the constraints of official discretion, he wrote about politics and politicians as he saw them in his materials, judging them by the scale of merit he had adopted in his early manhood. His moral standards were severe, but the high moral purity and independent judgement he admired was saved from the sort of *ad hominem* judgement which disfigures Croker's work, by his utilitarianism. Men's conduct (and Macaulay had a more indulgent role for women) is judged by its effects in the long term. 'An action for a hundred thousand pounds is in one sense a more momentous

---

[133] *LM*, iii. 286.   [134] *HE*, i. 319.   [135] Ibid., i. 482.

affair than an action for fifty pounds. But . . . a cause in which
a large sum is at stake may be important only to the particular
plaintiff and the particular defendant. A cause, on the other hand,
in which a small sum is at stake may establish some great
principle interesting to half the families in the kingdom'.[136]
So events in domestic life may in the long run be of more significance for the historian than the acts of kings and statesmen;
private morality, though practised in a narrow sphere, may
contain more lessons than the larger problems of statecraft. On
the other hand, intelligent moral choice presupposes a measure
of enlightenment and freedom: not much is to be learned from
the study of obscure lives where poverty and ignorance ensure
that no real choice is available.

This is why searching Macaulay's *History* for signs of popu-
list sympathies misses the point. He did not complacently
accept the fact that rulers generally keep better records than their
subjects, but neither did he feel obliged to explore the archives
for evidence about the very poor. As the arrangement and cataloguing of archives was only beginning in his day, he would
have had to turn archivist to do so. The bulk of the manuscript
sources Macaulay used in the first two volumes of the *History*
were the transcriptions bequeathed him by Mackintosh. He
acknowledged these as 'the rudest ore of history'.[137] But they were,
after all, another man's selection, enriching but hardly superseding
the plentiful memoir material. He did sit on the Board of the
Trustees of the British Museum, but there is no record that
he pressed, as a specialist would, for the purchase of materials
relevant to his work. The only manuscript public records
Macaulay used in the first two volumes of the *History* were in
his own office while he was Secretary of War, and concerned
the strengths of the army and navy under the Stuarts. But this
was a fortunate side-effect of his political life, not a window on
a new professional historiography. Indeed, one feels that if he
could have seen the mass of modern work based on the official
papers, which loom so large in the lives of the professional historian today, he would have deplored it. He would have been
especially dismayed by the divorce between literary and historical scholarship, because it was in literature that the aspirations

---

[136] *CHE*, iii. 19.   [137] *HE*, i. 302.

and disappointments of ordinary life left their mark. There was the corn which historians were, he thought, casting into the fire, while they kept the chaff, the 'despatches and protocols'.[138]

Macaulay contrived to make the *History* popular without being democratic, accessible without being vulgar, and he did so with a literary artistry which has never, as far as I know, been analysed.[139] In general, he held to the rule set out in the essay on History of avoiding general language and technical terminology if they tend to obscure human agency but he applies it in a great variety of ways. It is not merely that leading figures are vividly described; even obscure ones seem to belong to a scene that pulses with life. Measurements are conveyed where possible in terms of human effort. The rigours of coach travel in the late seventeenth century are expressed in a series of anecdotes about travellers' ordeals.[140] He will not say 'sixty years previously' if he can say, 'within the memory of the oldest man', or a variant of it. Urban squalor, which our economic historians would try to 'quantify', is conveyed in a vivid vignette.

In Covent Garden a filthy and noisy market was held close the dwellings of the great. Fruit women screamed, carters fought, cabbage stalks and rotten apples accumulated in heaps at the thresholds of the Countess of Berkshire and of the Bishop of Durham.[141]

It is not easy to convey an idea of the actions of men and women caught up in some common movement of social change. If the historian describes individuals he may lose sight of the group, but too great a concern with the group—class, church, or section— can imply that individuals have no will of their own. Gibbon's favourite device for overcoming this is metonymy, which blandly attributes a single identity to the group. 'The barren synagogue abhorred and envied the fecundity of the rebellious Church' is his way of summarizing the effects of the early Christians' abandonment of the Jewish rites.[142] Macaulay in his essays often uses this figure: I have quoted one example from his

---

[138] *CHE*, iii. 21; 258.
[139] Peter Gay's *Style in History*, ch. 3, 97–138, is the best treatment, but it inclines to a psychological explanation of the style rather than an analysis of its structure. It builds on William A. Madden 'Macaulay's Style' in *The Art of Victorian Prose* ed. Madden and G. Levine, (New York, 1968), 127–51.
[140] *HE*, i. 288–90.   [141] Ibid., i. 277.   [142] *Decline and Fall*, ii. 478.

'Milton'.[143] But metonymy is not specific. It overlays individual will with a single, pompous attribute, like a peerage conferred on a business tycoon. Macaulay in the *History* prefers what may be called metonymy's poor relation (though it has a more difficult name), synecdoche. By this, the group or institution is suggested not by its chief symbolic attribute but by a more characteristic part, as when we might say of an actor, 'we shall see his name in coloured lights'. Macaulay saw that this device suits a swiftly moving narrative. When he tells us that young noblemen joined the navy during the Dutch wars, he says, 'Mulgrave, Dorset, Rochester, and many others, left the playhouses in the Mall for hammocks and salt pork'.[144]

Still more skilfully he extends the device to portray common opinions. It is always hard to convey the way a theory or an outlook comes to distinguish a particular group of people. If one sets out their opinions accurately as abstract propositions, one credits all members with an implausible unanimity; but if one describes them as holding amorphous common attitudes one casts doubts on their cohesion. Macaulay can describe a group or movement with a string of examples which conveys both agreement and idiosyncrasy. It would need considerable scholarship to unravel the sources for his account, in his essay on Dryden, of how the affections of the metaphysical poets had driven true poetry into the theatre:

While the noble and the learned were comparing eyes to burning-glasses, and tears to terrestrial globes, coyness to an enthymeme, absence to a pair of compasses, and an unrequited passion to the fortieth remainder-man in an entail, Juliet leaning from the balcony, and Miranda smiling over the chess-board, sent home many spectators, as kind and simple-hearted as the master and mistress of Fletcher's Ralpho, to cry themselves to sleep.[145]

Perhaps it is too cleverly allusive to make a convincing case for simplicity. But in the *History* the same formula is used much more deftly, as in the famous description of Puritan prohibitions:

It was a sin to hang garlands on a Maypole, to drink a friend's health, to fly a hawk, to hunt a stag, to play at chess, to wear lovelocks, to put starch into a ruff, to touch the virginals, to read the Fairy Queen.[146]

[143] Above, Ch. 3, 74.   [144] *CHE*, iii. 278.
[145] *MW*, i. 203.   [146] *HE*, i. 69.

We do not need to know whether all these activities were actually forbidden. To make the Puritan odious it is enough to be told that he frowned on them. But the passage does raise the question whether Macaulay was condensing numerous actual examples from his well-stored memory, or creating them out of his imagination.

Macaulay's idea of the imagination is distinct from the English romantics' 'shaping spirit', or 'esemplastic power'. Where he uses the word in a critical context he associates it with the power to create unreal worlds and persuade people to believe in them. It was what he admired in Milton. As a faculty it was most active when the external world was shut out, which he suggests may be why Milton continued to write in his blindness. Everyone experiences it who indulges in building castles in the air.[147] Describing the way Bunyan's *Pilgrim's Progress* had stamped its imagery on all sorts of reader, he recalled the description of the straight and narrow path:

This is the highest miracle of genius, that things which are not should be as though they were, that the imagination of one mind should become the personal recollections of another. And this miracle the tinker [Bunyan] has wrought. There is no ascent, no declivity, no resting-place, no turn-stile, with which we are not perfectly acquainted.[148]

Seven years later, on his journey to Naples, the road through the Pontine marshes reminded him 'of the road in the Pilgrim's Progress running straight through the Slough of Despond, the Quagmire in the Valley of the Shadow of Death and the Enchanted Land'.[149] The romantic poets used images from nature to express states of mind. Macaulay's sensibility was urban. He drew on literary images to describe nature. But he also thought that the power of imagination faded with maturity, 'Our judgment ripens; our imagination decays'.[150] Milton's and Bunyan's achievements would not be repeated. Modern man had to be persuaded with fact; his moral lessons must be learned from actual examples. Imagination must take a subordinate role, that of making facts memorable. On the old method of writing history, he had said in 1828, the momentous revolutions always appear 'like supernatural afflictions, without warning or

---

[147] *MW*, i. 209.   [148] *CHE*, i. 411.
[149] Journal, i. fo. 290 (31 Dec. 1832).   [150] *MW*, i. 192.

cause'.[151] In fact they are usually the consequences of moral changes, which have permeated society thoroughly, well before they are acknowledged in any public measure. To explain these moral revolutions, the imagination could be called in aid of reason; it would be the faculty which impressed, or 'branded' the facts on the mind, and made them vivid. The writer who best demonstrated this combination of imagination and reason was Burke. Other politicians, Macaulay says in his essay on Hastings, knew the details of Indian administration, but Burke explained them.

In every part of those huge bales of Indian information which repelled almost all other readers, his mind, at once philosophical and poetical, found something to instruct or to delight. His reason analysed and digested those vast and shapeless masses; his imagination animated and coloured them. Out of darkness, and dulness, and confusion, he formed a multitude of ingenious theories and vivid pictures. He had, in the highest degree, that noble faculty whereby man is able to live in the past and in the future, in the distant and in the unreal. India and its inhabitants were not to him, as to most Englishmen, mere names and abstractions, but a real country and a real people.[152]

In 1849, considering the reviews of his first two volumes of his *History*, Macaulay thought the fact that they had been praised in such different places as Charleston and Heidelberg, proved that he had not addressed himself 'to mere local and temporary feelings', and he added: 'I am conscious that I did not mean to address such feelings, and that I wrote with a remote past and a remote future constantly before my mind'.[153]

That he thought this quite distinct from the task of the historical novelist is clear from his Italian journal. In Naples a snow fall prevented his going to Paestum so he stayed indoors reading Bulwer's *Last Days of Pompeii*. The classical scholar at once noticed the historical errors. Why had Glaucus failed to become a Roman citizen? Bulwer had exaggerated the spread of Christianity, and mistaken the Greek influence. But more interesting than these historical details is Macaulay's verdict on the historical novel generally. Bulwer's book, he says, has the usual faults of 'all works in which it is attempted to give moderns a glimpse of ancient manners'.

---

[151] *MW*, i. 281.   [152] *CHE*, iii. 433.
[153] Journal, ii. fo. 125 (2 Oct. 1849).

After all between us and them there is a great gulph. No learning can enable a man to clear that gulph. Strength of imagination may enable him to create a world unlike our own. But the chances are a thousand to one that it is not the world which has passed away. Perhaps those act most wisely who in treating poetically of ancient events, stick to general human nature, avoid gross blunders of costume and trouble themselves with little more.[154]

Clearly he was thinking ahead to the *History* and the dilemma of whether to be accurate or arresting. Complete immersion in the sources would lose the ordinary reader; but putting historic debates into a modern idiom would deceive him. In general Macaulay prefers paraphrase to direct quotation of original sources, as less liable to interrupt the flow of the narrative; but he gives direct speech in dramatic moments such as the Bloody Assize when it suits the violence of the action.

But what was 'general human nature'? Macaulay's habit of constructing dialogues enables him to give his readers a sense of divergent personalities in conflict, but his portraits, though often colourful, are not penetrating. He plainly had not the imagination to enter into the characters of even well-documented figures in the past in whom he suspected a vice: witness his portraits of Johnson and Boswell in the review of Croker, or the treatment of Marlborough in the *History*. Even when he set himself to draw a portrait, as he did with Tyrconnell, or Lord Mordaunt, he produced a bundle of contradictory qualities, the materials for a portrait rather than the portrait itself, in which the violent contrasts seem to have no necessary relation to the actions of the subject in question. The journal confirms the impression that he was more interested in morality than in character, happier in according praise or blame than in explaining motive. For he seems to have subscribed to the doctrine of associationism, which we find in J. S. Mill, according to which a man's moral standards are formed by the association of pleasure with some actions and pain with others. Every one who has observed the laws of association in himself, he says in one essay, 'knows that what is constantly presented to the imagination in connection with what is attractive will itself become attractive'.[155] This view demands that the historian should pay more attention to what is happening

---

[154] Journal, i. fos. 323–5; cf. Trevelyan, i. 471–2.
[155] *CHE*, iii. 260. Cf. *LM*, iii. 238 'The world is governed by associations'.

around a person than to what is happening inside him. If a person's moral values are wholly or largely shaped by the environment, it is a waste of time to make nice distinctions between individuals and more important to characterize the society that shapes them. One need not claim that Macaulay was as thoroughgoing an associationist as John Mill. But the theory's pedagogic side appealed to him because it credited the writer and the artist with a power in creating the values of a society, which confirmed his idea that great writing both shaped and outlasted political arrangements. This seems to me to explain his conviction that when a society changes, every one is affected; that under the Puritan's enforcement of piety every one became a hypocrite, that in the reaction brought by the Restoration, every one became a libertine. It is too mechanical to be persuasive.[156] One feels that custom and habit must have been more tenacious, especially in Stuart England, and that psychological variety will persist even in the most outwardly conforming society.

This brisk approach to individual psychology is not a great blemish in a narrative history, where even prominent figures make only brief appearances. It is a more serious fault in the main characters because they have imposed on them the double role of being themselves and representing larger processes. But it is just this ambiguity which provides the key to the structure of the *History*. If the Revolution of 1688 is to be shown to have a pivotal importance not just in English but in European history, its character as a palace coup must be played down, its character as a liberating moment in human development enhanced. A mere family quarrel, even one between crowned heads, might have some human interest, but not high drama. But showing the Revolution as the inevitable outcome of a growing spirit of independence, freedom, and confidence within English society would be undramatic as well as insular. So Macaulay deliberately understates (and in doing so slights the whole Whig historiographical tradition to which he is supposed to belong) the

---

[156] Macaulay's assumption that societies behaved like individuals in experiencing changes of mood emerges in many of his portraits. A good example is that of Thomas Wharton in Chapter XX. 'The history of his mind deserves notice: for it was the history of many thousands of minds. His rank and abilities made him so conspicuous that we are able to trace distinctly the origin and progress of a moral taint which was epidemic among his contemporaries'. *HE*, iii. 264.

factors which might seem to have pointed the way to a separate English constitutional development before the seventeenth century.

His opening chapters trace the emergence of Britain from the obscurity of an island on the edge of civilization: 'Nothing in the early existence of Britain indicated the greatness which she was destined to obtain' are the first words of the narrative proper.[157] A Germanic identity exists, but it carries no germ of a representative government, and Britain's rise to prominence is due to a series of lucky accidents and compromises between larger forces rather than any innate national genius. The Plantagenets were French. Had they succeeded in their aims English 'would have remained a rustic dialect . . . contemptuously abandoned to the use of boors'.[158] But salvation came with King John, to whose errors we owe Magna Carta. Macaulay's account of the formation of the English polity stresses its unity and its stability, but he insists that in so far as that stability had rested on a regard for tradition, so it had generated party spirit. In England, 'the dearest interests of parties have frequently been staked on the results of the researches of antiquaries. The inevitable consequence was, that our antiquaries conducted themselves in the spirit of partisans'.[159] Even Protestantism brought no emancipation. Far from making worship a matter of free choice, it produced a church, typified by Cranmer, more subservient to the royal will than any in Europe, Calvinist or Catholic.[160] So English reformers came to dislike the Elizabethan Church, and the persecution they suffered made them fanatical. A combined hatred of prelacy and kingship threatened to create a republican movement, but its excess of puritan zeal made many hanker after a strong monarchy. The resulting civil war brought no compromise but exhaustion. The restoration of the king was made possible by the restraint of Cromwell and the indecision of Monk, a cautious soldier without clear aims. The most positive feature of early modern England is the development of a national consciousness, a sturdy self-reliant outlook, which presages future greatness. But next to this, any gathering tradition of constitutionalism is understated, or attributed to chance or human failure. The

---

[157] *HE*, i. 11.   [158] Ibid., i. 19.
[159] Ibid., i. 28.   [160] Ibid., i. 51–2.

power of parliament in the seventeenth century owes more to James I's weakness and his son's duplicity than to public support. So the restoration of Charles II in 1660 is no triumph. The chapter closes with a deliberate bathos: 'the restored wanderer reposed safe in the palace of his ancestors'.[161]

The reign of Charles II is a period of domestic corruption and international humiliation. The corruption, as any reader who had followed Macaulay's essays could have predicted, is attributed to the Puritanism of the Commonwealth which produced a reaction in which every sort of vice was encountered. This time there was no restraining hand of religion. The Anglican Church had recovered power but not influence. 'It is an unquestionable and a most instructive fact that the years during which the political power of the Anglican hierarchy was in the zenith were precisely the years when national virtue was at the lowest point'.[162] The result was that every public man, Whig or Tory, Cavalier or Puritan, Anglican or dissenter was stained by the prevailing 'gross perfidy and corruption'. The only policy on which Charles II stood firm was that of ensuring his brother James's succession, and to do that he engaged in a foreign policy of sycophantic subserviency to Louis XIV which alienated the Protestant power of Holland. So his chief legacy was political strife. In this strife the Whig party was too weak to effect much, and mistakenly let itself be led by hotheads who turned from moderation and, in the hope of toppling James, chose to back a revolution led by the wrong man, Monmouth.[163]

In his journal in 1838 Macaulay had envisaged these two chapters gliding 'imperceptibly into the full current' of his narrative. That is actually what they do. They contain nothing that encourages a reader to feel he knows what will happen next. The description of England which follows in Chapter III portrays a country just emerging from barbarism. While he sets the scene Macaulay raises expectations by offering little glimpses forward into his own time, as if to make the reader want to leave the squalor of late seventeenth century England behind. He is not glorifying his own age in this chapter. He is setting out the main elements of that 'noiseless revolution' which, we remember, is to work its change alongside the political events we are about

---

[161] *HE*, i. 121.   [162] Ibid., i. 144.   [163] Ibid., i. 268.

to follow. The second paragraph of this chapter echoes the essay on History of 1828. Social progress, sketched in a sweeping survey of six centuries, is traced to the twin principles of the tendency of every experimental science towards perfection, and the wish of every individual to better his own condition. The gradual, inexorable change these two principles brought about, says Macaulay, 'seems at least as well entitled to the notice of a historian as any change of the dynasty or the ministry'.[164] No institutional changes, such as might be thought to have preserved or consolidated the progress made so far, are mentioned in this chapter. Along with the physical appearance of England in 1685, we are told of the English people who are to provide a sort of validating chorus to the chief actors in the narrative. Of course the voices in such a chorus need to be rational and progressive, so both clergy and country gentry are portrayed unflatteringly so that their testimony will be discredited in advance. But all classes are shown as part of a society which is savage and holds life cheap. The chapter ends with a stark warning that utopianism and nostalgia for a vanished past both rest on illusion.

So at last the stage is set for the drama of the Revolution. The English people have attained enough cohesion and education to feel dissatisfaction at the ways they have been governed to date. But their aspirations are still pulled this way and that, by one party which reveres the royalist past and by another which is corrupted by the dangerous appeal of violence and befogged by Puritan fundamentalism. It needs a crisis to clarify the issues, and that is provided by James II's blunders. He must be presented as the epitome of what is stupid and obscurantist in the era just expiring. In the opening months of his reign he behaves with a blind, dogmatic energy, but as his mistakes lose him supporters, his nerve fails and he becomes a pitiful victim of indecision. William III by contrast is a man of heroic moderation and self-control, whose personal virtues offer an attractive alternative to the vices of the court of Charles and James. His courageous openness converts the supporters of the old régime and ushers in an era of candour, self-reliance and progress. In constructing the dramatic contrast, Macaulay loses sight of the real

---

[164] Ibid., i. 217–19.

personalities in each case; awkward or inconvenient traits are smoothed away, and each man becomes a personification of forces of which he could at most have had only a dim intimation. The real men are to a large degree concealed by the theatrical role assigned them in the drama.

This is not the place to discuss the historiography of the Revolution of 1688, which could fill a separate book, and indeed has done. Macaulay's sources were long ago examined by Firth in a series of lectures posthumously published and this is still the best commentary.[165] Firth combined a love of literature with a scholar's thoroughness, and he wanted his audience to read Macaulay as a master of the lost art of narrative. But as he went through the *History of England* he concentrated on Macaulay's omissions and factual errors, and (at least in the form the lectures have come down to us) there is no final assessment of Macaulay the literary artist. In other words, he admired the craftsman, but he chose to criticize the scholar. There is a difference. A scholar working in George III's reign might criticize Sir Lewis Namier for having ignored evidence of popular radical feeling in the 1760s. But if he made a similar criticism of Alan Bennett's portrait of the King in *The Madness of George III*, he might be charged with missing the point.[166] But this is the sort of criticism Firth makes of Macaulay throughout his commentary, as if he was afraid to draw attention to the great man's love of dramatic effect, lest it weaken his standing as a scholar. In fact, many of Macaulay's omissions or expansions can be explained in no other way.

Take first an omission. Macaulay pays very little attention to the political philosophy of John Locke. We have in Chapter V a short account of the way he was deprived of his Studentship of Christ Church, and in VI an admission that in the *Letter on Toleration* Locke still thought there ought to be no toleration for Catholics. In Chapter XXI there is a brief mention of Locke's part in the restoration of the currency. But there is no mention of the *Second Treatise on Government* with its contractual theory of the origin of government and its argument for

---

[165] Sir Charles Firth, *Commentary on Macaulay's History of England* (ed. Godfrey Davies, 1938).

[166] Alan Bennett's 'The King and I', in *Writing Home* (1994), 227–40 has an ingenuous admission of the historical liberties taken for dramatic effect.

revolution. Locke's connection with Shaftesbury is mentioned, but not his close co-operation with the Exclusionists or the Rye House Plotters. In a reputedly Whig history this is decidedly odd. Firth's explanation is Macaulay's 'aversion to abstract theory', and he cites in support of this his contempt for the works of Filmer and Harrington.[167] It might be thought that the mention of Filmer's patriarchal theory at least merited a glance at Locke's refutation of it; but the absence of such a reference can hardly be due to an aversion to theory. Macaulay's controversial writings show a considerable taste and talent for theory.

Elsewhere in the *History* moreover, he could indulge in a digression because a piece of abstract argument has caught his imagination. Pascal's *Lettres Provinciales* do not seem, on the face of it, to call for a prominent place in an explanation of the Revolution of 1688. We first hear of them in Macaulay's essay on Ranke where, after a colourful account of the origin of the Jesuits and their role in the Counter-Reformation, he says briefly that they never recovered from the injury received in the struggle with the Jansenists of Port-Royal.[168] But in that essay the two passages are far apart. In the *History*, the first of these, the account of the Jesuits, is extended and elaborated. The Jesuits' struggle with Port-Royal comes immediately after the account of Jesuit missions around the world, and in this later version Macaulay praises Pascal's polemic, indeed he borrows his account of Jesuit casuistry from Pascal's ironic dialogues.[169] This version however does not claim that the Jesuits were defeated, only that their credit was so damaged that there was for them 'nothing left but to oppress the sect [the Jansenists] which they could not confute'.[170] And so, having lost credit with the educated classes, they came to rely on the secular power. Louis XIV took up their cause, and accordingly they became his instruments in foreign affairs. Through them he controlled the conscience of James II, and the agent of this control 'the chief representative of the Jesuits at Whitehall' was Fr. Edward Petre. 'Of all the evil counsellors who had access to the royal ear, he bore, perhaps, the largest part in the ruin of the House of Stuart'.[171]

---

[167] Firth, op. cit., 138.   [168] *CHE*, iii. 249.
[169] *HE*, i. 552.   [170] Ibid., 554.   [171] Ibid., 555.

Why should Macaulay omit a key document in the Exclusionists' struggle against James II, a classic work of political theory by a Whig philosopher, but paraphrase and give prominence to a polemic by a French Jansenist who, though a genius, wrote it as a contribution to a dispute among French Catholics of which even educated Englishmen were unaware? Given Macaulay's memory we can rule out ignorance, and in the light of the other references to Locke, inadvertence. The only other explanation that can be offered is that Macaulay knew what he was doing, and saw that he must maintain the moral and rhetorical balance of his narrative. To give prominence to Locke's treatise would be to lend respectability to Shaftesbury, already blackened in Macaulay's imagination by Dryden's satirical portrait and so lowered to a level below the Earl of Sunderland. It would suggest that the Exclusionists' faction had after all room for a sober academic philosopher, and that, far from 'standing aloof' from their 'rash councils' he actually approved their revolutionary aims.[172] Pascal however provided evidence not only of Jesuit practice but by implication of Jesuit motives in supporting Louis XIV. But rhetorically the passage has another function. The evidence of James II's subservience to Louis is actually rather thin. He was much more independent of French subsidy than Charles II had been. He was also absurdly confident until quite late in his reign that William of Orange, as his son-in-law, could represent no threat. In the event, William was able to invade England regardless of France, because Louis's concerns were in Alsace. Father Petre was not the most senior Jesuit in England and was easily overruled by Sunderland.[173] But by presenting the Society of Jesus as the most formidable organization in the Catholic World, Macaulay sought to make Petre seem more influential than he was, and James's actions could be attributed to a 'Jesuitical cabal', and thereby given a greater international significance than they actually had.[174]

One could give other examples of Macaulay's idiosyncratic variations of emphasis, but it would be tedious. The main point is that they are the result of conscious artifice, by a mind confident

[172] HE, i. 417.
[173] J. Miller, *James II: A Study in Kingship* (1977), 149–50; J. P. Kenyon, *Robert Spencer, Earl of Sunderland 1641–1702* (1958), 122–3, & chs. *passim*.
[174] HE, i. 559.

in its aims, magnificently stored and fully in control of its material. Those who search Macaulay's pages, as Firth did, for what he has omitted and sources he has missed are likely to underrate this overall design. The fact that we have no equivalent for Macaulay of Gibbon's *Autobiography*, and that he did not explain this design in letters or journal should not deceive us. The more an artist talks or writes about his intentions the more entitled we are to suspect he has fallen short of them.

The design becomes steadily clearer in the essays after 1834. Indeed, its main elements are there in *The Lays of Ancient Rome*. Like the *Lays*, the *History* blends the romantic and the utilitarian, Burkean Toryism and philosophic radicalism. In describing the 'remote past', Macaulay follows Burke, lavishing all the resources of his imagination on bringing historic personalities and their actions vividly before his readers. The main theme of Burke's defence of tradition, in his later writings at least, is that, while political institutions may have faults, they ensure the stability which makes civil society possible, indeed that advocates of precipitate reform may endanger both order and civility. The reason Macaulay thought Burke 'the greatest man since Milton' was that, alone among the politicians of his day, Burke saw that civility or culture (to use a later coinage) was more important than political ambition, in fact that if political life did not foster the activities of the writer, the poet and the artist, it was futile. The *History of England* is in that sense consistent with the theme of the *Reflections on the Revolution in France*. It is designed to associate the ordinary reader with the achievements of his nation's past, to make him a witness of the events that have shaped his world. But reverent awe is not enough. Modern England is confident and expansive. Its new readers have an appetite for innovation and adventure, as well as an affection for the past. They want to know where they are going. Macaulay's skill as a narrator lies in masking his final objective and avoiding explicit prediction: not the least important legacy of his childhood was a revulsion from prophecy. The 'remote future' is only hinted at in occasional glances forward, but it nevertheless provides the controlling motif of a steady progression towards a rational society, produced by free institutions, technological improvement, and commercial prosperity. This is the utilitarian theme, more cerebral and less obvious than the Burkean one perhaps, but equally important. Both are conveyed dramatically. As in a play, the characters unfold and the theme becomes clear through their actions. One may enjoy the plot unreflectingly; but the lesson sinks in and remains.

Macaulay judged his own work against his original aims, and realized he had fallen short of them. But that does not mean that those aims had fundamentally changed. Some foretaste of what Macaulay hoped to achieve appears in the 1828 essay on History. In the perfect historian's narrative, he tells us, 'some transactions are prominent; others retire'. He goes on: 'But the scale on which he represents them is increased or diminished, not according to the dignity of the persons concerned in them, but according to the degree in which they elucidate the condition of society and the nature of man'.[175] This explains not only the rough familiarity with which he assesses kings and their ministers, but also the recourse to the views of poets, playwrights, and essayists for evidence which he always thought more valuable than the political. It also explains why, when the first two volumes of the History were published and awaited the public's verdict, he was more inclined to trust his readers' reaction as reflected in sales than the opinions of his critics. If the book was popular, he had succeeded in that original aim of giving to truth those attractions which had been usurped by fiction. Quite consistently with this aim, he compared his success with that of Byron and Scott, Dickens and Thackeray. In the event, most critics succumbed to the popular enthusiasm. The major exception was John Wilson Croker. Now we must ask why.

[175] MW, i. 277.

8

Riposte

The events for which one generation cares most, are often those of which the next knows least.

BAGEHOT

I

On 18 November 1848 Macaulay corrected the last proofs of the first two volumes of his *History of England* and sent them back to Longmans. In the last sheets, he had contrasted the English Revolution of 1688 with the continental revolutions of this year. The very word 'revolution', he noted, had acquired a violent association at odds with the decorum and pomp of the proceedings which established William and Mary on the throne.[1]

All around us the world is convulsed by the agonies of great nations. Governments which lately seemed likely to stand during ages have been on a sudden shaken and overthrown. The proudest capitals of Western Europe have streamed with civil blood . . . Europe has been threatened with subjugation by barbarians, compared with whom the barbarians who marched with Attila and Alboin were enlightened and humane. The firmest friends of the people have with deep sorrow owned that interests more precious than any political privileges were in jeopardy, and that it might be necessary to sacrifice even liberty in order to save civilisation. Meanwhile in our island the regular course of government has never been for a day interrupted. The few bad men who longed for license and plunder have not had the courage to confront for one moment the strength of a loyal nation, rallied in firm array round a parental throne. And, if it be asked what has made us differ from others, the answer is that we never lost what others are wildly and blindly seeking to regain. It is because we had a preserving revolution in the seventeenth century that we have not had a destroying revolution in the nineteenth.[2]

---

[1] *HE*, ii. 212–13.   [2] Ibid., ii. 214.

Actually the horrors were already receding. 'This strange and awful year', Macaulay told his brother Charles, 'is ending better than a few months ago there seemed reason to expect . . . In France and Germany the friends of order are getting the upper hand'.[3] But in the *History*, the contrast between European anarchy and English order was retained, presumably for its emotional resonance. The *History* made its début at precisely the time when the English public was realizing that it must see liberty sacrificed if civilization was to be saved. By late November the Constitution of the French Republic was completed and overwhelmingly accepted by the Chamber. John Mill called it 'a digest of the elementary doctrines of representative democracy', but the influential paper the *Morning Chronicle* said, more presciently, that it had been framed 'only that a President who is its creature, may drive a coach and six through it'.[4] Further east, the 'friends of order' were more successful. On 6 November Londoners had learned that Vienna, which for a month had been in the hands of a radical-led mob, had capitulated to the army of Windischgraetz. A week later news came that General Wrangel had 'pacified' Berlin. English liberal opinion was not even very sympathetic to the parliament at Frankfurt. When its Leipzig delegate, Robert Blum, was executed in Vienna by Windischgraetz for taking part with the radical demonstrators, the *Chronicle* said that if 'the Chartist member for Nottingham', Feargus O'Connor, were ever caught armed behind a barricade in the Faubourg St Antoine, it would not feel English honour had been compromised if he were transported to Algeria or the Antipodes.[5]

The tone of the *History of England* undoubtedly reflected the experience of the propertied classes during the 1840s, experience which found expression in a distaste for radicalism and a rallying to traditional symbols of order. But since 1846 the traditional party divisions had been disrupted, and no single party reflected faithfully the new public mood. Radical newspapers had become moderate Whig, Whig ones had become Peelite, conservative ones were threatened with failure. The great Whig organ the *Morning Chronicle* had, after the proprietorship of Sir John Easthope, become a Peelite newspaper, proclaiming the great

[3] *LM*, iv. 383. [4] *MC*, 22 Nov. 1848, 4. [5] Ibid., 17 Nov. 1848.

truths of political economy, while being strongly anti-Whig.[6] Before the publication of Macaulay's two volumes, it carried a leader abusing the Whigs and hoping he had not produced a 'party pamphlet' praising such an unprincipled party.[7] A week later a four-column review complimented Macaulay not merely for renouncing politics 'at the very meridian of his career' and taking to literature, but for holding a just balance between the two parties in the text of the *History* itself:

Never was an historian better fortified than Mr Macaulay against those tendencies which have, more or less, warped the minds of nearly all the writers who had preceded him, and which have given a fatal Whig or Tory twist to every popular version of our constitutional annals.[8]

Plainly the *Chronicle* thought free trade rested on scientific economics, whereas Whiggism was the creed of a dying faction, and that condemning Whiggism and praising Macaulay were not inconsistent. But Peelism was a precarious foundation for a newspaper, especially if, as turned out, there was in fact no chance of uniting the Tory party's old leadership with its rank and file. A newspaper, like a review, needed to give its readers a feeling that it was in touch with the men in power. If the men it praised were not in power, its authority was weakened. The *Chronicle* was by the year of Peel's death in serious straits financially, and had in fact only a decade of independent life before it.

The only protectionist newspaper was the *Morning Post*, in which the young Disraeli under the patronage of Lyndhurst, had made his début as the scourge of the radicals, and which under C. E. Michele had from 1842 been a critic of the economic policies of Peel. By 1848 however the *Post* was in difficulties.[9] Michele had bought out the shareholders with money borrowed from his paper supplier, T. B. Crompton, who wanted payment. Michele, according to Lockhart, had approached Lord George Bentinck, who had offered him £15,000, but Crompton had refused the offer. 'It does not now pay even for its paper', Lockhart reported, '& will go for a song some day soon, if anyone will even give a song . . . If it goes what we still call our Party

---

[6] S. Koss, *The Rise and Fall of the Political Press in Britain* (1981), i. 74–5; 86–8.
[7] MC, 22 Nov. 1848, 4.   [8] Ibid., 30 Nov. 1848, 5–6.
[9] S. Koss, op. cit., i. 78–81. W.H. Hindle, *The Morning Post 1772–1937* (1937) is very slight.

will be without either a head in the lower house or an organ in the Daily press'.[10] A month later Bentinck had resigned the leadership of the Protectionists. In the *Quarterly* camp there was also perplexity about how to proceed. Lockhart was as alarmed as Croker by the revolutions of 1848; he even feared a general European war; but he saw that the nature of the debate had changed, and that the rapidity with which political news travelled had meant that readers now took their political opinions more from newspapers than from reviews. Should the reviews then deal more with general literature, inviting the sort of readers who would turn to them for relief from politics?[11] What would the *Quarterly*'s traditional readers, the parson and the squire, think of that? What would Croker, who had now unquestioned control over the political side of the review, say if his authority was, as in 1842, challenged? Characteristically Lockhart could not decide between the intransigent conservatism which had been the *Quarterly*'s traditional line, and the more purely literary policy on which his opinion would have had more weight. In November 1848 when the revolutionaries were failing everywhere, Lockhart was naturally reluctant to alter the *Quarterly*'s allegiance to monarchy, church, and the landed interest.

One must feel sorry for Lockhart. He was a man of letters swept, by his father-in-law's social ambitions, into a branch of literature in which he would always feel at a disadvantage. His sympathies were with the struggling writers of Grub Street,[12] but his politics took him into the political clubs and salons where poverty was a reproach and literary talent (of which he had much) was held cheap. His letters suggest that he had neither the cynicism to exploit his connections nor the confidence to defend the standards of the art he knew best. His despondency was increased by a personal scandal which involved his son Walter's gambling debts. He took a break in Paris, and on his return to London fell ill. So at the very time when Macaulay's *History* was making its impact on the press, the *Quarterly* had no strong hand at the helm. Perhaps he also recalled the row over the review of

<hr>

[10] CPC, Lockhart to Croker, 4 Nov. 1848.
[11] CPC, vol. iv, Lockhart to Croker, 6 May 1848.
[12] His memoir of Theodore Hook (*QR* lxxii, no. 143, May 1843) is a good example.

Macaulay's *Lays*. From his sick-bed he wrote Croker a letter about reviewing Macaulay, in which his fear that the *Quarterly* might lose reputation by condemning a popular success and his fear of upsetting an old colleague were about equally balanced. In 1846 he had helped Croker prepare a new edition of his Boswell,[13] and he now urged that, as that edition had carried Croker's replies to Macaulay's charges, there was no need to carry over the ill-feeling into a new review. Macaulay was 'one of the most vigorous writers of his time & I think any disparagement of his intellectual powers wd tell only against the review.' Besides, he added, 'I have learned to be very sensible that violence nowadays does not answer as well as it did thirty years ago'. That would have been clear editorial guidance for most contributors, but Lockhart (perhaps to soothe Croker's feelings) could not resist his own criticisms of Macaulay's book which in effect encouraged his correspondent to write the review in his old style.

'If you could do it [the *History*] pure justice nothing more is wanted to give the Author sufficient pain. He has written some very brilliant Essays—very transparent with artifice—& I suspect not over honest in scope and management, but he has written *no history*: & he has I believe committed himself ingenuously in 2 or 3 points which duly exposed wd. confound him a good deal & check his breeze from Eldorado.'

There was Macaulay's 'bitter hatred of the Church of England', his low estimate of the clergy of the Restoration period, and his treatment of 'the Whig criminals Sidney & Russell'. Lockhart admitted he was reading the book 'with breathless interest in spite of occasional indignations', but he concluded with an odd verdict. 'In short I doubt if Macaulay's book will go down as a standard addition to our *historical* library, though it must always keep a high place among specimens of English rhetoric.'[14]

Croker's reply showed that, unlike Lockhart, he had been reading the reviews. He was much clearer in setting out the pros and cons. He began by deprecating Lockhart's fears of criticizing a success, hinting gently that they went some way to confirming 'that the Tory party is cowed', and forecasting that the public's reaction to such a review would be to say that the *Quarterly* had

[13] CPC, Lockhart to Croker, 18 May 1846 (vol. iii, fos. 89, 90).
[14] CPC, Lockhart to Croker, 12 Jan. 1849 (vol. iv, fos. 65, 65a); mostly in Brightfield, *Croker*, 368–9.

praised Macaulay because he was a Whig, rather than point out 'his prejudices, partialities, and misrepresentations—of all of which it seems to me, from the extracts I have seen in the papers, there is a large stock.' Croker also denied that he was moved to pay off old scores. He *had* disliked Macaulay: 'his very person and countenance displeased me'. But in their parliamentary conflict his feelings of dislike had been 'if not lost, at least overpowered, by my sense of the brilliancy of his talents.' He had replied to the review of Boswell, he said, only because Macaulay had republished the original review. He assured Lockhart that the parliamentary clash would not prejudice him and that in any article he might write on the *History of England* he would have to resist the temptation to be too kind. But then he added that he would 'on full consideration' rather not take on the review. This part of the letter is arresting, not least because it contains a condensed statement of Croker's conception of the duty of the historian. He knew that if he followed his usual method, any review would be hard work. 'My right hand has forgot some of its cunning to do the thing well. I should have to read over again much that I have forgotten, and to endeavour to acquaint myself with much that I never knew.' This was not mere modesty. He had just published his edition of Lord Hervey's *Memoirs*. His editorial work had made him most familiar with eighteenth century sources, and with the French Revolution. Besides, his method was analytical. He wanted to distinguish, he wrote:

History properly so called, from history moralized or dramatized as by Shakespeare and Scott or made anecdotal like, as I presume from the extracts, Macaulay's. History should be a statue, cold, colourless, if you will, but giving the limbs and features, the forms and dimensions with unalterable, severe mechanical exactness; and not a picture to be coloured to the artist's eye, to be seen in a particular light, and to be helped out with accessories of detail selected not for truth but for effect. I admit that such pictorial history is more amusing; but does it really give you a truer view of the state of things? I doubt . . .

Exposing the errors of such pictorial history was, however, arduous:

To examine a work after this fashion, to discover, to analyze, to decompose the anecdotal colouring or discolouring, and to separate the general course of events from the exceptive instances which the anecdotal historians build so much upon, could take more learning and more leisure than I could now bring to the task.

This was a just assessment of his method. It was too exhaustive and analytical for the large, colourful narrative, and there is a hint that Croker was aware that Macaulay was more familiar with his chosen period than he was himself. On the other hand, while proclaiming his own disinclination, he warned Lockhart that it would be better that the *Quarterly* carried no review at all than one which compromised its principles and by flattering Macaulay showed the public it had gone soft. It should be possible, he said, to write a review which gave praise where it was deserved, and yet was frank about the work's faults. So the letter leaves one with the feeling that Croker wanted to expose Macaulay even if the work was done by someone else.[15]

Lockhart must have been at a loss. His major contributor had said both that he bore Macaulay no grudge *and* that the *Quarterly*'s tradition must be upheld; that he himself would not review the book *and* that it should be possible to find some reviewer who would give credit where credit was due. If Lockhart repeated his mistake over the *Lays of Ancient Rome* and sent the *History of England* to another reviewer, there could be an explosion. But he was sensitive to the implied charge of capitulation, and actually as worried as Croker at the threat of revolution and the spread of scepticism. So he soothed his friend's feelings by urging him to take his time to read the book and then decide whether to review it, and he suggested that they could invoke help.[16] Croker was not easily persuaded. He hesitated until early February and then replied that if Lockhart and Murray (who was apparently not averse to attacking the sales of his rival Longman) did not fear the effects of a review of Macaulay, he would start work. He made one condition, 'that I am to have your unreserved assistance'. Without that, he said, he could not go on. He added, 'You may stand as a kind of umpire between Macaulay and me'.[17]

---

[15] NLS, Lockhart MSS, 927 no. 59, fos. 106–7. Brightfield, 369–72, correctly in my view, treats this as a reply to that already quoted, but the MS date is 11 Jan. 1849. The safest inference is that Lockhart was too ill to date the original letter correctly.

[16] CPC, Lockhart to Croker, 12 Jan. 1849 (Lockhart vol. iv. fo. 64).

[17] NLS, Lockhart MSS 928, no. 30, fo. 41 Croker to Lockhart n.d. 'W(est) M(olesey) 8th'.

The review took a long time to prepare. Other experts were asked for their opinions. Various clergy obliged. Bodley's librarian, the delightfully-named Bulkeley Bandinel, was consulted on editions of sources. The manuscript began as jottings made as Croker read, and these were sent to Clowes the printer in 'fascicules', each given a letter of the alphabet, A to N. Once printed these went to Lockhart for scrutiny. It is not clear whether he shaped them into a continuous argument. A final page proof was circulated, which survives, and is seventeen pages longer than the final article. No other article in their long collaboration took up so much correspondence, Lockhart urging a polite tone but adding his own censure, Croker affecting sorrow that such a detestable book obliged him to be severe.[18] By March it was complete, and the *Quarterly* containing it appeared early in April.

Perhaps if the friends in Albemarle Street had been able to eavesdrop in Paternoster Row they might have been in greater haste, for the longer the review took, the greater were Macaulay's sales. Probably both author and publisher were surprised by these. In September 1848 they had agreed that for 6,000 copies of the *History*, Macaulay would be paid £500 a year for five years starting in January 1849; but that if that number of copies were sold before the end of that period, Longman would pay him two-thirds of the profits (after the expenses of printing and binding) on all subsequent volumes.[19] The 6,000 mark was soon reached and passed; the first two editions of 3,000 each went rapidly, and in January 1849 a third edition of 5,000 was printed.[20] In his journal, Macaulay had confided his fears. 'As compared with excellence the work is a failure. But as compared with similar books I cannot think it so.'[21] But early reviews were laudatory. Besides the *Chronicle*'s, there was high praise from the *Examiner*, the *Morning Herald* and the *Globe*.[22] Macaulay noted in his journal that Scott's *Lay of the Last Minstrel* had sold 2,250 in the first year, *Marmion* 2,000 in a month, but his own

[18] CPC, Lockhart letters vol. iv., fos. 80, 81, (14, 15 Mar. 1848); NLS, Lockhart MS 927, fo. iii. Croker to Lockhart, 2 Mar. 1849; g28, fo. 26, 9 Mar. 1849.
[19] Longman Archive, Reading University, MS II. 68–8. Agreement d. 18 Sept. 1848.
[20] Ibid., Impressions Book fos. 123, 126, 134; for sales, see Divide Ledger D. 4, fos. 375–6.
[21] TCM Journal, i. fo. 407 (18 Nov. 1848).
[22] *Examiner*, 30 Dec. 1849; *Morning Herald, Globe*, 7 Dec. 1849.

History 3,000 in ten days.[23] By 10 January, when Lockhart was still looking for a reviewer, and wondering if he had the strength to do the work himself, the second edition had gone, and 1,250 copies ordered of a third. The buoyant confidence at Longman's communicated itself to Macaulay. Early in February he received the famous delegation of Quakers who came to protest at his treatment of William Penn. His journal entry reads:

Lord Shelburne, Austin & Milman to breakfast. A pleasant meal. Then the Quakers five in number. Never was there such a rout. They had absolutely nothing to say. Every charge against Penn came out as clear as any case at the Old Bailey. They had nothing to urge but, what was true enough, that he looked worse in my history than he would have looked on a general survey of his whole life. But that is not my fault. I wrote the history of four years during which he was exposed to great temptations, during which he was the favourite of a bad King, & an active solicitor in a most corrupt court. His character was injured by his associations. Ten years before or ten years later he would have made a much better figure. But was I to begin my book ten years earlier for William Penn's sake? The Quakers were extremely civil. So was I. They complimented me on my courtesy & candour. But I am afraid they would qualify their compliments if they knew how I laughed at them after their departure.[24]

An amusing cartoon celebrating the Quakers' discomfiture soon appeared in *Punch*, showing Macaulay repelling his critics with a gigantic pen.[25] So confident did the Longman camp become that in late February the rumour circulated that, after doing some work on his review, Croker had given it up.[26] On 12 March Longman assured Macaulay that there would be no attack in the *Quarterly*. They plainly felt that the *History*'s spectacular sales put it beyond the power of any review to harm.

But they had surely also expected an act of retaliation. The quarrel in parliament, which had added the spice of personal

---

[23] TCM Journal, 12 Dec. 1848.

[24] TCM Journal, i. fos. 491–2; Trevelyan, (ed.) i. 188–9 where the last sentence is omitted. Lockhart wrote to Croker on 9 Feb. 1849 an account of the interview which he had had from Milman, [MS in possession of Mr T.L.G. Landon].

[25] *Punch*, vol. 16 (1849), 72; William Tallack, 'Macaulay and the Friends' in *Bulletin of Friends' Historical Society of Philadelphia*, vol. vii, no. 3 (May, 1927), 91–7. For what the Quakers were prevented from saying, see J. Paget 'The New Examen' in *Paradoxes and Puzzles, Historical, Judicial and Literary* (Edinburgh and London, 1874), 134–210.

[26] Journal, i. fo. 519, 24 Feb. 1849.

antagonism to the ancient rivalry of two reviews and two publishing houses, had been recalled to men's minds by the republication, in 1846, of Macaulay's essay on Croker's *Boswell*. People expected Croker to take revenge, and we feel drawn to do the same. From Samuel Rogers's sour joke about attempting murder and achieving suicide, until our own day, Croker's review of Macaulay has been judged as a failed reprisal. The reply which accompanied the second edition of his *Boswell* has been ignored. In fact, the material in the *Quarterly*'s review of Macaulay was not all Croker's; and one reason readers have found it tedious is that it is relentlessly detailed, and that is because, on the main issue of the significance of the Revolution of 1688, he and Macaulay broadly agreed.

II

Croker evidently expected that in reviewing the *History of England* he would be dealing with a work by a radical Whig. He looked on Russell's government as the feeble mouthpiece of Irish Repealers and Radicals, and till early 1848 it had included Macaulay. But he must have noticed that nearly all the reviewers of the first two volumes of the *History* commented on its political impartiality. As he read them himself he would have seen that they conveyed a view of the Revolution of 1688 which was very close to his own. Both men, as we have seen, were in their different ways admirers of Burke. Croker read the French Revolution in the light of the *Reflections on the Revolution in France* and his view of the Whigs was deeply influenced by *A Letter to a Noble Lord*. Macaulay had scarcely less admiration for Burke the writer. There are passages even in his early articles in which we hear Burke's great melody scored for brass. They recur in the *History of England*. 'People will not look forward to posterity, who never look backward to their ancestors'.[27] That is Burke. Macaulay adds some adjectives to extend the timescale: 'A people which takes no pride in the noble achievements of remote ancestors will never achieve anything worthy to be remembered with pride by remote descendants'.[28] Even in his interpretation of the Revolution of 1688 Macaulay follows Burke's

---

[27] *Reflections*, (Oxford, World's Classics edn.), 36.   [28] [*Works*. ii. 585].

argument against Price. James II's systematic flouting of the law led prominent men of both parties to favour a minor deviation from the strict succession, and in doing so vindicated existing laws and notions of constitutional propriety. At no point was there a question of a popular mandate, though the whole transaction conferred a great benefit on all Englishmen. Croker could hardly dissent from this general interpretation.

But he also found a view of political parties very like his own. In 1838, as we saw, he told Brougham that the two great antagonist principles at the root of all government were those of stability and experiment, that the former was a tory and the latter a whig principle.[29] He would have found much the same distinction in Macaulay's first chapter where 'the corporate existence of the two great parties which have ever since alternately governed the country' is dated to September 1641.

Everywhere there is a class of men who cling with fondness to whatever is ancient, and who, even when convinced by overpowering reasons that innovation would be beneficial, consent to it with many misgivings and forebodings. We find also everywhere another class of men sanguine in hope, bold in speculation, always pressing forward, quick to discern the imperfections of whatever exists, disposed to think lightly of the risks and inconveniences which attend improvements, and disposed to give every change credit for being an improvement. In the sentiments of both classes there is something to approve. But of both the best specimens will be found not far from the common frontier. The extreme section of one class consists of bigoted dotards: the extreme section of the other consists of shallow and reckless empirics.[30]

In the early months of the Long Parliament, Macaulay goes on, the Commons made a concerted attack on the abuses of royal government. But after the recess of 1641 it became clear that 'a great schism was latent', and from that moment the parties began their contention. At first they were called Cavalier and Roundhead, later Tories and Whigs, 'nor does it seem that these appellations are likely soon to become obsolete'. But lest the reader think he is taking sides, he adds that both parties were necessary to the country.

[29] See above, Ch. 3.   [30] *HE*, i. 82.

It would not be difficult to compose a lampoon or a panegyric on either of these renowned factions. For no man not utterly destitute of judgment and candour will deny that there are many deep stains on the fame of the party to which he belongs, or that the party to which he is opposed may justly boast of many illustrious names, of many heroic actions, and of many great services rendered to the State. The truth is that, though both parties have often seriously erred, England could have spared neither. If, in her institutions, freedom and order, the advantages arising from innovation and the advantages arising from prescription, have been combined to an extent elsewhere unknown, we may attribute this happy peculiarity to the strenuous conflicts and alternate victories of two rival confederacies of statesmen, a confederacy zealous for authority and antiquity, and a confederacy zealous for liberty and progress.

The great safeguard against anarchy on the one side and despotism on the other was that the parties' views overlapped, and the fanatics on each side were in a minority:

. . . The great majority of those who fought for the crown were averse to despotism, and the great majority of the champions of popular rights were averse to anarchy. Twice, in the course of the seventeenth century, the two parties suspended their dissensions, and united their strength in a common cause. Their first coalition [in 1660] restored hereditary monarchy. Their second coalition rescued constitutional freedom [in 1688].[31]

This view of party as resting in the last resort on temperament and not on a continuity of doctrine or a common organization, explains why Macaulay felt free to distribute praise and blame between members of both parties; why for instance he has a strong respect for Danby, but not Shaftesbury, and why he dislikes Marlborough even though he was a Whig. But it also explains why Croker could not attack the *History of England* primarily as the work of a Whig apologist.

The bulk of Croker's review is directed at Macaulay's alleged misuse of sources. He starts by saying that he had hoped, as he agreed with Macaulay on the beneficial effects of the Revolution of 1688, to have been able to meet him 'on the neutral ground of literature'.[32] It turned out, however, that what was novel in Macaulay's *History* was not new fact (for he had added little

---

[31] *HE*, i. 83–4.   [32] *QR*, lxxxiv, no. 168 (Mar. 1849), 549.

to the findings of Dalrymple, Fox, and Mackintosh) but a new narrative method. He had sought to imitate the historical novel, in particular the example of Scott, but the only way he could give his historical characters any semblance of life was by imposing on them his own prejudices, or, as Croker expresses it, 'hating the individuals of the opposite party as bitterly, as passionately, as if they were his own personal enemies'.[33] This charge is not the prelude to an exposure of Macaulay's political opinions as they had influenced his view of the past. For Croker goes on to say that he is not going to discuss broad historical developments, or issues of political interpretation in the *History*. As Macaulay had said nothing new, nothing his predecessors had not said before him, a critic's dispute would be with them, with Burnet, Dalrymple, Mackintosh and the others, and not with Macaulay himself. This was Croker's reason for concentrating on what he calls 'the humbler but more practical and more useful task'[34] of exposing Macaulay's treatment of details. It was an odd decision. For if in declaring for his own trusted method he was free to skirt around the large area of constitutional history on which he and Macaulay agreed, he also seriously limited the scope of his own argument. Try as he might, Croker could not confine his criticism to issues of literary technique: politics would keep intruding. Purely literary shortcomings could not be separated from charges of vulgarity and bad taste; liberties with sources became tangled (as they usually did in Croker's historical criticism) with the graver faults of plagiarism and bad faith; and what started out as a critique of the historian as novelist was compromised by the unavowed conviction that Macaulay was all along defending the Whigs.

Many of Croker's criticisms are shrewd. As a former political opponent he was much more aware than later writers on Macaulay of the similarities between the style of the speeches and that of the *History*. At the start of the review he says that while in parliament Macaulay was 'though not quite an orator, and still less a debater, the most brilliant rhetorician in the house'.[35] That was true. Even a Whig like Greville admitted that Macaulay's speeches were 'harangues and never replies'.[36]

---

[33] Ibid., 552. [34] Ibid., 554.
[35] Ibid., 549. [36] Greville, ii. 203.

Croker goes on to observe that the style of the *History* is forceful and clear and carries its readers with 'something of the sorcery which a brilliant orator exercises over his auditory'.

But it also has in a great degree the faults of the oratorical style. He deals much too largely in epithets—a habit exceedingly dangerous to historical truth. He habitually constructs a piece of what should be calm, dispassionate narrative, upon the model of the most passionate peroration—adhering in numberless instances to precisely the same specific formula of artifice. His diction is often inflated into fustian, and he indulges in exaggeration till it sometimes, unconsciously no doubt, amounts to falsehood.[37]

Croker gives many examples of this habit of exaggeration, as when Burnet, the original source, says William of Orange 'was that day hunting' and Macaulay turns it into 'William was many miles off after a stag',[38] which Croker calls 'this low phrase'. Again, when he came to describe Princess Anne's escape from Whitehall with Bishop Compton's help in November 1688, Macaulay wrote: 'The coach drove instantly to Aldersgate Street, where the town residence of the Bishops of London then stood, within the shadow of the dome of the Cathedral'. Croker's comment is: 'Noble! But unluckily, there was no dome either before that time, nor at that time, nor for some years later'.[39]

Croker also objects to history being made picturesque, partly because 'vulgar' details of clothes and furniture and food do not affect the action of the main characters, but also because such illustrative material must take the place of more serious analysis and explanation. In taking his inspiration from Scott, Macaulay had seen that history with these trappings would be more popular, but in spite of his 'constant endeavour to give from all the repositories of gossip that have reached us a kind of circumstantial reality to his incidents, and a sort of dramatic life to his personages', the result is not 'a substantial addition to history properly so called; on the contrary, he seems to have willingly taken it as he found it'.[40] This seems to miss Macaulay's aim and so to underrate his skill. A good story-teller may tell a familiar

---

[37] *QR*, lxxxiv, no. 168 (Mar. 1849), 553.   [38] Ibid., 558.
[39] Ibid., 584. Macaulay removed the dome from later editions.
[40] Ibid., 552.

story but do it with greater skill than any predecessor; the point is whether and how his method is an improvement. But Macaulay was actually, as we saw, very alert to the differences between a fictional and a historical narrative. History tells us of men and women doing things which no fictional writer would attempt for fear of losing his readers' respect. After describing in detail in Chapter VI, James II's strange infatuation with Catherine Sedley and the attempts of Clarendon and Rochester to use her influence with the King to strengthen the Church party, he comments:

So much is history stranger than fiction; and so true is it that nature has caprices which art dares not imitate. A dramatist would scarcely venture to bring on the stage a grave prince, in the decline of life, ready to sacrifice his crown in order to serve the interests of his religion, indefatigable in making proselytes, and yet deserting and insulting a wife who had youth and beauty for the sake of a profligate paramour who had neither. Still less, if possible, would a dramatist venture to intro-duce a statesman [Rochester] stooping to the wicked and shameful part of a procurer, and calling in his wife to aid him in that dishonourable office, yet, in his moments of leisure, retiring to his closet, and there secretly pouring out his soul to his God in penitent tears and devout ejaculations.[41]

The passage, with its revealing shift from fiction to drama, suggests the real point of Macaulay's taste for local detail. As the past is so unfamiliar, and involves people whose motives we cannot share, we need the details of their everyday lives to give their actions body and location, just as the most realistic stage dialogue needs at least some scenery to give it context and help us enter into the issues involved. Croker's criticism would have been more to the point if, instead of accusing Macaulay of imitating fiction, he had conceded that the story was vividly told and considered what ulterior purpose the component parts served. Whatever Macaulay had done with the existing narrat-ives, he had certainly not taken them as he found them.

Croker devotes twenty-four pages to the famous third chapter. He is puzzled why Macaulay chose 1685 as a point at which to examine English society. 'No worse point of time

---

[41] *HE,* i. 564.

could have been chosen', he says, 'for tracing the obscure but very certain connection between political events and the manners of a people'. Either 1660 or 1688 would have been better as ushering in new eras. He then has some fun with Macaulay's illustrations, showing that four-fifths of the examples in the chapter date from after 1685 and some from much earlier. The whole chapter in fact is like 'an old curiosity shop, into which . . . the knick-knacks of a couple of centuries are promiscuously jumbled'.[42] Macaulay had cited Swift and Gay to illustrate the squalor of London streets, where a gutter or 'kennel' ran down the middle, and the pedestrian kept to the wall to avoid the splashes of the carriages. 'The mild and timid gave the wall. The bold and athletic took it.' Croker pointed out that the same custom prevailed in Shakespeare's England, and cited the opening scene in *Romeo and Juliet*.[43] Equally absurd, says Croker, is Macaulay's offering, as evidence of the coarseness and insecurity of life in the late seventeenth century, events and practices which could be matched by similar ones in quite recent times. What could his motive be in muddling up the chronology? Croker suggests two: 'the embellishment of his historical romance' and 'a wish to exhibit England *prior to the Revolution* as in a mean and even barbarous and despicable condition'.[44]

Croker followed this up with an exposure, doubtless prompted by his clerical correspondents, of Macaulay's treatment of the Church and the country gentry. Macaulay knew that he had written provocatively about the Church, but it is clear from his journal that he expected the counter-attack from the Tractarians and ultra Evangelicals.[45] This gives the clue to his aims in Chapter III. In asserting that, as a result of the Reformation, the clergy had lost status and that by the seventeenth century they were looked on 'as, on the whole, a plebeian class',[46] he was questioning the high gentlemanly status which the Tractarians in his own day claimed for their order; and in pointing out their poverty he was suggesting that poverty and ignorance are the soil in which dogmatism and intolerance flourish. The rural clergyman was a Tory and a bigot.

---

[42] *QR*, lxxxiv, no. 168 (Mar. 1849), 579.   [43] Ibid., 584.
[44] Ibid., 585–6.   [45] TCM, Journal i. fo. 434, 7 Dec. 1848.
[46] *HE*, i. 253.

Having lived in seclusion, and having little opportunity of correcting his opinions by reading or conversation, he held and taught the doctrines of indefeasible hereditary right, of passive obedience, and of non-resistance in all their crude absurdity.[47]

The passage makes quite clear Macaulay's admiration for a learned clergy; but he insists that such men, 'men familiar with all ancient and modern learning . . . whose address, politeness and knowledge of the world qualified them to manage the consciences of the wealthy and noble', were to be found in the cities and the universities.[48] Croker and Lockhart (and one must include Lockhart because his insistence on the irreligious character of the *History* did much to colour the review) were committed to a *via media*, neither Tractarian nor ultra-evangelical, neither Catholic nor Dissenting, and they felt obliged to defend the Church of the Reformation settlement, as if it had never been the product of doctrinal compromise.[49] A critical account of how the Church originated seemed to them an assault on the Church in their own day. Macaulay's utilitarianism involved a relativist view of the social benefits of religion. Where, as was the case in modern England, political institutions are liberal, priestcraft and superstition are objectionable; but in the Middle Ages what now seems objectionable was wholesome. 'There is a point in the life both of an individual and a society at which submission and faith, such as at a later period would be justly called servility and cruelty, are useful qualities'.[50] Priestly fanaticism may be a good thing if it acts as a curb on princely absolutism. But to Croker such a position was shockingly cynical. 'Such forever is Mr. Macaulay's principle of art. It is not the elimination of error that he seeks for, but an artistic balance of conflicting forces'.[51] In the Reformation period, he continues, this search for contrasts involves a denigration of Anglicanism. Macaulay 'awards to the Catholics the merit of unity and consistency; to the Calvinists, of reason and independence; to the Anglicans, the lowest motives of expediency and compromise'.[52] So when he comes to describing the clergy in Charles II's reign, he chooses to portray

[47] Ibid., i. 258. [48] Ibid., i. 257.
[49] CPC, Macaulay file, Croker to Bishop Philpotts, 14 Mar. 1849 (copy).
[50] HE, i. 43. [51] QR, lxxxiv, no. 168 (Mar. 1849), 570.
[52] Ibid., 571.

their ignorance and social degradation, rather than their learning, piety, and high social standing.

As with the Church, so with the gentry. Croker was indignant at Macaulay's portrayal of the country gentry as a class of bucolic boors, summed up in the notorious sentence: 'The gross, uneducated, untravelled country gentleman was commonly a Tory'.[53] Even admirers of the third chapter do not claim that Macaulay was making a purely factual statement, and Croker shows that the whole picture of the class, and Macaulay's bland claim that he had taken it 'from sources too numerous to be recapitulated' and could be judged only by 'those who have studied the history and the lighter literature of that age', was an evasion, since no imaginative literature, light or grave, could be a substitute for fact.[54]

The review has taken up fifty pages before we have reached the fourth chapter, and the narrative proper of James II's reign, and the tone now changes. Up to now the stress has been mainly on Macaulay's methods as a historian. In the last pages of the review the charge is more openly political. Croker notes that from 1685 Macaulay's narrative relies on the unfinished history of Mackintosh, but that he fails to acknowledge the debt, and he shows by a series of parallel passages from the two historians that Macaulay often uses Mackintosh's own phrases, and that, where he differs from him it is in the direction of exaggeration and invention. Croker thought he had exposed a settled, systematic habit of plagiarism.[55] From what we know of the workings of Macaulay's memory, we would be more inclined to say that the borrowings were unconscious. This would be quite consistent with his supplementing the meagre details of social life to be found in historians and memoir writers with vivid examples from the plays and pamphlets he had read.

But Croker goes on to claim that Macaulay's liberties with the authorities have a consistent political motivation, and this is a much more serious charge than any made by Macaulay's later critics. Firth for example, claims only that Macaulay's 'perception of moral defects is much keener in the case of a Tory than in that of a Whig'.[56] Croker says that Macaulay gathers and

[53] HE, i. 250.   [54] Ibid., 251 n., QR, lxxxiv, no. 168 (Mar. 1849), 601.
[55] Ibid., 603–6.   [56] Firth, Commentary, 261.

aggravates any charges, true *or* false, against Tories, and softens and conceals even undeniable ones against Whigs, and that he does so in so 'dexterous' a manner as to 'keep up some show of impartiality'.

The reproach, well or ill founded, which he thinks most likely to damage the character of any one he dislikes, is repeated over and over again in hope that the iteration will at last be taken for proof, such as the perfidy of Charles I., the profligacy and selfishness of Charles II., the cold and cruel stupidity of James, the baseness of Churchill, the indecent violence of Rochester, the contemptible subserviency of his brother, Clarendon, and so on through a whole dictionary of abuse on every one whom he takes or mistakes for a Tory, and on a few Whigs whom for some special reasons of his own he treats like Tories. On the other hand, when he finds himself reluctantly forced to acknowledge even the greatest enormity of the Whigs—corruption—treason—murder—he finds much gentler terms for the facts; selects a scapegoat, some subaltern villain, or some one whom history has already gibbeted, 'to bear upon him all their iniquities', and that painful sacrifice once made, he avoids with tender care a recurrence to so disagreeable a subject.[57]

Croker illustrates this from the work of Dalrymple. The letters of Louis XIV's ambassador, Barillon, which Dalrymple edited, showed that payments had been made by the French king to the Whigs, notably Lord William Russell and Algernon Sidney, who were later involved in the Rye House plot to assassinate Charles II and his brother. Croker accuses Macaulay of dismissing Russell's treason and Sidney's corruption, 'with a censure so gentle as to sound like applause',[58] then ignoring them and finding a scapegoat in Ralph Montague. Montague had secured Danby's acquiescence in French policy by getting him a French bribe, then exposed him to impeachment. So he, Montague, became the villain in a transaction which actually included Russell and Sidney. Macaulay had omitted to mention that Montague was Russell's brother-in-law. He had then applied the same formula in describing Monmouth's rebellion, which was, says Croker, 'but the continuation and catastrophe of the Rye House Plot'.

[57] *QR*, lxxxiv, no. 168 (Mar. 1849), 611.   [58] Ibid., 612.

For that plot Lord Russell and Algernon Sidney had suffered, and these two martyrs, having been early canonized by the revolutionary Whigs, have been still worshipped—though with a less bold devotion since the discovery of Barillon's despatches—by that same party of which the Russell family have been from the Revolution to this day the great and powerful head.

The rebellion confirmed the claims of the Crown lawyers who prosecuted the Whig 'Martyrs' Russell and Sidney. Macaulay had tried to show 'that Monmouth had no premeditated design of rebellion, that he had given up all thoughts of public life, and that he was at least a reluctant victim of the scheming and plotting of the mischievous people about him'.[59] He had played down the role of Grey, but was savage to Ferguson, the Judas of Dryden's satire, *Absolom and Achitophel*. Croker also questions Macaulay's attempt to exonerate William of Orange from any connection with Monmouth's rebellion. If he had none, he asks, why was Grey made an earl after the Revolution, and Ferguson given a sinecure in the royal household? Finally, Croker casts doubt on Macaulay's heroic portrait of William III. The world, he says, has been content to consider William as 'a great soldier and statesman and the opportune though irregular instrument of a necessary revolution'. But Macaulay had stressed his private virtues, and made a romance out of his relations with Mary, to whom he was in fact cruel and ungrateful. His relationship with Elizabeth Villiers was quite comparable to Charles II's with Lady Castlemaine.[60] Far from being content in the role of Mary's consort, he wanted to be King of England in his own right.

Croker ends the review with a protest at Macaulay's devotion to the picturesque, even though he admits it makes the *History* an attractive and absorbing story-book. His last lines echo Lockhart's original verdict:

We protest against this species of *carnival* history; no more like the reality than the Eglintoun Tournament or the Costume Quadrilles of Buckingham Palace; and we deplore the squandering of so much melodramatic talent on a subject which we have hitherto reverenced as the figure of Truth arrayed in the simple garments of Philosophy. We are ready to admit an hundred times over Mr. Macaulay's literary powers

[59] *QR*, lxxxiv, no. 168 (Mar. 1849), 615.   [60] Ibid., 626.

—brilliant even under the affectation with which he too frequently disfigures them. He is a great painter, but a suspicious narrator; a grand proficient in the picturesque, but a very poor professor of the historic. These volumes have been, and his future volumes as they appear will be, devoured with the same eagerness that *Oliver Twist* or *Vanity Fair* excite—with the same quality of zest, though perhaps with a higher degree of it;—but his pages will seldom, we think, receive a second perusal—and the work, we apprehend, will hardly find a permanent place on the historic shelf—nor ever assuredly, if continued in the spirit of the first two volumes, be quoted as authority on any question or point of the History of England.[61]

III

Macaulay read Croker's review early in April at Lichfield, where he was on tour with the Trevelyans. 'I opened it with some anxiety', he admitted, 'which soon changed into the most profound contempt. Poor miserable creature. He has not hit a single blot. If he had known all that he might and ought to have known he might have produced a very annoying article. As it is his spite is a matter for mirth'.[62] A week later after a visit to Longman's, where they were preparing a fifth edition, he reported:

'General contempt for Croker's article . . . Really, he has done me a great service. I apprehended a strong reaction, the natural effect of such a success, and if hatred had left him free to use his very slender faculties to the best advantage, he might have injured me much. He should have been large in acknowledgment—should have taken a mild and expostulating tone—should have looked out for real blemishes which, as I too well know, he might easily have found. Instead of that he has written with such rancour as to make everybody sick, [with such inaccuracy that he has committed ten times as many blunders himself in eighty pages as he has been able to detect in my thirteen hundred pages, —and, above all, he has obviously grudged me the praise to which every body else, however hostile, owns me to have a claim. Envy itself therefore is ashamed to applaud him. He merely irritates the public curiosity to see more of my book.] I could almost pity him. But he is a bad—a very bad man—a scandal to politics & to letters.'[63]

---

[61] Ibid., 630.   [62] TCM Journal, i. fo. 566, 7 Apr. 1849.
[63] Ibid., fos. 574–6. The brackets are pencilled in the MS and correspond to the lines Trevelyan omitted in the *Life*, ii. 195.

G. O. Trevelyan, quoting these comments in part, tried to suggest that Macaulay brushed aside Croker's criticisms and that these were in themselves rancorous and trivial. As the article (unlike the more matured criticisms of John Paget, Walter Bagehot, or Gladstone) was never reprinted, most people who have heard of it at all have done so from Trevelyan's biography. But even Trevelyan was too embarrassed to quote his uncle's angrier phrases, and anger, in a man of Macaulay's complacency, is likely to be the only evidence that criticism has gone home. There is a lot of personal abuse in Macaulay's journals, and sometimes it is contradicted by his own more considered judgements. A month before calling Croker 'a scandal to politics and letters' he had read the edition of Lord Hervey's *Memoirs* and called it (though he could not bring himself to name the editor) 'a most able & entertaining book of memoirs'.[64]

Many contemporaries read Croker's review as a mean-spirited riposte for Macaulay's review of his *Boswell*,[65] and there may be some self-deception in Croker's disclaimer to Lockhart that he felt no personal resentment. But the idea of a personal duel may obscure the fact that the two reviews are very dissimilar in method and intention. Macaulay's early polemics are literary commando raids. They seem devised to achieve surprise, to shock and demoralize, but they do not occupy the ground or much alter the course of the conflict, which is why they can still be enjoyed out of context as feats of polemic. Croker's reviews are all part of a larger, less dramatic but more unremitting campaign, conducted by a man with no illusions about the enemy's strength or his own, and while they are meant to inflict damage, there is no energy wasted on personalities or rhetorical display. Critical exposure is the point: they deal with the writer's veracity, not his skill. The best points are scattered rather artlessly, like explosives with delayed detonations. Macaulay's reaction betrays this disparity. He saw at once that Croker had not copied his own method, and he was relieved. Instead of holding his reader with a display of wit, ridicule, and sarcasm, Croker had given him a long and unrelentingly detailed catalogue of errors, and Macaulay concluded that what was not

---

[64] Journal, i. fo. 457, 18 Mar. 1849.
[65] e.g., *Scotsman*, 14 Apr. 1849, 3, cols. 1–3.

enthralling must be boring and ineffective. It was the characteristic response of a man used to talking down his critics.

In Albemarle Street they were afraid Croker had been too severe. Lockhart had all along urged a style of condescending banter, free of personal imputations. 'You wd produce infinitely more effect of damage were every bitter word & unparliamentary imputation cut out',[66] he told Croker; and receiving another 'fascicule', he commended its tone as 'calm and playful such as is suitable for the *novelist*', meaning of course the author of the *History of England*.[67] But when the review was receiving adverse comments in the newspapers, he had second thoughts. Murray, who regularly passed on customers' comments, reported that two of Croker's references to Macaulay's career had caused offence and the implication was that the review would have been better without them.[68] One of these was a passing reference to Macaulay's mistake in calling Alice Lisle 'the Lady Alice', which Croker said, was strange in one who had been 'a guest at "*Windsor Castle*"'—a sly reference to the episode when Macaulay as a minister had written his constituents a letter addressed 'Windsor Castle', a gaffe which caused some unkind comment.[69] The other was more serious, and concerned Croker's protest at Macaulay's claim that Marlborough had from his youth been a miser: 'Already his private drawers contained heaps of broad pieces which fifty years later remained untouched'.[70] Croker, pointing out that the story was one which Pope (who hated Marlborough) had given Joseph Spence, who put it in his *Anecdotes*, reproached Macaulay for sneering at a young man's keeping his earliest earnings, and added that in Churchill's day there was no India 'to which an aspirant to station and fame might retire for a while to secure by honourable thrift an honourable independence, and thereby the power and liberty of action to realize the prospects of an honest ambition'.[71] Neither example seems specially offensive. The first was a joke; the second a shrewder thrust, not denying Marlborough's avarice, but reminding the historian that his Indian gains called for a

---

[66] CPC, vol. iv, fo. 80, 14 Mar. 1849.   [67] Ibid., fo. 81, 15 Mar. 1849.
[68] CPC, Lockhart vol. iv, Lockhart to Croker 18 Apr. 1849.
[69] LM, iii. 303 for the original letter; Trevelyan [pb. edn.] i. 19–21.
[70] HE, i. 699. The passage was removed from the later editions.
[71] QR, lxxxiv. no. 168, 610.

little more charity towards a young man with great ambition but no money. 'Honourable thrift' and 'honourable independence' are surely not insulting phrases. There were also slighting references to Macaulay's official experience, such as the comment on an ex-Secretary-at-War devoting an amount of space to the topography of Sedgmoor quite out of proportion to what was in the event a mere skirmish.[72] But these were legitimate comments on a public man's judgement. Another reviewer found the article 'very amusing', adding, 'none but the author can call it an unfair review'.[73]

Croker rejected the notion that he had been too severe. He was convinced he had proved what he called Macaulay's 'bad faith' by setting out the parallel passages from Mackintosh, and he expected a reply.[74] By the time the newspapers were commenting on his review, he had come to regret that he had given way to Lockhart's pleas for restraint. 'You and Mr Lockhart insisted on a milder treatment than I originally would have adopted', he told Murray, 'you were no doubt right and nothing will be lost by courtesy of language but be assured the general tone of admiration of all the critiques is but a temporary illusion, a *feu de paille* & the proofs of plagiarism & bad faith— forgery in fact which I have in my sleeve are worse than any that I produced'.[75] There was a reply, but not from Macaulay himself. The historian scribbled a few pages of notes 'sufficient to smash twenty Crokers' and sent them off to his friend Empson, Napier's successor as editor of the *Edinburgh*, and these were worked up into a reply by another contributor, named Moncrieff, which are feeble, and which Lockhart thought unworthy of a further notice.[76] So both sides could feel the contest had been a draw; Lockhart and Croker might have told themselves there were still a few shots in their locker; Macaulay

[72] *QR*, lxxxiv. no. 168, 621 sq. He would have been able to expand this point had he been able to see Macaulay's account of Churchill's capture of Cork and Kinsale in Ch. XVI.

[73] CPC, Macaulay file; Edward Cheney to J. W. Croker, n.d. (1849). Cheney wrote for the *Quarterly* and was the author of the article on 'Revolutionized Italy' which preceded Croker's review.

[74] Murray MSS, to John Murray 'Good Friday' [i.e. 6 Apr.] 1849.

[75] Ibid., no date 'W[est] M[olesey] Saturday'.

[76] *TCM*, Journal, i. fo. 588, 4 Apr. 1849; *ER*, vol. xc., no. 181 (July 1849), 249–92. Of these, 281–90 were clearly the materials sent by Macaulay, and perhaps account for the pages taken from vol. II of his journal after fo. 8.

and Empson that the *Quarterly*'s broadside had done no irreparable damage.

Nor did the reaction occur for which the *Quarterly* reviewers had hoped. It was not only that educated opinion was no longer divided broadly into two parties, so that neither quarterly could any longer rely on its views finding an obedient echo among newspapers of the same political sympathy. It was also a fact that the Year of Revolutions had produced a widespread revulsion at social and political upheaval which old Whigs, middle class radicals, Peelites, and Protectionists all felt. The *History of England* reflected this fear. It made no concessions to radicalism, it described a preserving revolution in a manner that only an unrepentant Jacobite could quarrel with, and it did so in a tone of boastful insularity which a popular readership could share.

Against this happy anticipation of the prevailing mood, Croker's criticisms could make little impression. He had undertaken the review before he realized how large was the area of common agreement. Then, instead of reappraising Macaulay's *History* in the light of his earlier opinions, his speeches and reviews, he had laid the political issues on one side, to concentrate on the way Macaulay had used his authorities. As he worked however, he had been torn between accusing Macaulay of writing history like a novelist, which seems to have been Lockhart's preferred theme, and accusing him of political partisanship, which was the natural outcome of his own memories. So the humour was stifled by the bitterness. The hard-won catalogue of factual errors and stylistic flaws, and their piecemeal despatch in 'fascicules' to the printer did not, one suspects, do much for the coherence and force of this argument. Important criticisms were made in passing, almost in parenthesis, and small ones at tedious length. Single examples of faults are noted, but not the pervading habits they illustrate.

So, for instance, Croker notes Macaulay's habit of embroidering an episode with extraneous names and associations, but omits to say what rhetorical purpose it served. In Chapter VI Macaulay gave a portrait of that extraordinary man, Charles Mordaunt, third Earl of Peterborough:

Already he had given abundant proof of his courage, of his capacity, and of that strange unsoundness of mind which made his courage and capacity almost useless to his country. Already he had distinguished himself as a wit and a scholar, as a soldier and a sailor. He had even set his heart on rivalling Bourdaloue and Bossuet. Though an avowed free thinker, he had sate up all night at sea to compose sermons, and had with great difficulty been prevented from edifying the crew of a man of war with his pious oratory.[77]

The footnote refers to 'Teonge's Diary'. Croker looks it up and finds that it contains 'nothing about "*free thinking*"—nothing about *Bourdaloue* and *Bossuet*—nothing about *sermons* (in the plural)', but that once, when on a man of war, Mordaunt, learning that the chaplain was ill, had asked the captain's leave to preach, and sat up till 4 a.m. to write his sermon; which the chaplain frustrated by getting up and rebuking the young man who, in pique, 'set to work with a hammer and nails and the parson, to spite him, would have no prayers'. 'The story', says Croker, 'needs no exaggeration; and is indeed spoiled by Mr Macaulay's unauthorised additions'.[78] But surely the real point is that the passage is spoiled only for the reader who has access to the original source; for those who have not, it is a mere feature of a larger portrait and in that portrait the reference to Bourdaloue and Bossuet alongside free thinking, cunningly sows a doubt about the integrity of a man who, though he helped William of Orange become King, later quarrelled with him. Croker, in his indignation at the selective use of a source, misses the larger prejudice which it betrays.

A similar closeness of focus helps explain Croker's relative indifference to the two features of Macaulay's *History* which struck contemporaries and have figured largely in the estimates of subsequent critics, his materialism and his puritanism. Croker is very aware of Macaulay's brashness. He notes the colloquialisms, the vulgar abuse of certain characters and the stress on material wealth. He observes that for Macaulay the worst insult that can be levelled at the clergy and the gentry is that they were poor.[79] But again the detail inhibits the wider and more humane indictment. It is as if there had been no critics of the selfish cant of wealth on the Tory side; no Southey or Coleridge, no Oastler

---

[77] *HE*, i. 534. Louis Bourdaloue (1632–1704) was a Jesuit who preached before Louis XIV.
[78] *QR*, lxxxiv, no. 168, 565.   [79] Ibid., 597.

or Bull, no Carlyle or Newman, on whose indignation it might have been profitable to draw. Yet Macaulay's idea of social progress is broadly utilitarian. Men, he implies, need peace and a level of prosperity before they can prefer long-term benefits to short-term ones. While they languish in barbarism they are lucky if they have a wise ruler to keep order or a priesthood to tend the flame of literature and civilization. But these two securities against anarchy must give way once men have caught a glimpse of a better state of society and tasted the rewards of free choice, namely material prosperity. This had been his theme as early as the Reform debates, as Croker must have heard.

'Civilisation will proceed. Wealth will increase. Industry and trade will find out new seats. The same causes which have turned so many villages into great towns, which have turned so many thousands of miles of fir and heath into cornfields and orchards, will continue to operate. Who can say that a hundred years hence there may not be, on the shore of some desolate and silent bay in the Hebrides, another Liverpool, with its docks and warehouses and endless forests of masts? Who can say that the huge chimneys of another Manchester may not rise in the wilds of Connemara?'[80]

Of course, in the *History* Macaulay's powers of graphic description tend to conceal his commitment to this overall philosophy, and he is too great a master of narrative suspense to want to accord a large role to the operation of laws of development determining or at least restricting men's actions. What betrays his belief in such a process is his judgement of men and women, not as individuals but as types. He disliked the courtier, corrupted by the caprices of power, fawning in his advice, unreliable in his services; and he liked upright, stoical men of action, whose economical speech and austere manners promise an end to profligacy among rulers and distrust in their subjects. James II and his court conform to the first type, William of Orange and his friends to the second. One represents a low morality being superseded, the other a more advanced morality being ushered in. Croker, as we have seen, was quite alert to the uneven treatment Macaulay accords to James II's private life and to William's, but he draws no general conclusion from it, only that

---

[80] *Speeches*, 32; 5 July 1831.

Macaulay reserves his insults and libels for those who oppose his hero.

This point is closely related to Macaulay's fundamental puritanism. Croker's objection to Macaulay's portrait of Marlborough illustrates it. As a young man, John Churchill had bought an annuity with £5,000 given him by the King's mistress, the Duchess of Cleveland. So Macaulay calls him 'a levier of contributions from ladies enriched by the spoils of more liberal lovers'.[81] Croker thinks this is unfair: a young man with 'no fortune but his good looks and sword'[82] might fall into temptation, he pleads, but this was surely a single instance. So a priggish charge receives a hardly less priggish defence, and the wider issue is avoided. The point is not that Croker, the friend and counsellor of those Regency *roués* the Marquis of Hertford and Viscount Lowther, ought to have attempted a defence of Churchill's amours in particular and cavalier morality in general. The important point concerns each man's range of sympathy. Croker, who would have thought it a moral evasion to explain a man's behaviour by reference to his social background, was quite unable to see any pattern of social prejudices in the views of his opponent. Thanks to his puritanism, Macaulay cannot bring himself to see any good in Churchill, but neither can Croker offer Cavalier habits as an extenuation.

How old-fashioned Croker's type of criticism had become emerges from a comparison with another writer, no less respectable, but a generation younger. Walter Bagehot's essay on Macaulay was written only seven years after Croker's review. It is based on four volumes of the *History of England*, not two, but it uses no other material not also available to the older man. (Trevelyan's biography was still, as Carlyle would have said, hidden in the womb of time). Bagehot moreover had as strong a sense as Croker had of the fragmentary nature of historical evidence. 'The data of historical narratives', he says in the essay on Macaulay, 'are a heap of confusion'. If literature is the fragment of fragments, history is 'a vestige of vestiges'.

. . . few facts leave any trace of themselves, any witness of their occurrence; of fewer still is that witness preserved; a slight track is all anything leaves, and the confusion of life, the tumult of change sweep even

---

[81] *HE*, i. 354.   [82] *QR*, lxxxiv, no. 168, 609.

that away in a moment. It is not possible that these data can be very fertile in certainties.[83]

This is very close to Croker's view of historical evidence and his scepticism of the veracity of a fluent narrative.

Yet Bagehot did not feel threatened by social change. He had a sense of social dynamics, of forces of stability and change operating independently of the political system, of classes co-existing in a genial discord. He finds Macaulay's narrative overheated and rhetorical, and instead of picking over the 'heap of confusion' piece by piece as Croker does, he penetrates at once to the psychology of the writer who insists that life is so dramatic. What sort of mind is it that can make so much out of such unpromising material? Bagehot finds the answer in what he calls Macaulay's 'inexperiencing nature'. He lived in books and abstracted himself from life. Even India made no discernible change in him. 'He is so insensible to passing objects, that they leave no distinctive mark, no intimate peculiar trace'.[84] Even in politics he had never 'thrown himself upon action, he has never followed trivial details with an anxious passion'. His oratory had not changed: 'the theme of a schoolboy is not more devoid of the salt of circumstance'. His mind was on great figures in the past and on posterity, not on his contemporaries. 'He regards existing men as painful prerequisites of great-grandchildren'.[85] This indifference to experience, Bagehot says, accounts for Macaulay's lack of sympathy for the Cavalier. For the Cavalier lived in the present; his was an enjoying, unreflective nature, which clung to tradition and authority because nothing less could curb and channel all that 'eager tumultuous disposition'. But Macaulay saw only its faults:

Its license affronts him; its riot alienates him. He is forever contrasting the dissoluteness of Prince Rupert's horse with the restraint of Cromwell's pikemen. A deep enjoying nature finds no sympathy. The brilliant style passes forward: we dwell on its brilliancy, but it is cold. He has no tears for that warm life; no tenderness for that extinct joy. The ignorance of the Cavalier, too, moves his wrath: 'They were ignorant of what every schoolgirl knows' . . .[86]

---

[83] *Literary Studies* 2 vols. (Everyman edn. 1920), ii. 229.
[84] Ibid., 201–2.   [85] Ibid., 205.   [86] Ibid., 210.

For a critic who knew so little of Macaulay's private life this is acute. If Bagehot had known what we know, would he not have seen (even if as a good Victorian he might have refrained from saying it) that the historian remained emotionally a schoolboy, and that the Cavalier stood for a way of life which he dreaded? Macaulay's censure sounds manly and gruff, but it had the function of keeping all unruly, all sensual nature at a safe distance whether in the past or the present. He never outgrew the warm affections of the family circle of his childhood, and just as he repeatedly tried to rekindle its glow, by re-reading favourite childhood books and revisiting old haunts, so his emotional life was a long drawn-out cooling, as one by one the members of that circle died or departed. Of emotional life outside the family he had no direct experience, and he was harshly unsympathetic to those who had, in his view, abused family values.

If Croker could not see, what was so plain to Bagehot, the social sympathies which informed Macaulay's historical portraits, how can we be sure that he was right in accusing Macaulay of writing an insidious apology for the Whig party? If his vision was limited on one issue, why should we consider it penetrating on another? Croker was actually a much more searching critic of politics than Macaulay: no one could accuse his political writings of lacking 'the salt of circumstance'. His long parliamentary service had not so much frustrated a youthful literary ambition; it had made it too heavily political. Every work of literature had to be judged by its political effects. Macaulay's mind remained curiously innocent of political ambition and the intricate stratagems which accompany it. Gladstone attributed this to his 'living habitually with men of congenial mind', adding that parliament left little mark on him: 'the comparatively few hours he spent there, most commonly with his thoughts ranging far abroad, could not have largely entered into, or perceptively modified, the habits of his mind'.[87] Nevertheless this aloofness from the political arena was an advantage to the historian. Historical understanding demands distance from the material studied, even gaining from the dilapidations of time. It is, in Coleridge's phrase, 'a lantern in the stern'.

[87] *QR*, cxlii, no. 283 (July 1876), 21; *Gleanings*, ii. 296.

Croker never accepted this. He thought it was as urgent to remind his readers of the treachery of Lord William Russell as it was to expose the incompetence of Lord John Russell as biographer of the poet Thomas Moore. Macaulay had been a member of the Russell administration and so was at least complicit in the long Whig tradition of encouraging revolution. The occasional criticism of Whigs in the *History of England* should deceive nobody. They were merely devices to deceive readers into thinking the author impartial.

Of course, if one were to go by appearances, Croker was right. Macaulay owed his political career to the Whigs. He had sat for a Whig nomination borough. He had served in Whig governments. His family had enjoyed Whig preferment. Soon after the first two volumes of the *History* appeared his brother John received a rich living from Russell.[88] In the following year his youngest brother Charles was appointed Secretary to the Board of Health.[89] All these favours might very well account for the fact that Macaulay tempered his censure when dealing with the ancestors of prominent Whigs. Yet to present occasional courtesy as evidence of a fundamental bias is to underrate Macaulay's art. He never approved of the extremists of the party even in the days of Shaftesbury's leadership or before Monmouth's rebellion, and he was careful to exonerate his hero, William III, from the suspicion of complicity with either party. The point of a Great Deliverer is that he must be, like Rousseau's lawgiver, dissociated from the hint of any responsibility for the evils he cures. William is not a Whig King. He is a hero above party, which is why it is important to deny he had any concerns in common with the Whig exiles and Monmouth. Macaulay saw that Whig partisanship, in the narrow sense, would compromise the drama of James II's isolation and eventual fall.

A similar consideration seems appropriate in connection with another prominent figure, the Marquis of Halifax, called 'the Trimmer'. Contemporaries remarked on Macaulay's high opinion of Halifax. Lord John Russell himself accused Macaulay of being a Trimmer (a charge the historian politely deflected with a reference to Burnet),[90] and Professor Hamburger has argued

[88] *LM*, v. 50–1.   [89] Ibid., 169; TCM, Journal iii. fo. 7.   [90] *LM*, v. 6.

that this fellow-feeling with Halifax provides the key to Macaulay's own political opinions.[91] I rather doubt if Macaulay's
conception of a narrative, with its preoccupation with that
'artistic balance of conflicting forces' which Croker noted,
would have allowed him to identify with any political argument
in so rigid a way. He was in fact rather critical of Halifax's con-
trariety, which so limited his practical impact. But that is surely
what makes the Trimmer so useful in a dramatic narrative.
Halifax surely has a dramatic role in Macaulay's story, besides
his historic one. He serves as critical commentator on the other
actors, his aloofness and deliberate inaction serving to inform
the audience what to approve and disapprove. Is it too fanciful
to suggest that Macaulay, who loved *Hamlet*, may have seen in
Halifax a figure who could be used as a Horatio? For all his respect
for Halifax's intellect, he gives him no vital role in the action.
He seems to serve chiefly as a measure of the folly of party
politics.[92]

   If even Croker with his strongly political motivation made
an unconvincing case for treating the *History of England* as a
Whig party history, it may be because Macaulay succeeded in
being more impartial than later readers have been prepared to
admit. A book which won praise from Francis Jeffrey and Lord
John Russell as well as from the Duke of Wellington and Bishop
Phillpotts cannot have been grossly one-sided. Yet we continue
to think of Macaulay as the quintessential Whig historian. The
reason lies in the ambiguity of the term. 'Whig' has a modern,
more general sense, denoting an approach to the past which subordinates it to the concerns of the present. A history is called
whiggish, according to this usage, if it allows modern values and
modern habits of conduct to affect the way historic figures and
societies are studied and presented. Academic historians use the
word whenever they perceive that an episode or a figure in the
past has been described with insufficient sympathy or understanding of the conditions of the period in question; and they
imply and sometimes boldly assert the superiority of their understanding of a period over that of an economist, a sociologist,
a political commentator, or even a lawyer. The disagreement
corresponds to a distinction made by Michael Oakeshott, between

---

[91] J. Hamburger, *Macaulay and the Whig Tradition* (Chicago and London,
1976), chs. 5 and 6.
[92] *HE*, i. 190–3.

the historian's view of the past and that of the practical man who
'reads the past backwards'. The practical disposition reads into
the past the concerns of the present. The historian by contrast
studies it for its own sake, quite shut off from present concerns.
'He loves it as a mistress of whom he never tires and whom he
never expects to talk sense'.[93] The practical approach to the past
is whig in the attenuated sense of Butterfield's essay. The professional historian ('the historian' of Oakeshott) is by occupation and often conviction anti-whig. Now Macaulay straddles
this distinction. If we call him whig we imply that he had an exclusively practical interest in the past, whereas there is good reason
to believe that he used it as an escape. It was indeed a mistress
to him; he loved it as a relief from the strenuous decisions of
political life. But he did expect it to talk sense, or in other words
to yield lessons for the guidance of the present. If we stress his
whiggism we must add that he was a romantic who wanted the
past to have a popular appeal. If we focus on the romantic and
escapist side we must not ignore those elements in his work which
led Arnold to call him 'the great apostle of the Philistines'—
his crude certainty, his bourgeois identification of respectability
with worldly success, and his complacency about the benefits of
material progress.

On the whole the reputation of philistinism seems to me to
derive more from the essays, which he knew were ephemeral
and which were written in a deliberately arresting style, than
the *History of England*, which was his real claim on posterity.
There the practical man predominates over the romantic and the
judgements are much more subordinated to a single theme, the
long-term national benefits of the Revolution of 1688. Narrow
political partisanship was incompatible with this theme, not
only because the Revolution was secured by men of both parties, but also because Macaulay sensed, rightly, that the reading
public was no longer interested in such sectional loyalties, and
he must deliver a message of wider national importance.[94] His

---

[93] *Rationalism in Politics and other Essays* (1962), 147, 166.

[94] Macaulay's Journal has some surprisingly forceful expressions of national
pride. Reading Wolfe Tone's Memoirs on 14 Aug. 1849, he asked himself why he
liked Tone, and why 'an Irishman's or Frenchman's hatred of England does not excite
in me an answering hatred? I imagine that my national pride prevents it. England
is so great that an Englishman cares little what foreigners think or how they feel
towards her.' TCM, Journal ii. fos. 72–3.

reviewers generally agreed that the *History* was remarkably even-handed in its treatment of Whig and Tory.[95] Its popularity was harder to explain. Macaulay did not write as a democrat, for a popular audience. Those grateful working men in Dukinfield who sent him their vote of thanks were listeners, not readers. Many critics, following Croker, have claimed Macaulay was imitating Scott. Lockhart may have encouraged the attribution. 'Scott has been the great inspirer and misleader of all our recent history writers, French and English', he wrote,[96] and this judgement has been repeated ever since. It is however only partially true of the young Macaulay, and it became progressively less true as his career progressed.

In a general sense, he may have absorbed Scott's feeling for the way societies change, with one ruling group finding its energies flagging, its convictions losing touch with political and social changes, until it is replaced by a younger group, with different ideas, a clearer vision of society's needs, and greater *élan*. In one of his earliest speeches Macaulay made this process the main argument for parliamentary reform, and his words could describe a favourite theme of Scott's:

All history is full of revolutions, produced by causes similar to those which are now operating in England. A portion of the community which had been of no account expands and becomes strong. It demands a place in the system, suited, not to its former weakness, but to its present power. If this is granted, all is well. If this is refused, then comes the struggle between the young energy of one class and the ancient privileges of another.[97]

But Macaulay had already seen that for the historian he wanted to be, this process provided only half the story. In the 1828 essay on History, he praised Scott for making his readers aware of the social changes narrative historians had ignored; but he wanted the historian to assimilate those to the political narrative. He complained that for a true picture of a given period the reader had to go to separate authorities, the informed eyewitness and the novelist's evocation: he had 'to look for the wars

[95] *Spectator*, 9 Dec. 1848, 1187.
[96] CPC, Lockhart letters vol. iv. fo. 175, Postscript to letter of 9 Mar. 1849, fo. 78.
[97] *Speeches*, 8–9, 2 Mar. 1831.

and votes of the Puritans in Clarendon, and for their phraseology in Old Mortality; for one half of King James in Hume,
and for the other half in the Fortunes of Nigel'.[98] The emphasis
on a central narrative was already there, but Macaulay had
not learned how hard it would be to blend the doings of famous
personages with 'the short and simple annals of the poor'. The
solution would in fact take him away from Scott, and indeed
even in the 1828 essay there is a hint of impatience at Scott's
fondness for inserting little scholarly footnotes and appendices
with references, to show that a particular episode was founded
on actual fact. Macaulay's case is, that if a historical episode is
interesting enough for fiction, it would be still more interesting
as history.

His maturer views grew still more critical. He saw that Scott's
nostalgia for past forms, his chivalrous feeling for doomed ways
of life, fed toryism and reaction. Scott's last years pointed the
moral. Abbotsford was a symbol of ostentation and extravagance
which, by making him write too much for money, ensured the
deterioration of his genius.[99] But above all, Macaulay turned
against Scott's romantic vision of Scotland with its separatist
allure. It may be that in doing so he was expressing a reaction
against events in Ireland and in his own constituency, Edinburgh, in the 1840s. But whatever the cause, the fact is that the
History of England is strongly nationalist, a truly English history,
which treats the Gaelic peoples as if Scott had never written. There
is indeed little of this in the first two volumes which deal with
the Revolution in England, and in any case neither Croker the
Irish nor Lockhart the Scots Protestant had any reason to make
a case for the Stuart cause. By the time Macaulay published
Volumes III and IV in which he dealt directly with Ireland and
Scotland, Lockhart was dead and Croker silent. But the point
they might have made was forcibly made by John Paget in his
essays on the Highlands of Scotland and the Massacre of
Glencoe.[100] Paget called Macaulay's treatment of the Highlander
'a parricidal onslaught by a son of the Highlands on the people

---

[98] MW, i. 278.
[99] LM, iii. 245–6. Macaulay was declining Napier's request that he review
Lockhart's Life of Scott.
[100] 'The New Examen' in Paradoxes and Puzzles, 32–100.

and the land of his fathers;[101] and he accused him of taking the responsibility for the massacre off the shoulders of William III and piling it all on to those of the Master of Stair. The most chilling aspect of Macaulay's account of the Glencoe atrocity is not his exoneration of William III for not noticing the order he was signing, but the way he exaggerates the savagery of Highland clan society so as to make the reader feel the massacre was characteristic of that primitive world, and quite incidental to the King's policy in Scotland. Paget's method is more selective than Croker's and so more telling. But it offers two sharply-focused examples of the general point, that Macaulay's theme is the development of national unity, and this ruled out nostalgia for simple ways of life among peoples who had escaped the benefits of civilization. The Jacobites, so sympathetically portrayed by Scott, must be shown to have been mistakenly devoted to a discredited dynasty and an obscurantist political system. Presenting the Highland 'tribes' (as Macaulay calls them) as noble and virtuous was to romanticize barbarism.

It needed a Scottish Whig to point this out most forcibly. Francis Jeffrey was once described by Macaulay as 'more nearly an universal genius than any man of our time', and he read the proofs of the first two volumes. His verdict was that Macaulay had proved 'beyond all future contradiction' three great matters; that the Stuart tyranny had been intolerable, that a revolution was necessary, and that it had been effected with remarkably little bloodshed by William III. Macaulay had done this, Jeffrey claimed, 'not by eloquent and lively writing, but by a patient and copious accumulation and lucid arrangement of facts and details, often separately insignificant, but constituting at last an *induction* which leaves no shade of doubt as to the conclusion'. For Jeffrey it was a triumph of fact over fiction. In three months he said, the *History* had

scattered to the winds, and swept finally from the minds of all thinking Englishmen, those lingerings of Jacobite prejudice, which the eloquence and perversions of Hume, and the popular talents of Scott and other writers of fiction, had restored to our literature, and but too much familiarised to our feelings, in the last fifty years. This is a great work, and a great triumph, and ought, I think, so to be hailed and rejoiced in.[102]

---

[101] 'The New Examen' in *Paradoxes and Puzzles*, 80.
[102] Lord Cockburn, *Life of Lord Jeffrey* 2 vols. (Edinburgh 1852), ii. 46.

That was exactly Macaulay's aim, and it explains why, when he learned of his spectacular sales, it was with Scott's success that he compared himself. Returning from Longman's on 12 December 1848 he records, 'Black says that there has been no such sale since Sir Walter's novels'. In March 1849 he wrote to his brother Charles, 'The sale of my book has been enormous,— twelve thousand copies in three months. None of Sir Walter's novels went faster'. The historian had indeed recovered the materials the novelist had appropriated, and he had shown that he could tell a complex story well which he had not invented.

If it is wrong to attribute the popularity of Macaulay's *History* to his imitating the methods of Scott, how do we explain it? When people say the *History* carries a political message they can mean two different things. Macaulay was a politician, and he could count on a wide readership both because he had been a Cabinet Minister as well as a popular reviewer. Politics in his lifetime was such a magnet for the ambitious careerist that an example of an able man forsaking a high position in politics for literature was in itself a curiosity. The *Morning Chronicle*'s claim that he had done so at the meridian of his career was, however, an exaggeration. He had always been a reluctant politician. He enjoyed the privileges and reputation of office, but he had not the tact or the commitment to want to be a minister for very long, and he could never have led a Cabinet. The only reputation he valued was literary: 'I have escaped public life'[103] he had written in November 1848, as if he now faced trial as a writer alone.

Yet the conviction that great literature outlasted political fame did not make the *History* non-political, even if reviewers, bored with the party stalemate, thought it rose above party politics. Macaulay may not have followed political events with 'an anxious passion', but he had a keen eye for literary success and failure, and he observed contemporary writers' reputations with the same shrewd attention which he gave to the movement of his railway shares. An entry in his journal, for 30 September 1849 reads:

Odd that Pendennis is not out yet. David Copperfield is out, but might as well have staid in. Dickens is a mine worked out, I fear. He can

---

[103] Journal, i. fo. 407, 18 Nov. 1848.

no more contend with Thackeray than the Potosi shafts with the new diggings in California. Will that be my case? If it be I hope that I shall have the sense to discover that it is so. Angry that Longman does not send my account.[104]

What he called writing 'with the year 2000 and even the year 3000 in my mind'[105] meant aligning himself with the opinions of the middle-class liberal readership of his day, exactly the readership which Thackeray is said to have respected, to the eventual detriment of his reputation. It meant siding with the town against the country; with commerce and industry against the gentry and the Church, and above all pandering to the prevailing moral cant of domesticity against the loose ethics of the Stuart court. But he did this without (despite Croker) identifying with any party in the state, and by carefully burying his own preferences in vivid imagery and well chosen example. His targets —Stuart monarchy, the landed aristocracy, the High Church party—had all passed the zenith of their power. Of course, Macaulay's treatment of these institutions offended men like Croker and Phillpotts who had spent their lives defending them. They could hardly have admitted that Macaulay had been studiously moderate. But to men at the other end of the political system, Macaulay seemed over-cautious. John Stuart Mill thought he 'ministered to English conceit', adding 'only in some degree, for he never "goes the whole" in anything'.[106]

Macaulay did indeed minister to English conceit. The whole *History* is filled with pride in England's achievements. But he also conveyed the message that only a free people can acquire a responsible government and progressively improve it so that its benefits extend to all classes. Of course this theme was not new. Parts of it are to be found scattered in many liberal writers of the time. Macaulay's version of it was memorable, and has lasted, for three reasons. One is that he was the first to tell the whole story of the Revolution of 1688, weaving together memoirs, official correspondence, pamphlets and plays and poetry, all in a single grand narrative, a narrative in which so many

---

[104] Journal, ii. fo. 143.   [105] Ibid., i. fo. 430, 4 Dec. 1848.
[106] *Collected Works*, xiv, 6, 27 Jan. [1849]. Mill was of course still buoyed up with optimism that the Second Republic in France would show Europe that a democracy could be stable.

different lives, from such a variety of occupations, were brought together in seemingly simultaneous action, that his readers felt they were hearing the full story for the first time and that it was written for them. The second quality is the insistent clarity of the prose.[107] There is less vehement argument in the *History* than in the *Essays*, more memorable description, and the vocabulary is more plain and accessible; but the range of topics is much wider, so that the transitions between each must be more carefully contrived. The *Essays* sometimes exasperate with their dogmatic renderings of the obvious. The *History of England* almost never does. The third quality is related to this clarity of expression, and it is narrative suspense. Macaulay conveys such a wide variety of scenes in such rich detail, and with such a fine sense of the time and place at which particular facts or characters should be introduced, that the reader feels that he is being invited to judge for himself. Irony and ridicule, the stock weapons of the *Essays*, are sparingly used, as if the author was reluctant to obtrude his own views. The reader does not have to work to gather the facts: they are paraded before him in a succession of scenes, interspersed with courteous expositions of the more difficult issues, and high-minded observations on the grosser forms of behaviour under scrutiny. Some episodes are truly 'branded' on to the mind, and not a few became subjects for Victorian historical painters.[108] It is this pictorial quality which surely explains the *History*'s longevity as a classic. Some histories are superseded, not only because new evidence is found to discredit their assertions, but also because time makes their argument and terminology obsolete. A generation passes, and they are literally unreadable. Macaulay's *History* has not suffered this fate. It is still read with pleasure by students and the general reader and even recommended by professional historians familiar with the work of Macaulay's many critics. The reason is that Macaulay immerses his readers in what he wants them to know. They may change their minds later, but they have had an experience which has stamped itself on their memory and shaped all their subsequent

[107] Taine's tribute to this is still the best, in his *Histoire de la littérature anglaise*, v. ch. iii, §7; English trans. H. van Laun (4 vols., 1886), iv. fos. 269–74. But Taine was thinking of the *Essays* which he thought demonstrated Macaulay the orator; whereas it seems to me that the *History* is more indebted to his love of drama.

[108] *MW*, i. 280.

views of the subject. They have encountered that rare thing, a work of history which is also a work of art.

By contrast, Croker's work is largely forgotten. In part this is because his reputation, never based on any marked taste for publicity, went down with the protectionist cause he supported. It might have been otherwise, if there had been a central work of literature to counteract the politics. He had the diligence, the acuteness, and the range of interests which better-known writers lack. He wrote lucidly and often memorably. But he distrusted the imagination without which it was impossible to lift his writing out of the daily routine of political commentary. In these pages I have tried to understand and explain his sincere and laborious life. But his quarrel with Macaulay is a reminder that posterity is not kind to mere critical acuteness, which it is inclined to attribute to malice, whereas it will forgive any faults in a writer if he leaves behind him a work of art.

Bibliography

1. MANUSCRIPT SOURCES

Aberdeen Papers (British Library, London)
William Blackwood Papers (National Library of Scotland, Edinburgh)
Brougham Papers (University College, London)
Bryce Papers (Bodleian Library, Oxford)
Croker Papers (William L. Clements Library, University of Michigan)
Croker Papers (William R. Perkins Library, Duke University, North Carolina)
Croker Papers (correspondence with Thomas Casey) University of Florida Libraries, Gainesville, Florida
Derby Papers (Liverpool Central Reference Library)
Isaac D'Israeli Papers (Bodleian Library, Oxford)
Goulburn Papers (Surrey Record Office, Kingston upon Thames)
Sir James Graham Papers (British Library)
Hertford Papers (British Library)
Theodore Hook letters (University of Chicago Library)
Houghton Papers (Trinity College, Cambridge)
J. G. Lockhart Papers (National Library of Scotland)
Lonsdale Papers (Cumbria Record Office, Carlisle)
Macaulay Papers (Trinity College, Cambridge)
Zachary Macaulay Papers (Huntington Library, San Marino, California)
Murray Manuscripts (Mr John Murray, 50 Albemarle Street, London)
Macvey Napier Papers (British Library)
Sir Robert Peel's Papers (British Library)
Stanhope Papers (Centre for Kentish Studies, Maidstone)
Wellesley Papers (British Library)
Wellington Papers (Southampton University Library)
Wilberforce Papers (Bodleian Library)

2. NEWSPAPERS AND PERIODICALS

Blackwood's Magazine
Edinburgh Review
Examiner
Fortnightly Review
Morning Chronicle

Morning Herald
Morning Post
Punch
Quarterly Review
Spectator
The Times
Westminster Review

3. PRINTED SOURCES, MEMOIRS, AND CORRESPONDENCE

Unless otherwise indicated, the place of publication is London.

Anderson, William Eric K. (ed.), *The Journal of Sir Walter Scott* (Oxford, 1972).

Arnold, Matthew, *Friendship's Garland* (1903).

Arbuthnot, C., *The Correspondence of Charles Arbuthnot* ed. A. Aspinall, (Camden Society, 3rd ser. vol. lxv; 1941).

Arbuthnot, Harriet, *The Journal of Mrs Arbuthnot, 1820–1832* ed. F. Bamford and the Duke of Wellington, 2 vols. (1950).

Aspinall, A. (ed.), *The Formation of Canning's Ministry February to August 1827*, (Camden Society, 3rd ser. vol. lix; 1937).

—— (ed.), *Three Early Nineteenth Century Diaries* (1952).

Brougham, Lord, *The Life and Times of Henry, Lord Brougham, written by himself*, 3 vols. (Edinburgh and London, 1871).

Campbell, Lord John, *Lives of Lord Lyndhurst and Lord Brougham* (1869).

—— *Life of John, Lord Campbell*, by Mary S. Hardcastle, 2 vols. (1881).

Cockburn, Lord, *Life of Lord Jeffrey with a Selection from his Correspondence*, 2 vols. (Edinburgh, 2nd edn., 1852).

[Croker, John Wilson], *Sketch of the State of Ireland, Past and Present* (1808, repr. in *Correspondence and Diaries*), vol. i (2nd edn., 1885).

—— *Stories Selected from the History of England, from the Conquest to the Revolution, for Children* (1817).

[——] *The New Whig Guide* (1819).

[——] (ed.), *Letters of Mary Lepel, Lady Hervey, with a Memoir and Illustrative Notes* (1821).

[——] (ed.), *Royal Memoirs of the French Revolution . . . with Historical and Biographical Illustrations by the Translator* (1823).

[——] (ed.), *Letters from Horace Walpole to the Earl of Hertford during his Lordship's Embassy in Paris* (1825).

[——] *Two Letters on Scottish Affairs from E. Bradwardine Waverley, Esq., to Malachi Malagrowther, Esq.* (1826).

—— (ed.), *The Life of Samuel Johnson, LL.D., including A Journal of a Tour to the Hebrides, by James Boswell, Esq., a New Edition with Numerous Additions and Notes* (1831).

[——] *Answers to the Edinburgh Reviewer of Croker's Boswell, Selected from Blackwood's Magazine* (1831).

—— *The Speech of the Rt. Hon. J.W. Croker on the Reform Question on Friday March 4, 1831* (1831).

—— *The Speech of the Rt. Hon. John Wilson Croker on the Question that 'The Reform Bill Do Pass', Tuesday 22nd September 1831* (1831).

—— *Resolutions moved by Mr Croker on the Report of the Reform Bill, March 14, 1832* (1832).

[——] *Letter to a Noble Lord who voted for the Second Reading of the Reform Bill, on the Amendments which it may be expedient to make in the Committee* (1832).

—— (ed.), *Johnsoniana; or Supplement to Boswell: being Anecdotes and Sayings of Dr Johnson, collected by Piozzi, Windham, Parker . . .* (etc), 2 vols. (1835).

—— (ed.) *Memoirs of the Reign of George II, from His Accession to the Death of Queen Caroline, by John, Lord Hervey, edited from the original manuscript at Ickworth* (1848).

—— *Correspondence between the Rt. Hon. John Wilson Croker and the Rt. Hon. Lord John Russell, on some passages of Moore's Diary, with a postscript . . . explanatory of Mr. Moore's acquaintance and correspondence with him* (1854).

—— *Essays on the Early Period of the French Revolution . . .* reprinted from the 'Quarterly Review', with additions and corrections (1857).

—— *Correspondence and Diaries of the late Rt. Hon. John Wilson Croker*, ed. Louis J. Jennings, 3 vols. (1884).

Disraeli, Benjamin, *Coningsby* (1844).

—— *Sybil* (1845).

—— *The Life of Benjamin Disraeli, Earl of Beaconsfield*, ed. W. F. Monypenny and G. E. Buckle, 2 vols. (1929).

—— *Letters*, ed. J. A. W. Gunn et al., 4 vols. (Toronto, 1982–?).

Disraeli's Reminiscences, ed. Helen M. Swartz and Marvin Swartz (1975).

Gladstone, W. E., *Gleanings of Past Years, 1843–78*, 7 vols. (1879).

Greville, Charles C. F., *The Greville Memoirs 1814–1860*, ed. L. Strachey and R. Fulford, 8 vols. (1938).

Haultain, A. (ed.), *Reminiscences* by Goldwin Smith (New York, 1910).

Hobhouse, Henry, *The Diary of Henry Hobhouse (1820–1827)*, (ed. A. Aspinall) (1947).

Holland, Henry Richard, Lord Holland, *Memoirs of the Whig Party during my Time*, 2 vols. (1852–4).

—— *The Holland House Diaries, 1831–1840*, ed. A. D. Kriegel (1977).

Kebbel, T. E. (ed.), *Selected Speeches of the late Rt. Hon. The Earl of Beaconsfield*, 2 vols. (London, 1882).

Knutsford, Lady, *Life and Letters of Zachary Macaulay* (1900).

Laughton, John Knox, (ed.) *Memoirs of the Life and Correspondence of Henry Reeve*, 2 vols. (1898).

Lewis, George F., *Letters of Sir George Cornwall Lewis, Bart . . .* (1870).

[Lockhart, John Gibson], *Peter's Letters to his Kinsfolk*, 3 vols. (Edinburgh and Glasgow, 1818).

[——] *Reginald Dalton* (Edinburgh and London, 1823).

—— *Memoirs of the Life of Sir Walter Scott, Bart*, 7 vols. (Edinburgh and London, 1837–8).

[Macaulay, Margaret], *Recollections of a Sister of T. B. Macaulay*, (1864).

Macaulay, Thomas Babington, *Lays of Ancient Rome*, (1842).

—— *Critical and Historical Essays*, 3 vols. (1843), (4th edn., 1846).

—— *Miscellaneous Writings*, ed. T. F. Ellis, 2 vols. (1860).

—— *The Works of Lord Macaulay*, ed. Lady Trevelyan, 8 vols. (1866).

—— *The History of England*, 3 vols. (Everyman edn. 1906).

—— *Critical and Historical Essays*, 2 vols. (Everyman edn. 1907).

—— *Lord Macaulay's Legislative Minutes*, ed. C. D. Dharker (Oxford, 1946).

—— *Selected Writings*, ed. J. Clive and T. Pinney (Chicago and London, 1972).

—— *The Letters of Thomas Babington Macaulay*, ed. Thomas Pinney, Cambridge, 6 vols. (1974–81).

—— *Napoleon and the Restoration of the Bourbons*, ed. J. Hamburger (1977).

—— *Life and Letters of Lord Macaulay*, ed. G. O. Trevelyan, 2 vols. (1876), (repr. Oxford, 1978).

Mackintosh, Robert J., *Memoirs of the Life of Sir James Mackintosh*, 2 vols. (1836).

Matthew, H. C. G., (ed.), *The Gladstone Diaries*, 14 vols. (Oxford, 1968–94).

Maxwell, Sir Herbert (ed.), *The Creevey Papers* (1905).

Mill, James, *History of British India*, 3 vols. (1817).

—— *History of British India*, ed. W. Thomas (Chicago and London, 1975).

—— and Macaulay, Thomas Babington, *Utilitarian Logic and Politics: James Mill's Essay on Government, Macaulay's critique, and the ensuing debate*, ed. J. Lively and J. Rees (Oxford, 1978).

Mill, J. S., *Autobiography*, ed. J. Stillinger (Boston, 1969, Oxford, 1971).

—— *The Collected Works of J. S. Mill*, ed. J. Robson et al., 31 vols. (Toronto, 1963–1991).

Moore, Thomas, *The Journal of Thomas Moore*, ed. Wilfrid S. Dowden, 6 vols. (East Brunswick, N.J., 1982–3).

Morley, John, *The Life of William Ewart Gladstone*, 3 vols. (1903).

Moultrie, John, *Poems*, 2 vols. (1876).

Mozley, T., *Reminiscences chiefly of Oriel College and the Oxford Movement*, 2 vols. (1882).

Newman, J. H., *Apologia pro Vita Sua*, Oxford, World's Classics, edn. (1964).

Parker, C. S., *Life and Letters of Sir James Graham, 1792–1861*, 2 vols. (1907).

Paston, George [Emily Morse Symonds], *At John Murray's: Records of a Literary Circle 1843-1892* (1932).

Peel, Sir R., *Speeches of the late Rt. Hon. Sir Robert Peel*, 4 vols. (1853).

—— *Memoirs of the Rt. Hon. Sir Robert Peel*, ed. Lord Stanhope and E. Cardwell, 2 vols. (1856, 1857).

—— *Sir Robert Peel, from his Private Papers*, ed. C. S. Parker, 3 vols. (1891–99).

—— *The Private Papers of Sir Robert Peel*, ed. G. Peel (1920).

Pellew, The Hon. G., *The Life and Correspondence of the Rt. Hon. Henry Addington, First Viscount Sidmouth*, 3 vols. (1847).

Ray, Gordon N. (ed.), *Letters and Private Papers of W. M. Thackeray*, 4 vols. (Cambridge, Mass., and London, 1945; Supplementary vols. 1 and 2, ed. Edgar F. Harden, 1994).

Robinson, H. C., *Henry Crabb Robinson on Books and their Writers*, ed. Edith J. Morley, 3 vols. (1938).

Romilly, S. H., *Letters to 'Ivy' from the First Earl of Dudley* (1905).

Russell, George W. E., *Collections and Recollections* (1903).

Smiles, S., *A Publisher and his Friends: Memoir and Correspondence of the late John Murray*, 2 vols. (1891).

Smith, Nowell C., *The Letters of Sydney Smith*, 2 vols. (Oxford, 1953).

Stanhope, Philip Henry, 5th Earl, *Notes of Conversations with the Duke of Wellington, 1831–1857* [1886] Oxford, World's Classics edn. (1947).

Trevelyan, George Macaulay, *Sir George Otto Trevelyan: A Memoir* (1932).

Trevelyan, George Otto, *The Competition Wallah* (2nd. edn., 1866).

—— *The Marginal Notes of Lord Macaulay* (1907).

West, Algernon, *Recollections 1832 to 1886*, 2 vols. (1899).

4. SECONDARY SOURCES AND WORKS OF REFERENCE

Aarsleff, Hans, *The Study of Language in England 1780–1860* (Princeton N.J., 1967).

Arnold, Matthew, *Culture and Anarchy*, ed. J. Dover Wilson (Cambridge, 1932).

Aspinall, Arthur, *Lord Brougham and the Whig Party* (Manchester, 1927).

Bagehot, Walter, *Biographical Studies*, ed. R. H. Hutton, (1895).
—— *Literary Studies* 2 vols. (Everyman edn. 1911).
Barnes, Donald, G., *A History of the English Corn Laws from 1660 to 1846* (1930).
Baxter, Stephen B., *William III* (1966).
Ben-Israel, Hedva, *English Historians and the French Revolution* (Cambridge, 1968).
Blake, Robert, *Disraeli* (1966).
Brightfield, Myron F., *Theodore Hook and His Novels* (1926).
—— *John Wilson Croker* (Berkeley, Calif., and London, 1940).
Brock, Michael G., *The Great Reform Act* (1973).
Brose, Olive, *Church and Parliament: The Reshaping of the Church of England 1828–60* (Stanford and London, 1959).
Burrow, John W., *A Liberal Descent: Victorian Historians and the English Past* (Cambridge, 1981).
Butler, Marilyn, *Romantics, Rebels and Reactionaries: English Literature and its Background* (Oxford, 1982).
Butterfield, Herbert, *The Englishman and his History* (1944).
—— *George III and the Historians* (1957).
—— *The Whig Interpretation of History* (1959).
Campbell, Ian, *Thomas Carlyle* (1974).
Campbell, Lord J., *Life of John, Lord Campbell*, ed. Mary S. Hardcastle, 2 vols. (1881).
Cannadine, David, *G. M. Trevelyan: A Life in History* (1992).
Carswell, John, *The Descent on England: A Study of the English Revolution of 1688 and its European Background* (1969).
Chadwick, Owen, *The Victorian Church Part I, 1829–1859* (1971).
Clark, George Kitson, *Peel and the Conservative Party, 1832–41* (1929).
Clive, John, *Scotch Reviewers: The 'Edinburgh Review' 1802–1815* (1957).
—— *Thomas Babington Macaulay: The Shaping of the Historian* (Cambridge, Mass., 1973).
Cobban, Alfred, *Edmund Burke and the Revolt against the Eighteenth Century* (2nd edn., 1960).
Collini, Stefan, Winch, Donald, and Burrow, John W., *That Noble Science of Politics: A Study in Nineteenth-Century Intellectual History* (Cambridge, 1983).
Conacher, James Blennerhasset, *The Peelites and the Party System, 1846–52* (1972).
Crowe, Ian (ed.), *Edmund Burke: His Life and Legacy* (Dublin, 1997).
Culler, A. Dwight, *The Victorian Mirror of History* (New Haven and London, 1985).

Davis, Richard W., *Dissent in Politics 1780–1830: The Political Life of William Smith, M. P.* (1971).

Doyle, William, *The Oxford History of the French Revolution* (Oxford, 1989).

—— and Haydon, Colin, eds., *Robespierre* (Cambridge, 1999).

Elliott, Marianne, *Wolfe Tone: Prophet of Irish Independence* (New Haven and London, 1989).

Evans, Eric J., *Sir Robert Peel: Statesmanship, Power and Party* (1991).

Edwards, Owen Dudley, *Macaulay* (1988).

Falk, Bernard, *'Old Q's' Daughter: The History of a Strange Family* (1951).

Feiling, Keith, *Sketches in Nineteenth Century Biography* (1930).

—— *The Second Tory Party 1714–1832* (1959).

Firth, Charles H., *A Commentary on Macaulay's History of England* (1938, repr. 1964).

Fontana, Biancamaria, *Rethinking the Politics of Commercial Society: The Edinburgh Review 1802–32* (Cambridge, 1985).

Forster, Edward Morgan, *Marianne Thornton, 1797–1887: A Domestic Biography* (1956).

Foster, Roy F., *Modern Ireland, 1600–1972* (1988).

Gash, Norman, *Politics in the Age of Peel: A Study in the Technique of Parliamentary Representation 1830–50* (1953).

—— *Mr Secretary Peel* (1961).

—— *Reaction and Reconstruction in English Politics 1832–52* (Oxford, 1965).

—— *Sir Robert Peel* (1972).

—— *Lord Liverpool: The Life and Political Career of Robert Banks Jenkinson, Second Earl of Liverpool 1770–1828* (1984).

Gay, Peter, *Style in History* (1974).

Gray, Dennis, *Spencer Perceval 1762–1812: the Evangelical Prime Minister* (1963).

Halsband, Robert, *Lord Hervey: Eighteenth Century Courtier* (Oxford, 1973).

Hamburger, Joseph, *Macaulay and the Whig Tradition* (Chicago and London, 1976).

Hawes, Frances, *Henry Brougham* (1957).

Hill, George Birkbeck, *Dr Johnson, His Friends and his Critics* (1878).

—— *The Letters of George Birkbeck Hill*, ed. Lucy Crump (1906).

Hilton, A. J. Boyd, *Corn, Cash, Commerce: The Economic Policies of the Tory Governments, 1815–1830* (1977).

—— *The Age of Atonement: The Influence of Evangelicalism on Social and Economic Thought, 1795–1855* (Oxford, 1988).

Hindle, W. H., *The Morning Post, 1772–1937* (1937).

Hinde, Wendy, *George Canning* (1973).

—— *Castlereagh* (1981).

Houghton, Walter E., *The Wellesley Index to Victorian Periodicals, 1824–1900*, vol. i (1966).

Hudson, Derek, *A Poet in Parliament: The Life of Winthrop Mackworth Praed 1802–1839* (1939).

Iggers, C. C., *The German Conception of History* (1968).

Ingamells, J., *The 3rd Marquess of Hertford as a Collector* (1983).

Jerman, B. R., *The Young Disraeli* (1960).

Johnson, Edgar, *Sir Walter Scott: The Great Unknown*, 2 vols. (1970).

Kaplan, Fred, *Thomas Carlyle: A Biography* (1983).

Kenyon, John P., *Robert Spencer, Earl of Sunderland 1641–1702* (1958).

Kerr, Donal A., *Peel, Priests, and Politics: Sir Robert Peel's Administration and the Roman Catholic Church in Ireland, 1841–1846* (Oxford, 1982).

Knight, Charles, *Passages of a Working Life during Half a Century*, 3 vols. (1864).

La Valley, Albert J., *Carlyle and the Idea of the Modern* (New Haven and London, 1971).

Lang, Andrew, *Life of John Gibson Lockhart*, 2 vols. (1897).

Lang, Timothy, *The Victorians and the Stuart Heritage: Interpretations of a Discordant Past* (Cambridge, 1995).

Levine, George, *The Boundaries of Fiction: Carlyle, Macaulay, Newman* (1968).

Lockhead, Marion, *John Gibson Lockhart* (1954).

Longford, Lady Elizabeth, *Wellington: The Years of the Sword* (1969).

—— *Wellington: Pillar of State* (1972).

McDowell, Robert Brendan, *Ireland in the Age of Imperialism and Revolution 1760–1801* (Oxford, 1979).

—— and Webb, D. A., *Trinity College Dublin, 1592–1952, an Academic History* (Cambridge, 1982).

Machin, George Ian T., *The Catholic Question in English Politics 1820–1830* (Oxford, 1964).

—— *Politics and the Churches in Great Britain, 1832–1868* (Oxford, 1977).

Mandler, Peter, *Aristocratic Government in the Age of Reform: Whigs and Liberals 1830–1852* (Oxford, 1990).

Marsh, Peter (ed.), *The Conscience of the Victorian State* (1979).

Mathiez, Albert, *The Fall of Robespierre, and Other Essays* (1927, repr. New York, 1968).

Matthew, H. C. G., *Gladstone 1809–1874* (Oxford, 1986).

McCord, Norman, *The Anti-Corn Law League 1838–46* (1958).

Meacham, Standish, *Henry Thornton of Clapham* (Cambridge, Mass., 1964).

Mellon, Stanley, *The Political Uses of History: A Study of Historians in the French Restoration* (Stanford, Calif., 1958).

Millgate, Jane, *Macaulay* (1973).

Miller, John, *James II: A Study in Kingship* (1977).

Mitchell, Austin, *The Whigs in Opposition 1815–1830* (Oxford, 1967).

Mitchell, Leslie G., *Holland House* (1980).

—— *Lord Melbourne 1779–1848* (Oxford, 1997).

Moore, Doris Langley, *The Late Lord Byron* (1961).

New, Chester W., *The Life of Henry Brougham to 1830* (Oxford, 1961).

Newbould, Ian D. C., *Whiggery and Reform* (1990).

Newsome, David, *The Parting of Friends: A Study of the Wilberforces and Henry Manning* (1966).

Newton Dunn, William, *The Man who was John Bull* (1996).

O'Brien, Conor Cruise, *The Great Melody: A Thematic Biography of Edmund Burke* (1992).

O'Leary, Patrick, *Sir James Mackintosh: The Whig Cicero* (Aberdeen, 1989).

Owen, C. Hugh, *The Lowther Family* (Chichester, 1990).

Paget, John, *Paradoxes and Puzzles, Historical, Judicial and Literary* (Edinburgh and London, 1874).

—— *The New Examen*, ed. W. Churchill (1934).

Patterson, Melville Watson, *Sir Francis Burdett and his Times (1770–1844)*, 2 vols. (1931).

Pocock, John G. A., *Virtue, Commerce and History: Essays on Political Thought and History, Chiefly in the Eighteenth Century* (Cambridge, 1985).

Prest, John M., *Lord John Russell* (1972).

—— *Politics in the Age of Cobden* (1977).

Ray, Gordon N., *Thackeray: The Uses of Adversity, 1811–1846* (New York and London, 1955).

—— *Thackeray: The Age of Wisdom, 1847–1863* (New York and London, 1958).

Read, Donald, *Peel and the Victorians* (Oxford, Blackwell, 1987).

Reardon, Bernard M. C., *Religious Thought in the Victorian Age: A Survey from Coleridge to Gore* (2nd edn., 1995).

Ridley, Jane, *The Young Disraeli, 1804–1846* (1995).

Roberts, Michael, *The Whig Party 1807–1812* (1939).

Rosenberg, John D., *Carlyle and the Burden of History* (Oxford, 1985).

Rosselli, John, *Lord William Bentinck: The Making of a Liberal Imperialist* (1974).

Shattock, Joanne, *Politics and Reviewers: The Edinburgh and the Quarterly in the Early Victorian Age* (Leicester, 1989).

Shine, Hill and Chadwick, Helen, *The Quarterly Review under Gifford: Identification of Contributors, 1809–1824* (Chapel Hill, N.C., 1949).

Smith, Ernest A., *Lord Grey, 1764–1845* (Oxford, 1990).

Speck, William A., *Reluctant Revolutionaries: Englishmen and the Revolution of 1688* (1989).

Stephen, Leslie, *Hours in a Library*, 3 vols. (1899).

Stewart, Robert, *The Foundation of the Conservative Party, 1830–1867* (1978).

—— *Henry Brougham 1778–1868: His Public Career* (1985).

Stokes, Eric T., *The English Utilitarians and India* (Oxford, 1959).

Thomas, William E. S., *The Philosophic Radicals: Nine Studies in Theory and Practice, 1817–1841* (Oxford, 1979).

Thompson, Edward and Garratt, Geoffrey Theodore, *The Rise and Fulfilment of British Rule in India* (1934).

Thompson, John M., *Robespierre* (2nd edn., 1939).

Tollemache, Lionel and Beatrix, *Safe Studies* (1884).

Tolley, Christopher, *Domestic Biography: The Legacy of Evangelicalism in Four Nineteenth-Century Families* (Oxford, 1997).

Ward, J. T., *Sir James Graham* (1967).

Ward, Thomas H., *History of the Athenaeum* (1926).

Winstanley, Denys Arthur, *Early Victorian Cambridge* (Cambridge, 1955).

Ziegler, Philip, *Life of Henry Addington, first Viscount Sidmouth* (1965).

5. ARTICLES AND ESSAYS

Ashley, Maurice, 'King James II and the Revolution of 1688: Some Reflections on the Historiography', in H. E. Bell and R. L. Ollard (eds.), *Historical Essays 1600–1750 Presented to David Ogg* (1963).

Beales, D. E. D., 'Parliamentary Parties and the Independent Member, 1810–1860', in R. Robson (ed.), *Ideas and Institutions of Victorian Britain: Essays in Honour of George Kitson Clark* (1967).

Bebbington, D. W., 'The Life of Baptist Noel: Its Setting and Significance', *Baptist Quarterly* (1971–2).

Best, G. F. A., 'The Evangelicals and the Established Church in the Early Nineteenth Century', *Journal of Theological Studies*, x. (1959).

Browning, A., 'Macaulay', *Historical Journal* ii. (1959).

Burrow, John W., 'The Uses of Philology in Victorian England', in R. Robson (ed.), *Ideas and Institutions of Victorian Britain: Essays in Honour of George Kitson Clark* (1967).

Clive, J., 'Macaulay's Historical Imagination', *Review of English Literature* Issue no. 4 (1960), 9–19.

Close, D. H., 'The Formation of a Two-party Alignment in the House of Commons between 1832 and 1841', *English Historical Review*, lxxxiv (1969), 257–77.

Conacher, J. B., 'Peel and the Peelites, 1846–50', *English Historical Review*, lxxiii (1958), 431–52.

DeBeer, E. S., 'Macaulay and Croker: The Review of Croker's Boswell'; *Review of English Studies* n.s., x. 40 (1959), 388–97.

Dinwiddy, J., 'Charles James Fox as Historian', *Historical Journal*, xii. (1969), 23–34.

Dreyer, F. A., 'The Whigs and the Political Crisis of 1845', *English Historical Review*, lxxx (1965), 514–37.

Fairlie, S., 'The Nineteenth-Century Corn Law Reconsidered', *Economic History Review*, xviii (1965), 562–73.

Fisher, H. A. L., 'The Whig Historians', Raleigh Lecture (1928).

Fraser, G. S., 'Macaulay's Style as an Essayist', *Review of English Literature* Issue no. 4, (1960), 9–19.

Fraser, P., 'Party Voting in the House of Commons 1812–1827', *English Historical Review*, lxxxi (1983), 763–84.

Gash, N., 'Peel and the Party System, 1830–1850', *Transactions of the Royal Historical Society*, 5th ser., i. (1951), 47–69.

—— 'The Organisation of the Conservative Party 1832–46', *Parliamentary History*, i (1982) and ii (1983).

Ghosh, P., 'Macaulay and the Heritage of the Enlightenment', *English Historical Review*, cxii (1997), 358–95.

Hawkins, A., ' "Parliamentary Government" and Victorian Political Parties, *c*.1830–80', *English Historical Review*, civ (1989), 638–9.

Hilton, A. J. B., 'Peel: A Re-appraisal', *Historical Journal*, xxii (1979), 585–614.

Kemp, B., 'The General Election of 1841', *History* (1952), 148–57.

—— 'Reflections on the Repeal of the Corn Laws', *Victorian Studies*, v. (1962), 182–204.

MacIntyre, A. D., 'Lord George Bentinck and the Protectionists: A Lost Cause?', *Transactions of the Royal Historical Society*, xxxix (1989), 141–65.

Madden, William A., 'Macaulay's Style' in *The Art of Victorian Prose*, ed. George Levine and William Madden (1968).

Millgate, Jane, 'Father and Son: Macaulay's *Edinburgh* Debut', *Review of English Studies*, xxi (1970), 159–67.

Munby, A. N. L., *Macaulay's Library* (1966).

—— 'Germ of a History: Twenty-three Pages of a Macaulay Cambridge Prize Essay', *Times Literary Supplement* (1969), 469.

Newbould, I. D. C., 'Sir Robert Peel and the Conservative Party, 1832–41: A Study in Failure?' *English Historical Review*, xlviii (1983), 529–57.

Robson, Robert, 'Trinity College in the Age of Peel', in R. Robson (ed.), *Ideas and Institutions of Victorian Britain: Essays in Honour of George Kitson Clark* (1967).

Sirkin, G. and N. R., 'The Battle of Indian Education: Macaulay's Opening Salvo', *Victorian Studies*, xiv (1971), 407–28.

Stokes, E. T., 'Macaulay: The Indian Years 1834–8', *Review of English Literature*, i. (1960), 41–50.

Thomas, William E. S., 'Religion and Politics in the Quarterly Review, 1809–1853', in Stefan Collini, Richard Whatmore, and Brian Young (eds.), *History, Religion and Culture: Essays in British Intellectual History 1750–1950* (Cambridge, 2000).

Thompson, M. A., *Macaulay*, Historical Association (1959).

Trevor-Roper, H. R., *The Romantic Movement and the Study of History* (1969).

6. UNPUBLISHED THESES

Bradley, Ian, 'The Politics of Godliness: Evangelicals in Parliament' (Oxford D.Phil thesis 1974).

Breiseth, C., 'British Conservatism and French Revolutions: John Wilson Croker's Attitudes to Reform and Revolution in Britain and France' (Cornell Ph.D. thesis 1964).

Index

Whig party:
  'appropriation' and 119
  Brougham and 80–1
  and Canning ministry 46–7, 81
  changing policies of 53–4
  decline of, after 1846 158
  defined 5, 77–8
  Exclusionist origins of 270
  free trade and 157–8
  and French revolution 41
  and French war 203
  and Lichfield House compact 104, 106
  Mahon on 53–4, 143–4
  and parliamentary reform 46–8
  Peel's opposition to 106–9
  and radicalism after 1815 77
  and reform crisis (1831–2) 139–40
Wilberforce, William 62, 81, 88

William III, King of England 5, 242, 249, 250, 259
  role in HE 271–2, 290, 296, 303, 307
William IV 47, 236
Wilson, Horace Hayman 150
Winch, Donald 70
Windischgraetz, Prince Alfred 278
Wordsworth, William 251
  TBM on 157
  quoted 190
Worontzow, Count 179
Wrangel, General 278
Wraxall, Sir Nathaniel 178–9
Wycherley, William 251

Xenophon 211

Zichy de Ferraris, Countess Charlotte, née Strachan 17